A·N·N·U·A·L E·D·I·T·I·O·N·S

Early Childhood Education

03/04

Twenty-Fourth Edition

EDITORS

Karen Menke Paciorek

Eastern Michigan University

Karen Menke Paciorek is a professor of early childhood education and coordinator of graduate education at Eastern Michigan University in Ypsilanti. Her degrees in early childhood education include a B.A. from the University of Pittsburgh, an M.A. from George Washington University, and a Ph.D. from Peabody College of Vanderbilt University. She edits, with Joyce Huth Monro, *Sources: Notable Selections in Early Childhood Education* and is the editor of *Taking Sides: Clashing Views on Controversial Issues in Early Childhood Education* (McGraw-Hill/Dushkin). She has served as president of the Michigan Association for the Education of Young Children and the Michigan Early Childhood Education Consortium. She presents at local, state, and national conferences on curriculum planning, guiding behavior, preparing the learning environment, and working with families. She currently serves as a school board trustee for the Northville Public Schools, Northville, Michigan.

Joyce Huth Munro

American Association of Colleges for Teacher Education

Joyce Huth Munro is Associate for Professional Issues and Liaison at the American Association of Colleges for Teacher Education in Washington, D.C. She has been an administrator and professor at colleges in Kentucky, South Carolina, and New Jersey. Her current writing and research focuses on discovering what makes quality teacher education programs. She is coeditor, with Karen Menke Paciorek, of *Sources: Notable Selections in Early Childhood Education* (McGraw-Hill/Dushkin). At regional and national conferences, she presents seminars on innovative methods of teacher education and curriculum design. Dr. Munro holds an M.Ed. from the University of South Carolina and a Ph.D. from Peabody College at Vanderbilt University.

McGraw-Hill/Dushkin

530 Old Whitfield Street, Guilford, Connecticut 06437

Visit us on the Internet
http://www.dushkin.com

Credits

1. **Perspectives**
   Unit photo—© 2003 by PhotoDisc, Inc.
2. **Child Development and Families**
   Unit photo—Courtesy of Louis Raucci.
3. **Care and Educational Practices**
   Unit photo—© 2003 by Cleo Freelance Photography.
4. **Guiding and Supporting Young Children**
   Unit photo—© 2003 by PhotoDisc, Inc.
5. **Curricular Issues**
   Unit photo—Courtesy of McGraw-Hill/Dushkin.
6. **Trends**
   Unit photo—© 2003 by Sweet By & By/Cindy Brown.

Copyright

Cataloging in Publication Data
Main entry under title: Annual Editions: Early Childhood Education. 2003/2004.
1. Early Childhood Education—Periodicals. I. Menke Paciorek, Karen, comp. II. Munro, Joyce H.   Title: Early Childhood Education.
ISBN 0–07–283815–9   658'.05   ISSN 0272–4456

Twenty-Fourth Edition

Cover image © 2003 PhotoDisc, Inc.
Printed in the United States of America   1234567890BAHBAH54   Printed on Recycled Paper

Editors/Advisory Board

Members of the Advisory Board are instrumental in the final selection of articles for each edition of ANNUAL EDITIONS. Their review of articles for content, level, currentness, and appropriateness provides critical direction to the editor and staff. We think that you will find their careful consideration well reflected in this volume.

To the Reader

In publishing ANNUAL EDITIONS we recognize the enormous role played by the magazines, newspapers, and journals of the public press in providing current, first-rate educational information in a broad spectrum of interest areas. Many of these articles are appropriate for students, researchers, and professionals seeking accurate, current material to help bridge the gap between principles and theories and the real world. These articles, however, become more useful for study when those of lasting value are carefully collected, organized, indexed, and reproduced in a low-cost format, which provides easy and permanent access when the material is needed. That is the role played by ANNUAL EDITIONS.

Early childhood education is an interdisciplinary field that includes child development, family issues, educational practices, behavior guidance, and curriculum. *Annual Editions: Early Childhood Education 03/04* brings you the latest information in the field from a wide variety of recent journals, newspapers, and magazines. In selecting articles for this edition, we were careful to provide you with a well-balanced look at the issues and concerns facing teachers, families, society, and children. There are four themes found in readings chosen for this twenty-fourth edition of *Annual Editions: Early Childhood Education.* They are: (1) the consistent and concerted effort required by all involved to guide young children's behavior, (2) the ongoing debate over the most appropriate way for children to acquire literacy skills for a lifetime of reading proficiency and enjoyment, (3) how high-quality experiences provided by qualified teachers shape a young child's early learning, and (4) the effect of policy on the quality of programs for young children. It is especially gratifying to see issues affecting children and families covered in magazines other than professional association journals. The general public needs to be aware of the impact of positive early learning and family experiences on the growth and development of children.

Continuing in this edition of *Annual Editions: Early Childhood Education* are selected World Wide Web sites that can be used to further explore topics addressed in the articles. These sites will be cross-referenced by number in the topic guide. We have chosen to include only a few high-quality sites. Students are encouraged to explore these sites on their own, or in collaboration with others, for extended learning opportunities.

Given the wide range of topics included, *Annual Editions: Early Childhood Education 03/04* may be used by several groups—undergraduate or graduate students, professionals, parents, or administrators—who want to develop an understanding of the critical issues in the field.

The selection of readings for this edition has been a cooperative effort between the two editors and the advisory board members. We appreciate the time the advisory board members have taken to provide suggestions for improvement and possible articles for consideration. We couldn't produce this book without the assistance of many. The production and editorial staff of McGraw-Hill/Dushkin ably support and coordinate our efforts. This book is used at more than 550 colleges and universities throughout the country. We realize this is a tremendous responsibility to provide a thorough review of the current literature—a responsibility we take seriously. Our goal is to provide the reader with a snapshot of the critical issues facing professionals in early childhood education.

To the instructor or reader interested in the history of early childhood care and education programs throughout the years, we invite you to view our other book, also published by McGraw-Hill/Dushkin. *Sources: Notable Selections in Early Childhood Education,* 2nd edition (1999) is a collection of 46 writings of enduring historical value by influential people in the field. All of the selections are primary sources that allow you to experience firsthand the thoughts and views of these important educators. Available also is the first edition of *Taking Sides: Clashing Views on Controversial Issues in Early Childhood Education.* This book is also published by McGraw-Hill/Dushkin and edited by Karen Menke Paciorek. Twenty controversial issues facing early childhood professionals or parents have been selected. The book can be used in a seminar or issues course.

We are grateful to readers who have corresponded with us about the selection and organization of previous editions. Your comments and articles sent for consideration are welcomed and will serve to modify future volumes. Take time to fill out and return the postage-paid *article rating form* on the last page. You may also contact either of us at karen.paciorek@emich.edu or jmunro@aacte.org

We look forward to hearing from you.

Karen Menke Paciorek

Karen Menke Paciorek
Editor

Joyce Huth Munro

Joyce Huth Munro
Editor

Contents

UNIT 1
Perspectives

Five selections consider developments in early childhood education.

1. **Overview of Existing Policies and Programs for Young Children,** *Preschool For All: Investing in a Productive and Just Society,* Committee for Economic Development, 2002

   When the American public starts to view early childhood education as an economic investment then, and only then, will the *funding* necessary for *quality programs* for all children begin to become available. The role of the *federal government* and the states in providing the incentive for businesses and communities to invest in young children can be crucial.

2. **Does Universal Preschool Pay?,** *Business Week,* April 29, 2002

   Strong advocates of all children entering school ready to succeed support *universal preschool* offerings. However, many question the government using *federal funds* to support preschool. *Achievement* for all children, especially *at-risk children,* will only be attained when *quality* preschool experiences are available to all.

3. **Eager to Learn—Educating Our Preschoolers: Executive Summary,** Barbara Bowman, M. Suzanne Donovan, and M. Susan Burns (eds.), *National Research Council,* 2000

   An esteemed committee of early childhood educators compiled a list of 19 recommendations to guide us in providing optimal *learning* experiences for children aged 2 to 5. Included are recommendations on appropriate *curriculum, policy, teaching,* and *technology.*

4. **How Do Education and Experience Affect Teachers of Young Children?,** Susan Kontos and Amanda Wilcox-Herzog, *Young Children,* July 2001

   Three research studies point out that developmentally cohesive *teacher preparation programs* are most effective in preparing *teachers* of the young. The *quality* of the *learning environment* for the children is related to the specialized education that the teachers have received.

5. **Concern Turns to Preschool Facilities,** Linda Jacobson, *Education Week,* January 16, 2002

   Throughout America, many of our youngest citizens spend their days in cramped, dirty, and unsafe *environments* that are not conducive to quality learning experiences. The *equipment and materials* along with the physical setting play a key role in the *health and safety* of the children. Greater attention to detail is needed if young children are to have high-quality environments in which to learn.

The concepts in bold italics are developed in the article. For further expansion, please refer to the Topic Guide and the Index.

UNIT 2
Child Development and Families

Nine selections consider the effects of family life on the growing child and the importance of parent education.

The concepts in bold italics are developed in the article. For further expansion, please refer to the Topic Guide and the Index.

UNIT 3
Care and Educational Practices

Eleven selections examine various educational programs, assess the effectiveness of several teaching methods, and consider some of the problems faced by students with special needs.

Unit Overview   60

15. **Who's Watching the Kids?,** Clara Hemphill, *Working Mother,* April 2002

Across America, the **quality** of child care is very uneven. Centers in many states may exceed the maximum staffing ratios for **infants** and **toddlers.** One of the points made in this article summarizing the ninth annual report on **child care** is that the **federal subsidy** has increased for **low-income** families, yet child care remains unaffordable for **middle-income families.**   62

16. **Creating Home-School Partnerships,** Keri Peterson, *Earlychildhood News,* January/February 2002

Of all the partnerships an early childhood program can establish, none is more important than with parents. **Research** shows that engaging families in school activities can increase children's **academic progress** as well as foster positive **behaviors.** When parents spend time assisting with homework and monitoring activities, everyone benefits. To maximize **parental partnerships, teachers** must first be trained in family **diversity** and communication.   66

17. **For America's Infants and Toddlers, Are Important Values Threatened by Our Zeal to "Teach"?,** Eleanor Stokes Szanton, *Young Children,* January 2001

The values that **families** and teachers transmit to **infants and toddlers** are largely shared by all Americans. Yet, perhaps the most important value of this uniquely American cluster of characteristics is **diversity.** Eleanor Stokes Szanton believes that national characteristics can be unintentionally threatened if **child care** programs ignore choice, exploration, and self-expression.   69

18. **All They Do Is Play? Play in Preschool,** Angie Dorrell, *Earlychildhood News,* March/April 2000

Valuable **learning** takes place during children's **play.** As they engage in preschool center play, children enhance their **creativity.** They also develop **language** and practice **social** skills. Angie Dorrell notes that an important **teachers'** role is to ensure that every center has good equipment and materials.   75

19. **10 Signs of a Great Preschool,** Irene Daria-Wiener, *Parents,* September 2001

Irene Daria-Wiener provides the fundamentals for identifying **quality** in **preschool** programs. She emphasizes **learning centers** as a valuable approach for **teaching** such aspects of the curriculum as **art,** language, and **blocks.**   79

20. **Study: Full-Day Kindergarten Boosts Academic Performance,** Debra Viadero, *Education Week,* April 17, 2002

Children who attend full-day **kindergarten** perform well on standardized **tests** and they are not likely to be held back in later grades. The **academic** gains of these children continue through **primary** grades. This **research** also confirms other positive cost benefits of kindergarten.   81

The concepts in bold italics are developed in the article. For further expansion, please refer to the Topic Guide and the Index.

UNIT 4
Guiding and Supporting Young Children

Seven selections examine the importance of establishing self-esteem and motivation in the child and consider the effects of stressors such as dealing with grief.

The concepts in bold italics are developed in the article. For further expansion, please refer to the Topic Guide and the Index.

UNIT 5
Curricular Issues

Ten selections consider various curricular choices. The areas covered include play, developmentally appropriate learning, emergent literacy, motor development, technology, and conceptualizing curriculum.

The concepts in bold italics are developed in the article. For further expansion, please refer to the Topic Guide and the Index.

The concepts in bold italics are developed in the article. For further expansion, please refer to the Topic Guide and the Index.

UNIT 6
Trends

Six selections consider the present and future of early childhood education.

The concepts in bold italics are developed in the article. For further expansion, please refer to the Topic Guide and the Index.

Topic Guide

This topic guide suggests how the selections in this book relate to the subjects covered in your course. You may want to use the topics listed on these pages to search the Web more easily.

On the following pages a number of Web sites have been gathered specifically for this book. They are arranged to reflect the units of this *Annual Edition*. You can link to these sites by going to the DUSHKIN ONLINE support site at *http://www.dushkin.com/online/*.

ALL THE ARTICLES THAT RELATE TO EACH TOPIC ARE LISTED BELOW THE BOLD-FACED TERM.

Academics
16. Creating Home-School Partnerships
20. Study: Full-Day Kindergarten Boosts Academic Performance
22. Measuring Results
44. Accountability Shovedown: Resisting the Standards Movement in Early Childhood Education

Accountability
44. Accountability Shovedown: Resisting the Standards Movement in Early Childhood Education
46. Putting Money Where It Matters
47. 'All Children Can Learn': Facts and Fallacies

Achievement
2. Does Universal Preschool Pay?
11. Developing High-Quality Family Involvement Programs in Early Childhood Settings

Aggressive behavior
28. Reinforcement in Developmentally Appropriate Early Childhood Classrooms
29. Bullying Among Children
30. Use the Environment to Prevent Discipline Problems and Support Learning

Arts
19. 10 Signs of a Great Preschool

Assessment
22. Measuring Results
45. Class-Size Reduction in California

At-risk children
2. Does Universal Preschool Pay?
41. Salting the Oats: Using Inquiry-Based Science to Engage Learners at Risk
47. 'All Children Can Learn': Facts and Fallacies

Behavior
9. Gender Expectations of Young Children and Their Behavior
14. Cartoon Violence: Is It as Detrimental to Preschoolers as We Think?
16. Creating Home-School Partnerships
26. Guidance Techniques That Work
27. Guidance & Discipline Strategies for Young Children: Time Out Is Out
29. Bullying Among Children
30. Use the Environment to Prevent Discipline Problems and Support Learning

Blocks and games and toys
19. 10 Signs of a Great Preschool
21. The Child-Centered Kindergarten: A Position Paper
25. The Silencing of Recess Bells
34. Blocks as a Tool for Learning: Historical and Contemporary Perspectives
40. Children Are Born Mathematicians: Promoting the Construction of Early Mathematical Concepts in Children Under Five

Books
13. Talking to Kids About Race
21. The Child-Centered Kindergarten: A Position Paper
31. Helping Children Cope With Stress in the Classroom Setting

Bullying
29. Bullying Among Children

Child care
15. Who's Watching the Kids?
17. For America's Infants and Toddlers, Are Important Values Threatened by Our Zeal to "Teach"?

Child development
7. Look Who's Listening
9. Gender Expectations of Young Children and Their Behavior
12. No Time for Fun
17. For America's Infants and Toddlers, Are Important Values Threatened by Our Zeal to "Teach"?
23. Different Approaches to Teaching: Comparing Three Preschool Program Models
25. The Silencing of Recess Bells

Classroom management
28. Reinforcement in Developmentally Appropriate Early Childhood Classrooms
29. Bullying Among Children

Class size
45. Class-Size Reduction in California
46. Putting Money Where It Matters

Cognitive development
32. Children and Grief: The Role of the Early Childhood Educator

Constructivist curriculum
23. Different Approaches to Teaching: Comparing Three Preschool Program Models
24. Examining the Reggio Emilia Approach to Early Childhood Education

Cost, educational
43. The "Failure" of Head Start

Curriculum
3. Eager to Learn—Educating Our Preschoolers: Executive Summary
19. 10 Signs of a Great Preschool
34. Blocks as a Tool for Learning: Historical and Contemporary Perspectives
36. Using Documentation Panels to Communicate With Families
40. Children Are Born Mathematicians: Promoting the Construction of Early Mathematical Concepts in Children Under Five

Developmentally appropriate practice
21. The Child-Centered Kindergarten: A Position Paper

World Wide Web Sites

The following World Wide Web sites have been carefully researched and selected to support the articles found in this reader. The easiest way to access these selected sites is to go to our DUSHKIN ONLINE support site at *http://www.dushkin.com/online/*.

AE: Early Childhood Education 03/04

The following sites were available at the time of publication. Visit our Web site—we update DUSHKIN ONLINE regularly to reflect any changes.

General Sources

Children's Defense Fund (CDF)
http://www.childrensdefense.org

At this site of the CDF, an organization that seeks to ensure that every child is treated fairly, there are reports and resources regarding current issues facing today's youth, along with national statistics on various subjects.

Connect for Kids
http://www.connectforkids.org

This nonprofit site provides news and information on issues affecting children and families, with over 1,500 helpful links to national and local resources.

Eric Clearing House on Elementary and Early Childhood Education
http://www.ericeece.org

This invaluable site provides links to all ERIC system sites: clearinghouses, support components, and publishers of ERIC materials. You can search the massive ERIC database and find out what is new in early childhood education.

National Association for the Education of Young Children
http://www.naeyc.org

The NAEYC Web site is a valuable tool for anyone working with young children. Also see the National Education Association site: *http://www.nea.org.*

U.S. Department of Education
http://www.ed.gov/pubs/TeachersGuide/

Government goals, projects, grants, and other educational programs are listed here as well as many links to teacher services and resources.

UNIT 1: Perspectives

Child Care Directory: Careguide
http://www.careguide.net

Find licensed/registered child care by state, city, region, or age of child at this site. Site contains providers' pages, parents' pages, and many links.

Early Childhood Care and Development
http://www.ecdgroup.com

This site concerns international resources in support of children to age 8 and their families. It includes research and evaluation, policy matters, programming matters, and related Web sites.

Global SchoolNet Foundation
http://www.gsn.org

Access this site for multicultural education information. The site includes news for teachers, students, and parents as well as chat rooms, links to educational resources, programs, and contests and competitions.

Goals 2000: A Progress Report
http://www.ed.gov/pubs/goals/progrpt/index.html

Open this site to survey a progress report by the U.S. Department of Education on the Goals 2000 reform initiative. It provides a sense of educators' future goals.

UNIT 2: Child Development and Families

Administration for Children and Families
http://www.acf.dhhs.gov

This site provides information on federally funded programs that promote the economic and social well-being of families, children, and communities.

I Am Your Child
http://www.iamyourchild.org

Rob Reiner's I Am Your Child Foundation features excellent information on child development.

Internet Resources for Education
http://web.hamline.edu/personal/kfmeyer/cla_education.html#hamline

This site, which aims for "educational collaboration," takes you to Internet links that examine virtual classrooms, trends, policy, and infrastructure development. It leads to information about school reform, multiculturalism, technology in education, and much more.

The National Academy for Child Development
http://www.nacd.org

The NACD, an international organization, is dedicated to helping children and adults reach their full potential. Its home page presents links to various programs, research, and resources into such topics as learning disabilities, ADD/ADHD, brain injuries, autism, accelerated and gifted, and other similar topic areas.

National Parent Information Network/ERIC
http://npin.org

This clearinghouse of elementary, early childhood, and urban education data has information for parents and for people who work with parents.

National Safe Kids Campaign
http://www.babycenter.com

This site includes an easy-to-follow milestone chart and advice on when to call the doctor.

Parent Center
http://www.parentcenter.com/general/34754.html

Parenting resources can be found at this site as well as information for assisting children who are facing stressful situations as a result of terrorism.

Zero to Three
http://www.zerotothree.org

Find here developmental information on the first 3 years of life—an excellent site for both parents and professionals.

www.dushkin.com/online/

UNIT 3: Care and Educational Practices

Canada's Schoolnet Staff Room
http://www.schoolnet.ca/home/e/

Here is a resource and link site for anyone involved in education, including special-needs educators, teachers, parents, volunteers, and administrators.

Classroom Connect
http://www.classroom.com/login/home.jhtml

A major Web site for K–12 teachers and students, this site provides links to schools, teachers, and resources online. It includes discussion of the use of technology in the classroom.

The Council for Exceptional Children
http://www.cec.sped.org/index.html

Information on identifying and teaching gifted children, attention deficit disorders, and other topics in disabilities and gifted education may be accessed at this site.

National Resource Center for Health and Safety in Child Care
http://nrc.uchsc.edu

Search through this site's extensive links to find information on health and safety in child care. Health and safety tips are provided, as are other child-care information resources.

Online Innovation Institute
http://oii.org

A collaborative project among Internet-using educators, proponents of systemic reform, content-area experts, and teachers who desire professional growth, this site provides a learning environment for integrating the Internet into educators' individual teaching styles.

UNIT 4: Guiding and Supporting Young Children

Child Welfare League of America (CWLA)
http://www.cwla.org

The CWLA is the United States' oldest and largest organization devoted entirely to the well-being of vulnerable children and their families. Its Web site provides links to information about issues related to morality and values in education.

National Network for Family Resiliency
http://www.nnfr.org

This organization's home page will lead you to resource areas of interest in learning about resiliency, including General Family Resiliency, Violence Prevention, and Family Economics.

UNIT 5: Curricular Issues

Association for Childhood Education International (ACEI)
http://www.udel.edu/bateman/acei/

This site, established by the oldest professional early childhood education organization, describes the association, its programs, and the services it offers to both teachers and families.

California Reading Initiative
http://www.sdcoe.k12.ca.us/score/promising/prreading/prreadin.html

The California Reading Initiative site provides valuable insight into topics related to emergent literacy. Many resources for teachers and staff developers are provided.

Early Childhood Education Online
http://www.ume.maine.edu/ECEOL-L/

This site gives information on developmental guidelines and issues in the field, presents tips for observation and assessment, and gives information on advocacy.

International Reading Association
http://www.reading.org

This organization for professionals who are interested in literacy contains information about the reading process and assists teachers in dealing with literacy issues.

Phi Delta Kappa
http://www.pdkintl.org

This important organization publishes articles about all facets of education. By clicking on the links in this site, for example, you can check out the journal's online archive, which has resources such as articles having to do with assessment.

Reggio Emilia
http://ericps.ed.uiuc.edu/eece/reggio.html

Through ERIC, link to publications related to the Reggio Emilia approach and to resources, videos, and contact information.

Teachers Helping Teachers
http://www.pacificnet.net/~mandel/

Basic teaching tips, new teaching methodologies, and forums for teachers to share experiences are provided on this site. Download software and participate in chats. It features educational resources on the Web, with new ones added each week.

Tech Learning
http://www.techlearning.com

An award-winning K–12 educational technology resource, this site offers thousands of classroom and administrative tools, case studies, curricular resources, and solutions.

UNIT 6: Trends

Awesome Library for Teachers
http://www.neat-schoolhouse.org/teacher.html

Open this page for links and access to teacher information on everything from educational assessment to general child development topics.

Future of Children
http://www.futureofchildren.org

Produced by the David and Lucille Packard Foundation, the primary purpose of this page is to disseminate timely information on major issues related to children's well-being.

National Institute on the Education of At-Risk Students
http://www.cfda.gov/public/viewprog.asp?progid=1062

The institute supports a range of research and development activities to improve the education of students at risk of educational failure due to limited English proficiency, race, geographic location, or economic disadvantage. Access links and summaries of the institute's work.

Prospects: The Congressionally Mandated Study of Educational Growth and Opportunity
http://www.ed.gov/pubs/Prospects/index.html

This report analyzes cross-sectional data on language-minority and LEP students and outlines what actions are needed to improve their educational performance. Family and economic situations are addressed plus information on related reports and sites.

We highly recommend that you review our Web site for expanded information and our other product lines. We are continually updating and adding links to our Web site in order to offer you the most usable and useful information that will support and expand the value of your Annual Editions. You can reach us at: *http://www.dushkin.com/annualeditions/.*

UNIT 1

Perspectives

Unit Selections

1. **Overview of Existing Policies and Programs for Young Children**, Preschool For All: Investing in a Productive and Just Society
2. **Does Universal Preschool Pay?** *Business Week*
3. **Eager to Learn—Educating Our Preschoolers: Executive Summary**, Barbara Bowman, M. Suzanne Donovan, and M. Susan Burns
4. **How Do Education and Experience Affect Teachers of Young Children?** Susan Kontos and Amanda Wilcox-Herzog
5. **Concern Turns to Preschool Facilities**, Linda Jacobson

Key Points to Consider

- Should the federal government pay for preschool so all children can attend prior to entering kindergarten? If so, how will this affect private companies in the business of providing early care and education?

- What are the most harmful factors affecting children and families today?

- To effect real change in education, what are three key recommendations that should be enacted according to the National Research Council?

- Describe the post-secondary education and experience of early childhood teachers that are most beneficial in bringing about change in the educational system.

- What should be the minimum requirements for individuals who want a career working with young children?

- For optimal learning to occur, describe the ideal learning setting in which young children should spend their day.

 **Links: www.dushkin.com/online/**
These sites are annotated in the World Wide Web pages.

Child Care Directory: Careguide
   http://www.careguide.net
Early Childhood Care and Development
   http://www.ecdgroup.com
Global SchoolNet Foundation
   http://www.gsn.org
Goals 2000: A Progress Report
   http://www.ed.gov/pubs/goals/progrpt/index.html

The focus for the first unit, Perspectives, is on providing quality learning experiences and settings for all young children. The unit begins with "Overview of Existing Policies and Programs for Young Children," from "*Preschool for All: Investing in a Productive and Just Society*," published by the Committee for Economic Development. It is followed by "Does Universal Preschool Pay?" When families have access to a preschool program that is conducive to stimulating the learning of their child, they are most fortunate. According to the National Day Care study, only one in seven programs provides such optimal care and education. That means the majority of children in America who attend preschool programs are not receiving the care or education that will be necessary for fully enhancing their learning abilities. The debate over offering universal preschool to all children has drawn the attention of many politicians and business leaders. Will the availability of preschool for all children ensure they enter school ready to learn and have higher achievement levels? Many people question spending money on preschool programs that appear, to the untrained eye, to be large blocks of time to just play. The fact that Alexandra Starr's article was published in *Business Week* highlights the importance of this issue to our country and its economic development.

The unit ends with "Concern Turns to Preschool Facilities" by Linda Jacobson from *Education Week*. Until we are willing to invest the dollars necessary to provide learning settings that are not only safe but inviting and challenging, children will not achieve at the level required for future school success. The days of relegating young, innocent children to damp, dimly lit basements should be long over. Children need learning environments, staffed by qualified early childhood educators, that will allow them to flourish as they build a strong foundation for future learning.

The 2000 release of *Eager to Learn—Educating our Preschoolers: Executive Summary* by the National Research Council (NRC) has been widely cited. Never have we known so much about the importance of young children's participation in appropriate educational experiences including quality early childhood programs and curricula where they are given opportunities to reflect, predict, and question. This will lay a strong foundation for the skills that will be most needed as children progress through the education system. It will cause those teachers who use a canned or pre-determined curriculum to rethink their approach to providing educational experiences for young children. Children need a learning atmosphere where they are given responsibility for being active participants in the development of the learning experiences, not merely passive bystanders who do what the teacher has carefully planned and prepared. It's what the editors call the "potluck" versus "dinner party" approach to planning and teaching. At a potluck, everyone contributes something to the meal, as opposed to a dinner party where one person determines the menu and prepares the meal for all the participants. Children deserve learning experiences that reflect a potluck approach over the teacher-directed dinner-party method. Children can contribute to their learning when given opportunities.

In many U.S. states, the requirements for adults wanting to work in pre-public school programs do not include hours in child growth and development or any post-secondary education but only a criminal background check involving crimes against children. Requirements for teachers vary greatly from state to state. As a public, we are willing to accept the lack of formal preparation for teachers of children under the age of 5, but we want teachers in kindergarten through 12th grade to hold college degrees and teacher certifications. On this front, much improvement is needed. Along these lines, Susan Kontos and Amanda Wilcox-Herzog reviewed the literature on teacher preparation and experience and its effects on learning opportunities made available for the children in their care. Their findings are reviewed in "How Do Education and Experience Affect Teachers of Young Children?" Not surprisingly, they found that teachers who have had more formal preparation in classrooms have received high-quality ratings. There is a relationship between specialized education for teachers of young children and the quality of educational experiences they provide.

Enjoy reading this section, which provides a view of important issues facing early childhood education today.

1

Chapter 2

Overview of Existing Policies and Programs for Young Children

To appreciate the deficiencies in how the United States approaches early learning, it is necessary first to understand what current arrangements look like and why they work the way they do. The nation has a patchwork of early care and education opportunities that evolved to meet different and traditionally separate objectives: fostering child development (giving young children access to education and other services that would prepare them for formal school) or meeting labor market needs (providing working families with child care). Today there is growing recognition of the significance of early learning for efforts to improve K–12 education, while changing patterns of work and welfare have created new incentives to provide early education to the growing number of young children who spend time in out-of-home care. While education and care for young children are, therefore, increasingly intertwined activities, public policies still tend to reflect their separate origins as either child development or labor market programs.

BACKDROP: CHANGING SOCIETAL PERSPECTIVES ON EDUCATION, WORK, AND WELFARE

Changing societal perspectives on education, work, and welfare make the education and care children receive before they enter school of growing importance for the general public and not just for parents. Education reformers increasingly recognize that their efforts to improve student achievement are affected by differences in children's development that are already evident when formal schooling begins. With most parents, mothers as well as fathers, now working, employers know that it is more important than ever for their employees to have access to high-quality child care arrangements to help them balance their work and family responsibilities. New welfare policies require low-income mothers of even very young children to work.

Efforts to reform elementary and secondary education have drawn attention to early education. There is growing emphasis on holding schools accountable for successfully educating *all* of their students. Reformers are increasingly aware that gaps in knowledge and skills are already evident when children enter kindergarten. Narrowing these gaps (especially those linked to children's race and family incomes) after children enter school has proven to be one of educators' most intractable challenges.

Ensuring that all students receive an adequate education may depend crucially on ensuring that they enter school ready to learn. In fact, courts in two states have recently ordered state officials to provide preschool education to children at risk of later educational problems. Plaintiffs in school finance lawsuits challenged the legality of state school funding laws on the grounds that insufficient and inequitable funding denied some students their constitutional rights to an adequate education.[a] In finding for the plaintiffs, courts in New Jersey and North Carolina included in their mandated remedies the provision of publicly-funded preschool programs for at-risk youngsters.[1] (The North Carolina court specified access for 4-year-olds, while the court in New Jersey included 3-year-olds as well.) Since school finance policies are under legal challenge in many states, it is likely that court-ordered preschool for at least some children will spread beyond New Jersey and North Carolina.

Access to preschool can also help families balance child-rearing and work. While individuals may still debate whether changing patterns of work and family are desirable, the irreversible reality is that it is now the norm in the United States for women to work. This is true of all women, including mothers of children who have not yet reached kindergarten age. Between 1950 and 2000 the civilian labor force participation rate of women 20 years of age and over increased from 33 to 60 percent. In 2000, 73 percent of women with children were in the labor force, including 72 percent of those with children 3- to 5-years-old and 61 percent of those with children under age 3.[2]

Moreover, public policy has shifted in its expectations about low-income mothers' participation in the workplace.

Women's Labor Force Participation Rate: 1950-2000

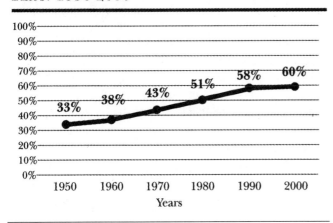

Source: U.S. Department Of Labor, *Report On The American Workforce*, (Washington, D.C.: Department of Labor, 2001), p. 126, table 5.

Labor Force Participation Rate of Women with Children: 2000

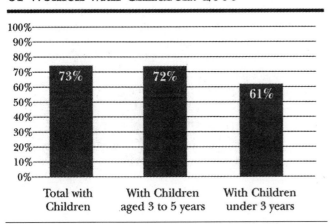

Source: U.S. Department Of Labor, *Report On The American Workforce*, (Washington, D.C.: Department of Labor, 2001), p. 127, table 6.

In the early 1990s over 90 percent of mothers receiving Aid to Families with Dependent Children ("welfare") were not in the paid labor force. Prior to 1996 states were not allowed to require public assistance recipients who were single parents caring for infants to participate in work-related activities.[3] This stipulation changed with passage of the Personal Responsibility and Work Opportunity Reconciliation Act (PRWORA). As of October 1999 most states still continued to exempt individuals with very young children from participating in work activities, but 16 states set the age limit at 3 to 6 months and 4 had no criteria for exemptions. In 23 states mothers of children over age 1 could be required to work. Only 5 states had an age limit higher than age 1.[4] Thus most single mothers became subject to PRWORA's assumption that adults, even those

with young children, should be self-supporting and that public benefits should be contingent on meeting work or work preparation requirements.

WHO CARES FOR AMERICA'S PRESCHOOLERS?

Because the United States has not approached the provision of early care and education in a systematic way, there is little routine and up-to-date information about who cares for young children. Another consequence of the nation's unsystematic approach is the lack of any universally accepted classification scheme for early care and education providers that would definitively describe the services they offer. The situation is further complicated by the fact that many young children are in multiple arrangements: for example, a child may spend part of the week in a child care center or preschool program and another part in a family day care setting (in a non-relative's home) or being cared for by relatives. Despite these difficulties, an overview of preschool arrangements can be pieced together from a variety of special (and not always strictly comparable) surveys.

In 1999, 59 percent of 3- to 5-year-olds who had not yet entered kindergarten participated in some kind of center-based program, variously called day care, nursery school, prekindergarten, preschool, and Head Start. The older the child, the more likely he or she was to be enrolled in a center-based program for at least some part of a week: 46 percent of 3-year-olds, 69 percent of 4-year-olds, and 76 percent of 5-year-olds. Just 23 percent of these children had parental care only: 31 percent for 3-year-olds, 18 percent for 4-year-olds, and 14 percent for 5-year-olds.[5] The remaining children were more likely to be cared for by relatives or in family day care settings operated by non-relatives than in center-based programs. Infants and toddlers were more likely than preschoolers to be in family-based rather than center-based care.

Center-based providers vary in the extent to which they are organized to provide educational experiences for preschool children and whether they offer services on a full- or part-day basis. There are no hard and fast rules distinguishing centers, but those labeled "day care" are more apt to be full-day programs meeting the child care needs of working parents (i.e., 9 to 10 hours a day). Nursery schools, prekindergartens, preschools, and Head Start are more apt to include instruction as an important and integral aspect of their service and, like many public kindergartens, may be part-day programs (2–4 hours) operating only during the regular school year. Even when educationally-oriented providers offer "full-day" services, full-day generally refers to the length of the typical elementary/secondary school day (6–7 hours) rather than the 9 to 10 hours offered by centers oriented to the child care needs of working parents.

The number of centers caring for children who have not yet entered kindergarten is unknown but totals well over 100,000.[b] The Children's Foundation 2001 survey of child centers found 111,506, based on reports from state child care licensing offices.[6] However, states differ in the extent to which they include or exclude educationally-oriented preschool programs from their child care licensing require-ments.[c] The Foundation also reported that there were 304,958 regulated family child care homes in 2000, mostly serving six or fewer children,[7] and estimated that there were 4 unregulated family day care homes for every regulated one.[d]

Center providers operate under a variety of auspices. Some are operated by nonprofit groups, including religious organizations. Some are profit-making businesses, both single centers and large corporate chains. In some places the public school system offers prekindergarten classes, although often these are open mainly to children who are at risk of not being ready to succeed in school because of poverty, limited English, disabilities, or other factors.

States have the primary responsibility for setting standards for and regulating early care and education providers. The major exception is that the federal government requires that the states have basic child care safety and health require-ments in place in order to receive funds from the Child Care Development Fund (see the next section). Even here, states set the health and safety requirements as well as procedures for ensuring the compliance of both regulated and nonregu-lated providers; and states vary in the extent to which their practices are consistent with recommendations of experts.[8] More generally, states differ in their rules about which providers are subject to regulatory standards and what standards must be met. As noted above, there are substantial numbers of providers (especially family-based providers but also including some centers) who are eligible for public subsidies but are exempt from any regulation except basic health and safety rules.

WHO PAYS FOR EARLY CARE AND EDUCATION?

In keeping with the traditional view that early care and education are individual consumer goods rather than an investment with important public benefits, families bear the largest responsibility for providing care and education for preschool children.

It is estimated that in 2001, public and private spending on early care and education for children from birth to age 5 will total $50–55 billion, with parents paying 50–55 percent, the federal government paying 25–30 percent, and state and local governments paying 15–20 percent. Corporate and philanthropic investments could amount to 1–5 percent but are difficult to estimate.[9] If the unpaid time of mothers and fathers engaged in child care is considered, the parental share is obviously much higher. Other costs that are not included in this total are those of relatives and

others who take care of children on an unpaid basis or at a below-market rate.

It is impossible, given the structure of current funding policies, to identify the resources going specifically to support early education for 3- and 4-year-olds as distinct from child care for children from birth to age 4 or 5. Even the $50+ billion cited above must be seen as a ballpark rather than a precise figure, since funding programs may cover school-age children as well and seldom provide good estimates of the age break-down of beneficiaries.

The two important considerations to keep in mind about early care and education funding are that, unlike elemen-tary and secondary education, (1) families still bear the largest share of costs, and (2) the federal government is a significantly more important partner than the states in *funding* (as opposed to providing or administering) early care and education. This latter fact is easily obscured by the state's lead role in administering programs and in the wide discretion states have to structure program parameters. But the American approach to financing early care and education has evolved quite differently from our approach to financing public elementary and secondary education. In the latter case, states and localities bear 93 percent of the burden of funding public schools, parents pay nothing, and the federal government only contributes about 7 percent. As important as this marginal federal money is to many elementary and secondary schools, federal funding policies have a far greater influence on the availability of early education opportunities.

Federal Funding

Most of the federal funding that subsidizes education and care for children under age 5 comes from 2 programs, Head Start and the Child Care Development Fund (CCDF). The former has its origins in the 1960s' efforts to expand educational opportunity by giving disadvantaged children a "head start" in school. CCDF is designed to support working parents by helping them with the costs of child care. Reflecting their different goals, the two programs operate in quite different ways.

Head Start. Head Start provides grants to local agencies to provide comprehensive early childhood developmental, educational, health, nutritional, social, and other services to low-income children and their families. Ninety percent of participants must be from families whose income is below the poverty line or from families who are eligible for public assistance. Most Head Start programs are half-day and part-year. While children from birth through kinder-garten are eligible, only 6 percent of the 857,664 children enrolled in FY 2000 were under age 3. Fifty-six percent were age 4. (The remainder were age 3 (33 percent) or age 5 (5 percent)). Nationwide, 1,535 Head Start grantees provided services in 18,200 centers at an average cost of $5,951 per child.[e] Head Start appropriations have risen rapidly over the last decade, from $1.6 billion in 1990 to $6.2 billion in 2001.[10]

Head Start is the oldest of the federal early care and education programs, having enrolled its first children in 1965. With strong roots in the Community Action Program of the War on Poverty, Head Start has traditionally given local grantees wide flexibility in program structure. Grantees must comply with federal program standards, which Congress in 1998 modified to place more emphasis on school readiness.

CCDF. The Child Care Development Fund was formed during the 1996 welfare reform by consolidating several existing child care programs. The fund provides grants to states for subsidizing the child care costs of eligible families and for improving the overall quality and availability of child care services. Some CCDF funds are subject to matching requirements.

States give CCDF subsidies in the form of certificates or outright cash to parents to purchase child care services or through grants and contracts to providers who enroll eligible children. In FY 1999 only 11 percent of the children participating in CCDF were served through grants or contracts; 83 percent were served through certificates and 6 percent through cash to parents. In that year 29 percent of CCDF children were served in settings "legally operating without regulation," as distinguished from regulated settings.[11] Eligible settings include centers, family day care homes, and relatives if they live in a separate residence. Federal law requires that CCDF providers comply with applicable state or local health and safety requirements but otherwise leaves it up to states to set licensing standards and determine reimbursement rates.

Parents share responsibility for paying child care fees, on a sliding scale basis, although states may waive fees for families below the poverty line. States set subsidy levels and fee schedules.

Children up to age 13 who reside with a family whose income does not exceed 85 percent of the state median income are eligible to participate; however, states are free to set lower eligibility limits, and most do. Parents must be working or in education or training or the child must be in need of protective services.

Federal funding for CCDF in FY 2001 was $4.5 billion. The General Accounting Office (GAO) estimates that 1.3 million children under age 5 participated in CCDF in FY 1999 and that 70 percent of total budget authority for the program went for children in this age group.[12]

Although children benefiting from CCDF may receive care that helps them prepare for school, school readiness is not an explicit goal of the program. There are no national performance standards for services or staff other than the basic requirements noted above that states must have and enforce health and safety rules.

Other federal funding. Head Start and CCDF provide roughly three-quarters of the federal subsidies available for early care and education. Smaller but still important subsidies flow from Temporary Assistance for Needy Families (TANF), from special education programs, and from Title 1 of the Improving America's Schools Act.[13]

Under TANF, the program that replaced Aid to Families with Dependent Children in the 1996 reform of federal welfare legislation, states can use some of their welfare block grant on child care. TANF in recent years has been an important source of child care funds, reaching 350,000 children under age 5 in FY 1999 at an estimated cost of $1.3 billion.

Children with disabilities get federal aid under "special education" programs. GAO reports that 1.1 million children under age 5 participated in special education in FY 1999, but these figures cover 3 different programs and may include duplicated counts of students. Total spending on special education services for children under age 5 was $835 million.

Title 1 grants for supplemental educational and related services to educationally-disadvantaged children in low-income areas mostly are spent by local districts on elementary education, but about 300,000 children under age 5 benefited from Title 1 funds in FY 1999.

In addition to these direct expenditure programs, several tax credits and exclusions help families and employers pay for employment-related dependent-care expenses. Unlike direct federal early care and education programs, tax benefits are not targeted to lower-income families.

State And Local Funding

Prekindergarten. As of 1998–99, 42 states (including the District of Columbia) invested in state prekindergarten initiatives offering regularly-scheduled group experiences for young children to help them learn and develop before entering elementary school.[14] Beyond this fundamental similarity, the initiatives were quite diverse:

- Some programs were available only in public school settings, while others (such as Georgia's) made use of a variety of settings.
- Some states only supplement federal Head Start programs, while others have developed separate initiatives. A number of states sponsor multiple initiatives.
- Georgia offers prekindergarten to all 4-year-olds whose parents want them to participate. To qualify to participate, Georgia Pre-K providers must offer services 5 days a week, for at least 6.5 hours per day, for 36 weeks a year. Providers are reimbursed $2,219 to $3,475 annual per child. Georgia officials estimate that approximately 63,500 4-year-olds, or 58 to 60 percent, are participating, with another 12,000 4-year-olds enrolled in Head Start centers that are not Pre-K providers.
- New York and Oklahoma have launched school-district-based initiatives to open prekindergarten to all 4-year-olds, regardless of income, but not all districts

GEORGIA'S PREKINDERGARTEN PROGRAM PROVIDERS

In 1993 Georgia established a prekindergarten program for 4-year-olds with funds from the state lottery. Originally targeting at-risk children, in 1995 the program was opened to all children whose parents want them to participate. Eligible providers include:

Public Schools	Private Schools
Department of Family Services	Head Start Agencies
For-Profit Child Care Agencies	Nonprofit Child Care Agencies
Hospitals	Vocational/Technical Schools
Universities	Churches
Atlanta Job Corp	Military Bases
YMCAs and YWCAs	

SOURCE: Karen Schulman, Helen Blank, and Danielle Ewen, *Seeds of Success: State Prekindergarten Initiatives—1998–1999* (Washington, D.C.: Children's Defense Fund, 1999), p. 186.

in these states participate. New York, which restricts district participation because of limited funding, appears to be currently serving roughly a quarter of its 4-year-olds and Oklahoma around half.

- Enrollment rates in states that restrict access to prekindergarten reach or exceed 20–30 percent in a few cases, but generally are much lower.[f] These states have adopted varying approaches to setting priorities about whom to serve. Most state programs are limited to low-income families and children with other risk factors. (Even then, most states do not serve all eligible children.) Some states focus on serving all children in selected communities, generally chosen because they are home to significant populations of disadvantaged families.

- Some states limit a child's eligibility for prekindergarten to one year. Others define eligible children to include both 3- and 4-year-olds or even all children from birth to age 5.

- Many state pre-K initiatives offer only part-day (2 to 4 hours a day), part-year services, although there are exceptions such as Connecticut, Massachusetts, and Hawaii.

- Some initiatives (particularly those that follow a public school model and focus on public school settings) focus comparatively narrowly on education goals, while others provide a more comprehensive array of services including health care and various family supports.

- States may distribute pre-K funds directly to providers or may distribute them to communities or school districts, which in turn distribute funds to individual providers. Hawaii and Arizona distribute some or all funds directly to parents.

- Many but not all state pre-K initiatives require providers to meet quality standards that are higher than the state's child care licensing standards. For example, New York State has no pre-service requirements for teachers in child care centers, while prekindergarten teachers are required to be certified in elementary education.[15]

In 1998–99 states spent approximately $1.7 billion on their pre-K initiatives and served 750,000 children.[16] Total state spending was quite uneven: the 10 highest spending states accounted for over three-quarters of state spending on pre-K initiatives, although they accounted for just over one-half the pre-K age population. The 5 top spending states (California, Georgia, Illinois, New York, and Texas) accounted for about half of all state pre-K spending.[17] State spending per enrolled pupil varied widely as well, from $7,000 in Connecticut (for children enrolled in full-day programs) to less than $2,000 in 14 state initiatives. While the various initiatives are not directly comparable, in that they cover different services, a sense of the meaning of these average expenditure levels can be gained by comparing them with the $5,147 average annual cost in the federal Head Start program in FY 1998.[18] Some states require localities to provide matching funds or permit them to supplement state money. These additional local dollars may come from school districts or from community programs and organizations.

Child care. Most state spending on child care is actually federal money, from federal appropriations for CCDF or from state decisions to transfer money from the TANF block grant to CCDF or to spend TANF funds directly for child care. In addition to meeting their required state match for these funds, however, states do expend some of their own

FULL-DAY, FULL-YEAR PREKINDERGARTEN INITIATIVES

Several states provide the necessary funding for full-day and/or full-year prekindergarten for eligible children and also require that it be offered by at least some percentage of programs.

Connecticut reimbursed providers $7,000 per child in 1998–99 for children participating for the full day and full year. The state also required that at least 60 percent of available prekindergarten slots be for full-day/full-year participation, to meet the needs of full-time working families. Based on local planning processes that were required to assess the need for these programs, several communities decided to go beyond minimum requirements and have all their prekindergarten programs operate on a full-day, full-year basis. Connecticut's program is open to all 3- and 4-year-olds where offered, but is limited to school districts with high concentrations of poverty. About 6,300 children were served in school year 2001–02, roughly 7 percent of the state's population of 3- and 4-year-olds.

Massachusetts requires that at least one-third of the children participating in its prekindergarten initiative be provided with full-day classes. This requirement reflects the initiative's orientation toward meeting the needs of working families. The state also promotes full-day/full-year programming by encouraging local councils under its Community Partnerships for Children to consider the range of schedules faced by working families (including irregular as well as regular shifts) in implementing their prekindergarten programs. Approximately 21,800 children from moderate and low-income families participated in prekindergarten in 2001–02, roughly 13.5 percent of the state's 3- and 4-year-olds.

Hawaii's Preschool Open Door program funds full-day programs for all participating children, although only for 9 months a year. The state provided funds directly to parents, who could choose the program their children attended. This might be a prekindergarten program, although it could also be a child care program that met only child care licensing standards. Hawaii's program served approximately 800 3- and 4-year-olds from low-income families in 1999–00, roughly 2.5 percent of the relevant age group.

In all 3 cases, while the states provided funding for extended programs, they also required parents to pay fees on a sliding scale basis.

In 1998–99 several other states (California, Florida, and Maryland) reported providing some support for extended hours in their prekindergarten programs, although they did not require programs to offer extended hours.

SOURCE: Karen Schulman, Helen Blank, and Danielle Ewen, *Seeds of Success: State Prekindergarten Initiatives 1998–99* (Washington, D.C.: Children's Defense Fund, 1999), pp. 129–30; Nancy K. Cauthen, Jane Knitzer, and Carol H. Ripple, *Map and Track: State Initiatives for Young Children and Families, 2000 Edition* (New York, NY: National Center for Children in Poverty, Columbia University, 2000); unpublished information from *Education Week.*

funds on child care. The exact amount, especially the portion directed to preschool-age children, is hard to pinpoint. State and local spending on early care and education combined is estimated to have been about $8 to $10 billion in 1999.[19]

State child care spending tends to benefit low-income families and to take the form of vouchers or direct payments to providers. States sometimes draw on general revenues for child care funding but may also depend on a variety of other revenue sources. For example, Kentucky and Maine devote part of their tobacco settlement money to child care; and California uses funds raised by taxes on cigarettes and other tobacco products for a range of "early childhood development services," including child care. Massachusetts and Kentucky give individuals, when registering and licensing motor vehicles, the option of designating part of their fees to support child care. Missouri funds its Early Childhood Development, Education and Care Fund from gambling fees. Georgia funds its pre-K program, as well as college education, from a state lottery. Over half the states have tax credits or deductions for child and dependent care.[20]

Notes

a. Unlike the federal constitution, virtually every state constitution includes some kind of "education clause" specifying education as a government function and requiring legislatures to create public schools that provide education variously described as "thorough and efficient" or "ample" or "adequate." Many state school finance systems are under legal challenge for failing to support an "adequate" education for all students.

b. This figure compares to roughly 80,000 public elementary and secondary schools.

c. For example, some states exclude preschools and prekindergartens, which may be regulated by different agencies. Some states exclude religiously-affiliated centers from licensing requirements.

d. States have varying rules about which family child care homes must be regulated. Many exempt homes caring for a small number of children.

e. Head Start centers often provide a broader range of services to children and their families than do other early childhood centers or public schools, so annual per-child Head Start costs are not directly comparable to costs incurred by other early education providers.

f. Reliable data on enrollment rates in prekindergarten programs are not available. We have made rough estimates based on unpublished information provided to us by the staff of *Education Week,* who collected enrollment numbers from states. The problem in estimating enrollment rates is in knowing what denominator to use, since states may allow children younger than four to enroll but the extent of their eligibility to participate is difficult to determine.

Notes

1. *Hoke County v. State of North Carolina/State Board of Education,* 95 CVS 1158 (Hoke II, October, 2000); *Abbot v. Burke,* 748 A2d 82 (2000).

2. U.S. Department of Labor, *Report on the American Workforce* (Washington, D.C.: U.S. Department of Labor, 2001), pp. 126–127, tables 5–6.

3. R. Kent Weaver, *Ending Welfare as We Know It* (Washington, D.C.: Brookings Institution Press, 2000), p. 20.

4. State Policy Documentation Project, *Work Requirements: Exemptions as of October 1999,* available at <**http:// www.spdp.org/tanf/exemptions.pdf**> Accessed June 21, 2001.

5. National Center for Education Statistics, *Digest of Education Statistics, 2000,* NCES-2001-034 (Washington, D.C.: U.S. Department of Education, January 2001), table 48.

6. The Children's Foundation, *Child Care Center Licensing Study Summary Data,* available at <**http://www. childrensfoundation.net**/ Accessed June 12, 2001.

7. The Children's Foundation, *Child Care Center Licensing Study Summary Data,* available at <**http://www. childrensfoundation.net/**> Accessed June 12, 2001. Estimate of the number of unregulated family care homes provided to CED by Children's Foundation staff.

8. U.S. General Accounting Office, *Child Care: State Efforts to Enforce Safety and Health Requirements,* GAO/HEHS-00-28 (Washington, D.C.: U.S. General Accounting Office, January 2000).

9. W. Steven Barnett, "Funding Issues for Universal Early Education in the United States" (draft, Center for Early Education, Rutgers University, March 30, 2001). Figures updated for CED by author.

10. U.S. Department of Health and Human Services, Head Start Bureau, *2001 Head Start Fact Sheet,* available at <**http:// www2.acf.dhhs.gov/programs/hsb/about/fact2001.htm**>. Accessed July 5, 2001.

11. U.S. Department of Health and Human Services, Child Care Bureau, *FY 1999 CCDF Data Tables and Charts,* available at <**http://www.acf.dhhs.gov/programs/ccb/research/99acf800/**> Accessed July 12, 2001.

12. U.S. General Accounting Office, *Early Education and Care: Overlap Indicates Need to Assess Crosscutting Programs,* GAO/HEHS-00-78 (Washington, D.C.: U.S. General Accounting Office, April 2000), pp. 13–15.

13. U.S. GAO, *Early Education and Care,* pp. 13–15.

14. Karen Schulman, Helen Blank, and Danielle Ewen, *Seeds of Success: State Prekindergarten Initiatives 1998–1999* (Washington, D.C.: Children's Defense Fund, September 1999), p. 13.

15. Schulman, Blank, and Ewen, *Seeds of Success;* The Center for Career Development in Early Care and Education, Wheelock College, *Child Care Licensing: Qualifications and Training for Roles in Child Care Centers and Family Child Care Homes: 2000 Summary Sheet,* available at <**http://www.nccic.org/cctopics/ cclicensing00.pdf**> Accessed September 13, 2001.

16. Schulman, Blank, and Ewen. *Seeds of Success,* p. 16.

17. Schulman, Blank, and Ewen, *Seeds of Success,* p. 87; The Center for Career Development in Early Care and Education, Wheelock College, *Child Care Licensing.*

18. Schulman, Blank, and Ewen, *Seeds of Success,* pp. 33–5.

19. W. Steven Barnett, "Funding Issues for Universal Early Education," p. 10.

20. Anne Mitchell, Louise Stoney, and Harriet Dichter, *Financing Child Care in the United States: An Expanded Catalog of Current Strategies 2001 Edition* (Kansas City, MO: Ewing Marion Kauffman Foundation, 2001).

DOES UNIVERSAL PRESCHOOL PAY?

Support for the idea is growing, but the tab will be high

Two years ago, Vice-President Al Gore declared that if elected President he would spend $50 billion a year to offer pre-kindergarten to the country's 8.3 million three- and four-year-olds. With the U.S. at war and George W. Bush in the White House, odds are that Uncle Sam won't be paying to send toddlers to school just yet.

But just in the past month, early childhood education has suddenly moved to the political front burner again. In early April, Bush announced that his Administration would begin integrating early literacy skills into the curriculum of Head Start, the federal program that serves poor children. He also earmarked $45 million for research into the most effective techniques for teaching young children. Senators Edward M. Kennedy (D-Mass.) and George V. Voinovich (R-Ohio), meanwhile, want to parcel out $1 billion per year over five years to bolster state education programs aimed at kids from infancy to age five. Their goal: to accelerate a move already under way in the states, which have more than doubled their pre-kindergarten spending in the past decade, to $1.7 billion, according to the Children's Defense Fund, a Washington (D.C.) group. State pre-K programs now serve three-quarters of a million children.

The idea of exposing very young children to letters and numbers has been gaining momentum because of the ongoing school-reform movement. As experts search for ways to improve kindergarten through 12th grade (K-12), they have become increasingly convinced that many kids don't start school prepared to learn. This view has been bolstered by research showing that children absorb many basic cognitive skills between the ages of three

STARTING SCHOOL AT AGE THREE

Universal preschool education is on the political front burner again

NUMBER OF CHILDREN There are 8.3 million three- to five-year-olds in the U.S., many of whom get little formal exposure to reading or numbers.

COST Preschool would run $4,000 to $5,000 a year per kid, or $33 billion to $42 billion if every child were enrolled in a voluntary program. Head Start costs roughly $6,600 a year.

BENEFITS Studies show that early learning helps poor children, which experts say is evidence that middle-class kids would benefit as well, although less so. Poor three- to five-year-olds who get high-quality basic education consistently score about five percentage points higher on school tests through age 21 than those who get no early schooling. Only 30% repeat a grade, vs. 56% of those with no schooling. And some 35% attend college by age 21, vs. 14% of other poor kids.

WHO'S ON THE BANDWAGON President Bush wants to spend $45 million to study the best early-childhood teaching techniques. Senators Kennedy and Voinovich have proposed a $1 billion-a-year plan to fund state early education programs for all kids under five. The Committee for Economic Development, a business group, is pushing a national preschool program for all three- to five-year-olds.

and five. Transforming day care into preschool takes advantage of these crucial years, especially for poor children, who are most likely to fall behind in school. "You simply can't talk about closing the achievement gap without talking about pre-K," says Andrew Rotherham of the Progressive Policy Institute, a centrist think tank.

Proponents point out that most other developed countries guarantee an education to their three- to five-year-olds. France, Belgium, and Italy provide free preschool to everyone in this age group, including immigrants, who often lag other children. "A lot of children [in the U.S.] are starting school behind their peers, and in many cases they never catch up," says Isabel V. Sawhill, a senior fellow at the Brookings Institution.

Most of the hard evidence demonstrates that poor kids see the most enduring gains from preschool. Middle-class kids who attend pre-K show higher cognitive skills, including math and language abilities, as well as better social skills, says a 1999 study by a team of 10 researchers from the University of North Carolina and three other universities. But by age eight, which is as far as the study goes, most middle-class kids with no preschool have narrowed the gap. As a result, it isn't clear just how valuable widespread preschool would be for every American toddler. "The data on how much kids benefit is not very encouraging," says David F. Salisbury, an education expert at the libertarian Cato Institute, which opposes publicly funded pre-K.

Nonetheless, pre-K is gaining popularity in part because so many households these days face work-family conflicts. With more mothers working, 64% of three-to five-year-olds now go to some kind of day-care center, i.e., outside the home and not with a neighbor or family member. Most centers are private, and their quality varies widely. A recent study in four states found that 70% provide mediocre care, while one in eight is so inadequate as to actually endanger children's health or safety.

Still, the hodgepodge of nursery schools and child care that working families now use provides a platform on which a more comprehensive preschool system could be built. Rather than expanding K-12 schools to include pre-K, existing day-care centers could be upgraded, says Walter S. Gilliam, an education expert at the Yale University Child Study Center. Most of the state initiatives have involved improving existing programs rather than attempting to start new public preschools. Only one state, Georgia, now offers universal pre-K—but only to four-year-olds.

Another key building block for early childhood learning: lifting teacher skills. Currently, fewer than half of the states have minimum requirements for instructors in child-care centers. Low salaries are a big hurdle, too: Day-care employees earn about $16,000 a year, often less than a parking lot attendant. The result: a 30%-plus annual turnover rate, vs. 13% or so for K-12 teachers, who are paid more than

twice as much. A universal preschool system would make more money available for instructor pay.

The point on which there's strong consensus is that disadvantaged kids profit from early learning. As it is, Head Start serves more than 900,000 poor three- and four-year-olds. But the part-day program that focuses on health care and nutrition along with education is chronically underfunded. The $6.5 billion-a-year budget means it can't accommodate three of five eligible children. But those who do get in come out ahead. Only 30% of four-year-olds whose mothers are on welfare could count to 20 out loud or write their name correctly, according to an Apr. 16 study of kids in California, Connecticut, and Florida. By comparison, 53% of Head Start children—a comparable demographic group—could count to 20, and 66% could write their first names.

Programs that offer more education than Head Start reap even better results. The most thorough study, called the Carolina Abecedarian Project (after the ABCs), followed 111 disadvantaged North Carolina kids for 21 years. Half were enrolled in a high-quality educational program from infancy to age five, while the control group got only nutritional supplements. All the children attended comparable public

schools from kindergarten on. The result: Those who attended preschool were less likely to drop out of school, repeat grades, or bear children out of wedlock. By age 15, less than a third had failed a grade, vs. more than half of the control group. At age 21, the preschoolers were more than twice as likely to be attending a four-year college.

The big question about preschool, of course, is where to find the money. A universal program could be done for less than Gore's $50 billion proposal. But it still would run up to $42 billion a year, according to a new study by the Committee for Economic Development, a New York City-based group of blue-chip corporations. The price tag could be lower if some of the cost were borne by middle-class families, many of whom already are paying for day care.

Still to be debated is whether preschool is the best use of public funds for kids who aren't from poor families. No one has done a cost-benefit analysis to see if middle-class kids would be helped more by, say, extra money for K-12 schools instead. In the meantime, though, it's clear that as long as learning officially starts only in kindergarten, millions of children will fall behind before they even reach the schoolhouse door.

By Alexandra Starr in Washington

Eager to Learn—
Educating Our Preschoolers:
Executive Summary

Children come into the world eager to learn. The first five years of life are a time of enormous growth of linguistic, conceptual, social, emotional, and motor competence. Right from birth a healthy child is an active participant in that growth, exploring the environment, learning to communicate and, in relatively short order, beginning to construct ideas and theories about how things work in the surrounding world. The pace of learning, however, will depend on whether and to what extent the child's inclinations to learn encounter and engage supporting environments. There can be no question that the environment in which a child grows up has a powerful impact on how the child develops and what the child learns.

Eager to Learn: Educating Our Preschoolers is about the education of children ages 2 to 5. It focuses on programs provided outside the home, such as preschool, Head Start, and child care centers. At this, the threshold of a new century, there can be little doubt that something approaching voluntary universal early childhood education, a feature of other wealthy industrialized nations, is also on the horizon here. Three major trends have focused public attention on children's education and care in the preschool years:

1. the unprecedented labor force participation of women with young children, which is creating a pressing demand for child care;
2. an emerging consensus among professionals and, to an ever greater extent, among parents that young children should be provided with educational experiences; and
3. the accumulation of convincing evidence from research that young children are more capable learners than current practices reflect, and that good educational experiences in the preschool years can have a positive impact on school learning.

The growing consensus regarding the importance of early education stands in stark contrast to the disparate system of care and education available to children in the United States in the preschool years. America's programs for preschoolers vary widely in quality, content, organization, sponsorship, source of funding, relationship to the public schools, and government regulation.

Historically, there have been two separate and at times conflicting traditions in the United States that can be encapsulated in the terms *child care* and *preschool*. A central premise of this report, one that grows directly from the research literature, is that *care and education cannot be thought of as separate entities in dealing with young children*. Adequate care involves providing quality cognitive stimulation, rich language environments, and the facilitation of social, emotional and motor development. Likewise, adequate education for young children can occur only in the context of good physical care and of warm affective relationships. Indeed, research suggests that secure attachment improves social and intellectual competence and the ability to exploit learning opportunities. Neither loving children nor teaching them is, in and of itself, sufficient for optimal development; thinking and feeling work in tandem.

Learning, moreover, is not a matter of simply assimilating a store of facts and skills. Children construct knowledge actively, integrating new concepts and ideas into their existing understandings. Educators have an opportunity and an obligation to facilitate this propensity to learn and to develop a receptivity to learning that will prepare children for active engagement in the learning enterprise throughout their lives. This report argues, therefore, that promoting young children's growth calls for early childhood settings (half day or full day, public or private, child care or preschool) that support the development of the full range of capacities that will serve as a foundation for school learning. As the child is assimilated into the culture of education in a setting outside the home, early childhood programs must be sensitive and responsive to the cultural contexts that define the child's world outside the school or center, and they must build on the strengths and supports that those contexts provide.

CONTEXT OF THE REPORT AND COMMITTEE CHARGE

As Americans grapple with decisions about early childhood education that many European countries have already made, we can draw on certain advantages. We have a strong research community investigating early childhood learning and development and production evidence on which to base the design, implementation and evaluation of programs. And we have a tradition of experimentation and observation in preschools that gives us access to a wealth of experience in early childhood education.

The Committee on Early Childhood Pedagogy was established by the National Research Council in 1997 to study a broad range of behavioral and social science research on early learning and development and to explore the implications of that research for the education and care of young children ages 2 to 5. More specifically, the committee was asked to undertake the following:

- Review and synthesize theory, research, and applications in the social, behavioral, and biological sciences that contribute to our understanding of early childhood pedagogy.
- Review the literature and synthesize the research on early childhood pedagogy.
- Review research concerning special populations, such as children living in poverty, children with limited English proficiency, or children with disabilities, and highlight early childhood education practices that enhance the development of these children.
- Produce a coherent distillation of the knowledge base and develop its implications for practice in early childhood education programs, the training of teachers and child care professionals, and future research directions.
- Draw out the major policy implications of the research findings.

The study was carried out at the request of the U.S. Department of Education's Office of Educational Research and Improvement (Early Childhood Institute) and the Office of Special Education Programs, the Spencer Foundation, and the Foundation for Child Development. An important motivation for sponsors of the study is to help public discussion of these issues move away from ideology and toward evidence, so that educators, parents, and policy makers will be able to make better decisions about programs for the education and care of young children....

RECOMMENDATIONS

What is now known about the potential of the early years, and of the promise of high-quality preschool programs to help realize that potential for all children, stands in stark contrast to practice in many—perhaps most—early childhood settings. In the committee's view, bringing what is known to bear on what is done in early childhood education will require efforts in four areas: (1) professional development of teachers, (2) development of teaching materials that reflect research-based understandings of children's learning, (3) development of public policies that support—through standards and appropriate assessment, regulations, and funding—the provision of quality preschool experiences, and (4) efforts to make more recent understandings of development in the preschool years common public knowledge. The committee proposes recommendations in each of these areas.

Professional Development

At the heart of the effort to promote quality early childhood programs, from the committee's perspective, is a substantial investment in the education and training of those who work with your children.

Recommendation 1: Each group of children in an early childhood education and care program should be assigned a teacher who has a bachelors' degree with specialized education related to early childhood (e.g., developmental psychology, early childhood education, early childhood special education). Achieving this goal will require a significant public investment in the professional development of current and new teachers.

Sadly, there is a great disjunction between what is optimal pedagogically for children's learning and development and the level of preparation that currently typifies early childhood educators. Progress toward a high-quality teaching force will require substantial public and private support and incentive systems, including innovative educational programs, scholarship and loan programs, and compensation commensurate with the expectations of college graduates.

Recommendation 2: Education programs for teachers should provide them with a stronger and more specific foundational knowledge of the development of children's social and affective behavior, thinking, and language.

Few programs currently do. This foundation should be linked to teachers' knowledge of mathematics, science, linguistics, literature, etc., as well as to instructional practices for young children.

Recommendation 3: Teacher education programs should require mastery of information on the pedagogy of teaching preschool-aged children, including:

- Knowledge of teaching and learning and child development and how to integrate them into practice.
- Information about how to provide rich conceptual experiences that promote growth in specific content areas, as well as particular areas of development, such as language (vocabulary) and cognition (reasoning).
- Knowledge of effective teaching strategies, including organizing the environment and routines so as to promote activities that build social-emotional relationships in the classroom.
- Knowledge of subject-matter content appropriate for preschool children and knowledge of professional standards in specific content areas.

- Knowledge of assessment procedures (observation/performance records, work sampling, interview methods) that can be used to inform instruction.
- Knowledge of the variability among children, in terms of teaching methods and strategies that may be required, including teaching children who do not speak English, children from various economic and regional contexts, and children with identified disabilities.
- Ability to work with teams of professionals.
- Appreciation of the parents' role and knowledge of methods of collaboration with parents and families.
- Appreciation of the need for appropriate strategies for accountability.

Recommendation 4: A critical component of preservice preparation should be a supervised, relevant student teaching or internship experience in which new teachers receive ongoing guidance and feedback from a qualified supervisor.

There are a number of models (e.g., National Council for Accreditation of Teacher Education) that suggest the value of this sort of supervised student teaching experience.

Recommendation 5: All early childhood education and child care programs should have access to a qualified supervisor of early childhood education.

Teachers should be provided with opportunities to reflect on practice with qualified supervisors.

Recommendation 6: Federal and state departments of education, human services, and other agencies interested in young children and their families should initiate programs of research and development aimed at learning more about effective preparation of early childhood teachers.

Recommendation 7: The committee recommends the development of demonstration schools for professional development.

The U.S. Department of Education should collaborate with universities in developing the demonstration schools and in using them as sites for ongoing research:

- on the efficacy of various models, including pairing demonstration schools as partners with community programs, and pairing researchers and in-service teachers with exemplary community-based programs;
- to identify conditions under which the gains of mentoring, placement of preservice teachers in demonstration schools, and supervised student teaching can be sustained once teachers move into community-based programs.

Educational Materials

Recommendation 8: The committee recommends that the U.S. Department of Education, the U.S. Department of Health and Human Services, and their equivalents at the state level fund efforts to develop, design, field test, and evaluate curricula that incorporate what is known about learning and thinking in the early years, with companion assessment tools and teacher guides.

Each curriculum should emphasize what is known from research about children's thinking and learning in the area it addresses. Activities should be included that enable children with different learning styles and strengths to learn.

Each curriculum should include a companion guide for teachers that explains the teaching goals, alerts the teacher to common misconceptions, and suggests ways in which the curriculum can be used flexibly for students at different developmental levels. In the teacher's guide, the description of methods of assessment should be linked to instructional planning so that the information acquired in the process of assessment can be used as a basis for making pedagogical decisions at the level of both the group and the individual child.

Recommendation 9: The committee recommends that the U.S. Department of Education and the U.S. Department of Health and Human Services support the use of effective technology, including videodiscs for preschool teachers and Internet communication groups.

The process of early childhood education is one in which interaction between the adult/teacher and the child/student is the most critical feature. Opportunities to see curriculum and pedagogy in action are likely to promote understanding of complexity and nuance not easily communicated in the written word. Internet communication groups could provide information on curricula, results of field tests, and opportunities for teachers using a common curriculum to discuss experiences, query each other, and share ideas.

Policy

States can play a significant role in promoting program quality with respect to both teacher preparation and curriculum and pedagogy.

Recommendation 10: All states should develop *program* standards for early childhood programs and monitor their implementation.

These standards should recognize the variability in the development of young children and adapt kindergarten and primary programs, as well as preschool programs, to this diversity. This means, for instance, that kindergartens must be readied for children. In some schools, this will require smaller class sizes and professional development for teachers and administrators regarding appropriate teaching practice, so that teachers can meet the needs of individual children, rather than teaching to the "average" child. The standards should outline essential components and should include, but not be limited to, the following categories:

- School-home relationships,
- Class size and teacher-student ratios,
- Specification of pedagogical goals, content, and methods,
- Assessment for instructional improvement,
- Educational requirements for early childhood educators, and
- Monitoring quality/external accountability

Recommendation 11: Because research has identified content that is appropriate and important for inclusion in

early childhood programs, *content* standards should be developed and evaluated regularly to ascertain whether they adhere to current scientific understanding of children's learning.

The content standards should ensure that children have access to rich and varied opportunities to learn in areas that are now omitted from many curricula—such as phonological awareness, number concepts, methods of scientific investigation, cultural knowledge, and language.

Recommendation 12: A single career ladder for early childhood teachers, with differentiated pay levels, should be specified by each state.

This career ladder should include at a minimum, teaching assistants (with child development associate certification), teachers (with bachelor's degrees), and supervisors.

Recommendation 13: The committee recommends that the federal government fund well-planned, high-quality center-based preschool programs for all children at high risk of school failure.

Such programs can prevent school failure and significantly enhance learning and development in ways that benefit the entire society.

The Public

Recommendation 14: Organizations and government bodies concerned with the education of young children should actively promote public understanding of early childhood education and care.

Beliefs that are at odds with scientific understanding—that maturation automatically accounts for learning, for example, or that children can learn concrete skills only through drill and practice—must be challenged. Systematic and widespread public education should be undertaken to increase public awareness of the importance of providing stimulating educational experiences in the lives of all young children. The message that the quality of children's relationships with adult teachers and child care providers is critical in preparation for elementary school should be featured prominently in communication efforts. Parents and other caregivers, as well as the public, should be the targets of such efforts.

Recommendation 15: Early childhood programs and centers should build alliances with parents to cultivate complementary and mutually reinforcing environments for young children at home and at the center.

FUTURE RESEARCH NEEDS

Research on child development and education can and has influenced the development of early childhood curriculum and pedagogy. But the influences are mutual. By evaluating outcomes of early childhood programs we have come to understand more about children's development and capacities. The committee believes that continued research efforts along both these lines can expand understanding of early childhood education and care, and the ability to influence them for the better.

Research on Early Childhood Learning and Development

Although it is apparent that early experiences affect later ones, there are a number of important developmental questions to be studied regarding how, when, and which early experiences support development and learning.

Recommendation 16: The committee recommends a broad empirical research program to better understand:

- The range of inputs that can contribute to supporting environments that nurture young children's eagerness to learn;
- Development of children's capacities in the variety of cognitive and socioemotional areas of importance in the preschool years, and the contexts that enhance that development;
- The components of adult-child relationships that enhance the child's development during the preschool years, and experiences affecting that development for good or for ill;
- Variation in brain development, and its implications for sensory processing, attention, and regulation, are particularly relevant;
- The implications of developmental disabilities for learning and development and effective approaches for working with children who have disabilities;
- With regard to children whose home language is not English, the age and level of native language mastery that is desirable before a second language is introduced and the trajectory of second language development.

Research on Programs, Curricula, and Assessment

Recommendation 17: The next generation of research must examine more rigorously the characteristics of programs that produce beneficial outcomes for all children. In addition, research is needed on how programs can provide more helpful structures, curricula, and methods for children at high risk of educational difficulties, including children from low-income homes and communities, children whose home language is not English, and children with developmental and learning disabilities.

Research on programs for any population of children should examine such program variations as age groupings, adult-child ratios, curricula, class size, and program duration. These questions can best be answered through longitudinal studies employing random assignment. In developing and assessing curricula, new research must also continue to consider the interplay between an individual child's characteristics, the immediate contexts of the home and classroom, and the larger contexts of the formal school environment.

Recommendation 18: A broad program of research and development should be undertaken to advance the state of the art of assessment in three areas: (1) classroom-based assessment to support learning (including studies of the impact of methods of instructional assessment on pedagogical technique and children's learning); (2) assessment for diagnostic purposes; and (3) assessment of program quality for accountability and other reasons of public policy.

Research on Ways to Create Universal High Quality

Recommendation 19: Research to fully develop and eval-uate alternatives for organizing, regulating, supporting, and financing early childhood programs should be conducted to provide an empirical base for the decisions being made.

The current early childhood system is fragmented, lacks uni-form standards, and provides uneven access to all children. Numerous policy choices have been proposed. This research would inform public policy decision making.

CONCLUSION

At a time when the importance of education to individual ful-fillment and economic success has focused attention on the need to better prepare children for academic achievement, the research literature suggests ways to make gains toward that end. Parents are relying on child care and preschool programs in ever larger numbers. We know that the quality of the programs in which they leave their children matters. If there is a single crit-ical component to quality, it rests in the relationship between the child and the teacher/caregiver, and in the ability of the adult to be responsive to the child. But responsiveness extends in many directions: to the child's cognitive, social, emotional, and physical characteristics and development.

Much research still needs to be done. But from the com-mittee's perspective, the case for a substantial investment in a high-quality system of child care and preschool on the basis of what is already known is persuasive. Moreover, the consider-able lead by other developed countries in the provision of quality preschool programs suggests that it can, indeed, be done on a large scale.

Barbara Bowman, M. Suzanne Donovan, and M. Susan Burns (eds.)

How Do Education and Experience Affect Teachers of Young Children?

Susan Kontos and Amanda Wilcox-Herzog

How do teachers excel at their "craft?" Can we teach individuals to be experts, or are good teachers" genetically predisposed" to their abilities via personality or some other factor? Perhaps teaching is learned on the job, by experience, rather than through educational programs. Or perhaps the answer is all of the above.

Early childhood educators continue to discuss teacher/caregiver qualifications and ways to encourage best practice across groups of professionals who bring a variety of qualifications to their work (Johnson & Mc-Cracken 1994). It is crucial to inform those discussions with relevant research as support for, if not a counterbalance to, expert informed opinions. This Research in Review synthesizes what we know from research about how general education, specialized education, and experience relate to early childhood professionals' practices in teaching young children.

Education

Education refers to the level of formal schooling an early childhood professional has attained, regardless of the content. For example, an early childhood teacher with a bachelor's degree in business has more formal schooling (though less specialized education) than a teacher with an associate's degree in early childhood education. Because many early childhood educators enter the field with little or no specialized education, researchers have been interested in whether level of education, independent of content, is related to teachers' teaching practices. In other words, researchers have attempted to determine if teachers with more education exhibit behaviors that better exemplify best practice.

This article divides practice into two components: teachers' interactions with children and the overall quality of the classroom learning environment. Note that we often use the term *teacher* for the sake of simplicity, while acknowledging the importance of the caregiving function in early childhood education as well as the respect due to those early childhood professionals who prefer the term *caregiver* and/or *family child care provider*.

Teachers' interactions with children

A classic study conducted by Berk (1985) focused on the relationship between teacher education and teacher behavior toward children in child care settings. She found that teachers with college degrees were more likely than those without a degree to encourage children, make suggestions to them, and promote their verbal skills.

These three studies demonstrate that not only are specialized education and quality associated, but there may also be a causal relationship between them (that is, a change that can be attributed to education).

Another classic study, the National Day Care Study (Ruopp et al. 1979), demonstrated that caregiver education was positively associated with social interaction, cognitive/language stimulation, and conversation with children. The National Child Care Staffing Study (Whitebook, Howes, & Phillips 1990), a large, multisite study, found that education was the caregiver background variable that best predicted caregiver behavior (sensitivity, harshness, detachment). On the other hand, a more recent large, multisite study of infant/toddler care (NICHD Early Child Care Research Network [ECCRN] 1996) found no relationship between teachers' education and the frequency or ratings of positive caregiving.

Kontos and colleagues (1995) demonstrated similar relationships between interactions and formal education for family child care providers and for teachers in centers. In this study, level of formal schooling was significantly positively related to observer ratings of provider sensitivity and observations of responsive involvement with children but negatively related to observer ratings of detachment and providers' self-ratings of restrictiveness.

The learning environment

The Staffing Study (Whitebook, Howes, & Phillips 1990) revealed that teacher education was positively associated with "appropriate caregiving," a subscore of the

Early Childhood Environment Rating Scale (ECERS—Harms & Clifford 1980), which is a frequently used measure of overall classroom quality. Consistent with the Staffing Study, three other studies demonstrated a relationship between teachers' general education and the quality of the learning environment. Scarr, Eisenberg, and Deater-Deckard (1994), Phillipsen et al. (1997), and Epstein (1993) all found statistically significant associations between general education and scores on the ECERS (Harms & Clifford 1980) and /or the ITERS (Infant/Toddler Environment Rating Scale—Harms, Cryer, & Clifford 1990). A study of family child care providers produced similar results; provider education and global family child care quality as measured by the Family Day Care Rating Scale (FDCRS) (Harms & Clifford 1989) were significantly related.

Taken together, these studies demonstrate that better educated teachers and family child care providers work in classrooms or homes with higher quality ratings than do those with less education. It is tempting, but not valid, to assume that educated teachers create higher quality classrooms. These correlational studies do not allow us to determine the direction of effects, even though it may make intuitive sense that teachers with more education create higher quality classrooms. Maybe it is simply that better quality centers are able to hire staff with more education.

Specialized education

Teachers' formal schooling may or may not focus on child development and/or early childhood education. Specialized education may also take place outside of formal schooling (via workshops and other means). Many states allow teachers to do their work with little if any specialized education (Phillips, Lande, & Goldberg 1990). Thus, it is important to know if specialized education is related to how well they are likely to do their job. We turn now to that issue.

The learning environment

Studies examining the relationship between specialized education and the quality of the classroom or home child care learning environment (Whitebook, Howes, & Phillips 1990; Epstein 1993; Scarr, Eisenberg, & Deater-Deckard 1994; Cost, Quality, and Child Outcomes Study Team 1995; Kontos et al. 1995) have found consistent positive correlations using such instruments to measure quality as the ECERS (Harms & Clifford 1980), FDCRS (Harms & Clifford 1989), or the ITERS (Harms, Cryer, & Clifford 1990). One study (Scarr, Eisenberg, & Deater-Deckard 1994) also included the Assessment Profile (Abbott-Shim & Sibley 1987). The small to moderate but statistically significant correlations indicated that teachers' specialized education accounts for some, but not all, of

the variation in the quality of learning environments they provide.

Taken together, these studies demonstrate that better educated teachers and family child care providers work in classrooms or homes with higher quality ratings than do those with less education.

Three studies measured quality before and after training with comparison or control groups (quasi-experimental designs). DeBord and Sawyers (1996) examined the impact of specialized education on the quality of care provided by 22 family child care providers, some of whom were affiliated with a child care association. They found that providers unaffiliated with a child care association initially displayed lower quality ("minimal," on average, according to the FDCRS) but increased to "good" following training. Affiliated providers were rated as "god" to start with and did not change following training. In a second study conducted by Cassidy and her colleagues (Cassidy et al. 1995; Cassidy & Buell 1996), teachers who obtained 15–20 credit hours of course work at the junior college level had higher quality ECERS scores at post-test than the control group that did not receive the course work. Finally, quality of family child care, as measured by the FDCRS, increased significantly following Family to Family training (offered to family child care providers in 40 U.S. communities as part of Dayton Hudson Foundation's quality child care initiative) and was higher than that of a comparison group of regulated providers who did not participate in this training program (Kontos, Howes, & Galinsky 1997). These three studies demonstrate that not only are specialized education and quality associated, but there may also be a causal relationship between them (that is, a change that can be attributed to education).

Teachers' interactions with children

The studies that we review next examined the relationship between teachers' behaviors with children and their specialized education. A follow-up analysis of Staffing Study data (Howes, Whitebook, & Phillips 1992) indicated that specialized education at the college level was important for teachers' competent interactions with infants and toddlers (as measured by the appropriate caregiving subscale of the ITERS), in contrast to preschool teachers who seemed to do well with a college degree in *any* subject *or* specialized education at the college level. Howes (1983) demonstrated that center-based caregivers with more specialized education played more with children and were less restrictive. In addition, family child care provider with more specialized education also played more with children and showed more responsivity, results consistent with those reported by Kontos and colleagues (1995). Kaplan and Conn (1984) reported that, following 20 clock hours of training in child development distributed across an average of seven sessions, teachers used more activities than before to facilitate social-emotional development, had better arranged and more plentiful materials, and spent more time in "physical child care" (not defined, but considered positive). Their study had no control group, however, so it is not possible to infer that the observed changes can be attributed to the intervention.

These data suggest that coherent teacher preparation programs (regardless of length or cost of the program) are more effective in preparing teachers than are more ad hoc educational experiences.

Arnett (1989) observed the behavior of 159 child care teachers in Bermuda with four different levels of specialized education ranging from no training to extensive training (a college degree in early childhood education). Results demonstrated that teachers with degrees were more warm and less punitive and detached in their interactions with children than teachers in the other three groups. Teachers with mid-range training consisting of two or four courses in child development were more positive and less punitive and detached than teachers with no training. Thus, Arnett demonstrated that some specialized education is good for the quality of teachers' interactions with children but more is even better.

Several studies were unable to show a relation between specialized education and teacher interactions with children. Cassidy and Buell (1996) reported that, in spite of increased ECERS scores following specialized education, there was no change in the amount of responsive language used by teachers/caregivers. In other words, the course work appears to have influenced overall classroom quality but not the quality of teacher's verbalizations with children. Family to Family training did not change providers' sensitivity or responsivity of the caregivers' interaction with the children, although quality was enhanced (Kontos, Howes, & Galinsky 1997). Thus, results regarding the association between specialized education and teacher interactions with children are mixed in studies using quasi-experimental designs.

One problem with research examining the effects or correlates of teacher education and specialized education is that the two factors tend to be intertwined. In other words, teachers with more formal education were also more likely to have more specialized education. Berk (1985), for instance, demonstrated differences in teacher interactions with children between teachers with specialized education and those with high school diplomas (in favor of the former). However, she was unable to show that specialized education was superior to a degree in a non-child-related field.

Another problem is that amount of formal and specialized education tends to be calculated as continuous vari-

ables (that is, actual years of education) rather than categorized into groups such as teachers with a high school diploma, teachers with an associate degree, teachers with a bachelor's degree, and so on. As a result, we can use these studies to investigate relationships between teachers' education and other variables, but we cannot get from them policy-relevant information telling us which category of education (formal or specialized) makes a significant difference to practice.

Howes (1997) conducted a study that attempted to address both of these two research problems. Using data from two large investigations of child care, Howes classified teachers into five categories by crossing categories of formal education with categories of specialized education and including in the study only teachers who fit into those predetermined categories. These categories were high school diploma with workshops, Child Development Associate (CDA) training, some college with some early childhood education courses, associate degree (AA) in early childhood, and an undergraduate or graduate degree in early childhood. Groups were compared for teacher sensitivity (Arnett 1989) and involvement (Howes & Stewart 1987). Results from both studies indicated that teachers with bachelor's degrees in early childhood education or higher were the most sensitive and involved teachers compared to all other groups. Teachers with AA degrees and CDA credentials were more sensitive and involved than teachers with some college or high school plus workshops, however. These data suggest that coherent teacher preparation programs (regardless of length or cost of the program) are more effective in preparing teachers than are more ad hoc educational experiences.

One study reported results contrary to the studies above. The National Institute of Child Health and Human Development (NICHD) Study of Early Child Care (1996) examined predictors of positive caregiving in settings with infants and toddlers. Specialized education was not among the statistically significant predictors for that age group. Instead, positive caregiving was predicted by group size and child-adult ratio.

There is a considerable amount of evidence that specialized training is related to the quality of the learning environment for children and to the quality of teachers' interactions with children.

Summary

There is a considerable amount of evidence that specialized training is related to the quality of the learning environment for children and to the quality of teachers' interactions with children. Two studies (Cassidy et al. 1995; Kontos et al. 1997) used quasi-experimental designs that allow us to infer causality between specialized education and practice. These two studies indicate that global indicators of quality may change somewhat (at least statistically, if not observably), but that observations of teachers' interactions with children revealed no change as a function of specialized education. It may be that researchers are not observing the kinds of behaviors that are likely to change as a function of specialized education. Two studies (Howes, Whitebook, & Phillips 1992; NICHD/ECCRN 1996) found different results for infants/toddlers compared to preschoolers; Howes found specialized education most important for work with infants, whereas the NICHD/ECCRN study found specialized education more important for work with preschoolers.

Experience

Some people believe that education, either general or specialized, is unrelated to effective teaching of young children. In the opinion of many, practical experience is the key to good teaching (Berk 1985). Experts in the early childhood field have described stages of teacher development, focusing essentially on level of experience (Katz 1972). What do research findings point to regarding the relationship between teaching experience and abilities?

Practices

Evidence from research on the relationship between teacher experience and practices appears to be mixed. For example, in Arnett's Bermuda study (1989), experience was unrelated to the sensitivity of teachers' interactions with children. The Staffing Study (Whitebook, Howes, & Phillips 1990; Howes, Whitebook, & Phillips 1992) found that experience failed to predict the quality of the learning environment or teacher behavior. Similarly, experience was not a predictor of positive caregiving in child care settings with infants and toddlers, according to the NICHD ECCRN study (1996).

Howes (1983), on the other hand, found that more experienced teachers in both family child care and center-based care were more likely to exhibit developmentally appropriate caregiving behaviors. Family child care providers with more experience were more likely to restrict toddlers and display negative affect with them. Center caregivers with more experience were more likely to play with toddlers and less likely to ignore their requests. Thus, some positive correlates of experience have been demonstrated.

Less positive results for experience were reported by the Family Child Care and Relative Care study (Kontos et al. 1995). A small negative but statistically significant association ($r = -.17$) was found between family child care providers' years of experience and the quality of care provided (as measured by the FDCRS). In addition, providers with more experience were rated by observers as more harsh and detached, and they rated themselves as

more restrictive. In this study, experience was related to less desirable characteristics in family child care providers.

Evidence from research on the relationship between teacher experience and practices appears to be mixed.

In Epstein's (1993) study of High/Scope training, experience was a highly significant predictor of overall classroom quality, as measured by the ECERS. However, both groups of teachers in her study—those receiving inservice training and the comparison group—were highly educated, had received a lot of specialized education and were highly experienced, which makes it impossible to disentangle the unique effects of experience. Although confounding education and specialized education is an across-the-board problem, the Epstein sample is unique in that it added experience to the mix.

The complexity of the issue is apparent when we examine another study in which moderate experience appears to be the key (Phillipsen et al. 1997). In this case, results indicated that when teachers had less than three years of experience, they were more sensitive with children and worked in classrooms of high quality; and when teachers had more than three years of experience, classroom quality and teacher sensitivity were lower. According to this study, there may be an optimum level of experience beyond which its effectiveness becomes questionable.

In general, the results relating experience to practice are mixed and rather weak.

Summary and implications: What does research tell us?

In a nutshell, our review of the research can be summarized in three sentences:

• Teachers' formal education correlates with overall classroom quality and, less often, with effective teacher behavior.
• Specialized education may be causally related to overall classroom quality, and it is correlated with effective teacher behavior.
• Teachers' experience cannot be consistently linked to overall classroom quality or effective teacher behavior.

What does this mean for the field of early childhood education and for teachers working in that field?

The research reviewed here essentially supports the concept behind the career lattice developed as part of NAEYC's professional development program (see Johnson & McCracken 1994). Although the research does not support experience as an important influence on practice, it does show how relating increased job responsibilities to educational background (general and specialized) is a sound approach. As the career lattice concept illustrates, specialized education *and* experience provide opportunities for early childhood professionals to add breadth to their expertise and also move up in responsibility and pay.

Family child care providers with more experience were more likely to respond positively to toddlers' social bids and were less likely to restrict toddlers and display negative affect with them. Center caregivers with more experience were more likely to play with toddlers and less likely to ignore their requests.

Education and specialized education are considered to be "regulatable" variables in the child care world. In other words, they represent aspects of the child care environment that can be regulated by states. In most states, however, teachers in early childhood settings not affiliated with public schools are subject to little or no regulation regarding their educational qualifications. In some states the standards utilize education and experiential requirements. For instance, teachers in California can get child development permits to work based on a mix of experience and education. Teachers and aides are not required to hold specialized degrees if they have the right blend of experience and course work. Research does not support this approach.

In light of research demonstrating that education and specialized education are linked to program quality, it makes sense for states to upgrade regulations regarding teachers' educational background. For this to happen, teachers, administrators, and other child advocates (including parents) need to make known to state policymakers the positive impact of teacher education on the learning potential of early childhood classrooms (as measured by overall classroom quality and teacher behavior). Advocacy for teacher qualifications will go a long way toward enhancing the educational background of the early childhood teacher workforce. At issue are specialized education experiences as well as credentials that may go along with these experiences, such as specialized licensure that documents the merits of the educational experiences.

Advocacy takes time, however. In the interim, it is crucial for teachers and administrators to put in place temporary voluntary standards for teacher educational qualifications that go beyond the current state regulatory requirements. Even though states may not require early childhood teachers to have postsecondary education or specialized education, teachers and administrators can recognize their value and seek out education for themselves as well as promote the hiring of staff with more education than is required. Moreover, according to Howes's

study (1997), seeking out teacher preparation programs of various types (CDA training, associate degree, bachelor degree) is a better strategy than simply taking a hodgepodge of relevant courses and workshops as they become available.

One problem in the field is recruiting and retaining qualified teachers (Johnson & McCracken 1994). Even if teachers and administrators value and seek out education, the poor wages typical in early childhood education lead to high turnover, especially among educated teachers who have other work alternatives that pay better. Some administrators are even hesitant to hire teachers with specialized education and/or licensure for fear they will ultimately lose them to a better paying job (for example, teaching in public school). Thus, qualifications are compromised for the potential of greater continuity among staff. Advocacy for worthy wages is therefore a crucial strategy for obtaining and maintaining a qualified early childhood workforce. NAEYC and the Center for the Child Care Workforce both have ongoing advocacy activities that early childhood educators can join.

Even though states may not require early childhood teachers to have postsecondary education or specialized education, teachers and administrators can recognize their value and seek out education for themselves as well as promote the hiring of staff with more education than is required.

Another problem is providing access to specialized education for early childhood professionals who cannot afford and/or do not choose to quit their jobs to upgrade their education. To meet the needs of inservice professionals, the field will need to rely more and more on distance education strategies. Some distance programs have already begun to appear. For instance, using distance techniques. Pacific Oaks College in Pasadena, California, offers a master's degree in early childhood education and Ivy Tech State College in Indiana offers an associate's degree in child development. These programs are not the correspondence courses that we have been familiar with in the past. These new programs utilize new technology, including the Internet and the World Wide Web, in addition to print, occasional classroom meetings, and other strategies. It will not be long before there are accessible, affordable programs for early childhood educators to obtain specialized education.

Finally, we should point out that, although research tells us that specialized education is important, it tells us nothing about what content is most important and needed, who (administrators, head teachers, assistant teachers, or aides) is most likely to benefit from education, and what pedagogical methods are most effective in changing beliefs and behaviors of teachers (Kagan & Neuman 1996). These are concerns toward which future research must be directed.

To meet the needs of inservice professionals, the field will need to rely more and more on distance education strategies. These new programs utilize new technology, including the Internet and the World Wide Web, in addition to print, occasional classroom meetings, and other strategies.

References

Abbott-Shim, M., & A. Sibley. 1987. *Assessment profile for early childhood programs*. Atlanta, GA: Quality Assist.

Arnett, J. 1989. Caregivers in day-care centers: Does training matter? *Journal of Applied Developmental Psychology* 10: 541–52.

Berk, L. 1985. Relationship of caregiver education to child-oriented attitudes, job satisfaction, and behaviors toward children. *Child Care Quarterly* 14: 103–29.

Cassidy, D., & M. Buell. 1996. Accentuating the positive? An analysis of teacher verbalizations with young children. *Child and Youth Care Forum* 25: 403–14.

Cassidy, D., M. Buell, S. Pugh-Hoese, & S. Russell. 1995. The effect of education on child care teachers' beliefs and classroom quality: Year one evaluation of the TEACH early childhood associate degree scholarship program. *Early Childhood Research Quarterly* 10: 171–83.

Cost, Quality, and Child Outcomes Study Team. 1995. *Cost, quality, and child outcomes in child care centers: Technical report*. Denver: Economics Department, University of Colorado, Denver.

DeBord, K., & J. Sawyers. 1996. The effects of training on the quality of family child care for those associated with and not associated with professional child care organizations. *Child and Youth Care Forum* 25: 7–15.

Epstein, A. 1993. *Training for quality: Improving early childhood programs through systematic inservice training*. Monographs of the High/Scope Educational Research Foundation. Ypsilanti, MI: High/Scope.

Harms, T., & R. Clifford. 1980. *Early Childhood Environment Rating Scale*. New York: Teachers College Press.

Harms, T., & R. Clifford, 1989. *Family Day Care Rating Scale*. New York: Teachers College Press.

Harms, T., D. Cryer, & R. Clifford. 1990. *Infant/toddler Environment Rating Scale*. New York: Teachers College Press.

Howes, C. 1983. Caregiver behavior in center and family day care. *Journal of Applied Developmental Psychology* 4: 99–107.

Howes, C. 1997. Children's experiences in center-based child care as a function of teacher background and adult : child ratio. *Merrill-Palmer Quarterly* 43: 404–25.

Howes, C., & P. Stewart. 1987. Child's play with adults, toys, and peers: An examination of family and child care influences. *Developmental Psychology* 23: 423–30.

Howes, C., M. Whitebook, & D. Phillips. 1992. Teacher characteristics and effective teaching in child care: Findings from the National Child Care Staffing Study. *Child and Youth Care Forum* 21: 399–414.

Johnson, J., & J. McCracken, eds. 1994. *The early childhood career lattice: Perspectives on professional development*. Washington, DC: NAEYC.

Kagan, S.L., & K.M. Neuman. 1996. The relationship between staff education and training and quality in child care programs. *Child Care Information Exchange* (January): 65–70.

Kaplan, M., & J. Conn. 1984. The effects of caregiver training on classroom setting and caregiver performance in eight community day care centers. *Child Study Journal* 14: 79–93.

Katz, L. 1972. Developmental stages of preschool teachers. *Elementary School Journal* 73: 50–54.

Kontos, S., C. Howes, & E. Galinsky. 1997. Does training make a difference to quality in family child care? *Early Childhood Research Quarterly* 11: 427–45.

Kontos, S., C. Howes, M. Shinn, & E. Galinsky. 1995. *Quality in family child care and relative care*. New York: Teachers College Press.

NICHD (National Institute of Child Health and Human Development) Early Child Care Research Network. 1996. Characteristics of Infant child care: Factors contributing to positive caregiving. *Early Childhood Research Quarterly* 11: 269–306.

Phillips, D., J. Lande, & M. Goldberg. 1990. The state of child care regulation: A comparative analysis. *Early Childhood Research Quarterly* 5: 151–79.

Phillipsen, L., M. Burchinal, C. Howes, & D. Cryer. 1997. The prediction of process quality from structural features of child care. *Early Childhood Research Quarterly* 12: 281–303.

Ruopp, R., J. Travers, F. Glantz, & C. Coelen. 1979. *Children at the center: Final report of the National Day Care Study*. Cambridge, MA: Abt Associates.

Scarr, S., M. Eisenberg, & K. Deater-Deckard. 1994. Measurement of quality in child care centers. *Early Childhood Research Quarterly* 9: 131–51.

Whitebook, M., C. Howes, & D. Phillips. 1990. *Who cares? Child care teachers and the quality of care in America. Final report of the National Child Care Staffing Study*. Oakland, CA: Child Care Employee Project.

Susan Kontos, Ph.D., *is professor of child development and family studies at Purdue University in West Lafayette, Indiana. Susan teaches in the undergraduate and graduate programs and conducts research on the developmental outcomes of classroom processes for young children.*

Amanda Wilcox-Herzog, Ph.D., *is an assistant professor of human development/psychology at California State University at San Bernardino. Amanda primarily teachers human development and early childhood education classes and has taught children ranging in age from birth through eight.*

From *Young Children*, July 2001, pp. 85–91. © 2001 by the National Association for the Education of Young Children. Reprinted by permission.

Concern Turns to Preschool Facilities

BY LINDA JACOBSON
San Francisco

With no playground of its own, the Tenderloin Childcare Center sometimes has its 36 preschoolers walk past boarded-up buildings and homeless men sleeping in doorways to reach a subway station, where the youngsters catch a ride to a city playground.

Traveling back and forth from the playground to the child-care center—located on the first floor of a brick apartment building that used to be a YMCA hotel—is not something the children or the teachers look forward to. But there is no alternative.

"It can be one of the most challenging parts of the day," Graham Dobson, the administrative coordinator of the center, said of the trek.

Efforts are growing to pay for preschool facility improvements

The lack of a playground is just one of the many facility needs that this center, and others like it around the country, have to go without. And the potential dangers and depressing physical characteristics of many such centers have some early-childhood policymakers saying it's time to start focusing more attention on improving the quality of the nation's child-care and preschool facilities.

The Tenderloin Childcare Center, for instance, is housed in the former YMCA hotel's ballroom on the building's first floor. Once an ornate hall with high ceilings, it's now just a large room with peeling paint that has been turned into three make-shift classrooms like cubicles in an office.

The old stage in the ballroom has children's climbing structures and soft mats behind a floor-to-ceiling safety net, which keeps the youngsters from falling off the stage. In the large room, voices echo across the open space, and children playing loudly in one area can drown out the voices of teachers trying to talk or read books to other children.

"We have to juggle the space around a huge amount," Mr. Dobson said as he tried to talk over the sound of small toilets flushing outside the cluttered office he shares with another director.

'An Invisible Issue'

The condition of facilities for preschool-age children rarely receives the same emphasis from advocacy organizations as the call for qualified and well-compensated early-childhood teachers, said Cheryl D. Hayes, the executive director of the Finance Project. The Washington-based policy-research and technical-assistance organization focuses on services for children and families.

"It's a little bit of an invisible issue," Ms. Hayes said.

Efforts are growing, however, to bring not only attention to the issue, but new financing to help programs find higher-quality facilities or upgrade their current buildings and classrooms.

For example, the Tenderloin center, which serves poor children, some of whom are from homeless families, was a prime candidate for help from the Child Care Facilities Fund, a nonprofit lender based in Oakland, Calif. The fund works with the San Francisco mayor's office and private donors to improve and expand early-childhood-education facilities in that city.

Early this year, the center will move to a fully renovated site a few blocks away that has two floors of classrooms, office space, a staff meeting room, a gathering room for parents—and finally, an outdoor playground.

It's a step other directors of early-childhood facilities would like to take, but can't because of budget constraints.

In many centers, teachers and classroom assistants have to walk children to other parts of the building to use the restroom because no such facilities are nearby. That is frustrating for teachers, especially those in understaffed centers, where it is difficult to take one child to the restroom while also monitoring the other youngsters.

And preschool teachers rarely have break rooms, where they can unwind and compare notes, or adequate storage space, which means that supplies are often scattered all over the place.

"You need at least a healthy and safe space, if not stimulating and developmentally appropriate," said September Jarrett, the director of the Child Care Facilities Fund.

Experts say better facilities raise teacher morale.

Beyond those basics, some experts say better facilities can significantly improve the attitudes of early-childhood educators toward their work and toward the children they teach.

"I think there is growing evidence that facilities are more important than were previously thought," said Carl Sussman, who runs a Boston-based community-development consulting group. He is a founding member of the National Children's Facilities Network, an organization working to improve early-childhood facilities throughout the country.

Finding the Money

The San Francisco city government, which already had a history of providing financing for child-care facilities, approached the Low Income Housing Fund, a national financial institution based in San Francisco that focuses on community development, about operating such a program specifically for such facilities.

With what Ms. Jarrett now describes as a "layered cake" approach, the Child Care Facilities Fund pieces together a variety of different sources of public and private money to pay for anything from heating repairs to brand-new buildings.

In a pioneering move, the city secured its primary source of funding for major child-care construction and renovation projects from the U.S. Department of Housing and Urban Development. The money is loaned to child-care providers, who have to repay 20 percent of the debt over 10 years. The other 80 percent is paid for by San Francisco's department of human services.

About $8.6 million in what is known as Section 108 funding—federal dollars that can be used for community development projects—is being used to develop child-care space that will eventually serve almost 600 more children, according to Ms. Jarrett.

San Francisco, where real estate costs are among the highest in the United States, is also among the most unlikely places for a wave of child-care construction to be taking place.

In fact, shortly after the fund was created, real estate costs in the city "went through the roof," Ms. Jarrett said. Even churches that had been renting space to child-care providers for years were saying they could make more money by leasing the space to someone else or developing it as something other than a child-care center.

Many of the new facilities are now part of larger subsidized-housing developments throughout the city, such as the new Heritage Homes community in the Visitacion Valley, which is the southernmost part of the city and county. When complete, the development, which includes townhouses for low-income families, will also have a new center for 45 children attached to a senior housing facility.

"If you're going to build low-income housing, you've got to have a child-care angle," Ms. Jarrett said.

Providers in need of smaller improvements are not left out. The facilities fund also provides smaller grants of up to $20,000 for needs such as playground improvements or emergency equipment purchases.

One such provider is Cruz Fernandez, who runs a home-based Montessori program on the first floor of her house in the Oceanview neighborhood here. She opened her business in 1999, using borrowed materials. A $4,500 grant from the facilities fund has allowed her to buy new child-size furniture and the expensive, durable materials that are an essential part of a Montessori education.

"When I first heard about [the grants], I couldn't believe it," Ms. Fernandez said. And, she added, the children are proud of the new equipment. "They take care of it," she said.

Beyond San Francisco

Other places around the country also have come up with different ways of paying for early-childhood facilities.

The facilities fund in the San Francisco area was modeled after work done by the Illinois Facilities Fund, a community-development financial institution in Chicago that began making real estate loans to nonprofit organizations, including child-care centers, about 12 years ago.

It wasn't until 2000, however, that Chicago officials agreed to put a significant amount of money—$25 million—into building child-care facilities to serve children from low-income families. That, combined with a $25 million match being raised by the fund, has helped pay for 16 building projects.

Like the Child Care Facilities Fund used in San Francisco, the Illinois fund also has smaller "loan products" for providers who need to make minor improvements.

Back east in Connecticut, school readiness legislation passed in 1997 fostered a much greater demand for classroom space. But unlike other states, Connecticut is financing preschool construction in much the same way that school districts build schools—by issuing 30-year revenue bonds. That approach has generated more than $40 million for the construction of 19 new facilities in the state's 21 "priority," or high-need, districts.

The state also appropriated $2.5 million to pay 80 percent of the interest on the bonds. Providers were responsible for 20 percent. That funding has now been exhausted, and supporters are hoping the legislature will renew the program.

On the other hand, in New Jersey—where the state supreme court in 1998 ordered the state education department to provide early-childhood programs in 30 needy districts—advocates for early-childhood education say the state has been a stumbling block rather than a supporter on facilities issues.

"... some [facilities] are in parking lots, some are on school grounds, taking up playground space."

The poor condition of facilities in those districts has become a key part of the debate over how to improve the quality of pre-school facilities across the state.

"There is a major problem with the amount of facilities and the quality of these facilities," said Joan M. Ponessa, the director of research at the Education Law Center in Newark, which represents all the children in the 30 districts that were part of the state supreme court ruling.

While funding for school construction, including preschool facilities, has been passed by the New Jersey legislature, districts have not been given permission from the state to build permanent buildings for early-childhood programs. Instead, the state ordered districts to use trailers to house the programs. But many of the urban schools, Ms. Ponessa said, don't have space for trailers.

As a result, she said, some programs "are in parking lots," and "some are on school grounds, taking up playground space."

Policymakers Interested

The quality of child-care facilities is an issue that is beginning to attract attention from policy-makers at the federal level, too. Last year, the Department of Health and Human Services awarded $2.5 million to 10 different organizations around the country—from Alaska to Maryland—that will provide technical assistance to providers to help them renovate or build child-care facilities.

Research on how facilities affect what happens in early childhood classrooms is almost nonexistent

But Sens. Christopher J. Dodd, D-Conn., and Mike DeWine, R-Ohio, would like the federal government to do much more. Last year, they introduced a bill that would provide $250 million over five years to improve and build child-care facilities. The proposed Childcare Facilities Financing Act would be targeted toward low-income areas.

The bill did not move out of committee last year, though, and Ms. Jarrett acknowledged that even though many policymakers agree that more public money is needed to improve child-care programs, it's hard to predict when money might be available.

Many of those concerned with improving facilities also would like to see more included on the issue as part of the accreditation process for early-childhood programs.

But Alan Simpson, a spokesman for the National Association for the Education of Young Children, a Washington-based organization that accredits early-childhood programs, said that while the association "might like more programs to be in facilities that were designed for that purpose, we're not in a position to demand it."

Moreover, because local building codes vary tremendously, it would be hard for the NAEYC or other organizations to write one set of facility standards for the whole country, said Trinita Logue, the president of the Illinois Facilities Fund.

'Out of the Basement'

Research on how facilities affect what happens in early-childhood classrooms is almost nonexistent.

A landmark 1995 study by researchers from four universities, known as the "Cost, Quality, and Outcomes" study, found, however, that many classrooms—especially those for infants and toddlers—did not meet basic sanitary requirements and were even dangerous to children.

And child-care experts emphasize that the physical features of a facility can have an effect on how the teachers do their work.

"We really believe that if you respect the adult, that trickles down to the children," Ms. Logue said.

A recent example to support her belief comes from the School for Young Children, a laboratory preschool at St. Joseph College in West Hartford, Conn.

When students in a child-study course observed youngsters at play at the school, they found that the adults in the school, which was in the basement of a college building, were interacting with the children during only about 3 percent of the observations.

While that figure was comparable to earlier research on adult involvement in play, the college students and their faculty adviser, Carlota Schechter, were still disturbed by the results. So they observed the children again. But this time, the program was in a new facility, an old elementary school that was renovated to serve the needs of young children. This time, the percentage of observations in which teachers were interacting with children during playtime jumped to 22 percent.

Astounded by the increase, Ms. Schechter and the director of the program met with the teachers, who attributed the difference to their move to the new site. In the old facility, the children's spots for storing their personal items, the restrooms and sinks, and the phones were all down the hall, which forced the teachers to leave the room frequently.

"In the new space, teachers do not need to leave the room to monitor these activities, and thus there is much more time for teachers to be interacting with children in the classroom," Ms. Schechter wrote in a proposal for a similar study that is now being conducted at a preschool in Hartford.

The teachers also noted that because the rooms in the new facility were larger, the children had more room to play—and, as a result, there seemed to be fewer disputes between children than there were in the other location.

"The feeling of coming out of the basement—literally out of the basement—raises teacher morale so much," Ms. Schechter said.

From *Education Week*, January 16, 2002, pp. 14-15. © 2002 by Education Week. Reprinted by permission.

UNIT 2
Child Development and Families

Unit Selections

Key Points to Consider

- What skills developed during the preschool years will be of most assistance as children grow and develop throughout life?

- Describe the role adults play in assisting children to develop a sense of right and wrong.

- What role do parents and the media play in gender identification?

- How do children benefit by having their fathers involved in their schools?

- What can parents and teachers do to help children develop tolerance for people of different races and cultures?

- Describe the effects on young children of viewing cartoon violence.

 **Links: www.dushkin.com/online/**
These sites are annotated in the World Wide Web pages.

Administration for Children and Families
http://www.acf.dhhs.gov

I Am Your Child
http://www.iamyourchild.org

Internet Resources for Education
http://web.hamline.edu/personal/kfmeyer/cla_education.html#hamline

The National Academy for Child Development
http://www.nacd.org

National Parent Information Network/ERIC
http://npin.org

National Safe Kids Campaign
http://www.babycenter.com

Parent Center
http://www.parentcenter.com/general/34754.html

Zero to Three
http://www.zerotothree.org

P arents may want academic skills to be the focus of their child's early childhood learning experiences, but when asked what skills will best prepare their child to be successful in life, there may be a different answer. "Skills for School Readiness— and Life" outlines six important attitudes and behaviors for success throughout life. The teachers' role in providing for the development of independence, compassion, trust, creativity, self-control, perseverance, and resilience is critical. In a similar vein, "What's the Difference Between Right and Wrong?" examines the development of moral reasoning. Teachers, parents, and administrators who focus solely on the development of the cognitive domains, ignoring the affective or social and emotional areas, are neglecting to educate the whole child.

Finally, after years of schools having "helping moms" or "room mothers," teachers are realizing the benefit of encouraging dads to participate in their children's education. "Encouraging Fathers to Participate in the School Experiences of Young Children: The Teacher's Role" by Barry Frieman and Terry Berkeley describes how fathers can become integral contributors to children's education. In one Chevy Chase, Maryland, school, Lena is envied by her peers for her father's active participation in her school. Her dad will accompany the class on trips, document learning opportunities with photographs, or share art with the class. His contributions are greatly appreciated by a teaching staff that recognizes the importance of fathers in the classroom. Lena's father is encouraged by the teacher's use of "moms or dads" in her conversations about families helping in the classroom. The most striking evidence for supporting dads in their children's education comes in the form of a 1997 study from the U.S. Department of Education. The researchers recognized the contributions mothers make as essential to the social and emotional well-being of children, but they found that the involvement by fathers may be critical to academic achievement. Although this study was done with students in grades 6–12, it is important to note that parent participation in the later grades hinges on their involvement in their children's preschool and primary education. Our job as early childhood educators is to encourage all parents, but especially fathers, to come into the classroom and to feel comfortable and useful during their visits. Lorenza DiNatale provides suggestions for getting families involved in their children's early education in her article, "Developing High-Quality Family Involvement Programs in Early Childhood Settings." By getting parents off to a positive start with their initial school volunteer experience, we are doing a huge favor for our colleagues who work with older children. Then as children move through the grades, their families will be accustomed to contributing to their children's education.

Often as editors, we find themes emerging from the hundreds of articles we read each year in professional journals as well as magazines aimed at the general public. This was the case this year as well. It took us back 20 years to the 1981 publication of David Elkind's *The Hurried Child.* Elkind reported on the practice in the early 1980s of parents pushing their children to grow up too quickly and missing childhood. Unfortunately, one of the articles chosen for this unit reports a similar theme. "No Time for Fun" show parents pushing their children to do more, achieve more, and grow up more quickly. Children are increasingly being denied the chance to participate in what many adults hold as their fondest childhood memories. Leisurely passing away the hours while attempting to dam up a little stream and float leaves and sticks, finding secret hiding places for games of hide-and-go-seek, or using every available cushion, pillow, and blanket to make a fort are memories many adults have of childhood. What will be your children's memories of their play experiences? Asking parents that question can cause some serious reflection on their part related to their hectic lifestyle and heavy reliance on technology for their children's leisure activity.

As early childhood educators, we must work with families to help them find the balance of appropriate extracurricular activities that will enable their children to live a rich and fulfilling life while still enjoying the period known as childhood. They will have years to engage in focused study but the years of childhood pass quickly. It is appropriate for teachers of young children to provide opportunities for families to explore their role in helping their children achieve in the future as well as fully participate in childhood. Articles, such as those included in this edition, can be summarized for parents and posted on a bulletin board or included in a newsletter. Parent discussion groups can have out-of-school activities as a discussion topic. Teachers can use their knowledge about child development to guide parents in making appropriate decisions regarding their children. Often parents, caught up in the frenzy of competing with other families, lose perspective of what is best for their own child. As a parent it is perfectly acceptable to say to a child, "No," "You're too young," or "Not in our family." Parents can also ask themselves why they are pushing their children to engage in activities that were never a part of their own childhood 20 or so years ago. Parents need to remember that, just as with walking and talking, each child has his or her individual time schedule for acquiring skills.

The terrorist attacks of September 11, 2001, caused the entire country to examine personal practices of discrimination based on peoples' skin color, race, dress, or cultural identity. Adults can help children develop healthy attitudes about people different from themselves by seeking experiences that expose children to different cultures and diversity. Helpful suggestions for beginning conversations with children about race are included in "Talking to Kids About Race." We encourage teachers to share these discussion topics with parents of young children.

independence
compassion
trust
creativity
self-control
perseverance
Skills for school readiness—and life

Quiz

Yes	No	
❐	❐	1. Children are ready for school when they know the letters of the alphabet and can sound out words.
❐	❐	2. Children entering kindergarten must know how to count to 20.
❐	❐	3. Children who are curious and creative will have lots of problems in school.
❐	❐	4. Children cannot be responsible for their own clothes, work, and lunch money in kindergarten.
❐	❐	5. Knowing how to make friends is less important in school success than knowing how to write your name.
❐	❐	6. Children cannot develop compassion until they reach high school.

If you answered yes to any of these questions, you may need to re-think your ideas about school readiness.

Too often early care and education teachers feel pushed to focus on academics. They may decide to drill letters and numbers. They may make flash cards and worksheets. They may order videos and computer programs that promise school readiness.

Let's take a step back and consider the skills children really need to succeed in school. Will 5-year-old Timmy succeed if he can count to 20 by rote on the first day of kindergarten? Or will he stand a better chance of success if he comes with a sense of self-confidence and trust? If he feels curious and creative? If he gets along well with others? If he has self-control and can finish what he starts? If he loves learning?

The truth is that if Timmy has the attitudes and behaviors that foster learning, he will likely learn what he needs to learn in every grade level. More than that, he will likely learn how to succeed in life.

The attitudes and behaviors children most need for school readiness are independence, compassion, trust, creativity, self-control, and perseverance. Our role as teachers is to create an environment where children can develop these traits.

Independence. Children begin learning independence as toddlers. They insist on doing things themselves one minute and wail in frustration the next. They say "no" and "mine" and resist taking a nap even when they can barely hold their eyes open.

Ideally by kindergarten, children are able to take some responsibility for their own success and failure. They discover that their actions have consequences and that they can influence those consequences by their actions. They learn to internalize motivation and don't

Readiness for life

Traits children need for school readiness extend throughout life.

Independence. We act independently when we make informed, competent decisions based on experience, information, and balanced judgment. We are willing to take reasonable risks, and look beyond "how we always do it" to improve a public or personal situation.

Compassion. Compassion enables us to recognize the humanity—and dignity—of all people. It is the characteristic that drives charity, volunteer work, tolerance, and mutual respect.

Trust. Trust allows us to accept our own worth, feel secure with friends, and have a positive, open outlook. We trust when we know the rules, want to abide by them, and expect consequences to certain behaviors.

Creativity. Creativity enables us to think through mental challenges and use negotiation techniques to solve social conflicts. It involves flexibility—not being locked into a routine for its own sake—and an eagerness to search for new answers and solutions.

Self-control. Self-control refers to the ability to think about a behavior and decide whether to act or not. Self-control enables us to be patient with ourselves and others.

Perseverance and resilience. We persevere by overcoming obstacles and solving problems. These qualities help us get to the bottom of the list—getting reports written, sweaters knit, cars manufactured, kitchens cleaned, and grass cut.

have to rely on rewards and praise to find success. They want to practice self-reliance—and show that they don't want or need the constant protection and supervision of adults. Encourage independence in the following ways:

- Give toddlers reasonable choices. "Do you want to read this book or that one?"
- Allow 18-month-old Jennie to use a spoon at mealtime but stand ready to help if she gets frustrated.
- Provide 3- and 4-year-olds with peanut butter, crackers, and plastic knives and let them prepare their own snack.
- Set up learning centers and let children choose activities within them. In the math center, for example, they might sort items by size, fit geometric shapes into a puzzle, or string beads in a pattern.

Compassion. Infants and toddlers regard themselves as the center of the universe. They are unable to understand the needs of others and can express only their own.

Ideally by kindergarten, children begin to empathize—to put themselves in another's place. Children begin to recognize the strengths and weaknesses of other people—and to share their sorrow or pride.

Encourage the development of compassion in the following ways:

- Talks about feelings. Give a name to pain, fear, anger, and joy, for example.
- Identify and encourage kindnesses, such as when Abby tries to console Abbot when he scrapes his knee.
- Make pet care more than routine by talking about feeling hungry, thirsty, or dirty.
- Encourage cooperative rather than competitive activities. Instead of challenging children to a foot race, plan an obstacle course that requires children to help each other squeeze through a cardboard box, for example.

Trust. When infants and toddlers have consistent, loving care they develop basic trust. They feel they are important members of the family or group and learn they can rely on adults for help in unfamiliar situations. Coupled with a desire for independence, trust enables children to feel the protection and support of adults as they explore, discover, and interpret the environment.

Ideally by kindergarten, children can understand the give-and-take of social situations. They are comfortable with the rules or "ways of doing" that keep them safe. They rely on our consistency to know what is expected of them and are eager to do things the right way.

Encourage the development of trust in the following ways:

- When a baby cries, respond as soon as possible.
- Follow daily routines for eating, play, and naps.
- Establish simple rules and enforce them consistently.
- Treat children fairly, with respect and consideration.
- Provide supervision to prevent biting, bullying, cruel teasing, and other violent behavior.

Creativity. Babies are born curious. They reach for objects and explore them with their mouths and hands. As toddlers, they get into everything and climb into interesting spaces.

Ideally by kindergarten, children are eager to work on and solve their own problems—in art and construction projects, computations, and social interactions. They approach ideas and tasks with initiative, playfulness, and inventive thinking. They ask lots of questions.

Encourage creativity in the following ways:

- Provide clay, paints, blocks, and other unstructured materials. Allow children time to explore the material without the need to make an object or paint a picture.
- Focus on the process, not the product. Avoid asking "What is it?" Rather say things like "Looks like you really enjoyed doing that" or "You worked hard on that."
- Ask open-ended questions. Instead of "Did you like the story?" ask "What did you like best about the story?"
- Notice and appreciate children's ideas. "Yes, Juan. We could take apart that old clock and see if we could make it work."
- Avoid rote learning and modeled projects that minimize individuality.

Self-control. Toddlers have little self-control. Ricky, for example, sees a truck and wants it. However, he does not have the intellectual or social skills to consider that Heddy is already playing with it and that he needs to wait for his turn.

Ideally by kindergarten, children understand and accept the need for rules—for their own sake and sake of others in community. They are learning the art of compromise and negotiation and can often see an event from someone else's point of view. Kindergarten children are usually able to identify their own property and respect the belongings of their peers. They are also able to take responsibility for simple tasks, have the self-control to stay focused, and follow through on a commitment.

Encourage self-control in the following ways:

- Model self-restraint. "I feel like eating a big bowl of ice cream right now, but I know I would feel too stuffed to move."
- Offer children choices.
- Consistently enforce simple rules.
- Offer to help children identify and deal with their frustrations. "Your face looks really angry,

Jacob. Shall we take some deep breaths before we talk about the problem?"
- Be clear about appropriate and inappropriate ways to express anger. "You can stamp your feet, Hannah, but I can't let you use your feet to kick Hank."

Perseverance and resilience. Toddlers learn to walk only after lots of trials and tumbles. Determination to succeed helps them ignore bumps and falls, and find success. When preschoolers dig canals in the sand, they learn cause and effect—what works and doesn't work.

Ideally by kindergarten, children have experience with problem-solving, brainstorming, and evaluating decisions. They can often use these skills to evaluate what went wrong with a project—and find the courage and determination to try again.

Encourage perseverance and resilience in the following ways:

- Encourage children to finish projects they begin—work a puzzle, build a structure, paint a picture, or play a game before quitting.
- Let children extend their projects over time—a block construction or multi-piece puzzle, for example, could take several days.
- Provide storage space for unfinished art projects.
- Avoid the temptation to do something for, rather than with, a child.
- Teach negotiation skills. "Cole and Bryan, how can you both play with the trike without fighting?"

Independence, compassion, trust, creativity, self-control, and perseverance—these attitudes are the real signs of school readiness. These are also the attitudes children need to grow into successful, competent adults. With these qualities, they will find satisfying jobs, form loving families, and be respected in society.

From *Texas Child Care*, Fall 2002, pp. 40-42. © 2002 by Texas Workforce Commission.

Look Who's Listening

New research shows babies employ many tricks to pick up language

BY RICHARD MONASTERSKY

Sitting in a dim laboratory at the Johns Hopkins University, David Wiggs peers at a flashing red light and listens intently to a series of sentences playing over a loudspeaker.

"Fluid ice is a difficult concept to grasp. Merchants used to trade ice for water. Weird ice no longer surprises anyone. The experts soon detected that it was flawed ice."

The words could be the rantings of a glaciologist on acid, but David doesn't raise an eyebrow. For this blue-eyed infant, the strange passage is just one small drop in a river of gibberish flowing past his ears every day.

In the nine months since his birth, David Wiggs (not his real name) has been wading through that stream of largely unintelligible sound. Now he is starting to navigate its pools and eddies. Succeeding in a task that no computer could tackle, the plump little boy has learned how to break the continuous flow of speech he hears from any person into discrete chunks—what we call words—even though he has no idea what most of the chunks mean.

And that's only his latest success. David has been picking up clues about how to pull apart and understand his native language ever since he floated in the womb. From the day he gulped his first breath, he could distinguish the rhythms of English from many other languages, simply from the memory of the muffled sounds that had filtered though his mom's belly.

Now the scientists studying language acquisition are growing up right along with David. Even as the youngster starts to cobble together an understanding of English, researchers are teasing apart the complex process of how children pick up language. Their discoveries challenge the work of earlier investigators, who tended to see the problem in stark terms of nature or nurture. Though that conflict still smolders, most scientists now recognize that both genes and environment must play a role. So researchers today concentrate on determining which abilities are bred into humans and which ones they develop through listening to the babble that surrounds them.

"We are starting to get a clearer picture about when things develop and about how they're developing," says Peter W. Jusczyk, a professor of psychology at Johns Hopkins. "So I do think there's a coherent middle ground that's forming here. Maybe we are moving more into a kind of a maturity."

A WAR IS OVER WORDS

Although philosophers have argued for centuries about innate knowledge, the modern debate over language started in 1957, when B. F. Skinner pushed his theory of stimulus response, or S.R., into the linguistic realm and published Verbal Behavior. In that work, the famous psychologist asserted that language parallels other types of behavior: Children are born as blank slates and learn language from their environment, through direct reinforcement from parents and others.

At that time, rival theories of psychological development couldn't gain a toehold in the United States, says Mr. Jusczyk. "You had Skinner beating everybody over the head, and all the S.R. theorists for a long time held sway in this country."

Their grip started to loosen in 1959, when Noam Chomsky, a professor of linguistics at the Massachusetts Institute of Technology, published a review of *Verbal Behavior* that aired his competing theory of language as an innate ability, a theory he expanded on in later writings. Infants are born with a universal grammar, he wrote, and the language heard early in life plays only a limited role, setting the cognitive switches inside the brain and tuning the universal grammar to a particular language—for instance, specifying that objects come after verbs in English but before verbs in Japanese.

Peter D. Eimas, now an emeritus professor of cognitive and linguistic science at Brown University, extended the "nativist" theory when he posited that children are born with a "phonetic feature detector" that is unique to humans and has evolved the specialized task of picking out phonemes—the building blocks of words—from speech.

The debate over learned versus innate faculties raged through the 1960's and 1970's. "There was a war here," says Mr. Jusczyk, who was an undergraduate student of Mr. Eimas at the time. But eventually the Chomskian revolution swept over the field of language research. "A lot of people jumped on the bandwagon," Mr. Jusczyk says, "and it was because, in some sense, the S.R. view was so extreme before."

In recent years, the pendulum of theory has swung again: not back to behaviorism, but toward a new position that examines how both innate abilities and subsequent learning play specific roles. The skirmish still flares up in scientific journals, though, revealing a deeply ingrained—if not innate—polarization.

Steven Pinker, a professor of psychology at M.I.T. who aligns himself with nativist theory, says researchers must move beyond the simplified form of the nature-nurture debate. "What we should be doing is figuring out what is innate, and not arguing whether innate stuff is important or unimportant and whether learning is important or unimportant. There has to be something innate—otherwise house cats would learn language the same way that children do. But a whole language can't be innate."

Jeffrey L. Elman, a professor of cognitive science at the University of California at San Diego, agrees, even though he lives on the other side of the theoretical divide. Many aspects of linguistic ability stem from our genes, he grants, but he wonders what the specific innate mechanisms are that make language possible, and whether they are unique to humans. "The road from the genome to relative clauses is very long, shrouded in clouds, and not at all an obvious one."

BORN LISTENERS

That road takes many twists in the first year of life, as infants pass through a series of stages and employ several techniques for dealing with the sounds coming out of their parents' mouths.

From their earliest moments of life, children seem tuned into the rhythms of language, the patterns of stress and pacing that make English distinct from, say, Russian. Studies by French researchers in 1998 showed that newborns have a knack—manifested by how frequently they sucked on a pacifier—for telling the difference between languages with different rhythms, although they have a harder time with ones that share a rhythmic pattern, like English and Dutch.

And newborns are born listeners, with an ability to hear differences between sounds that adults can't hope to match, says Patricia K. Kuhl, a professor of speech and hearing sciences at the University of Washington. She calls them "citi-

zens of the world," because they can perceive phonemes from all languages.

Adults, by contrast, have selective hearing. In experiments conducted over the past four years, Ms. Kuhl and her colleagues have documented that native Japanese speakers, for example, cannot distinguish between the phonemes "ra" and "la." English speakers, on the other hand, have a hard time telling the Mandarin Chinese phoneme "qi," which starts with something akin to a "ch" sound, from the phoneme "xi," which begins with a sound closer to "sh."

Young infants can hear them all, but that ability soon disappears, Ms. Kuhl and her graduate student, Feng-Ming Tsao, found in a study last year. The incessant speech that babies hear early on actually warps their ability to distinguish among sounds later. For babies raised by English speakers, Ms. Kuhl says, "by the time they get to their first birthday, their brains are quite strongly committed to the English way of listening."

Even as they are acclimating to their mother tongue, infants are also starting to take their first steps toward comprehending language. The key to that process involves learning how to pick out words from the rapidly flowing stream of normal speech.

GIVE HIM A BREAK

For the first few months of a baby's life, every day is like wandering around in a foreign country where the inhabitants jabber away in some unknown dialect. "If you're listening to a foreign language, it's very difficult to figure out where one word ends and another begins. If you're a baby, you have to cope with this same problem of segmenting the input," says Mr. Jusczyk.

Only after accomplishing that feat can infants start to associate meanings with individual words.

A decade ago, nobody knew when infants began to break the speech stream into individual words. Then, in 1995, Mr. Jusczyk and Richard N. Aslin, of the University of Rochester, perfected a technique for testing whether children could perform that task. They sat babies in a darkened room and had them listen to individual words, like "cup," "dog," and "bike."

Then the researchers played passages of speech, some of which contained the previously heard words. They measured how interested the babies were in the words by how long they gazed at a light that flashed repeatedly as each passage was played.

Six-month-old infants showed no preference for passages containing the previously heard words. But infants only seven weeks older than that listened significantly longer to those passages, indicating that they could distinguish words like "bike" within strings of speech, even though they may not have known their meaning.

"I never would have suspected that they could have picked up that information as rapidly as they did," says Mr. Jusczyk. "After I got the data, I was forced to deal with that fact."

Using the same method, cognitive psychologists set out to determine how babies could perform such preverbal tricks. The recent experiments have "really changed the landscape for what we think is going on inside infants' heads," says Jenny R. Saffran, an assistant professor of psychology at the University of Wisconsin at Madison.

Among babies' tools for decoding speech, one technique apparently involves a subconcious form of statistics. Simply put, babies can keep track of how many times they hear a sound. For example, when presented with the phrase "funny puppy," infants are more likely to group "fun" with "ny" rather than "ny" with "pup," because they have heard the combination "fun-ny" more often than they have heard "ny-pup."

Ms. Saffran and her colleagues demonstrated that capacity when they exposed infants to an artificial language consisting of words like "pabiku" and "tibudo" strung together randomly, without breaks. After only two minutes of listening, the babies had learned to segment the words from each other, simply because those combinations of phonemes appeared more frequently than did combinations that cut across words.

"Learners may behave somewhat like sponges," says Ms. Saffran. "If there are certain things that recur, you are just going to suck them up. You can't help it."

She and San Diego's Mr. Elman and others say such results argue against the nativist concept of infants as poor learners. But the nativists, including M.I.T.'s Mr. Pinker, say that interpretation is too simple.

In any case, infants can't live by statistics alone, because that would lead them astray quite often, says Mr. Jusczyk. In one example documented by a researcher, a mother urged her toddler to "behave," and the child shot back, "I am have." Because the word "be" often occurs on its own, the child had used that pattern to segment "behave" into two words.

Infants appear to have a whole range of other tricks, as Mr. Jusczyk has shown in recent experiments, including the one that young David participated in. That study, published last month in the *Journal of Experimental Psychology: Human Perception and Performance,* examined how infants regard sentences that include such phrases as "cold ice," "weird ice," and "fluid ice."

If the babies were simply keeping track of repetitions, then they should have reacted to the word "dice" as familiar, because each of the examples contained "d" followed by "ice." But in the study, eight-and-a-half-month-old infants did not exhibit any familiarity with "dice," reported Mr. Jusczyk and Sven L. Mattys, a lecturer in experimental psychology at the University of Bristol, in Britain. The babies' brains had latched onto some other aspect of language that overrode the circuits monitoring phoneme repetition. For instance, the "i" in "ice" sounds slightly different from the "i" in "dice," because speakers close off their windpipes before voicing the vowel in "ice."

ALGEBRA AT 7 MONTHS

If statistics won't get babies everywhere with language, they may try a little algebra. At least that's the way Gary F. Marcus describes the results of his study of seven-month-old infants.

An associate professor of psychology at New York University, Mr. Marcus let the babies listen to a repeating pattern of syllables that obeyed either an A-B-A or an A-B-B grammar, such as "ga ti ga" or "li na na." Then he played different syllables arranged in both patterns, such as "wo fe wo" and "wo fe fe." The infants reacted to the patterns they had heard before as if they were familiar, even though the syllables were completely new.

Such results, he says, show that infants develop algebra-like rules and can plug different sounds into the patterns they hear. Mr. Chomsky argues for the same type of "generalization" ability to explain how we can create, and also comprehend, completely novel combinations of words.

"Chomsky illustrated this with the now-famous sentence 'Colorless green ideas sleep furiously.' You can understand the syntax of that even if you've never heard it before," says Mr. Marcus.

While his research shows that infants have that ability early on, if not from birth, other studies challenge the nativist view that many of the language tools of infants are evolved specifically for that purpose.

Marc D. Hauser, a professor of psychology at Harvard University, has found that adult monkeys can match young infants in many of their cognitive abilities. In the March issue of *Cognition,* Mr. Hauser and his colleagues showed that a species called the cotton-top tamarin can perform the same statistical processing that infants

displayed in Ms. Saffran's test. More recently, tamarins have accomplished the pattern-identification task mastered by babies in Mr. Marcus's algebra study, says Mr. Hauser, who has yet to publish those data.

"Every time there's been a question raised and people have bothered to do the experiments, the animal data showed that the mechanism is similar," he says. The implication is that infants use general auditory tools for listening to and understanding speech—tools that we inherited from our primate ancestors and later co-opted for language. "They are not special to speech," says Mr. Hauser.

Researchers are now investigating how far they can push those general tools. Can tamarins actually learn more-complex grammatical patterns, the kinds that most interested Mr. Chomsky? asks Mr. Hauser. Ms. Saffran, meanwhile, has started to test whether simple statistical procedures can help in grammar acquisition, a point pushed by the anti-nativists.

In the laboratory at Johns Hopkins, all those issues are playing out beneath David's blond curls. He finishes the "weird ice" experiment without much fidgeting, and the tester rewards him by holding up a cuddly monkey puppet, which makes the baby scream. Too young for words, David sobs for a few minutes as the adults around him struggle in vain, trying to figure out what is going on inside his head.

WHAT'S THE DIFFERENCE BETWEEN RIGHT AND WRONG:

UNDERSTANDING HOW CHILDREN THINK

BY SANDRA CROSSER, PH.D.

"No! I can't share," shouted Ernie. Desperation could be heard in his voice as Ernie defensively attempted to gather all 147 blocks into his three-year-old arms. "I NEED them!" he protested. Ernie's sense

of fairness—right or wrong—had been violated by a request to share. Is Ernie a selfish, naughty child? Has he been spoiled? Probably not. A more likely explanation is that Ernie is simply thinking and behaving

normally in a way that exhibits his emerging sense of morality.

The experts tell us that morality involves thinking, feeling, and acting. Feelings of empathy and altruism and acts of sharing and compassion are coupled to and limited by the individual's cognitive development. How we feel, act, and think about good and bad are all parts of our morality.

A great deal has been written about emergent literacy and emergent numeracy as early childhood educators attempt to create and implement curricula that reflect developmentally appropriate practice in reading and mathematics. The young child is in the process of becoming a reader, a writer, or a mathematician. We try to understand those processes while realizing that they will be ongoing, continuing to develop in varying degrees over the child's lifetime.

In much the same way, preschoolers are emerging into the world of moral thought. How children think about right and wrong may be just as developmental as how children think about letters and numbers. Therefore, it is important to examine the young child's typical developmental progression of moral thought in order better to understand how to link emerging morality to developmentally appropriate practice. This article will focus on the young child's moral thinking. For that purpose, moral thought will be defined as thinking about right and wrong.

Is Taking off Your Hat Indoors a Moral Issue?

It is important to make the distinction between issues of morality and issues of social convention. While moral issues involve concepts such as justice, fairness, and human rights, issues that are conventions involve socially agreed-upon rules that are not moral in nature. Classroom rules such as taking off one's hat indoors, sitting on all four legs of a chair, or limits on the number of children allowed in a play area at any one time are all conventions which involve no moral issue. Even children as young as three years have been able to distinguish between moral and conventional issues (Nucci, 1981; Nucci & Nucci, 1982).

Developmental psychologists advise that it is important for teachers to discriminate between moral issues and issues of convention when dealing with discipline over rule infractions. When a child breaks a rule that is a convention, she is simply to be told that a rule was broken and to stop the action. No lectures, please. If, on the other hand, the infraction involves a moral issue, it is important for an adult to talk with the child about the implications of the action in regard to human rights and fairness. The wrong must be made right so that justice prevails.

Young children think of right and wrong in terms of...

Absolutes. Things are always good or always bad. It is unimportant whether an act was intentional or unintentional.

How much physical damage was done. The greater the damage, the worse the perception of the act.

Whether an act will evoke punishment. If an act will be punished then it is wrong.

Rules. Rules should never be broken. Breaking rules is viewed as wrong.

Their own perspective. Children have difficulty taking another person's view of an issue.

Piaget's View of Moral Development

Jean Piaget was perhaps the first to delve into the thought processes behind children's moral decision-making (Piaget, 1932/1965). While Piaget was not so concerned with what the child decided, he was interested in how the child arrived at the decision. In his wisdom, Piaget observed children playing games, told them stories involving moral dilemmas, and questioned them. He arrived at the conclusion that young children differ from older children in the ways they think about moral issues. The child's individual level of cognitive development, enhanced by informal interactions with other children, determines how the child characteristically thinks about right and wrong. Though Piaget's work was done many years ago, subsequent investigations have generally supported his findings.

Are You a Good Guy or a Bad Guy?

According to Piaget, preschoolers are in a stage called Morality of Constraint. In this stage, children tend to think of right and wrong in black and white terms. That is, an act is always right or always wrong. There are no shades of gray and there is no room to negotiate. People are good people or

people are bad. Good guys are always good and bad guys are always bad.

Typically, the young child will define the rightness or wrongness of an act in terms of whether or not it will evoke punishment. For example, it is wrong to take your brother's toy car because you will have to sit in the time-out chair. There is sure to be punishment, even if there is no one to witness the wrong, because the child in the Morality of Constraint stage believes in imminent justice. Accordingly, the child might believe that she fell and skinned her knee because she told a lie. The child believes justice will be served. There is always a payback.

Children in the Morality of Constraint stage are convinced of the sacred nature of rules. Rules must not be changed, even if they are simply rules for playing a game. However, it is right and fair to ignore rules if they interfere with one's individual benefit. This egocentric focus is termed relativistic hedonism and is evident when Ernie says, "I can't share the blocks. I need them!" However, Ernie would be incensed by the injustice of another child's hoarding of the blocks. Relativistic hedonism enables the child to take from others without feeling guilt because, "I need it." The child is not being bad or immoral. He is simply demonstrating normal moral development.

Step on a Crack, Break Your Mother's Back

The young child's egocentric nature is also evident as she mentally connects her own actions with unrelated events because she is not always accurate in her understanding of cause/effect relationships. Remember the old rhyme, "Step on a crack, break your mother's back"? Didn't we all avoid those cracks in the sidewalk and feel a twinge of guilt when we accidentally stepped on one? The young child's immature concepts of cause/effect relationships may link up with her natural egocentrism for sometimes emotionally devastating feelings of guilt as the child mistakenly blames herself for a divorce, illness, or other catastrophe.

This natural egocentrism is also tied to the preschooler's cognitive difficulty in taking another person's mental perspective, or thinking about how the other person feels. The child in the Morality of Constraint stage typically considers only one perspective... his own. It is not until the child is in elementary school that he can easily put himself in another person's shoes. And it is not until much later that he can comprehend multiple perspectives (Selman, 1980).

How Boys and Girls Differ in Moral Decision-Making

Carol Gilligan, a student of Kohlberg's, took issue with his finding that males tend to think in higher moral stages than do females. Gilligan (1982) embarked on research that led her to conclude that females think about moral issues in a manner that is different from, but not inferior to, males. In resolving moral dilemmas, females are typically less concerned with justice and more concerned with caring and maintaining relationships, even to the point of self-sacrifice.

Gilligan's point can be seen in children's free play. When boys are confronted with a conflict involving fairness they tend to argue it out or take their ball and go home. On the other hand, girls faced with conflict over fairness will try to resolve the issue through compromise. But if compromise fails, girls will generally change the activity rather than disband the group (Cyrus, 1993).

Preschoolers' typical level of cognitive development places other constraints on their moral thinking, as well. They tend to think about the wrongness of an act in terms of how much physical damage has been caused, without regard for whether or not the act was intentional or accidental. If Sammy spills water while trying to clean up the art table, he will be considered naughty regardless of his intention to help. The wrongness of the act is judged in direct proportion to the amount of damage, regardless of motive.

In the same way, it is difficult for the preschooler to understand the concept of an accidental wrong. It may be impossible to convince the young child that a classmate accidentally knocked down her block building or stepped on her toe because the area was crowded (Vasta, Haith & Miller, 1995).

Children in Piaget's Morality of Constraint stage tend to look at adult authority in a manner that is different from children who are a few years older. While older children evaluate whether or not an adult has earned

or deserves respect, young children tend to think that it is wrong to disobey an adult simply because the person is an adult. Age and status confer authority. This, of course, is one factor that makes young children so vulnerable to sexual abuse.

How children think about right and wrong may be just as developmental as how children think about letters and numbers.

Kohlberg's View of Moral Development

Several decades after Piaget described his work in the area of children's moral development, a young graduate student, Lawrence Kohlberg, began what would be a lifetime study of human moral development. Defining the concept of morality as justice, or fairness, he asked people to respond to a series of moral dilemmas. Based upon their reasoning, Kohlberg classified moral development into stages, which he believed were invariant and hierarchical. That is, we all pass through the stages in sequence, reaching higher levels of moral thought. However, some of us get stuck somewhere in the progression and never reach the highest levels of moral thinking (Kohlberg, 1984).

Like Piaget, Kohlberg believed that in order to move up the staircase of moral thought, we must possess the cognitive abilities to think about moral issues in more and more abstract ways. That is, cognitive development sets parameters around our ability to reason morally. However, moral development can be facilitated if the person is regularly exposed to reasoning that is slightly higher than the level on which he is thinking. This exposure resolves cognitive conflict and helps moral thinking to advance.

In Kohlberg's scheme, the preschool child is probably judging right and wrong based on the same factors Piaget described earlier. However, Kohlberg expanded the work of Piaget to include three levels: Preconventional, Conventional, and Postconventional. Preconventional and conventional levels of thought pertain to children and are described here. The postconventional level of thought is not described because it is beyond the grasp of children.

Preconventional Thought

When preschool children make moral decisions, Kohlberg would predict that those decisions would be based on avoiding punishment and satisfying one's immediate desires, from an egocentric perspective, and probably on the basis of a whim. This level is called preconventional thought.

Conventional Thought

At the intermediate level, conventional thought, development takes a turn from concern with egocentric morality to consideration for the needs of working and living together. The child begins to think in terms of pleasing others and doing what is helpful. The emphasis is on being a good boy or a good girl. Concern starts to move beyond self-interest to the good of the group. While this level of conventional moral thought is beyond that of most preschool children, it is the level toward which they are growing. According to Kohlberg, children should be exposed to moral thinking at this next higher level in order to facilitate that growth.

Kohlberg's theory remains strong but open to some criticism (Kurtines & Gewirtz, 1995). While the theory appears to hold true for Western culture, some Eastern cultures are not based on the same justice criterion posed by Kohlberg as the ultimate morality (Huebner & Garrod, 1991).

How to Help Children Develop Moral Thought and Action

1. Deal with problems appropriately.

When dealing with discipline problems, determine whether the infraction involves a moral issue or a social convention, and deal with the situation accordingly. If a moral issue is involved, be sure to talk with the child so that she understands the reasons her actions were wrong, lead the child to consider that the other person also has a perspective, and help the child decide how to right the wrong. Use reasoning rather than punishment. "I'm sorry" should be spoken only from the child's heart, never upon command.

2. Allow children to experience moral conflict. Schedule large blocks of free play time so that children may experience natural moral conflicts and practice working out their solutions.

3. Discuss moral dilemmas. Select stories involving moral dilemmas and talk about the perspectives of the various characters. Emphasize that people make mistakes. We are not always good or always bad.

4. Encourage children to change the rules. When playing a favorite game, encourage children to change the rules. Play the game in different ways, emphasizing that if all the players agree, it is OK to change the rules.

5. Involve children in making some class-room rules. Emphasize what is good for the group. Avoid having children decide on punishments because they will most likely prefer harsh, unrealistic punishments that do nothing to change behavior.

6. Encourage dramatic play and role playing. Dramatic play and role play enable children to stand in another person's shoes and promote the development of perspective-taking.

7. Explore the concept of intention and motive. Use stories and puppet skits. Discuss the character's motivations. Did Goldilocks try to break the Little Bear's chair? Why did it break? How did Little Bear feel? What could Goldilocks do to help Little Bear feel better?

8. Praise moral behavior. Make it a point to comment on the helpful nature of an act that promotes or assists other individuals within the group. Praise children for putting the needs of the group ahead of their own needs. Recognize children for being kind, fair, and helpful.

9. Use real dilemmas. Use real dilemmas and concrete classroom situations to discuss moral issues. Avoid the use of fables and maxims as they are too abstract for young children to comprehend fully.

Conclusion

Because young children are emerging moral thinkers constrained by their cognitive characteristics, the early childhood curriculum should provide opportunities for children to deal with moral issues and think about right and wrong in developmentally appropriate ways. Preschool teachers can promote children's moral development by dealing with issues of fairness, justice, human rights, and caring. In addition, the teacher who understands normal moral development will be aware of the reasons young children sometimes appear to be selfish and will recognize opportunities to promote the development of moral thinking in ways that match the child's cognitive level of functioning.

References

1. Cyrus, V. (1993). *Experiencing race, class, and gender in the United States.* Mountain View, CA: Mayfield Publishing Company.

2. Gilligan, C. (1982). *In a different voice: Psychological theory and women's development.* Cambridge, MA: Harvard University Press.
3. Huebner, a. & Garrod, a. (1991). Equilibration and the learning paradox. *Human Development, 34,* 261–272.
4. Kohlberg, L. (1984). *Essays on moral development, Volume II: The psychology of moral development.* San Francisco, CA: Harper & Row.
5. Kurtines, W. & Gewirtz, J. (Eds.) (1995). *Moral development: An introduction.* Boston: Allyn and Bacon.
6. Nucci, L. (1981). The Development of Personal Concepts: A Domain Distinct from Moral or Societal Concepts. *Child Development, 52,* 114–121.
7. Nucci, L. & Nucci, M. (1982). Children's Responses to Moral and Social Conventional Transgressions in Free Play Settings. *Child Development, 53,* 1337–1342.
8. Piaget, J. (1932/1965). *The moral judgment of the child.* (M. Gabain, Trans.) New York: Free Press. (Originally published 1932.)
9. Selman, R. (1980). *The growth of interpersonal understanding: Developmental and clinical analysis.* New York: Academic Press.
10. Vasta, R.; Haith, M.; & Miller, S. (1995). *Child psychology: A modern science.* New York: John Wiley & Sons, Inc.

Sandra Crosser, Ph.D., is a Professor at Ohio Northern University, Ada, Ohio.

From *Earlychildhood News,* May/June 2002, pp. 12-16. © 2002 by Excelligence Learning Corporation. Reprinted by permission.

GENDER EXPECTATIONS OF YOUNG CHILDREN AND THEIR BEHAVIOR

BY RAE PICA

Is it nature (biology) or nurture (environment) that determines personality and behavior? Are boys naturally more aggressive than girls? Are girls naturally more nurturing than boys? Or do the expectations of parents and society impose these behaviors, and others, on children of one gender or the other?

NATURE VERSUS NURTURE

There are, of course, inherent differences between girls and boys. We now know that male fetuses are a bit more active than female fetuses (Blum, 1999)—perhaps due to the extra dose they receive of the hormone called androgen, which has been linked to excitability (ASU Research, 1998). Also, human males can produce as much as 10 times more testosterone than females. Both of these hormones are associated with a stronger drive for rough-and-tumble play and competitiveness. In fact, when a baby girl's adrenal gland inadvertently elevates test-osterone levels (a condition known as congenital adrenal hyper-plasia), the girl also prefers cars and trucks and aggressive play (Blum, 1999).

Researchers have also found that just one year after birth, boys and girls show distinct toy preferences, with boys attracted to more mechanical or structural toys and girls gravitating toward toys that have faces and can be cuddled (Blum, 1999). Similarly, one study showed that when a barrier is placed between one-year-olds and something they want, the boys tend to try to knock down the barrier, while the girls look to their mothers for help.

Does this indicate that girls are naturally more passive and boys naturally more active? There are experts who disagree on the issue. It was Freud's belief that the answer lay exclusively with biology. That belief held strong until the 1960s and 1970s, when many academics (including John Money, a renowned sex researcher) began promoting the idea that *nurture* was the

stronger influence in an individual's developing sexual identity (Anselmo & Franz, 1995).

Katz (1986) has written that adults in all cultures respond differently to boys and girls from the time of birth, and that differences in behavior cannot be attributed to biological factors affecting gender. Gurian (1997), on the other hand, believes it is first biological differences that affect behavior and then cultural responses to that behavior that influence development. Most experts do agree, however, that it is difficult to determine how much of behavior is due to biology and how much to perceptions and expectations—and that "gender-specific behavior is a complicated mix of both nature and nurture" (Bryant & Check, 2000, p. 64).

PARENTAL INFLUENCE

It is true that, from birth, parents display very different expectations of each gender. A study conducted in 1974 showed that parents—especially fathers—described newborn girls as "softer, finer-featured, smaller, weaker, and more delicate" than boys. A follow-up study in 1995 showed similar results. And other studies in the 1970s and 1980s, in which infants were "disguised" in cross-gender clothing, demonstrated that parents brought trucks to the supposed boy babies and dolls to those they considered girls (Bryant & Check, 2000, p. 65). Gurian (1997) also tells us parents talk to, cuddle, and breastfeed their boy infants significantly less than their girl infants.

As children get older, parents tend to talk more to their daughters, encourage them to help others, and discourage autonomy. Boys, on the other hand, are encouraged to be fearless. One study used videotapes of children on a playground to determine parental responses. The results showed that mothers of daughters were more likely to see danger in their activity, and they intervened more quickly and more often than did mothers of sons (Morrongiello & Dawber, 2000). Mothers of daughters also issued more statements of caution, while mothers of sons offered more words encouraging risk-taking.

Strickland (1999) further points out that, when a baby boy falls down, parents make light of it, encouraging the child to get up and try again. On the other hand, when a baby girl takes a tumble, we "run over and scoop her up and make sure she's all right" (p.40).

Throughout childhood, boys tend to have more interaction with their fathers than girls, with vigorous physical activity predominant in that interaction (Beveridge & Scruggs, 2000). Boys also receive more encouragement from both parents and society to participate in physical activity.

ADVERTISING, MARKETING, AND TELEVISION

Parents, of course, are not the only ones in our society promoting gender stereotyping and inequality. Children are bombarded daily with television images promoting what they conceive to be the "norm": boys playing with cars, trucks, and action figures and girls playing with dolls. "Pink" aisles in the toy stores feature dolls, makeup, and miniature appliances, while "blue" aisles offer vehicles and war toys. Even modeling clay and building blocks are sold in different colors—bold for boys and pastels for girls (Kutner, 1998).

An examination of "boys'" toys and games shows they tend to promote problem solving and exploration—"key ingredients for gaining a sense of mastery and competence" (Giuliano, 2000). "Girls'" toys, on the other hand, limit exploration and discourage independence and problem solving.

One result of this media pressure is that, regardless of what they may have asked for, boys more often receive activity-oriented toys and games, while girls are given stuffed animals, toy houses, kitchen sets, and dress-up outfits. Researchers have found that despite what toys may be on their lists, children receive gender-specific toys (Zhumkhawala, 1997). Girls are then praised when playing with dolls. On the other hand, boys are ignored when they display nurturing behavior. Additionally, one study demonstrated that a high number of boys felt their fathers would think cross-gender play was "bad"; thus their toy choices were more stereotypical (Raag & Rackliff, 1998).

RESULTING BEHAVIOR

There is evidence that childhood play socializes and prepares children for different adult roles. Even before adulthood, however, the impact of early socialization is apparent. Though no one is sure why, children begin segregating by sex at about two-and-a-half-years-old, with girls pulling away first (Macoby, 1999). By age four, children play with others of the same sex about three times more often; by six, they play with same-sex friends about 11 times more often (Woolfolk, 2001).

Because researchers in such places as India, Mexico, Africa, and the Philippines have found the same pattern occurs in their areas—and because it is even seen among certain animals—there is reason to believe the phenomena is at least partly due to biology. However, research also shows that children as young as four begin presuming there are similarities within each gender (i.e., stereotyping). And even at such a young age, they already have very strong beliefs about what is and is not gender-appropriate; and they have no qualms about pressuring others to conform. Boys, especially, worry about being teased for having a girl as a friend.

Play styles, too, are drastically different. Girls play in small groups, closer to teachers, with cooperation and verbal interaction prevalent. Boys play in large, unstructured groups, spread out, with body contact and competition reigning. The result of all this is an increasingly stronger separation between "boy" activities and "girl" activities. And this separation can eventually impact adult behavior because they grow up with different habits, social skills, and expectations (Martin & Fabes, 2001).

How much can be attributed to androgen and testosterone isn't known. However, girls are often noticeably upset by the aggressive nature of boys' play. Might they be less upset—and more inclined to join in—had their parents and society encouraged them to be greater risk-takers, or if their toys had encouraged problem solving and adventure?

Research has shown that playing with boys and "their" toys—i.e., being considered a tomboy—distinguished between women who later became college athletes and those who didn't (Giuliano, 2000). These women, as girls, had also received more encouragement from all family members than did women who were not very involved in sports.

Lever (1976) contends that boys' play promotes business or professional careers for males, while girls' play promotes family careers for females. Along these same lines, Toyama (1977) found that successful female administrators were more likely to have played football and other team activities in childhood. Williams and McCullers (1983) determined that successful professional women with atypical careers (e.g., doctors and lawyers) were more likely to have had "masculine" play styles than those who took on the more gender-typical careers of nurses and court reporters. Coats and Overman (1992) looked at the childhood play styles of women in traditional occupations (e.g., teachers and librarians), somewhat nontraditional occupations (e.g., insurance agents or research associates), and highly nontraditional occupations (e.g., lawyers or doctors). Consistent with the other studies, they found that the women in nontraditional roles were more likely to have taken part in male play activities as children.

Potential is lost in other ways, too, as a result of perceptions and stereotypes. Because boys are louder and seem to possess more energy, society has assumed they have more emotional stamina. Science tells us the opposite is true. As it turns out, boys require a lot of emotional support and that, without it, lower IQs may result (Blum, 1999). By the same token, confinement seems to bring down IQ in girls.

WHAT TEACHERS AND PARENTS CAN DO

While we certainly do not want males and females to be alike in every way, we can try to provide equal opportunity for both girls and boys to reach their full potential as human beings. Some differences are biologically driven, but stereotypes are culturally imposed. Parents and teachers, therefore, must monitor their actions and words so as not to promote gender bias.

For example, parents can introduce gender-stereotypical toys, like trucks and dolls, to their children of both sexes. They should dress both their sons and daughters for active, outdoor play. Arranging play dates where boys and girls interact in structured activities seems to encourage more cooperative play between the sexes (Martin & Fabes, 2001).

Early childhood teachers can place stuffed animals and dolls of both genders in the housekeeping area and in the block area. Also, parents and teachers should avoid even such seemingly innocuous messages as use of words like snowman, when snowperson displays more gender equity (Zhumkhawala, 1997).

Role-playing activities in which children of both genders demonstrate the actions of police officers, hairstylists, chefs, homemakers, and other occupations traditionally associated with one gender or the other may be subtle but will make an impression on young children. Additionally, both parents and teachers can ensure boys and girls are praised equally—for achievement, not appearance—and that both girls and boys have equal opportunity and encouragement for physical play.

CONCLUSION

These solutions may seem too understated to make a difference. However, by playing with blocks, girls will gain experience and confidence in their math and science skills (Zhumkhawala, 1997). By participating more in physical activity, girls will gain greater confidence in their physical skills and will be better equipped to take risks. Boys who are encouraged to take part in "girl" activities are more likely to fully develop their nurturing and verbal skills, as well as fine motor coordination. When boys and girls play together (games like tee ball and jump rope can easily cross "gender lines"), girls learn assertiveness and boys learn to better cooperate and control their impulses (ASU Research, 1998). And we can help ensure the IQ of both genders remains at its full potential by encouraging autonomy in girls and by offering boys greater affection.

Teachers especially have opportunities to offer support to boys faced with teasing or rejection by other boys should they choose to engage in activities normally preferred by girls. And teachers can do much to educate and reassure parents, beginning perhaps by sharing this article with them. For teachers and parents, awareness is the first step toward eliminating gender bias.

REFERENCES

Anselmo, S., & Franz, W. (1995). *Early childhood development*, 2nd ed. Englewood Cliffs NJ: Prentice-Hall. ASU Research. (1998). Social structure on the playground. *ASU Research E-Magazine*.

Beveridge, S., & Scruggs, P. (2000). TLC for better PE: Girls and elementary physical education. *Journal of Physical Education, Recreation and Dance*, 71(8), 22–25.

Blum, D. (1999). What's the difference between boys and girls? *Life*, 22(8), 44–50.

Bryant, A., & Check, E. (2000). How parents raise boys and girls. *Newsweek* Special Issue, 64–65.

Coats, P.B., & Overman, S.J. (1992). Childhood play experiences of women in traditional and nontraditional professions. *Sex Roles*, 26, 261–71.

Giuliano, T.A. (2000). Footballs versus Barbies: Childhood play activities as predictors of sport participation by women. *Sex Roles*, 52, 134–42.

Gurian, M. (1997). *The wonder of boys: What parents, mentors, and educators can do to shape boys into exceptional men*. NY: J.P. Tracher.

Katz, L.G. (1986). Boys will be boys and other myths. *Parents*, March issue, p. 176.

Kutner, L. (1998). The gender divide. *Parents*, 73(4), 112–14.

Lever, J. (1976). Sex differences in the games children play. *Social Problems*, 23, 478–87.

Macoby, E. (1999). *The two sexes: Growing up apart and coming together*. Cambridge MA: Harvard University Press.

Martin, C.L., & Fabes, R.A. (2001). The stability and consequences of young children's same-sex peer interactions. *Developmental Psychology*, 37(3), 431–446.

Morrongiello, B.A., & Dawber, T. (2000). Mothers' responses to sons and daughters engaging in injury-risk behaviors on a playground: Implications for sex differences in injury rates. *Journal of Experimental Child Psychology*, 76(2), 89–103.

Raag, T., & Rackliff, C.L. (1998). Preschoolers' awareness of social expectations of gender: Relationships to toy choices. *Sex Roles*, 38 (9/10), 685–700.

Strickland, E. (1999). How to build confidence through outdoor play. *Early Childhood Today*, 13(7), 39–40.

Toyama, J.S. (1977). Selected socio-psychological factors as related to the childhood games of successful women. In M.L. Krotee (Ed.), *The Dimensions of Sport Sociology* (pp. 52–59). West Point NY: Leisure Press.

Williams, S., & McCullers, J. (1983). Personal factors related to typicalness of career and success in active professional women. *Psychology of Women Quarterly*, 7, 343–57.

Woolfolk, A. (2001). *Educational psychology*, 8th ed. Boston: Allyn & Bacon.

Zhumkhawala, S. (1997). Dolls, trucks, and identity: Educators help young children grow beyond gender. *Children's Advocate*, Nov/Dec, 6–7.

Rae Pica is a movement education consultant and an adjunct instructor with the University of New Hampshire. She is the author of 13 books, including the text *Experiences in Movement, the Moving & Learning Series*, and the recently-released *Wiggle, Giggle, and Shake: 200 Ways to Move & Learn*. Rae is nationally known for her workshops and keynotes and has shared her expertise with such groups as Children's Television Workshop, the Head Start Bureau, Centers for Disease Control, and Nickelodeon's *Blue's Clues*.

Working with Families

Encouraging Fathers to Participate in the School Experiences of Young Children: The Teacher's Role

Barry B. Frieman and Terry R. Berkeley

INTRODUCTION

Female teachers share the gender experience with the mothers of their students and as such they have some insight into how other women have developed into the role of mother. It is not as easy for female teachers, the overwhelming majority of early childhood educators, to relate to fathers. Teachers can maximize the participation of fathers in the school experiences of young children by understanding how men learn what it means to be a father, being sensitive to working fathers, trying to involve absent fathers, and encouraging positive parenting skills.

LEARNING HOW TO FATHER

Fathers, like mothers, do not start out with all the insights and skills needed to be an effective parent. Many begin with the first model they see, which is the behavior of their own parent. Using one's own fathering as a template for behavior can be growth enhancing or potentially destructive.

Teachers can play a key role by understanding that many fathers have not learned positive skills from their own fathers and by providing fathers with information about positive fathering. A teacher cannot assume that all men know how to father, just as they cannot assume that all women know how to mother. Many men have grown up with deficient models or absence of models of fathering in their families....

Teachers cannot assume that men know how to father. They can help by making educational materials about fathering available. Newsletters can include a column about fathering as well as one about mothering. The columns can be written by a male faculty member, counselor, or administrator with a female counterpart, preferably a father and a mother, or they can be reprinted from one of the many Internet sites that include material on fathering, mothering, and parenting. Even if parents are divorced, school personnel should send the newsletter, via mail if necessary, to the noncustodial parent.

Teachers can lobby with their school counselors to run an "informational" group for fathers, who are either custodial or noncustodial. These groups can help fathers explore their feelings about fathering with a skilled facilitator. Counselors will have a better chance of recruiting fathers to participate if the group is labeled as "educational" rather than a group "to share feelings" (Frieman, 1994).

Teachers need to be cautious when asking children to get information from their fathers. A child with a noncustodial father can often talk to his parent on the telephone, but children with absent fathers are put in a very embarrassing position when asked about their fathers.

WORK AND FATHERING

The traditional role of the father is that of the provider of the family. Fathers thought of their role as working hard to provide their children with the financial means to buy the necessities of life (LaRossa, 1997). Many men grew up with fathers who made sure that work obligations were satisfied, often at the expense of child obligations (McKenry, Price, Gordon, & Rudd, 1986). Men of the twenty-first century who want to place their child first and their work second are facing the reality that working women have had to deal with for decades. It is not easy, and often people have to make hard choices between their children and their careers.

Some men and women have no choice. Those working lower on the career ladder are faced with the ultimatum of "show up for work or lose your job." These parents often figure out ways to spend time with their children when they are out of work. Often, this might mean giving up personal time and devoting significant time outside of work to being with one's children....

People in professions are more likely to have choices about work hours. As college professors, the authors of this article have more flexible schedules. For example, one can teach at night and have a few hours during the afternoon to watch a field hockey game, or one can work late or on weekends to make up time that has been spent with children. However, even in the professions fathers may be faced with conflicts....

Teachers should be able to make provision for fathers who cannot take time off from work to be involved in their child's school experience. One way to do this is to have flexible times for fathers to visit the school. A pot of coffee brewing early in the morning can lure a father to drop his child off at school a few minutes early and stay for a cup of coffee and discuss his child's schooling and development. Other possibilities include making sure fathers know that they are important by providing time to speak with fathers either in person or communicating via e-mail or telephone. Also, teachers and administrators can make time to communicate to fathers via letters and newsletters (paper or electronic) that they are very welcome in their children's schooling, not just relegated only to special projects involving manual labor.

Working fathers would also benefit from early morning or late afternoon or evening conference hours so they could keep connected with their child's education. Fathers with flexible schedules could be invited to school to have lunch with their child or to share some time reading to a child's class, or tutor children in their child's class.

Anton found that he could not attend his daughter's evening violin concert at her elementary school. When he told this to his daughter's teacher, she invited Anton to come to the special day program that was presented to the other children in the school so he would still be able to see the performance. He was the only parent there. Because of the teacher's actions, he was able to watch his daughter play.

Teachers could also provide fathers with a list of low-cost weekend educational activities. Lists of suggested field trips, such as an excursion to the library, along with a list of possible books to read together, are particularly appreciated by fathers who see their children only during scheduled visitations. Suggested lists of good educational toys could be given to fathers to aid in birthday and holiday gift giving.

ABSENT FATHERS

It is an unfortunate fact that many fathers choose not to make themselves a part of the lives of their children....

Fathers can be physically absent from the home for reasons of divorce, remarriage, military service, incarceration, or work that requires travel. Some fathers although physically present are emotionally absent from their children. This includes the father who lives in the same home as his children but never emotionally connects with them. Other men choose to be both physically and emotionally absent from their children, have children and, then, take no interest in fathering. Often, these are the men or boys who have children but do not intend to live with the child's mother and their child as a family. They might occasionally visit their children or provide them with money, but they don't take part in the process of fathering. They are fathers in title only (Frieman, 2000).

Teachers can help children with absent fathers by involving males to serve as role models in the classroom, arranging for services for physically absent or noncustodial fathers, and altering the curriculum to make it male friendly (Frieman, 2000). Female teachers, aware that children need males in their lives, can involve surrogate "fathers" in the classroom lives of father-absent children. Volunteers can come from the ranks of retired

community members or volunteers from civic organizations. Of course, great care must be taken to ensure that any person entering the classroom to work with children is safe. Criminal background checks are one way to ensure that volunteers will do no harm to children. Male volunteers, similar to classroom helpers, will first have to be trained in how to relate appropriately to young children.

Routine phone calls reporting positive behaviors of their children, newsletters mailed home, and report cards mailed home are other ways to ensure that noncustodial fathers are involved in the school process. Children's books and stories used in the classroom can also help to present fathering in a positive light to children who have no active fathers. Many books present positive images of men and confront issues involving absent fathers. This literature represents the great diversity found in today's schools.

TEACHING POSITIVE PARENTING SKILLS

Teachers can play an important role in teaching positive parenting skills to all fathers. Some important issues that fathers need to learn are how to praise their children, how to put their children's needs first, and how to deal with mistakes.

Praising Children

Fathers need to learn how to give their children praise for accomplishments. It is easy to be supportive of a child when she or he does something so spectacular that others acknowledge the child's accomplishments. But it is just as important for a father to praise his children when they do ordinary things. The key is to let the child own the accomplishment and all of the resulting praise. Bill's story illustrates this point.

> After a wonderful singing performance by my daughter, one of the people in the audience came up to me and said, "Congratulations! She was wonderful." I replied, "Yes, I know. She works very hard at her music and deserves a great deal of credit for what she has accomplished."

Bill recognized that his daughter deserved the praise and not him. Similarly, when his younger daughter led her field hockey team to the playoffs, Bill quickly pointed out to other parents who congratulated him that it was his daughter who deserved the recognition for her hard work and leadership.

After each of his son's high school football games, Rodney would meet his coworker, Sam, very early before work for coffee. During this session, he would proudly give his colleague a complete description of his son's hard work and actions on the field, noting that he was proud of his son but was clear that the accomplishments belonged to his son.

Learning to praise their children might not be a natural thing to do for all fathers. Teachers can help fathers learn the appropriate responses to their child's victories and appropriate responses to other child actions. This can be modeled by praising daily "victories" that all children have in school when speaking to the child's father. An occasional phone call home or e-mail to the father to report that the child performed well, or worked especially hard during the day, can be helpful. In this way fathers can see a model that praises desirable behavior.

Ms. Rogers, a fifth-grade teacher, gave fathers a few file cards and asked them as they watched their child participate in the school play to note everything that their child did that was positive. Fathers were encouraged to write down these things and share them with their child after the performance. This exercise helped teachers to train fathers to look for the good in their own children.

Putting Children's Needs First

Many things that men need to learn in order to become more effective fathers run counter to the way men are normally socialized, especially being socialized to think that fathers are the most important members of the household. Particularly when a father has younger children and has to make a choice between whose needs get met—his or his child's—he needs to learn to value the child's needs above his own. The situations of two fathers illustrate this point:

Harry came home after a particularly hard day at work. He was physically exhausted having spent the day doing hard work. He wanted nothing more to enjoy the dinner his wife was making that night and then lie down and rest. As soon as he walked in the door, his first-grade daughter jumped on him and excitedly reminded him that this evening was the school skating party and that she would have a chance to have a special skate with her dad. Harry forgot about how tired he was and concentrated on how excited his daughter was to go skating with him.

Paul recalled, "At two in the morning I received a phone call from my daughter noting that she was stuck at a club in town and needed a ride home." The fact that he was tired did not matter. Most important to him was that his daughter called him and knew that he would be there for her. These fathers have placed their children's needs as first as a "way of life." They saw it as a regular part of fathering.

Weekly newsletters can highlight important events to children. A first-grade teacher, for example, sent a letter home announcing the annual parent-child "Olympics" in the school gym. Also with the announcement, she wrote a note home letting parents know how important the event was to their child and noting to fathers that their children were excited about participating together with their fathers. After the event all fathers who attended were issued a special "badge," which recognized their contributions to the school by attending the event. Fathers who attended other events and contributed to the classroom were also recognized in the school newsletter. Another teacher contacted the local community newspaper and had them write an article about the contributions that fathers were making to her classroom.

Concerned that some fathers might not be able to attend the traditional Thanksgiving lunch, one teacher in a neighborhood in which most of the men worked in the same factory contacted the factory manager and asked if the company would donate 1 hour of time so the men would be able to extend their lunch hour to be with their children. There were benefits to the students, the fathers, the school, and the factory.

Making Mistakes

Many men have a hard time accepting the fact that they can make mistakes in their fathering or parenting. Fathers may feel their authority is compromised if they back down from a decision. This is not true. Children respect a father who makes mistakes and corrects them, and they have greater respect for fathers who are this honest and sensitive with them.

Most caring men have done their share of insensitive things as fathers. Speaking as fathers ourselves, we usually figure out pretty quickly that we have made mistakes from the reactions of our children. When we make mistakes, we have learned to apologize and to ask our children what we could do next time to make sure that things work out differently. We also try to forgive ourselves. It is easy to berate oneself for making a mistake, but it serves no purpose. As fathers we try to learn from our mistakes. A parent is continually learning. The fact that fathering is a developmental process has allowed us to be even more excited about our children, about fathering, and about our growth as individuals.

When necessary, a father has to put his pride on the shelf and think of his child first. One might have to accept verbal abuse from someone in order to protect one's child. Divorced fathers have to maintain a business-like co-parenting relationship with their former wives, even if pride gets in the way when dealing with the "other" parent. Also, fathers should stay focused on the importance of protecting their children physically and psychologically. If it means getting psychologically punched, a father needs to take that punch rather than let it land on one's child. It is important to take the time to listen, to admit mistakes, to find better ways to do things, and then, to acknowledge to one's child how what they have said has been helpful to them.

Teachers must work to protect the pride of fathers by giving divorced fathers the chance to deal with the school independently of their former wives (Frieman, 1998). By understanding that one's pride might get in the way of involvement, teachers need to treat divorced fathers as if they were single parents, providing them with all information about their child independent of that given to mothers. This does not mean a teacher gets in the middle of parents; rather, the teacher offers information to each parent just to be sure everyone is appropriately informed.

CONCLUSION

If teachers, especially female teachers, understand the uniqueness of fathers, they will be better able to increase father involvement in their child's educational experience. By understanding the unique paths to fatherhood that many men take, teachers will be better able to engage fathers as allies in the educational experiences of their children. The benefits of such understanding will accrue to fathers, their children, their teachers, and the school community in which all participate.

REFERENCES

Frieman, B. B. (1994). Children of divorced parents: Action steps for the counselor to involve fathers. *Elementary School Guidance and Counseling, 28,* 197–205.

Frieman, B. B. (1998). What early childhood educators need to know about divorced fathers. *Early Childhood Education Journal, 25,* 239–241.

Frieman, B. B. (2000). *What teachers need to know about children at risk.* Boston: McGraw-Hill.

LaRossa, R. (1997). *The modernization of fatherhood: A social and political history.* Chicago: University of Chicago Press.

McKenry, P., Price, S., Gordon, P., & Rudd, N. (1986). Characteristics of husbands' family work and wives' labor force involvement. In R. Lewis & R. Salt (Eds.), *Men in families* (pp. 73–84). Beverly Hills, CA: Sage.

Barry B. Frieman and Terry R. Berkeley are from the Department of Early Childhood Education, Towson University.

Correspondence should be directed to Barry B. Frieman, Department of Early Childhood Education, Towson University, 8000 York Road, Towson, MD 21252; e-mail: bfrieman@towson.edu.

From *Early Childhood Education Journal,* Spring 2002, pp. 209-213. © 2002 by Early Childhood Education Journal.

Developing High-Quality Family Involvement Programs in Early Childhood Settings

Lorenza DiNatale

Tell me, I'll forget. Show me, I may remember. But involve me, and I'll understand.

These words, paraphrased from Confucius, form the motto of the Even Start Program at Cane Run School in Louisville, Kentucky. Educators have long understood the primary role of parents in the physical, moral, and emotional development of their young children. More recently, they have also acknowledged the importance of families' involvement in the education of their children.

When parents are involved, they have a better understanding of their role as their child's primary educators. Moreover, parents and teachers get to know and learn from each other, which results in children receiving more individual attention and curricula becoming more rich and varied.

Although I use the word *parent* in this article, I recognize that family members and other adults also hold responsibility for raising a child. Therefore, references to parents should be construed to include any adults who play an important role in a child's development and upbringing.

The need for strong partnerships

Many preschool and primary teachers understand the vital role parents play and the need for developing strong partnerships with families. Parents are the primary teachers and nurturers of their children. They provide appropriate environments and interactions that promote learning and help their children develop the skills and values needed to become healthy and successful adults. Two of the main purposes of an early childhood program are to support and strengthen the parent in this role and to provide the foundation for a family's ongoing involvement in their child's education.

NAEYC's revised statement on developmentally appropriate practice states that programs should support strong ties between child and family (Bredekamp & Copple 1997). Head Start is a national, federally funded, community-based program for children from families with low incomes and their parents. Head Start grantees are required to develop goals for children in collaboration with families and to involve parents in making decisions about both education and program management.

Research findings

Decades of research have shown that one of the most accurate predictors of achievement in school is not family income or parents' education level, but the extent to which parents believe they can be key resources in their children's education and become involved at school and in the community (Henderson & Berla 1994; Lewis & Henderson 1997; Powell 1998). Parent involvement in education benefits not only children and parents, but also teachers and overall program quality. When parent involvement is strong, teachers and program administrators are more likely to experience improvement in self-esteem, have higher morale, feel more job satisfaction, and hold greater respect for their profession (Epstein et al. 2002). Schools and programs with a high degree of consistent and meaningful parent involvement usually outperform similar programs without family involvement. Such schools tend to have more support from families and more respect in the community (Cavarretta 1998; Hatch 1998).

One of the most accurate predictors of achievement in school is the extent to which parents believe they can be key resources in their children's education and become involved at school and in the community.

In this technological age, we are all realizing how the school, the home, and the community are connected to each other and to the world at large. Kibel and Stein-Seroussi (1997) believe that a community can truly exist only when its members acknowledge their importance to each other, come together, and identify themselves by joint efforts to achieve mutual goals. An early childhood program is a community of families, teachers, and neighborhood residents accepting mutual responsibility for sustaining and enhancing relationships that promote children's success.

Basics of Family Involvement

Recruit volunteers. Provide parents with calendars listing special events or classroom projects, so they can plan ahead—and take off work, if necessary—for specific days and times to volunteer during the month.

Make volunteers feel welcome. Create a special place for parents to put their belongings. Greet volunteers as they enter the classroom and introduce them to the children.

Plan ways to involve volunteers. Survey parents about their interests and talents. Match volunteer assignments to parent interests when possible. Develop job descriptions that outline and clarify volunteer responsibilities.

Supervise volunteers. Set aside a regular time to talk to volunteers in person, on the phone, or through e-mail each week to plan and evaluate activities. Provide positive feedback and encouragement, and discuss concerns as they arise.

Steps to establishing quality parent involvement programs

If research has found that educators and parents agree that collaboration can be effective and beneficial and bring added resources to the classroom, then why are there not more successful parent involvement programs in early childhood settings? Barriers range from teachers' concerns over the ability of parents to maintain confidentiality to not knowing how to effectively recruit, use, or supervise volunteers. Parents often feel they do not have the time to volunteer or do not know what they can do to help. Teachers often feel they do not have the time to

prepare activities for volunteers. Although time and planning are needed to begin a program, the long-term results are well worth the initial investment.

Assessing needs

Establishing a successful family involvement program begins with assessing your program's volunteer needs. Develop a short survey or meet with other staff to determine where, besides the classroom (for example, the office, the kitchen, on the bus, the playground, at home), parents can make contributions and in what ways.

Planning for success

If you do not have a parent/volunteer coordinator on staff, work with the program administrator to seek the assistance of a volunteer coordinator from the local school district or another professional with a background in developing volunteer programs. This person could provide workshops or consultation on the basics of creating and maintaining a successful family involvement program (see "Basics" at left).

> **A first step in building a bridge between the culture at home and the one at school is for parents and teachers to talk often and get to know and understand each other's perspectives, behaviors, and interactions.**

Supporting cultural differences

Early childhood programs reflect the racial, ethnic, and cultural diversity of our society. When designing parent involvement programs that are inclusive of all families and respectful of cultural differences, it is important to consider parents' views of their children's development and behavior as well as their own roles and responsibilities as parents. A first step in building a bridge between the culture at home and the one at school is for parents and teachers to talk often and get to know and understand each other's perspectives, behaviors, and interactions. Teachers can ask parents how the

school can complement a family's beliefs and values rather than always expecting parents to adapt. Translators—friends, family members, or even other parents who are native speakers—can help foster communication if necessary.

> **Policies and practices should promote respect and appreciation for the cultures of all children and families.**

Policies and practices should promote respect and appreciation for the cultures of all children and families. One way to show respect is to ask parents to help create signs that hang on each entrance of the school and each classroom that say "Welcome" in all the languages spoken by families in the program. Written materials for families should be translated into languages spoken at home. Holiday celebrations should likewise be respectful and inclusive of the cultures of all families.

Respect for differences should be part of the planning and implementation of volunteer experiences. Some cultures prize cooperation and obedience within the group more than competition or individual achievement. Teachers should respect all parents' cultural values.

Orientation is the key

A well-planned orientation eases anxiety and confusion, alleviates fears, and increases the chances of parents maintaining a long-term relationship with the program. Orientation sets the tone and helps create the environment in which families will participate. An effective orientation familiarizes the parent or community member with the school's facilities and staff, the program's philosophy and curriculum, and relevant policies and procedures on confidentiality, discipline, and attendance, as outlined in a family handbook. Orientation should focus on volunteer job descriptions and expectations, how volunteers are supervised, and how volunteers should check in and record their hours, as required by Head Start.

INVOLVING PARENTS AT THE CENTER

Teachers and administrators know that the selection of toys and materials and the way the early childhood environment is organized are designed to accomplish the goals of the curriculum and enhance the child's social, emotional, cognitive, and physical development. It is important for parents to understand this as well and to know how their interactions with children in each area of the classroom facilitate learning and development. Here are some ways parent volunteers can support children in the classroom and outdoors.

Art

- Sit at the table and offer help, as needed, to children using scissors, glue, or clay.
- Talk to children about their artwork and show an interest in their creations.
- Help children write their names on their work.
- Replace paper at the easel and help children put on and take off smocks.
- Help children develop sensory abilities by exploring the concepts of color, pattern, texture, size, and shape.

Woodworking

- Show children the proper and safe way to use materials.
- Make sure children wear safety goggles and follow safety rules.
- Supervise the use of tools.
- Help children pound nails, steady a piece of wood, or hold a saw or hammer.

Blocks

- Help children start a building project and then encourage them to complete it on their own.
- Allow children to knock down their own buildings but not those of others.
- Help children explore basic math concepts such as *larger* and *smaller* and skills such as counting and grouping.

Dramatic play

- Join in the children's play, if invited, and make comments or ask questions to expand the play.
- Help children learn self-help skills such as grasping, snapping, buttoning, zipping, and tying so they can put on and take off clothes.
- Help children group objects in categories, such as separating cups and plates at cleanup time.
- Help children understand measurement by cooking a "make believe" family dinner by following recipe directions that call for adding ingredients by teaspoons, cups, and so on.

Manipulatives

- Sit at the table with children and assist them with puzzles and other table toys. Encourage children to try to complete more complex puzzles if they are ready.
- Sort and group materials with the children by color, shape, size, and other characteristics.
- Help children build eye-hand coordination as they thread beads or build with table blocks.

Music

- Sit on the floor and sing and/or play instruments with the children.
- Dance and do movement activities with children during group time.
- Imitate fingerplay actions with the children.
- Encourage children to share their favorite songs and fingerplays.

Library

- Hold up books while reading to children so they can see the pictures.
- Invite children to help turn the pages of big books.
- Use the felt board and felt pieces to lead children in retelling a story.
- Read to individual children during playtime.
- Talk with children about the pictures in books.
- Encourage children to join in with repetitive sounds and phrases from a story as they read it together.

Writing

- Write children's dictated stories and help them create their own books.
- Help children practice writing their names and individual letters.
- Read to children.

Science

- Let children help to fill or empty the water and sand tables.
- Encourage children to choose and add new materials to the area.

- Work with children as they pour and fill containers and notice the differences in weight of empty containers versus containers filled to different levels.
- Encourage children to discover what kinds of materials float and sink in water and discuss the possible reasons why.
- Help children with blowing bubbles, feeling different textures, or smelling mystery substances.

Outdoor Play

- Throw balls and play catch with children to help them coordinate eye and hand movements.
- Encourage children to look around the playground and talk about changes in plants and other living things outside as the seasons shift. Ask children to tell you what they are seeing and smelling.
- Help children climb on outdoor equipment and push children on swings.
- Set up and supervise an obstacle course with tires, boxes of different sizes, and so on. As children move through the course, point out when they are going "around," "over," "through," and "under" things.

Parents can also lead an art project, tell a story, teach a song or dance, or cook with the children using a recipe from their culture or a family favorite. They can help serve meals, assist at naptime by putting important notes in cubbies or comforting children who cannot sleep. They can assist on the playground, in the planning and chaperoning of field trips, and in developing events such as open houses, parent workshops and seminars, and book and health fairs.

It is also important to give families a voice in program development and decision making. Open access to teachers and the program's administrator, regularly scheduled family meetings, and the formation of committees to address specific issues or program concerns should be part of any family involvement program.

Involving families at home

Some parents cannot come to the center during the day to volunteer; however, there are many ways they can contribute from home. A parent with access to a computer might design and update the center's Web page, create a newsletter, or design forms and stationery. Other tasks a family might do at home include creating homemade learning games and toys for the classroom, reading and tape-recording stories or music, sewing costumes and uniforms for the dramatic play area, or making curtains for a puppet theater.

Teachers can support all children and families at home by preparing exploration kits for use at home. These kits can contain videos, books, learning toys or games, and index cards with parent-child activity ideas that focus on a particular topic. Circulate the kits until all families have had a turn. Teachers can also start a book- or toy-lending program with reading tips for parents and suggestions for using a toy to develop different kinds of skills.

To develop and sustain a feeling of camaraderie, belonging, and satisfaction, provide ongoing parent training, treat parents with respect, and provide activities throughout the year that demonstrate appreciation for their work.

Assessing progress

It is important to evaluate family involvement strategies on a regular and ongoing basis. This can be done informally through regular observation and conversations with parents. Use more formal surveys or interviews to assess the overall quality and success of a family involvement program. As a part of the evaluation process, recognize parents for their contributions both personally and publicly. To develop and sustain a feeling of camaraderie, belonging, and satisfaction, provide ongoing parent training, treat parents with respect, and provide activities throughout the year that demonstrate appreciation for their work.

What parents take with them

As children transition out of the early childhood environment, parents bring away with them the experiences and skills they learned from the child's initial exposure to school. Most important, parents also have a commitment to helping their child succeed in school. By investing in parents, we invest in children.

References

1. Bredekamp, S., & C. Copple, eds. 1997. *Developmentally appropriate practice in early childhood programs.* Rev. ed. Washington, DC: NAEYC.
2. Cavarretta, J. 1998. Parents are a school's best friend. *Educational Leadership* 55 (8): 12–15.
3. Epstein, J. L., M. G. Sanders, K. Clark Salinas, B. Simon, N. Rodriguez Jansorn, & F. L. VanVoorhis. 1997. *School, family, and community partnerships: Your handbook for action.* Thousand Oaks, CA: Corwin/Sage Publications.
4. Hatch, T. 1998. How community action contributes to achievement. *Educational Leadership* 55 (8): 15–16.
5. Henderson, A. T., & N. Berla. 1994. *A new generation of evidence: The family is critical to student achievement.* Columbia, MD: National Committee for Citizens in Education.
6. Kibel, B., & A. Stein-Seroussi. 1997. *Effective community mobilization: Lessons from experience.* Rockville, MD: U.S. Department of Health and Human Services.
7. Lewis, A. C., & A. T. Henderson. 1997. *Urgent message: Families crucial to school reform.* Washington, DC: Center for Law and Education.
8. Powell, D. 1998. Reweaving parents into the fabric of early childhood programs. *Young Children* 53 (5): 60–67.

For further reading

1. Campbell-Lehn, C. 1998. Finding the right fit: Creating successful volunteer job descriptions. *The Journal of Volunteer Administration* 26 (3): 22–29.
2. Coleman, M. 1997. Families and schools: In search of common ground. *Young Children* 52 (5): 14–21.
3. Diffily, D., & K. Morrison, eds. 1996. *Family-friendly communication for early childhood programs.* Washington, DC: NAEYC.
4. Goldberg, S. 1997. *Parent involvement begins at birth: Collaboration between parents and teachers of children in the early years.* Boston: Allyn & Bacon.
5. Harms, T., R. Clifford, & D. Cryer. 1998. *Early Childhood Environment Rating Scale.* Rev. ed. New York: Teacher's College Press.
6. Herr, J., & Y. Libby-Larson. 2000. *Creative resources for the early childhood classroom.* 3d ed. New York: Delmar.
7. Lee, L., & E. Seiderman. 1998. *Parent Services Project.* Cambridge, MA: Harvard Family Research Project.
8. Mulcahey, C. 2002. Take-home art appreciation kits for kindergartners and their families. *Young Children* 57 (1): 80–87.
9. U.S. Department of Education. 1996. *Reaching all families: Creating family-friendly schools.* Washington, DC: Author.

Lorenza DiNatale, M.S., is the parent involvement program coordinator for National PTA. She has taught preschool, supervised early childhood teachers, administered early childhood programs, and written a book for National PTA on how to develop a quality parent involvement program.

NO TIME FOR FUN

HOMEWORK IN KINDERGARTEN? PERSONAL COACHES FOR LITTLE LEAGUE? THE PRESSURES FACING CHILDREN TODAY ARE ENORMOUS. HERE'S HOW YOU CAN LIGHTEN THE LOAD—AND RESTORE FUN TO CHILDHOOD.

By Susan Garland

Last year, my daughter Kristina brought a note home from kindergarten telling parents that each child was expected to learn to recognize 150 words, 5 each night, by the end of the year. But whenever I sat down to help her study, she'd start to cry and flail, "I can't do it," she would sob.

I eased up, figuring there was no need to push her. After all, I didn't read until I was in first grade. Kristina, however, wouldn't let go. She worried that her classmates were moving ahead of her and that everyone would tease her if she fell behind. Her competitive drive motivated her to make some progress, but Kristina still didn't finish the project by June —a fact that bothered her even after her summer vacation began.

> **WE LIKE TO THINK OF CHILDHOOD AS AN IDYLLIC, CAREFREE TIME. BUT IN TODAY'S FAST-PACED, HIGH-ENERGY WORLD, CHILDREN FEEL PRESSURED AT EVER-YOUNGER AGES.**

Stressed-out over kindergarten?

Parents may love to think of childhood as an idyllic, carefree time. But child-development experts report that today's competitive, high-energy society is forcing kids to cope with stress and pressure at younger ages. Academic demands aren't the only source of tension. Well-meaning parents, eager to give their children every advantage, enroll even the youngest kids in so many activities that they need their own Palm Pilots to keep track. Moms and dads are so busy themselves that they often rush their children through everyday tasks, such as getting dressed and eating. Time for relaxed talk or play is at a premium in many American households.

What's more, children are relentlessly bombarded with information that unsettles them. Television news about school shootings, neighborhood violence, and environmental decay delivers the message that the world is a dangerous place. Meanwhile, the entertainment industry continues to target younger kids with sophisticated content that they're not ready to handle. And hours spent at fast-paced computer games can overwhelm even the best-adjusted child.

The resulting stimulation, frenetic pace, and demands to master so much so soon can leave kids overpowered by feelings of helplessness, child-development experts say. "When a child's sense of control over his world goes down, his level of stress goes up," says Georgia Witkin, Ph.D., an assistant clinical professor of psychiatry at the Mt. Sinai School of Medicine, in New York City, and author of *KidStress: What It Is, How It Feels, How to Help* (Penguin Paperback, 2000).

For some kids, the results are particularly disturbing: A study last June by the American Academy of Pediatrics found that 18.7 percent of children who visited pediatricians' offices in 1996 were identified as having psychological problems related to their social environment—up from 6.8 percent in 1979. And a 1999 Surgeon General's report found that 13 percent of children ages 9 to 17 suffered from anxiety disorders.

Researchers report that kids are showing the same symptoms of chronic stress as adults, including headaches, stomachaches, insomnia, and irritability. In some cases, stress is worsening such childhood health conditions as asthma and allergies. Landmark research by Bruce E. Compas, Ph.D., a professor of psychology, medicine, and pediatrics at the University of Vermont, in Burlington, has found links between stress and emotional and behavioral problems, including aggression and difficulties at school. Though researchers don't know for sure whether stress contributes to depression and anxiety disorders, they suspect that a link exists.

Some cases of childhood stress, of course, can be tied to divorce or to a parent's death or illness. But it's not just traumatic situations that send a child into a tailspin. Dr. Compas's research indicates that the cumulative effect of many smaller stresses—pressure to achieve academically, feelings of being excluded by peers, conflicts at home—can be just as harmful. "Little things are chronic," he says. "They keep coming back. They're more psychologically immediate."

Sources of Stress

In today's 24/7 world, the pressures on children are pervasive. To help kids get an edge in an increasingly competitive labor market, well-meaning parents are pushing children to learn more at earlier ages. School systems are trying to boost test scores in order to get more recognition and funding. Some parents even hire tutors so their 5-year-olds can keep up with the kindergarten curriculum.

Ted Feinberg, Ph.D., a former senior psychologist for a school district outside Albany, New York, recalls one worried mother who called him before her preschooler was to meet with education specialists at the elementary school that her son was to attend in the fall. All preschoolers in New York are screened for special needs and other issues. The mother wanted a copy of the screening test so she could prepare her child. "I told her that this was not entrance to college and not something to be anxious about," says Dr. Feinberg, who is now assistant executive director of the National Association of School Psychologists, in Bethesda, Maryland. The problem for her child, he says, is that "if a parent is anxious, there is a strong potential that the child will be anxious by association."

In a study of elementary-school children, Louis A. Chandler, Ph.D., an associate professor of educational and developmental psychology at the University of Pittsburgh, diagnosed many as suffering from stress, which was manifested in such ways as frequent temper outbursts and impulsive and stubborn behavior.

Dr. Chandler says he found that in most cases, the parents and the schools were pushing too much responsibility and decision making on the children. What appeared to be missing, he says, were sufficient stability, routine, and guidance from adults. The trend in the schools, says Dr. Chandler, is for "cooperative learning," in which even the youngest children work in teams to help each other learn, with the teacher often relegated to sideline monitor. Removing the teacher from a central authority role, Dr. Chandler says, can increase insecurity and anxiety, because "children are being forced to make choices without the strong guidance of adults."

Too Busy to Play

The pressures on kids continue after school. Many are being shuttled from ballet class to soccer practice, from religious school to violin lessons, with adrenaline pumping and meals grabbed on the go. Organized sports have replaced the casual neighborhood pickup game, so winning has become ever more important.

What's more, kids are increasingly exposed to unsettling news from around the world—about violence, wars, air pollution. Concerns about such dangers heighten their feelings of a lack of control over their life. "Television news scares the hell out of them," says Scott Poland, Ph.D., president of the National Association of School Psychologists. "They pick up a sense of fearfulness. It adds a bit of pessimism." A Montclair, New Jersey, mother recalls how her daughter "went through a period when she asked me every night before she went to sleep whether I thought acid rain was going to kill all the fish."

SIGNS OF STRESS

- Typical symptoms in kids include stomachaches, headaches, nervous behavior, irritability, frequent crying, fear of insomnia and going to bed alone, and bed-wetting. Extreme shyness could also be an indication.
- Changes in behavior can also signal stress. Is your usually outgoing and talkative child now quiet and sullen? Is a child who normally plays nicely with other kids now shoving and arguing? Is a child who used to head off to school happily refusing to go now?
- Experts suggest consulting a doctor if the behavior lasts more than two weeks or is affecting your child's diet or sleep. The physician can refer you to a mental-health specialist if needed.

Even in the safest communities, young kids worry about violence. When Patti Raber Max's son was 7, he was one such worrier. "On several occasions, as he went to bed, he told me in a very soft voice, 'I'm afraid of being shot,' " says Raber Max, of Potomac, Maryland. She suspects that he'd heard something on the radio news. "It's not as if we live in a crime-ridden neighborhood or he knew of any particular incident. I told him, 'I would never let anything happen to you. I will always protect you.' That seemed to help."

Coping Skills

Just as adults do, children have varying abilities to handle stress. Hereditary factors and environment both play a role. Some kids may be born with an inherent disposition toward fearfulness, though such a temperament at birth doesn't mean they'll always be timid.

A study by Jerome Kagan, Ph.D., a professor of psychology at Harvard University, found that about 20 percent of more than 450 infants reacted to stimulation with agitated limb movements and crying. By the time these "high reactive" children were 4½, 87 percent of them seemed to resemble typical children, though they were less extroverted. Dr. Kagan concluded that the environment can play a part in reducing anxiety. The children who showed high fear at all ages were most likely to develop anxious symptoms by the time they were 7.

Research by W. Thomas Boyce, M.D., a professor of epidemiology and child development at the University of California at Berkeley, arrived at similar conclusions. Over the course of several studies, Dr. Boyce found that between 15 and 20 percent of several hundred children ages 3 to 8 had "exaggerated biological responses" to various stressful events. Stressors included changes in the drop-off routine for children attending day care. Responses included higher-than-normal changes in blood pressure and heart rates and higher secretion levels of stress-related hormones. These children also had higher rates of respiratory illnesses and behavioral problems.

The good news, Dr. Boyce says, is that the evidence shows that these sensitive children can thrive in supportive conditions. His studies show that the stress-prone kids actually showed a lower rate of illness and behavior problems than other children when placed in low-stress settings.

Time to Chill

Obviously, parents can't protect their children from all stress, nor would they want to. But they can reduce the amount of stress as well as help kids manage the unavoidable pressures. The best thing parents can do is allocate regular quiet time to talk to their children. Discussing their day and their feelings can automatically reduce children's stress level.

Dr. Compas says parents should teach their kids problem-solving skills to handle stressful situations head-on. Dozens of academic studies, he says, show that children who "try to avoid the stress and suppress their feelings will do worse psychologically than those who confront the stress and face their feelings."

So a child who is being picked on at school, Dr. Compas says, will do better if he is able to talk about the situation with his parents, who can then help him figure out what to do about it. A child who seems preoccupied with pollution can be shown that she can do something to help the environment, perhaps signing up for a park-cleanup day with a parent.

IT'S BEST TO LIMIT AFTER-SCHOOL ACTIVITIES TO TWO A WEEK; AT THE VERY LEAST, THEY SHOULD BE SCHEDULED SO CHILDREN AREN'T RUSHED FROM PLACE TO PLACE.

Bettie B. Youngs, Ph.D., author of *Stress and Your Child* (Fawcett, 1995), says that parents can give their child a sense of control by helping her develop problem-solving skills: Identify the problem, brainstorm alternative solutions, evaluate possible consequences, and come up with a game plan. She also suggests that parents ask children at bedtime to discuss the best part of their day, which allows them to "focus on the positive and to stop

feeling anxious about things that didn't work."

Another important step: slowing the pace of your child's life. Some experts suggest that most children shouldn't participate in more than two extracurricular activities a week. At the very least, activities should be scheduled so children aren't rushed from place to place. Parents who need to place their children in after-school programs should be careful about piling on more activities in the evenings and on weekends.

Children should also be given lots of unstructured time, either by themselves or with friends at home. Downtime gives children a chance not only to relax but also to work out problems through play. "Kids need time to think, to be creative, to use their imagination," says Sheila Ribordy, Ph.D., a child psychologist in Chicago. "They need to learn how to entertain themselves."

Also, parents should help their youngsters choose a sport or another activity in which they can feel competent. Competitive baseball for an uncoordinated child is sure to raise frustration levels and hurt self-esteem. And lay off the pressure to excel. Instead of focusing on grades, parents should praise a child for persevering. "Parents should say, 'We don't expect you to be the best student in your class. You please us by being a loving son,' " Dr. Poland says. Turbo-charged parents don't do their kids any favors by turning them into

miniatures of themselves, he warns. "Kids who are very competitive in their early years often burn out by the time they reach high school," he says.

TOO MUCH PRESSURE CAN LEAVE A CHILD OVERWHELMED BY FEELINGS OF HELPLESSNESS.

Finally, it's important to become role models for our children. Stress levels can soar when parents are too busy for their children. Obviously, parents can't always avoid distractions, but a regularly short-tempered and harried parent can leave a child with a sense of helplessness. Not surprisingly, a child's stress level will soar if the parent is frantic. "Children are not getting a chance to learn from example how to de-stress," Dr. Witkin says.

So let your child see you at the kitchen table calmly pondering a crossword puzzle. Put away your briefcase in the evening, and read a novel. Go out with your kids after dinner for a long, leisurely walk. Not only will such measures help your child reduce the stress of contemporary life but they could do wonders for your stress levels as well.

From *Parents* magazine, April 2001, pp. 144-150.

Talking to Kids About Race

Children are quick to pick up racial biases from family members, friends, and TV. That's why it's so crucial to talk about issues like skin color and to dispel myths about race at an early age. Here's how to get started.

By Lori Miller Kase

When it came to race, Jennifer Seavey and her husband, who are white, had always tried to instill a sense of color blindness in their three children. "If we met someone who is black, our focus was 'Pretend you don't see any difference,'" says the Atlanta mom. But one day while she was driving, something her 6-year-old son, Drew, said to a black friend made Seavey rethink this philosophy. "You know what I used to think when I was little?" Drew asked his friend. "I used to think that God put us all in the oven, and you came out burned and we came out perfect."

Though Drew's friend didn't say anything, Seavey was mortified. "My stomach jumped into my throat, and I said, 'It's funny that you used to think that when you were little, but isn't it great that we know now that God makes people in all different colors?'" Then she quickly changed the subject. "I realized that because I had never talked to Drew about racial differences or given him an accurate explanation, he felt that he needed to explain it to himself," Seavey says.

Though very young children's queries about race are born of curiosity rather than prejudice, that racial innocence is short-lived. Kids are quick to absorb the biases around them and, when they enter school, those of society in general. "If you don't talk about race with young children, your

kids may ascribe greater importance to the differences they see in people than you want them to," says Phyllis Katz, Ph.D., director of the Institute for Research on Social Problems, in Denver. When Dr. Katz tracked the development of racial attitudes in children, she found that almost half of the 200 children had racial biases by age 6.

That's why it's crucial for parents of all races to respond openly and honestly to their young children's questions and misperceptions about skin color and other ethnic differences, no matter how awkward it may seem—and to continue to bring up these issues as their kids grow. You can't always control the racial stereotypes that children pick up from TV, movies, or classmates; if you don't live in a diverse community, it may also be difficult to expose your child to kids of other races. But by talking to your child early and often about racial differences—teaching him why prejudice is wrong and setting a good example yourself—you can raise him to be an accepting, tolerant person.

How Kids Learn Racial Attitudes

The preschool period is a key time for parents to nurture children's natural inclination to see people as individuals rather than

as stereotypes. By age 3 or 4, kids can identify skin color but still have little understanding of the concept of race, says Marguerite A. Wright, Ed.D., author of *I'm Chocolate, You're Vanilla* (Jossey-Bass, 1998). In fact, preschoolers are more likely to describe themselves as pink and peach or brown and chocolate than they are to use the terms black or white. "Children often learn about negative attitudes attached to other people's skin color before they can actually identify who is black and who is white," Dr. Wright says. Usually, it's because of conversations they've overheard in their home—among parents, older siblings, or others who spend time around them.

Dr. Wright recalls one black preschooler she interviewed named Josie, who had a surprisingly negative attitude toward white people for someone so young. Her hostility toward whites also encompassed light-skinned blacks: Because she was too young to understand racial categories, she simply grouped together those with similar skin color. Dr. Wright discovered that Josie's mother frequently portrayed whites as intent on mistreating blacks. Unfortunately, attitudes like this, when ingrained in a child early in life, are hard to shake later on.

Between the ages of 5 and 7, kids begin to pick up on the social meanings attached to skin color, says Dr. Wright, and start to become aware of other kinds of physical differences, such as eye shape and hair texture as well. They also start to adopt the prejudices of family members and friends, not to mention those depicted on television and in movies and popular music. In a study by psychologists Darlene Powell Hopson, Ph.D., and Derek S. Hopson, Ph.D., which used black and white dolls to assess the racial attitudes of young children, 65 percent of black children preferred to play with the white dolls—and more than three quarters of both black and white kids said that the black dolls "looked bad" to them.

An Honest Conversation

Answering your child's questions honestly and without embarrassment is the first step toward teaching tolerance. Here are a few basic principles.

Don't deny differences. "If your white child asks, 'Why does that kid have brown skin and I have light skin?' parents should not say 'There's really no difference.' Kids aren't color-blind, and they won't believe you," Dr. Katz says. "They're just trying to find out whether these differences mean anything." Instead, you could simply respond, "Because his mommy and daddy have brown skin" or "Skin color is passed down from parents and grandparents, and people are different colors depending on which part of the world their ancestors came from." You should also tell your child that people think and feel and enjoy a lot of the same things, even if they look different.

While researching their book *40 Ways to Raise a Nonracist Child* (HarperPerennial, 1996), Barbara Mathias and Mary Ann French found that black families tended to talk to their children much earlier in life about race than their white counterparts—probably because race is a much more salient issue for minorities. "I can't tell you how many white parents say to me, 'My child doesn't notice racial differences—why should I bring them up if he doesn't notice?'" Mathias says. "You should bring it up because they live in a society that does notice. And this society has a very powerful effect on a child."

Give straight answers. Never make a young child feel ashamed for bringing up racial issues or pointing out differences in skin color. By responding to kids' questions and comments in a matter-of-fact fashion, parents can pave the way for future candid conversations about race. For example, if your child points to a black woman at the grocery store and says, "Look, Mom, that lady's face is brown," don't be embarrassed and hush him up—take the opportunity to educate your child and explain why.

Similarly, if your child notices that Asian children have "different eyes," as my daughter once put it, you can explain that eyes come in many colors and shapes and that parents pass on something to their children that makes their eyes look like their own. "There's no need to bring in race if the child is just talking about a person's eyes," Dr. Wright says. "Adults think race, but children just think eyes or skin or whatever other characteristic. Keep your answers specific but truthful." Tailor your explanations to your child's questions and to his particular age and comprehension level.

Start early. Kappel Clarke, who is African-American, and his wife, Mabeline, who is Hispanic, anticipated how they would talk to their children about race before they even had their first daughter, Dánia, now age 8. "We knew that there are real issues that affect children born to biracial couples, so we decided to discuss as much about her background as possible during the early years so we would have a platform to stand on, one that she could be really proud of," says Clarke, a personal trainer at the Equinox Health Club, in New York City.

Clarke says that from the time Dánia was 3 years old, he and his wife have tried to make race a regular part of their conversation. "We wanted to avoid waiting until an incident happened before confronting these topics," Clarke says. But though he and his wife have told Dánia that some people will judge her by the way she looks, they try not to make race the biggest issue. "We try to develop her confidence in all aspects of her life."

Be reassuring. Sometimes children simply need to hear that it's okay to be different, especially if they are in the minority. Charlotte Wade, and African-American who is raising her niece Starkiesha in a predominantly Asian section of Oakland, California, recalls the day her niece came home from second grade and said, "There are only two students in the class who look like me." "We had never talked about race until this happened—in fact, it took me a while to understand what she was talking about," Wade remembers. "I said, 'You mean two little girls who have ponytails?' and she said, 'No, I mean little girls who are black like me.' I responded, 'That's okay. There don't have to be any students in your class who look like you so long as your teacher is teaching everybody.' Then Starkiesha asked, 'So it's okay that there's only three of us?' and I said, 'Yes, it is.'"

Don't overdo it. Maintaining a balance is important, says Dr. Wright, especially if you're a minority. Minority parents who dwell too much on race, particularly with very young children who can't yet process the information, may be doing them a disservice. For example, Dr. Wright says, she knows black parents who tell their children that they'll have to work twice as hard as white students do to succeed in school. "Some of them grow up thinking that they are destined to be treated unfairly and don't even bother trying," she says. "It handicaps a child, it really does."

Dealing With Prejudice

Despite our best efforts, we can't protect our children from the reality of prejudice and bigotry. Nor can we shield them from the stereotypes that are so prevalent in our society. Rachelle Ashour, a Virginia grammar-school teacher, recalls the eye-opening experience she had while teaching a predominantly black third- and fourth-grade class in Washington, D.C. "If you go into the gift shop of a museum with the kids, for instance, they really are watched more than other children are—it used to make me so angry," she says. "And the kids would pick up on it. They'd say, 'They're following me in the store because they think I'm going to steal something.' I'd say, 'They're just prejudiced.'" By acknowledging the racism, Ashour says, it gave her the opportunity to discuss with her students ways in which they might handle such situations.

According to experts, parents can help make children proud of who they are—and thus less affected by others' views of them—by giving them an understanding and appreciation of their heritage. Those of us who are minorities should surround our children with positive images of people who resemble them—both family portraits and pictures of our cultures' admirable achievers, says Drs. Darlene and Derek Hopson. But white parents, too, should explore their family's history, suggests

Reuel Jordan, dean of children's programs at the Bank Street College School for Children, in New York City. "Many white families think they don't have an ethnicity, that they are just American. But we encourage all families to get in touch with their heritage, which can help them understand other people's ethnicity."

Unfortunately, many families find themselves living in communities in which their kids are surrounded only by people who look just like them. "Young kids begin to develop attitudes toward people who are different from them very early on if they're not exposed to people from other environments and cultures," says Alvin F. Poussaint, M.D., a professor of psychiatry at Harvard Medical School and coauthor of *Raising Black Children* (Plume, 1992). Experts say they can easily develop an "us-them" mentality. Here's what you can do to help.

Monitor the media. When kids don't encounter people of other races in their day-to-day lives, their images of racial groups come mostly from television and movies. "What often happens is that white kids think that all blacks are athletes, because they see so many on TV, or that most black kids are comedians, because they've seen the black sitcoms," Dr. Poussaint says. Even the evening news, he says, which often shows policemen handcuffing blacks and Latinos, perpetuates stereotypes. It's up to parents to point these out to their children—and to counter such images by highlighting the many different ways in which people of all backgrounds have contributed to society.

Expose kids to various cultures. Dr. Poussaint says it is especially important for parents to expose their kids to other cultures through the books they read together, by attending shows or movies featuring musicians or actors of different races, and by providing toys and dolls that reflect the world's diversity. "When kids have dolls that aren't all black or all white, they begin to see that people come in different shades of color, with different shapes of eyes," Dr. Poussaint says. "This might encourage children to ask their parents questions. Later, if they hear derogatory terms, they'll know it's not the right way to refer to people."

Seek out diversity. Parents can also bring more diversity into their family's lives by looking for culturally mixed playgroups or enrichment classes for their young children—or by involving their older kids in after-school activities or sports teams that attract people of different backgrounds. And though your choice of public school may be dictated by where you live, you can seek out a preschool program that provides a multicultural education and draws a racially mixed group of kids.

Examine your own biases. Look at the examples that you set for your kids. No parent likes to think that she is prejudiced, but small actions can sometimes send negative signals to a child. When you take your children to the park, do you tend to sit only near people of your own race? If your father-in-law tells an ethnic joke at dinner, do you smile even if it makes you uncomfortable? Do you look for opportunities to expand the racial mix of your own group of friends and acquaintances? "If you teach your kids by example that people's differences are okay, that they should be valued—that we should take joy in them—then you are giving your children a gift," says Barbara Mathias. "You are giving them a tremendous advantage when they go out into the world."

Cartoon Violence: Is It as Detrimental to Preschoolers as We Think?

Kristen M. Peters and Fran C. Blumberg

INTRODUCTION

What impact does television content, specifically the violence presented in children's cartoons, have on 3- to 5-year-old children? Whether cartoons provide primarily good entertainment or bad examples of conflict resolution is difficult to readily determine. Policymakers and television networks acknowledge possible negative effects of cartoon violence on child viewers, as evidenced by the following initiatives:

1. The Children's Television Act (CTA) of 1990, which requires broadcasters to provide informative and educational programming for children;
2. V (Violence)-chip legislation that allows for the insertion of electronic blocking devices for adults to screen out shows rated for high violent and objectionable content; and
3. The National Cable Television Association's TV Parental Guidelines, a television program rating system that provides parents with information about violence, sexual situation, coarse language, and suggestive dialog in the programs (Banta, 2001; Federal Communications Commission, 1996; National Cable Television Association, 1996; Wright, 1995).

The necessity of these measures is questionable given preschoolers' fairly sophisticated understanding of moral violations, such as physically harming another individual (Wainryb & Turiel, 1993). The present research review critically examines the effects of cartoon violence on children's moral understanding and behavior for the purposes of enabling early childhood educators and parents to make informed decisions about what constitutes potentially harmful television viewing (Huston & Wright, 1998; Huston, Wright, Marquis, & Green, 1999).

HOW VIOLENT IS CHILDREN'S TELEVISION PROGRAMMING?

According to Huston and Wright (1998), preschoolers watch up to 30 hours of television per week. Four-year-olds, on average, watch 50-70 minutes of television a day, most of which is animated cartoons (Huston et al., 1999). This finding is noteworthy, as cartoon shows have been characterized as containing some of the highest levels of violent and aggressive content on television (Calvert, 1999; National Television Violence Study, 1997; Potter, 1999). For example, Gerbner, Morgan, and Signorielli (1993) examined television programming from 1973 to 1993 and found that 92% of children's Saturday morning programs contained some form of violence, as compared with 71% of prime time programs; the average number of violent scenes per hour was 23.0 as compared with 5.3 on prime time programs.

The National Television Violence Study (NTVS), funded by the National Cable Television Association, assessed television violence with the "goal of encouraging more responsible television programming and viewing" (1997, p. 1). The NTVS found that nearly two-thirds of serials for children contained violent acts. This situation may be further exacerbated by the current popularity of the Japanese cartoon genre called "anime" (e.g., *Cardcaptors, Batman Beyond*). This genre is characterized by fast action animation featuring numerous violent fight scenes (Rutenberg, 2001). As Rutenberg noted, anime is vastly popular among young viewers.

WHAT DO WE MEAN BY VIOLENCE AND HOW DO YOUNG CHILDREN RESPOND TO IT?

Clearly, violence sells—even among young children. Despite its widely perceived egregious effects, there is disagreement about how violence should be defined. One standard definition, adopted by the Cultural Indicators Project that was charged in 1967–68 with investigating television violence, is "the overt expression of physical force, with or without weapon, against self or other, compelling action against one's will on pain of being hurt or killed, or actually hurting or killing" (Gerbner, Gross, Jackson-Beeck, Jeffries-Fox, & Signorielli, 1978, p. 179). This definition excludes violence that is implausible or reflected in threats, verbal abuse, and comic gestures (Potter, 1999; Signorielli, Gerbner, & Morgan, 1995). Other researchers, such as Williams, Zabrack, and Joy (1982), distinguished between aggression and overt violence. Specifically, they characterized aggression as a "behavior that inflicts harm, either physically or psychologically, including explicit or implicit threats and nonverbal behaviors" and violence as "physically aggressive behaviors that do, or potentially could, cause injury or death" (p. 366).

Given differing conceptions of violence, it remains unclear as to whether aggressive acts committed by cartoon characters are truly violent (Condry, 1989). Given their fantasy-based content and unrealistic character actions, cartoons create a "gray world" as far as violence is concerned. In fact, adult television viewers perceive fantasy and cartoons as devoid of violence and not particularly disturbing or frightening (Potter, 1999). Major television networks (e.g., Kids WB) also characterize cartoon episodes as reflecting themes of good-versus-evil that emphasize the reinforcement of loyalty and punishment for selfishness (Rutenberg, 2001). Accordingly, violence and conflict between "good" and "evil" characters are appropriate because the end is justified by the means.

Not all television networks, however, adhere to a positive view of cartoon violence, as in the case of Nickelodeon's refusal to show anime cartoon genre (Rutenberg, 2001). Research shows that children perceive comic cartoons, in which the victim remains uninjured, as more violent and less acceptable than violence depicted without comic intent (Haynes, 1978). Bjorkqvist and Lagerspetz (1985) reported that preschoolers showed fear when they viewed violent cartoon scenes and were asked to recall scenes that were most anxiety producing. Paik and Comstock (1994) also suggested that cartoons might be harmful because young children have difficulty distinguishing reality from fantasy.

A longstanding concern in the study of children's social and emotional development is the nature of the relationship between television violence and aggressive behavior (Simmons, Stalsworth, & Wentzel, 1999). According to the American Psychological Association's review of research examining the effects of television violence (1985), when children watch programs with violent content, they demonstrate increases in aggressive attitudes, values, or behavior. Numerous studies have shown that preschoolers demonstrate increased aggressiveness after watching cartoon characters engaged in violent behavior (Bandura, Ross, & Ross, 1963a, 1963b; Paik & Comstock, 1994; Potts, Huston, & Wright, 1986; Sanson & DiMuccio, 1993).

These findings are theoretically consistent with Bandura's social learning perspective (Bandura & Walters, 1963), which contends that children learn behaviors by observing others' actions and the consequences of those actions. Actions resulting in a reward are presumably more likely to be learned than those resulting in punishment. Findings from Bandura and Huston (1961) indicate that for preschoolers, observation of aggressive models is a "sufficient condition for producing imitative aggression" (p. 317), regardless of the nature of the relationship between the model demonstrating the behaviors and the child. Similarly, preschool children may demonstrate overt aggressive behavior in their play and interactions with peers and adults after viewing cartoons containing violent and aggressive content (Bandura et al., 1963a, 1963b; Friedrich & Stein, 1973; Sanson & DiMuccio, 1993). Bandura et al. (1963a) concluded

that children modeled their aggressive behavior after video-taped characters and generalized this behavior to other forms of aggressive acts (i.e., aggressive gun play). Thus, the behavior of popular cartoon characters may serve as models for children with the accompanying message that aggressive behavior is justified, especially when the behavior is rewarded (Bandura et al., 1963b; Bjorkqvist & Lagerspetz, 1985).

The models that children view on cartoon programs, such as "superheroes," are often highly attractive and aggressive in their behaviors (Liss, Reinhardt, & Fredriksen, 1983; NTVS, 1997). The NTVS reported that for all types of programs, about a third of the perpetrators of violence demonstrated some good qualities, such as considering the needs of others, with which viewers might identify. For preschoolers, the actions of cartoon heroes are clearly visible on the screen and likely to be imitated in play (Liss et al., 1983). In cartoons, the characters' actions seldom result in negative consequences. For example, the NTVS reported that nearly 70% of the violent interactions depicted on children's programs revealed no pain on the part of characters. Of those violent interactions, nearly 60% featured unrealistic harm, or no harm. Additionally, less than half of these programs featured negative consequences for violent interactions. Thus, cartoon violence may provide young viewers with a faulty impression of the impact of violence and aggression in real-life situations.

There are also questions about the long-term effects of specific types of violence on children's behavior (Van Evra, 1998). Different theoretical perspectives have examined these effects. For example, Zillmann's excitation transfer or arousal theory (1971) contends that watching television violence and aggression arouses individuals who subsequently direct or "transfer" their energies into another activity, perhaps in behavior that may be inappropriate in their social environment. Berkowitz's cognitive neoassociation or cue theory (1984) suggests that ideas or "cues" portrayed in television violence (e.g., guns, particular kinds of characters and settings) send a signal to individuals, which increases the likelihood that they will behave aggressively when they experience the aggressive-eliciting cues in real-life situations (Potter, 1999). According to the Gerbner et al.'s cultivation theory (1978), heavy television viewing facilitates a mainstreaming effect in which children may regard what they see as an accurate representation of real-life situations (Calvert, 1999). Accordingly, children may acquire a distorted view of violence in the real world (Gerbner et al., 1978; Lometti, 1995). Drabman and Thomas (1974) suggested that by the time children are in elementary school, they may have become desensitized to the effects of violence on victims. This claim is best examined in the context of children's understanding of television content in general.

PRESCHOOLERS' INTERPRETATION OF TELEVISION CONTENT

Research has consistently indicated that preschoolers' comprehension of television content is relatively poor and may remain poor through age 8 (Bjorkqvist & Lagerspetz, 1985;

Condry, 1989). Four-year-olds recall more of the story line than peripheral television content, but may have difficulty identifying and differentiating central from incidental content (Van den Broek, Lorch, & Thurlow, 1996). Central content refers to content that is important to understanding a given story whereas incidental content refers to information that may embellish but not advance the understanding of a given story. Even 6-year-olds experience programs such as cartoons in a "fragmentary manner rather than a continuous story" (Bjorkqvist & Lagerspetz, 1985, p. 77). Hodapp (1977) found that 5- and 6-year-olds failed to transfer what they learned from educational programs to solving similar problems in real-life situations. Thus, preschoolers also may be unable to incorporate actions based on the violent behaviors of cartoon characters into their repertoire of social behaviors.

One contributing factor to this inability to transfer knowledge from media to daily life is children's understanding of reality versus fantasy. In general, researchers have found that when violent scenes are interpreted as real, they have a greater likelihood of resulting in subsequent aggressive behavior than when they are interpreted as unrealistic (Berkowitz, 1984; Huesmann, Lagerspetz, & Eron, 1984). Individuals tend to use cues such as animation to help them distinguish reality from fantasy (Condry, 1989). However, according to Flavell (1986), preschoolers may possess little or no understanding of the distinction between reality and fantasy, indicating that what they view on television may be perceived as "real." Even 6- and 7-year old children "appear to have difficulty understanding television conventions that violate real-world possibilities," for example, in understanding scene cuts and instant replays (Huston & Wright, 1998, p. 1020).

The character's motive and the consequence of violent actions may help the child viewer interpret events seen on television. According to Roberts and Bachen (1981), the portrayal of aggression on television, combined with a moral verbal message, may be too sophisticated for young children. Collins, Berndt, and Hess (1974) found that kindergarten children recalled the consequences of the characters' aggressive actions but were less able to identify the characters' motives for those actions. Children typically need adults' help to understand relationships between social acts portrayed on television and cues such as motives and consequences (Collins, Sobol, & Westby, 1981). Heroes or protagonists in cartoons, however, often use aggression while delivering moral lessons (Liss et al., 1983). Thus, children believe that there are immediate rewards for the antisocial behavior, especially when there is a lag between the violent behavior and subsequent punishment. This perception may promote inappropriate beliefs about the consequences of harming others.

PRESCHOOLERS' INTERPRETATION OF THE MORALITY OF VIOLENT ACTIONS

Consideration needs to be made of the preschoolers' perception of the portrayed violence and their understanding of con-

flict resolution in terms of its underlying morality. Simply observing a preschooler's aggressive behavior following the viewing of violent television does not provide information about how the child behaves in the context of real-life moral dilemmas. Situations presented in the world of cartoons may be specific to the domain of cartoons and, therefore, may be interpreted differently than violence in the domain of reality. Bjorkqvist and Lagerspetz (1985) found that 5-, 6-, and 9-year-olds tended to base their moral judgments of the "goodness" or "badness" of a cartoon character's behavior on their ability to identify with that character. Research findings indicate that preschoolers' moral reasoning abilities may be relatively advanced (Wainryb & Turiel, 1993). Bandura et al., (1963b) found that preschoolers could indicate the consequences of a character's actions, for example, that the character acted aggressively (e.g., engaged in a fight) to receive a reward (e.g., toys). They also tended to criticize that character's actions as morally wrong (e.g., selfish, mean).

Current views on the development of moral reasoning contend that young children are able to identify moral transgressions and breaches of social conventions. Moral transgressions, or violations of moral rules, are those actions that infringe on the rights, duties, or welfare of others (Wainryb & Turiel, 1993). Social-conventional rules pertain to acceptable behaviors within a specific social system (Wainryb & Turiel, 1993). Preschoolers may be able to identify and make distinctions between moral transgressions and social-conventional transgressions (Cassidy, Chu, & Dahlsgaard, 1997). In fact, preschoolers were found to recognize real-life dilemmas as well as identify, differentiate, and make inferences about the features of moral and social-conventional interactions presented in story form (Oppenheim, Emde, Hasson, & Warren, 1997; Smetana, 1981, 1985). Additionally, preschoolers conceptualized hypothetical and actual moral transgressions as more serious in nature and worthy of punishment than personal rules (i.e., those pertaining to an individual's subjectively perceived rights) or social-conventional violations (Smetana, Schlagman, & Adams, 1993; Tisak, 1993). Thus, researchers believe that preschoolers may be able to differentiate between moral and social-conventional transgressions and consider both in evaluating situations in real-life and hypothetical scenarios (Cassidy et al., 1997; Weston & Turiel, 1980). This understanding also may help preschoolers mediate between the effects of cartoon violence on the screen and in their lives beyond the screen.

CONCLUSION

To pinpoint the effects that the viewing of cartoon violence has on preschool children, it is essential to determine what children interpret and learn from what they watch. The bottom line is whether preschoolers understand that the consequences of cartoon transgressions differ from those of real-life transgressions. Accordingly, if preschoolers can differentiate between the appropriateness of cartoon actions versus similar actions in the real world, then the influence of cartoon violence may not be as detrimental as commonly accepted. Similarly, young children's imitation of cartoon characters' behaviors may be more situation-specific than an incorporation of the characters' actions into a long-term repertoire of social skills. These conclusions, while supported in our literature review, remain controversial.

What is less controversial is adults' role in helping young viewers interpret the violent content that they see in popular cartoons. This effort involves monitoring how violence is used to resolve interpersonal conflicts and the message communicated to the viewer about the appropriateness of this violence. For example, a superhero that always conquers her enemies through violent means that inflict minimal physical harm may leave children with the message that violent behaviors are justified and inconsequential. This type of message can be characterized as an informational assumption. According to Wainryb and Turiel (1993), informational assumptions influence how children and adults evaluate the morality of a given behavior or action. These assumptions are largely based in societally mandated beliefs, one's current understanding of the world, and interactions with significant others. For children, these significant others include adult caregivers. Accordingly, parents and educators play vital roles in influencing children's impressions of violent actions, violent actions as a means of conflict resolution, and the moral acceptability of that means of resolution.

Children's spontaneous impressions can be addressed in a variety of contexts, most notably, that of adults and children watching programs together, or co-viewing. Research indicates that co-viewing helps improve children's recall of the television program content (Watkins, Calvert, Huston-Stein, & Wright, 1980). Co-viewing also has been used as an instructional vehicle for adults to comment on program content as it is presented and to address children's potential questions about character motives and actions (Wright, 1995). Adults should use the co-viewing situation to not only address questions but also to model and discuss morally acceptable alternatives to resolving conflicts in both cartoon and real-life situations.

Clearly, cartoon watching will continue to be a popular and enjoyable preschool-age activity. The most frequently watched cartoons will continue to contain high levels of violent content. Our goal as early childhood educators and those interested in young children should be to use conflicts on cartoons as a learning opportunity to teach invaluable moral lessons applicable to real-life situations.

REFERENCES

1. American Psychological Association. (1985). *Violence on television*. Washington, DC: APA Board of Ethical and Social Responsibility for Psychology.
2. Bandura, A., & Huston, A. C. (1961). Identification as a process of incidental learning. *Journal of Abnormal and Social Psychology, 63,* 311–318.
3. Bandura, A., Ross, D., & Ross, S. (1963a). Imitation of film-mediated aggressive models. *Journal of Abnormal and Social Psychology, 66,* 3–11.
4. Bandura, A., Ross, D., & Ross, S. (1963b). Vicarious reinforcement and imitative learning. *Journal of Abnormal and Social Psychology, 67,* 601–607.
5. Bandura, A., & Walters, R. H. (1963). *Social learning and personality development.* New York: Holt, Rinehart, & Winston.
6. Banta, M. (n.d.). The V-(Violence) chip story. Retrieved on January 15, 2001, from National Coalition on Television Violence Web site: http://www.nctvv.org.
7. Berkowitz, L. (1984). Some effects of thoughts on anti- and prosocial influences of media events: A cognitive-neoassociationist analysis. *Psychological Bulletin, 95,* 410–427.
8. Bjorkqvist, K., & Lagerspetz, K. (1985). Children's experience of three types of cartoons at two age levels. *International Journal of Psychology, 20,* 77–93.
9. Calvert, S. L. (1999). *Children's journeys through the information age.* New York: McGraw-Hill College.
10. Cassidy, K. W., Chu, J. Y., & Dahlsgaard, K. K. (1997). Preschoolers' ability to adopt justice and care orientations to moral dilemmas. *Early Education and Development, 8(4),* 419–434.
11. Collins, W. A., Berndt, T. J., & Hess, V. L. (1974). Observational learning of motives and consequences for television aggression: A developmental study. *Child Development, 45,* 799–802.
12. Collins, W. A., Sobol, B. L., Westby, S. (1981). Effects of adult commentary on children's comprehension and inferences about a televised aggressive portrayal. *Child Development, 52,* 158–163.
13. Condry, J. (1989). *The psychology of television.* Hillsdale, NJ: Lawrence Erlbaum Associates.
14. Drabman, R. S., & Thomas, M. H. (1974). Does media violence increase children's toleration of real-life aggression? *Developmental Psychology, 10,* 418–421.
15. Federal Communications Commission. (1996). Children's Educational Television. Retrieved on February 8, 2001, from http://www.fcc.gov.
16. Flavell, J. H. (1986). The development of children's knowledge about the appearance-reality distinction. *American Psychologist, 41(4),* 418–425.
17. Friedrich, L., & Stein, A. H. (1973). Aggressive and prosocial television programs and the natural behavior of preschool children. *Monographs of the Society for Research in Child Development, 38* (4, Serial No. 151).
18. Gerbner, G., Gross, L., Jackson-Beeck, M., Jeffries-Fox, S., & Signorielli, N. (1978). Cultural indicators: Violence profile no. 9. *Journal of Communication, 30(3),* 176–207.
19. Gerbner, G., Morgan, M., & Signorielli, N. (1993, December). *Television violence profile No. 16: The turning point from research to action.* Unpublished manuscript, Annenberg School of Communication, University of Pennsylvania, Philadelphia.
20. Haynes, R. B. (1978). Children's perceptions of "comic" and "authentic" cartoon violence. *Journal of Broadcasting, 22,* 63–70.
21. Hodapp, T. V. (1977). Children's ability to learn problem-solving strategies from television. *The Alberta Journal of Educational Research, 23(3),* 171–177.
22. Huesmann, L. R., Lagerspetz, K. M. J., & Eron, L. D. (1984). Intervening variables in the television violence-aggression relation: Evidence from two countries. *Developmental Psychology, 20,* 746–775.
23. Huston, A. C., & Wright, J. C. (1998). Mass media and children's development. In W. Damon (Series Ed.) & I. E. Siegel & K. A. Renninger (Vol. Eds.), *Handbook of child psychology: Vol. 4. Child psychology in practice* (5th ed., pp. 999–1058). New York: John Wiley & Sons.
24. Huston, A. C., Wright, J. C., Marquis, J., & Green, S. B. (1999). How young children spend their time: Television and other activities. *Developmental Psychology, 35(4),* 912–925.
25. Liss, M. B., Reinhardt, L. C., & Fredriksen, S. (1983). TV heroes: The impact of rhetoric and deeds. *Journal of Applied Developmental Psychology, 4,* 175–187.
26. Lometti, G. E. (1995). The measurement of televised violence. *Journal of Broadcasting & Electronic Media, 39,* 292–295.
27. National Cable Television Association. (1996). TV Parental Guidelines. Retrieved on January 21, 2001, from http://www.ncta.com/tv.html.

28. National Television Violence Study (Vol. 1). (1997). Thousand Oaks, CA: Sage.

29. Oppenheim, D., Emde, R. N., Hasson, M., & Warren, S. (1997). Preschoolers face moral dilemmas: A longitudinal study of acknowledging and resolving internal conflict. *International Journal of Psychoanalysis, 78,* 943–957.

30. Paik, H., & Comstock, G. (1994). The effects of television violence on antisocial behavior: A meta-analysis. *Communication Research, 21,* 516–546.

31. Potter, W. J. (1999). *On media violence.* Thousand Oaks, CA: Sage.

32. Potts, R., Huston, A. C., & Wright, J. C. (1986). The effects of television form and violent content on boys' attention and social behavior. *Journal of Experimental Child Psychology, 41,* 1–17.

33. Roberts, D. F., & Bachen, C. M. (1981). Mass communication effects. *Annual Review of Psychology, 32,* 307–356.

34. Rutenberg, J. (2001, January 28). Violence finds a niche in children's cartoons. *New York Times* (CL 51, 647), A1, A19.

35. Sanson, A., & DiMuccio, C. (1993). The influence of aggressive and neutral cartoons and toys on the behavior of preschool children. *Australian Psychologist, 28,* 93–99.

36. Signorielli, N., Gerbner, G., & Morgan, M. (1995). Violence on television: The Cultural Indicators Project. *Journal of Broadcasting & Electronic Media, 39,* 278–283.

37. Simmons, B. J., Stalsworth, K., & Wentzel, H. (1999). Television violence and its effects on young children. *Early Childhood Education Journal, 26(3),* 149–153.

38. Smetana, J. G. (1981). Preschool children's conceptions of moral and social rules. *Child Development, 52,* 1333–1336.

39. Smetana, J. G. (1985). Preschool children's conceptions of transgressions: Effects of varying moral and conventional domain-related attributes. *Developmental Psychology, 21,* 18–29.

40. Smetana, J. G., Schlagman, N., & Adams, P. W. (1993). Preschool children's judgments about hypothetical and actual transgressions. *Child Development, 64,* 202–214.

41. Tisak, M. S. (1993). Preschool children's judgments of moral and personal events involving physical harm and property damage. *Merill-Palmer Quarterly, 39(3),* 75–390.

42. Van den Broek, P., Lorch, E. P., & Thurlow, R. (1996). Children's and adults' memory for television stories: The role of causal factors, story-grammar categories, and hierarchical level. *Child Development, 67,* 3010–3028.

43. Van Evra, J. (1998). *Television and child development* (2nd ed.). Mahwah, NJ: Lawrence Erlbaum Associates.

44. Wainryb, C., & Turiel, E. (1993). Conceptual and informational features in moral decision making. *Educational Psychologist, 28(3),* 205–218.

45. Watkins, B., Calvert, S., Huston-Stein, A., & Wright, J. C. (1980). Children's recall of television material: Effects of presentation mode and adult labeling. *Developmental Psychology, 6,* 672–674.

46. Weston, D. R., & Turiel, E. (1980). Act-rule relations: Children's concepts of social rules. *Developmental Psychology, 16(5),* 417–424.

47. Williams, T. M., Zabrack, M. L., & Joy, L. A. (1982). The portrayal of aggression on North American television. *Journal of Applied Social Psychology, 12,* 360–380.

48. Wright, J. C. (1995). Child viewers, television violence, and the First Amendment. *The Kansas Journal of Law and Public Policy, 4(3),* 33–38.

49. Zillmann, D. (1971). Excitation transfer in communication-mediated aggressive behavior. *Journal of Experimental Social Psychology, 7,* 419–434.

Kristen M. Peters and Fran C. Blumberg are from the Division of Psychological & Educational Services, Fordham University.

Correspondence should be directed to Fran C. Blumberg, Division of Psychological & Educational Services, Fordham University, 113 West 60th Street, Room 1008, New York, NY 10023; e-mail: kpeters@fordham.edu.

From *Early Childhood Education Journal,* Spring 2002, pp. 143-148. © 2002 by Early Childhood Education Journal.

UNIT 3

Care and Educational Practices

Unit Selections

Key Points to Consider

- What steps has your state taken to improve child-care staffing ratios, funding, regulations, and employee turnover this past year?

- Do you believe there is a uniquely American cluster of characteristics that should be fostered in child care? If so, what are some of those characteristics?

- Consider the scope and quality of child care in your state. What are the key factors you would use for ensuring quality care in your state?

- Identify an authentic community need that could be met by preschoolers, with the help of elementary-age children or senior citizens.

- Make a brief listing of the components of developmentally appropriate practice that you believe are vital.

- Which do you believe is more important: teaching or learning? Explain your reasoning.

- Find out if there have been changes over the past 5 years in the amount of time scheduled for recess for kindergarten, first, second, and third grade in a school district near you.

 **Links: www.dushkin.com/online/**
These sites are annotated in the World Wide Web pages.

Canada's Schoolnet Staff Room
http://www.schoolnet.ca/home/e/

Classroom Connect
http://www.classroom.com/login/home.jhtml

The Council for Exceptional Children
http://www.cec.sped.org/index.html

National Resource Center for Health and Safety in Child Care
http://nrc.uchsc.edu

Online Innovation Institute
http://oii.org

One of the things that makes teaching young children so rewarding in the United States is our understanding of quality care and educational practices. As a nation, we have many high-quality early childhood programs that are based on a rich knowledge of child development. However, despite advancing knowledge of good care and practice, the quality of child care across the nation remains uneven. This is the message of our first article, "Who's Watching the Kids," a summary of the results of *Working Mother*'s ninth annual survey. For families who can afford it, excellent child care is readily available. It is middle- and low-income families who must settle for less-than-adequate care. *Working Mother* magazine uses key factors, such as accreditation, group size, and safety, to identify the current status of child care in each state.

A hallmark of quality child care is strong home-school partnerships, and parental involvement in a wide variety of activities is the way to develop partnerships. When parents are engaged in school activities, children are better able to learn and grow and their teachers gain respect and appreciation of family cultures. "Creating Home-School Partnerships" gives valuable strategies for understanding family diversity as the beginning point for working closely with parents.

Understanding diversity is also the theme of "For America's Infants and Toddlers, Are Important Values Threatened by Our Zeal to Teach?" This article counsels teachers to maintain a balance of care and teaching in programs for infants and toddlers. If, as a nation, we value diversity, then heavy emphasis should be placed on choice and exploration, rather than on more direct teaching methods. Author Eleanor Szanton stimulates our thinking by asking an essential question: Which is more important, teaching or learning?

The time-honored method of learning in early childhood is play. Today, more than ever, the importance of play in learning needs to be reaffirmed. As preschools face pressure for children to excel academically, play is often eliminated unless teachers remain committed to its value. "All They Do Is Play? Play in Preschool" is an excellent reminder of the role of play centers in fostering language, mental, social, and physical skills.

Several articles in this unit focus on the need to balance children's developmental needs with academic achievement. The Association for Childhood Education International (ACEI) has developed a position paper underscoring the importance of "The Child-Centered Kindergarten." This professional organization continues to emphasize educating the whole child, responding to individual differences, and providing multiple opportunities for learning.

The results of a new study show that children who attend full-day kindergarten perform better on standardized tests than children who attend half-day. Another benefit is that fewer children in full-day kindergarten are retained. Unfortunately, what the study does not show is whether the curriculum is balanced between play and academics.

Despite ACEI's child-centered position, many schools are failing to educate the whole child. With increasing pressure to spend more time on academics in preparation for testing, children are being deprived of recess and informal social interaction times. The last article in this unit addressing balance is "The Silencing of Recess Bells." As implied by the title, there are consequences of eliminating recess in primary grades, and the results can be detrimental to development.

Appropriate practice in early childhood education depends on the teachers' own learning opportunities. As teachers grow to understand a wide range of educational practices, they are better equipped to provide effective education and care for young children. The foundation of early childhood care and education is constructivism, an approach that views learning as an interactive experience. When teachers adopt elements of constructivist practice, they begin to view children as active learners. Three divergent yet sound approaches to constructivist practice are discussed in this unit. "Different Approaches to Teaching: Comparing Preschool Program Models" presents the basics of Montessori and High/Scope. "Examining the Reggio Emilia Approach to Early Childhood Education" presents the project-based approach. All three of these approaches are examples of appropriate practice and care.

Good practice—activities that are appropriate for children's development, play that is active, and learning that is connected to real-world problems—has no shortcuts and cannot be trivialized. It takes careful thought and planning, using the latest knowledge of early childhood education, to make wise curriculum and practice choices. By working out specifics of routines and procedures, curriculum, and assessment that are suitable for young children, the early childhood professional becomes a reflective teacher. These are the essential tasks for a teacher interested in sound educational practice.

9TH ANNUAL REPORT

WHO'S WATCHING THE KIDS?

HIGH COSTS, STAFF TURNOVER, LOW STANDARDS. IS THIS HOW AMERICA SHOWS ITS COMMITMENT TO CHILDREN AND FAMILIES?

BY CLARA HEMPHILL

Nothing is more important to a mother than knowing that her children are safe, stimulated, and happy while she's at work. That's why Working Mother has researched the state of child care every year since 1993 to assess changes in the quality, availability, and affordability of this crucial social program. This year, in addition to highlighting the newest innovations in child-care programs across the country and the shortcomings in policy and financing, we visited a child-care center in Massachusetts, a state with policies that are regarded by experts as among the best, and another one in Texas, where inadequate care is more often the rule than the exception. The result is a snapshot of how the fundamentals of child care—staffing ratios, funding, regulations, and employee turnover—matter in the daily lives of children. We've also provided "The Child-Care Checklist" for tips on how to choose a child-care program for your little ones.

OVERALL CHILD-CARE QUALITY: UNACCEPTABLE

Despite political rhetoric emphasizing the importance of America's children and families, the quality of child care remains drastically uneven across the country, with many youngsters attending poor to mediocre centers that are understaffed, underregulated, and costly. And it's unlikely that

parents will see large-scale improvements soon: The slowing of the economy and a renewed emphasis on defense spending have once again put expanded child-care funding initiatives on the back burner.

Meanwhile, the percentage of working mothers with children under the age of 6 has grown dramatically over the past few decades, from 39 percent in 1975 to 64 percent in 2001, according to the U.S. Bureau of Labor Statistics. In addition, more mothers with infants are working—and infant care is particularly expensive and hard to find, given the need for additional staff. There are also more single mothers in the workforce than ever, including millions forced off welfare due to reform initiatives.

Federal subsidies for low-income families have increased by nearly $4 billion in the past five years as part of welfare reform. Those funds—$6 billion a year of the $9 billion now being spent on child-care subsidies—are paying for the care of nearly 2.2 million children a month, compared to 1.2 million children a month in 1997, the year before welfare reform was enacted.

Still, millions of working-class families can't get help, says Helen Blank, director of child care for the Children's Defense Fund, a Washington, DC-based advocacy group. "Many of them are working people who aren't eligible for subsidies. Families earning thirty thousand to fifty thousand dollars a year have a very hard time."

> **"THERE'S THIS FALSE ASSUMPTION THAT ONLY REALLY LOW-INCOME FAMILIES NEED HELP PAYING FOR CHILD CARE," SAYS ANNE MITCHELL.**

"There's this false assumption that only really low-income families need help," says Anne Mitchell, president of Early Childhood Policy Research.

And 2002 is shaping up to be a particularly difficult year. "Our fear is we'll lose some of the gains we've made," says Blank. "Revenues are down, the states don't have money, and they're threatening to decrease their contributions."

An official from the Administration for Children and Families agrees there is still work to be done. "And we don't want to give the impression that all the need has been met," she says. "But if you look at where we were five years ago, we have progressed in our ability to serve families of the working poor."

Indeed, a few states are tackling the issue of how to attract and keep good child-care workers in a troubled industry, one that's been plagued by low pay and high turnover. In an effort to improve staff retention, California, Illinois, and New

York, for example, are experimenting with plans to offer free or reduced college tuition to child-care workers.

North Carolina, one of the most innovative states, has devised an incentive plan that encourages child-care centers to improve quality by offering them higher subsidy rates for children in their care if they upgrade staff and other aspects of their programming. Oklahoma, the District of Columbia, Massachusetts, and South Carolina have also adopted similar incentives.

Another promising trend: Public prekindergarten programs are growing. Forty-two states have established some form of free pre-K for 4-year-olds, and three states—Georgia, Oklahoma, and New York—are developing "universal" pre-K for all children, regardless of family income. While some classes last only a few hours a day, many are incorporated into existing full-day programs. The benefit? Quality goes up because certified teachers, rather than less experienced child-care employees, teach the classes. And the price of care goes down because the pre-K classes are free.

Here, a look at how the most critical tenets of child care—staffing, quality, affordability, and availability—are affected by the lack of funding and political commitment, leaving millions of families, and millions of children, in a bind.

ADULT-TO-CHILD RATIOS: NOT ENOUGH GROWN-UPS

The overall child-care dilemma is painfully apparent in Texas, where the adult-to-child ratios are 1 to 13 for toddlers and 1 to 20 for 4-year-olds. And the situation isn't much better nationwide. Only 10 states and the District of Columbia have regulations for child-care centers that meet the maximum staffing ratios recommended by the National Association for the Education of Young Children: 1 to 4 for infants, 1 to 5 for toddlers, and 1 to 10 for 4-year-olds. And Texas isn't the most egregious offender: Alabama, Arkansas, Georgia, Idaho, Louisiana, New Mexico, and South Carolina have the worst adult-to-child ratios for infant care in the country.

In Texas, loose state regulations have led to a vigorous free market of private child-care centers, but even these find it hard to survive. "I'm between a rock and a hard place," says Philip Banks, the owner of Tutor Time Day Care Center in Dallas, a for-profit center that's part of a national chain. The center charges fees ranging from $175 a week for a baby to $120 a

week for a preschooler—higher than average for the area—but Banks says he barely breaks even. Some of the lower-income families who send their children here receive state subsidies in the form of vouchers to pay their tuition, but Banks says the subsidies don't meet his costs.

Banks prides himself on the improvements he's made since he bought the center, which cares for about 100 children, in 1997. He has increased salaries and offers health benefits, as well as tuition reimbursement for staffers who take courses in child development. He also gives workers free care for their own children and offers a retirement account after one year.

But while kids enjoy splashing in a shallow wading pool in the play yard attached to the center, or playing a game of ring-around-the-rosy with a teacher, there simply aren't enough arms to cuddle every child who needs attention. There are no field trips: It would be dangerous to take so many kids out with such little supervision. At naptime, dozens of sleepy preschoolers stretch out on blankets in one room, supervised by a single adult.

At lunchtime one day in the toddler room, children are seated in their group high chairs—tables with recessed plastic seats that allow one grown-up to feed six kids at once. Three staffers care for 20 children, ranging in age from 12 to 24 months. One passes out paper plates of grilled-cheese sandwiches, oranges, and string beans to the eight older children (ages 18 to 24 months), while two others tend to 12 little ones (ages 12 to 17 months).

The teachers are so busy feeding, changing, and cleaning the children that there is no time for chitchat—no time for the human interaction that is just as important to a child as being fed. Children sometimes cry for long periods without being consoled.

"Mommy?" calls a 19-month-old girl in pink-checked short overalls with big brown eyes. "Daddy?"

The teacher, Rebecca, sighs. "She just can't get adjusted," she says. But Rebecca doesn't have time to comfort her. She has seven other children to care for. They need to be fed, cleaned up, and put down for naps.

Not surprisingly, where adult-to-child ratios are high, the quality of care tends to be much higher. In Massachusetts, ratios are 1 to 5 for toddlers and 1 to 10 for preschoolers. The benefits accrued from this standard are evident at the Cambridgeport Children's Center in Boston. The teachers here have time to talk individually to their

charges and to help them learn to make friends. They read to them often, and there are frequent trips to the park and a nearby swimming pool. One class became fascinated with insects, so the teachers prepared lessons in which children investigated and wrote about various kinds of bugs.

"Hooray! Hooray! My school! I'm going to my school!" a 3-year-old girl shouts one morning on her way into the center, housed in a converted garage behind a house on a tree-lined street.

Her teacher, Zoe, is elbow-deep in homemade clay when the girl arrives. "Guys, I've just made the smoothest, bluest clay you've ever seen," Zoe says as she dishes out clumps to three children seated at a low table. The girl's mother kisses her goodbye, and the child settles down to work.

There is no baby room here; the director believes babies need more attention than almost any center can offer. In the preschool room for ages 3 and 4, there is one adult for every four kids.

The center isn't fancy, and a lot of equipment is homemade. The water table, where kids splash with measuring cups, was made by several fathers on a weekend, for example. But what Cambridgeport does offer is abundant interaction between children and staff. One day, when a child feels homesick before lunch, a teacher soothes her by helping her dictate a letter to her mother—a letter stuffed into her cubby for pickup time.

Care this good is possible in part because the center operates as a parent cooperative, very rare in the child-care world. Parents help hire teachers, are active fundraisers, and volunteer for maintenance chores on the weekends.

It's no wonder, then, that the waiting list to get into Cambridgeport is a long one. Some parents sign their children up at birth in the hopes of having space when the child turns 2 or 3.

But there is also a catch-22 at work here: When state regulations are strict, as they are in Massachusetts, fewer child-care providers can meet the rigorous standards, and parents are forced to scramble for available spots. When state standards are low, as they are in Texas, the supply of licensed child-care centers is high, but the overall quality is lower.

HIGH COSTS OF CHILD CARE

The struggle to find affordable, high-quality child care cuts across class lines, with middle-class families caught in a particu-

THE CHILD-CARE CHECKLIST

FIVE THINGS YOU NEED TO KNOW WHEN CHOOSING YOUR CHILD-CARE PROVIDER

1. DON'T BE FOOLED BY STATE LICENSING. Many parents mistakenly believe that if a center is licensed, it must be good. "Licensing is just a minimum floor of safety," says Faith Wohl, president of the Child Care Action Campaign. "It's not a guarantee of quality." Check out a center with your own eyes. And trust your instincts.

2. INSIST ON REASONABLE STAFFING RATIOS. Even the most loving caregiver is lost with too many children. Babies, in particular, need intense attention that very few centers can provide. A national study of chid care by the National Institute of Child Health and Development found that infants fared the best when each adult cared for only one child. The next best option: a caregiver in a family child-care home, who looks after one baby and two or three toddlers of preschoolers, says child-care expert Bruce Fuller of the University of California at Berkeley. By the time they are 2 or 3 years old, children benefit from being around other kids, and somewhat larger groups are desirable. The National Association for the Education of Young Children recommends one adult for every three babies, five toddlers, or eight 4-year-olds.

3. FIND A QUALITY CAREGIVER. Whether you're dealing with a child-care center, a nanny, or a neighbor, the most important consideration is the relationship between the caregiver and your child. You want someone who is not only attentive to your child's physical needs but will take the time to interact with him in meaningful ways, from playing peekaboo on the floor to helping him make friends.

4. LOOK FOR PLEASANT PLAY AREAS, WITH PLENTY OF TOYS AND BOOKS. Children don't need fancy equipment. In fact, beware of centers that emphasize glitz at the expense of staff salaries. But kids do need things to play with and comfortable areas in which to play. In a family child-care home, you want a room that's set aside exclusively for the children (as opposed to them having the run of the house). In centers, look for rooms big enough for kids to play in, as well of lots of books and an outdoor playground.

5. PARENTS SHOULD BE WELCOME AT ALL TIMES. Beware of centers that discourage your visits or participation—especially at the beginning, when you should be able to stay with your child until he's acclimated. And spend as much time as you can when you first look at a center, observing interactions; several hours is optimal.

larly frustrating bind. These parents can't afford high-quality care without government subsidies—and subsidies, including vouchers and Head Start, are generally available only for the very poor. "People at both ends of the income scale do better than those in the middle—and nobody does very well," says Faith Wohl, president of the Child Care Action Campaign.

Quality care is expensive. In fact, the Children's Defense Fund found that the average yearly cost of child care was more than double the cost of a year's state university tuition in urban areas in 11 states. At the Oxford Street Day Care Cooperative in Cambridge, Massachusetts, another nonprofit cooperative and one of the rare centers that offers quality care for babies, tuition for infants averages $20,000 a year. Even at that rate, the center requires parents to work in their children's classroom several hours a week and to help clean up on weekends—volunteer labor that helps keep operating costs lower and staff-to-child ratios at acceptable levels.

Some states are experimenting with ways to make care more affordable and to improve quality for all. "North Carolina is a state that's really trying to do better," says Mitchell. "The most significant thing is that North Carolina is spending a large amount of its own money, two hundred million dollars beyond the federal money it is receiving, to improve the quality of child care through staff education, raising childcare workers' wages, and helping families to afford care."

Tax credits are another way a state can make child care more affordable. The credits are much more valuable than standard tax deductions because parents get a dollar back for every dollar they spend. Some states have also made the credits "refundable," so even parents whose incomes are too low to be taxed receive a refund check. Minnesota, California, and New York are among the states with a refundable tax credit.

"WHERE'S MY TEACHER?" LOW PAY, HIGH TURNOVER

Turnover among child-care staff is a problem nationwide, largely because low wages make it difficult to attract and retain experienced, well-educated staff. Parking-lot attendants make more, on average, than child-care workers, according to the Center for the Child Care Workforce in Washington, DC. Researchers there say wages average less than $7 an hour in 23 states and less than $10 an hour everywhere else

except the District of Columbia. Year-to-year turnover averages 30 percent, and some centers have turnover as high as 100 percent in a year.

And turnover matters, because small children need to form an emotional bond with the person caring for them, experts say. Having caregivers come and go can be upsetting to small children; if the changes are extreme and the children are vulnerable, staff turnover may even harm their development.

Some states have taken modest steps to address the staffing crisis. California, Illinois, Washington, New York, Wisconsin, Oklahoma, and Georgia have allocated a share of state money to increase wages for child-care workers, according to the Children's Defense Fund. Rhode Island and North Carolina, meanwhile, have made more child-care staffers eligible for state-funded health insurance.

Rx FOR CHILD CARE: MONEY PLUS POLITICAL WILL

Can incremental efforts to improve America's child-care system really help? Economists Suzanne Helburn and Barbara R. Bergmann, the authors of a new book, *America's Child Care Problem: The Way*

Out (Palgrave), argue that what's needed is an expansive federal program that offers the middle class as well as the poor the help they need to make child care and early education affordable. "We, as a nation, need to realize that the need for child care is no different from the need for public schools," Helburn says.

The price tag for the authors' proposed program: $30 billion a year, two thirds the amount President Bush recently proposed for increased military spending next year.

But such a massive infusion of cash seems unlikely in the near term. Where does that leave the future of the nation's child-care system and the families who so badly depend on it?

Sharon Lynn Kagan, a professor of early childhood and family policy at Teachers College, Columbia University, is guardedly optimistic. Business and politics came together in a powerful coalition to drive improvements in the public school system, Kagan says, and leaders will soon realize that a nation that doesn't invest in its youngest children, too, is sacrificing its future.

"We need more money, to be sure," Kagan says. "But we also need to use the money we've got, and money we're asking for, more wisely. Right now, we're funding poor quality. We have to invest in professional development and expand the regulatory system because that improves quality. We've got the knowledge; we have to be a lot more strategic."

For a detailed look at care in your state, go to childrensdefensefund.org to request the "Children in the States" annual report.

From *Working Mother,* April 2002, pp. 32-35, 78. © 2002 by WMAC, Inc. All rights reserved.

creating home-school partnerships

BY KERI PETERSON

"Home-school partnerships command a lot of attention these days. The federal government has issued documents to help schools organize parent participation programs. Major reform efforts and educational interventions list parental involvement as an important ingredient. Scholarly writing on the topic abounds, and various publications offer guidance to schools or describe exemplary programs" (Finn, 1998, p. 20). "Early interventionists have recognized for many years that the most powerful, efficient, and effective system for making a lasting difference in the life of a child has always been the family" (Gage and Workman, 1994, p. 74). Schools often recognize this, but teachers all too frequently get discouraged and don't spend the needed energy to establish and nurture partnerships with parents. This article will explain what home-school partnerships are, discuss the benefits that home-school partnerships create, present barriers for effective home-school partnerships and, finally, offer suggestions for improvement of home-school partnerships.

WHAT DO HOME-SCHOOL PARTNERSHIPS LOOK LIKE?

Parental involvement can simply be categorized in two ways: parental engagement in school activities and parental engagement at home. Traditionally, parental engagement in school activities "has encompassed a variety of activities such as volunteering in the classroom, participating in parent conferences and home visits, communications between parent and teacher via phone, and written means, assisting with fundraising and special events, and participating on advisory boards. Essentially, parents have been invited and welcomed to be involved in the established structure of a program for their child" (McBride, 1999, p. 62). Parents engaged at home may look differently from one family to another, but may include "actively organizing and monitoring the child's time, helping with homework, discussing school matters with the child, and reading to and being read to by their children" (Finn, 1998, p. 20).

WHO BENEFITS FROM HOME-SCHOOL PARTNERSHIPS?

All of those involved (teacher, child, and parent) in home-school partnerships stand to gain from the relationship that is created between the school and the family. In a study conducted of nine kindergarten children who seemed headed for reading difficulties in first grade, Goldenberg concluded that "the earlier in a child's school career his/her parents become involved, and that involvement is sustained, the bigger the payoff" (Eldridge, 2001, p. 65).

Parental involvement benefits children both academically and in their behaviors and feelings about school. "The benefits for young children begin with greater gains in reading for those children whose parents are encouraged by the teacher to help with reading activities at home" (Eldridge, 2001, p. 65). In an elementary school in Oakland, CA, four classrooms piloted a Home-School Connections project in their classrooms. "Activities included frequent information updates, via phone and mail, family homework projects that encouraged reading at home, and a series of family seminars on such topics as homework help and reading. Parents felt free to visit the classrooms and to communicate with the teacher by phone. Although it is difficult to assess the direct impact of this close family connection, students in the pilot classrooms had some of the highest reading scores in the school" (Cohn-Vargas and Grose, 1998, p. 45). "Extensive research reviews find that the home environment is among the most important influences on academic performance" (Finn, 1998, p. 20). Simply put, the amount of time parents spend monitoring their children's activities and assisting their children with homework has a dramatic effect on how successful their children are academically. "Additionally, children of parents who are involved have a more positive attitude about school, improved attendance, and show better homework habits than do children whose families are less involved" (Eldridge, 2001, p. 65).

Parents that become involved in their child's schooling can benefit significantly from the experience. "Parents involved with school in parent-related activities show increased self-confidence in parenting, more knowledge of child development, and an expanded understanding of the home as an environment for learning" (Eldridge, 2001, p. 66). Involved parents report that they feel they should help their child at home, that they understand more about what the child is being taught, that they know more about the school program, and that they support and encourage their child's school work (Eldridge, 2001, pp. 65–66). "Additionally, involved parents show an increased appreciation for a teacher's merits and abilities and are more likely to view positively a teacher's interpersonal skills" (Eldridge, 2001, p. 66).

Parental involvement also affects the teacher. "A teacher who involves parents in children's learning is more likely to report a greater understanding of families' cultures, an increased appreciation for parental interest in helping their children, and a deeper respect for parents' time and abilities" (Eldridge, 2001, p.

66). Teachers who are committed to parental involvement tend to reap significant positive benefits in terms of parental perceptions of their merits. When parents and teachers connect, both will see significant and lasting effects in their appreciation and understanding of each other's efforts (Eldridge, 2001, p. 66).

BARRIERS TO HOME-SCHOOL CONNECTIONS

There are several barriers that prevent effective home-school connections from happening in many schools across our nation. Most of these barriers involve the school and the parents. In my experience as a primary classroom teacher, children have always enjoyed their parents' involvement and have, in fact, shown much enthusiasm for it.

One barrier to home-school connections is the lack of knowledge and training teachers have regarding parental involvement. "Despite the strong evidence supporting the importance of home-school collaborations, prospective teachers receive little training, information, or experience working with parents. Surprisingly few in-service programs have been designed to support teachers in expanding or improving their parent involvement efforts" (Brand, 1996, p. 76). Many teachers feel uncomfortable and awkward around parents and have had little training on how to overcome their feelings, let alone truly support and encourage home-school partnerships.

Another barrier to home-school partnerships is that many parents do not fully understand how valuable and important their interactions with their children are. Parents also don't feel they have the ability to truly help their child academically. "Many parents express a belief that their assistance is not needed by the schools or teachers" (Eldridge, 2001, p. 66). "Well-designed school opportunities and incentives for parent involvement may have only limited success if they do not also address parents' ideas about their role in children's education and their self efficacy for helping their children succeed in school" (Powell, 1998, p. 64). Researchers have discovered that children succeed in school more often when the home is emotionally supportive, when parents provide reassurance when their child encounters failure and when parents accept responsibility for assisting their children (Finn, 1998, p. 20). Barriers are created when homes and parents do not closely resemble these ideas.

"The reason some families don't become more involved in schools stems in part from parental perceptions of school. Menacker, Hurwitz, and Weldon (1988) reporting on home-school relations in inner-city schools, noted that most of the adults in these families had had unsuccessful or negative school experiences themselves, which contribute to their perception of the school as unresponsive" (Eldridge, 2001, p. 66).

Timing of home-school connections often creates a barrier for parents as well. "Time constraints and work schedules of parents have been found to be problems in involvement efforts" (Eldridge, 2001, p. 67). When schools do not offer programs that are flexible, such as evening events, participation levels decrease.

"Family circumstances also need to be addressed in attempts to remove barriers to participation in meetings" (Powell, 1998, p. 64). Schools that do not take into account child care arrangements and transportation barriers, for example, experience less parental involvement in home-school partnerships, especially with low-income families. In a recent study in 12 Baltimore schools, parental involvement increased by 10 percent when a high level of support (transportation to workshops, child care, meals, two meeting times) was offered to families. "It appeared that the additional 10 percent was a higher-risk group as measured by children's reading achievement and teacher ratings of the home educational environment" (Powell, 1998, p. 64). It is likely that there are many other barriers to effective home-school partnerships. It is important for schools to identify as many barriers as possible so that they may be eliminated in hopes of creating stronger partnerships with the families it serves.

SUGGESTIONS FOR IMPROVING HOME-SCHOOL PARTNERSHIPS

"Across all populations and programs, a major challenge is to develop ways of engaging parents that respond to a family's interests and life circumstances" (Powell, 1998, p. 63). "Our understanding of parent involvement needs to be on a continuum that allows for parent participation on a variety of levels and through a wide variety of activities" (Gage and Workman, 1994, p. 77).

"First and foremost, a teacher should create a classroom climate that is open and accepting of parents and is based on a partnership approach. In this way the barriers of parental reluctance and awkwardness are lowered, and those parents who know the school to be unresponsive can begin to experience the classroom in another way" (Eldridge, 2001, p. 67). In order to do this, more universities and school districts need to be better training teachers on parental involvement concepts so that home-school partnerships are natural for teachers. "The currently weak attention to teachers' demonstrated skills in relating to parents must be strengthened in professional education and state certification requirements. It appears that, among the many competencies required for effective work with parents, special emphasis should be given to skills in learning and appreciating the perspectives of families" (Powell, 1998, p. 66).

One important thought to remember that may help improve home-school partnerships is the idea of what home-school partnerships "look like."

"Teachers pay more attention to students whose parents are involved in school" (Finn, 1998, p. 23). Often, educators dismiss the work that families do at home with their children—forgetting that the "home environment is among the most important influences on academic performance" (Finn, 1998, p. 20). One suggestion for improvement, then, would be for educators to recognize the work that families do at home. "The most powerful form of parent involvement has the parent actively involved with the child at home in all ways that relate to optimal learning and growing" (Gage and Workman, 1994, p. 77).

Research indicates that as educators we need to be telling parents about how important their job is and how much what they do with their children at home affects their achievement in the classroom. "Many parents feel they lack, or do lack, the skills to guide their children's reading or schoolwork" (Finn, 1998, p. 22). Sup-

BARRIERS TO POSITIVE FAMILY-TEACHER PARTNERSHIPS

BY AMY SUSSNA KLEIN, ED.D., AND MARIAN MILLER, M.ED.

There are a number of barriers that can prevent positive family-teacher relationships from forming. Some of these common obstacles include:

- **Differences in backgrounds.** The family and teacher come from different cultures, languages, and socio-economic statuses.
- **Stress.** There is stress for both families and teachers. For example, long hours and little flexibility at work reduce the time available for teachers to work on family communication and for parents/caregivers to relate to school.
- **Differing Values.** The family and teacher lack a mutual set of values.
- **Differences in viewing roles.** Differing views of the role of the school for the child between the teacher and the parent or caregiver.
- **Types of experiences.** Prior experiences with families/teachers have set up differing expectations.
- **Notions of openness.** Lack of openness to outsiders entering their territory (home or school).
- **Differences in experiences.** A parent's experience in school (positive or negative) sets up some expectations for their own interactions with school/teacher for their own child.

- **Communication abilities.** Teachers or families lack the ability to identify and communicate key experiences, ideas, or issues.
- **Communication discomfort.** Families or teachers are uncomfortable about communicating their needs, or do not have enough fluency in the language.
- **Need to feel valued.** Parents and teachers perceive that their perspective and opinions are not valued.
- **Differences in viewing child's needs.** The school views the child (her learning and development) differently than the family does. The school's philosophy differs from the family's view of appropriate child rearing. For example: The family equates teaching with telling, and the teacher equates learning with doing. Or, behavior issues are handled one way at home and another at school (spanking at home, explaining at school). When the school clearly explains philosophy, families get a better sense of the match between home/school expectations.

Amy Sussna Klein, Ed.D., is President of ASK Education Consulting. She can be reached by email at Askeducation@cs.com.

Marian Miller, M.Ed., is a faculty member at Lesley College

porting and encouraging parents in their role as their child's first teacher is vital to their child's success.

"To serve the needs of diverse children and families, teachers often must seek support for children and families beyond the traditional walls of the school" (Hurd, Lerner and Barton, 1999, p. 74). Schools need to continue to rely on community agencies to help in the effort of educating our children. "Dryfoos (1990) finds that when collaboration occurs between the school and the youth- and family-serving agencies and the community programs in which the school is embedded, an integrated and comprehensive community-wide system is established" (Hurd, Lerner and Barton, 1999, p. 74). Head Start is a well-known leader of an integrated services model.

CONCLUSION

"Teaching, nurturing, and caring for children is a community process. When most effective, many constituents—parents, teachers, extended family, neighborhoods, agencies, and community partners—are engaged. In the best of worlds, all parties work together to support children in the context of their families" (Hurd, Lerner and Barton, 1999, p. 74).

REFERENCES

Brand, S. (1996). Making parent involvement a reality: Helping teachers develop partnerships with parents. *Young Children,* 51(2), 76–80.

Cohn-Vargas and Grose, K. (1998). A partnership for literacy. *Educational Leadership,* 55(8), 45–48.

Eldridge, D. (2001). Parent involvement: It's worth the effort. *Young Children,* 56(4), 65–69.

Finn, J. (1998). Parental engagement that makes a difference. *Educational Leadership,* 55(8), 20–24.

Gage, J. and Workman, S. (1994). Creating family support systems: In head start and beyond. *Young Children,* 49(7), 74–77.

Hurd, T., Learner, R., and Barton, C. (1999). Integrated services: Expanding partnerships to meet the needs of today's children and families. *Young Children,* 54(2), 74–79.

McBride, S. (1999). Family centered practices. *Young Children,* 54(3), 62–68.

Powell, D. (1998). Reweaving parents into the fabric of early childhood programs. *Young Children,* 53(6), 60–67.

Keri Peterson is a teacher in the four-year-old program at Early Learning Center, Tiffany Creek Elementary School, in Boyceville, WI. She is currently enrolled in the M.S. program at the University of Wisconsin-Stout.

Article 17

For America's Infants and Toddlers, Are Important Values Threatened by Our Zeal to "Teach"?

Eleanor Stokes Szanton

Editor's note: All Americans are aware of the diversity within the total U.S. population. In addition, many members of the early childhood community, and numerous other citizens, are aware that Americans do not *all* share *all* of the same values. Yet from the perspective of people living in other countries, there's a cluster of personal characteristics considered peculiarly American.

Some of us cherish all of these values, some of us dislike a few—or more than a few—of them. We may not agree on the ranking of these attributes—which attribute is more important than which. But even people who resent these values and characteristics acknowledge their existence.

In this thought-provoking article, the author discusses the values transmitted to the next generation by a majority of Americans and by many early childhood education leaders. They are reflected in NAEYC's standards of developmentally appropriate practice, which have evolved from the combined and refined input of many experts. The author points out how mainstream infant/toddler programs encourage these characteristics in

children. She worries that low quality programs may interfere with the development of characteristics deemed desirable by many Americans.

We know that many readers—and even some of NAEYC's leaders—will take exception to several of the assumptions and statements in this article. Therefore we think that it will be a powerful discussion starter for staff and early childhood education students. We invite you to think as you read (we have highlighted some things you may want to think about), talk over your thoughts with others, and write to us!

Americans by and large raise their children in a very distinctive way. That is perhaps surprising neither to those who endorse it nor to those who do not approve of it. What is fascinating is seeing just how early this process begins.

From more than 40 years of observation, practice, and study of infant/toddler care and education here and abroad, I have become very aware of those common values mentioned by John Hope Franklin. But I am surprised at how little they are dis-

cussed in research and practice. Typically child development specialists speak of certain *universals of development*—attributes that growing children share the world over. On the other hand they study the impact of *group differences* in child development—what it means to grow up in one ethnic group as opposed to another, to be poor instead of rich, White instead of Black, in a rural versus an urban setting. Researchers also study *individual differences* such as temperament, ability, and resilience. But in the process they largely ignore a distinction just as important as the others—*national characteristics* that many of us believe to be a valuable source of our strength as Americans.

Even with our diversity it is important to see just how much is shared in raising our children from infancy onward—both at home and in "good" early child care. In doing so, I believe that we develop in our children a set of characteristics that are functional for life in the United States and in this new century.

Indeed, it is especially important to understand how distinctively and functionally we raise our children, because that process is now being unintentionally threatened.

Studied	Ignored	Studied	Studied
Universals of development	National Characteristics	Cultural and group differences	Individual differences

This article discusses how early in a child's life values held by most Americans are transmitted in good group care and education. It suggests how much more those valued competencies will be needed in this new century. And it raises a red flag about the direction of an increasing number of programs for infants and toddlers that use teaching methods designed for older children, because in doing so they may ignore the natural developmental processes of infants and toddlers and affect the future success of these children in the national culture of which they are part.

Attitudes toward diversity

The concern about understanding and honoring differences is one of the values that unite most Americans and distinguish them from people of other nations. In this era and in this country, much emphasis is placed upon those differences. This is certainly fitting. We have a highly diverse nation. And we only need look at the ethnic strife around the world and at the hate crimes and other more subtle examples of inter-ethnic hostility in our own country to believe differences are important to recognize, understand, and honor.

What is striking is to see how much American attitudes toward diversity in child care may differ from those of others. The following example serves to highlight this difference.

Not many years ago, I visited a country in Eastern Europe, observing the infant/toddler child care centers. In that country often there were three or four infant or toddler rooms in one large building, together with preschool rooms. In one room I found a child of approximately eight months lying alone on a mattress in a kind of play pen. Her eyes were open and totally listless in expression, though she did watch what was going on. No one paid any attention to her. I thought she might be unwell. All the other children were free to walk or crawl around the play area.

As we went to look at the other children's rooms, that little girl stayed in my mind. About 45 minutes later, after we had finished looking at the other groups, I asked if I could go back to the first room—the room with the listless child. When we did, I found her still lying in exactly the same position, still watching, still listless. Still no one was paying attention to her. When I asked about her, I was told, "She's Albanian." It turned out that her Albanian mother, a minority in that country, had wanted her child to be "main-streamed" and had recently entered her in the program so that she could learn the language of the dominant culture from the beginning. The generally caring and committed staff simply did not know what to do with her. They wished her mother had decided to use one of the several Albanian child care centers that were available. They apparently planned to let her lie there as long as she "wanted to" lie alone. However, after I asked, one of the teachers picked her up and nuzzled her head in her neck. The child began to respond.

To most Americans, this is an appalling story. I do not say that this behavior—and worse—cannot happen in the United States. But it would never be held up as good practice. Demonstrating best practice and even good practice in the United States, a program would provide a primary teacher/caregiver of the same ethnic and linguistic background as the child. Failing that, the child's caregiver would have some diversity training and know something about the culture of this child, both from the family and from other sources (Lally et al. 1995; Bredekamp & Copple 1997).

There are excellent reasons for this attention to children's cultural backgrounds. In the words of one expert in infant/toddler development,

> Preschoolers have formed a somewhat well-developed "working sense of self," with likes and dislikes, attitudes, and inclinations. [In contrast] infants and toddlers are in the process of forming this preliminary sense of self. Part of what infants and toddlers get from caregivers are perceptions of how people act at various times in various situations (seen as how the infant should behave), how people act toward them and others (seen as how they and others should be treated), and how emotions are expressed (seen as how they should feel). The infant uses these impressions and often incorporates them into the self she becomes. (Lally 1995, 59)

That sense of self is both an individual one and a cultural one, with cultural expectations for how people act at various times in various situations, toward them and others, and how emotions are expressed. Young children also need to build the foundations of their own language.

There is another kind of diversity that our nation honors, and that is diversity of physical and mental ability. Awareness and respect for varying abilities is reflected in good practices in our inclusive infant/toddler programs. In many countries children with special needs, especially young ones, are hidden away or kept at home as an embarrassment to family and school. Since the mid 1970s we have moved to include children with special needs in preschool programs whenever possible, both to broaden opportunities for the children themselves and to enrich the entire group (Bryant & Graham 1993; O'Brien 1997).

Individualism and independence

Good practice in early childhood care and education in the United States places a heavy emphasis on adult-child interaction. Teachers and individual children talk to each other a lot as teachers encourage joint attention and elaborate on what the child is doing, naming the activity, setting it in context, scaffolding the child's interpretation of events. Individual differences in temperament are studied and respected. Our children become used to using caregivers and teachers as resources (*Discoveries of Infancy* 1992). In the United States good practice calls for low child-teacher ratios, responsive caregiving, and an individualized approach to early childhood education (Lally et al. 1995; Bredekamp & Copple 1997).

Japan offers a good example of a contrasting approach to early childhood education. In Japan there is much more emphasis on peer groups. (I speak now not of infants and toddlers, who until recently in that country have rarely been in group care, but of children three years and older.) Children are placed in "table groups" that go through several grades together. They take on chores early in life and remind each other of their duties. The child-teacher ratio is much higher, so teachers frequently use peer pressure rather than adult-child interaction to achieve their objectives (Lewis 1995). In many non-Western societies, small children quickly become one of many in a family group, often cared for by older siblings (LeVine et al. 1996).

Clearly some things are lost in the American approach to raising young children, primarily a strong sense of belonging to a group, strong group loyalty, early responsibility for other

children. However, the difference puts in high relief what is strikingly American—the importance of individual interplay between child and adult.

Choice and exploration

Hand in hand with valuing independence and individualism goes the high value assigned to individual choice and exploration. For better or worse, the larger society in the United States puts great emphasis on independence and the ability to accomplish things on one's own. That emphasis is apparent from the earliest years of care and education (Hansen, Kaufmann, & Saifer 1996). Researchers and other observers have noticed differences between the treatment of little boys and little girls on this point, with boys being more strongly encouraged to strike out on their own (Maccoby & Jacklin 1974). Nonetheless, when compared to children in other countries, independence is fostered in toddler girls, as well.

In child care in many countries, toys are presented to toddlers to play with. They may be stored out of children's reach and brought out for them. At the same time children in these settings learn amazingly early—in American eyes—what "Do not touch" means. The concept of babyproofing is more typically American. American infants and toddlers are generally allowed to crawl and move about freely in an environment where health and safety hazards have been removed. Playpens are discouraged. In early childhood centers toddlers are free to reach toys of their own choosing, placed on low, easily accessible shelves or the floor. Children are encouraged to explore and try new things.

A visitor from one of the countries of the former Soviet Union remarked after watching the young American children choose a name for their class's new bunny, "You are really teaching democracy! We would never ask children to vote on the rab-

bit's name." Whether encouraging toddlers to select from among toys or preschoolers to make simple decisions, we raise our children to be used to, and comfortable with, making their own choices.

Initiative

Initiative is another highly functional American trait. It goes in tandem with individualism, independence, choice, and exploration.

With the glaring and tragic exceptions of those forced here in slavery and those Native Americans already here, the United States was built by people—and their descendants—who were willing to leave everything they had known and come to some place entirely different. (Even those who felt they had no choice but to flee famine, persecution, or death were different from their relatives who chose not to flee. And many an African American family has tales of their forebears' escape and desperate survival through their wits and self-reliance.) The vast majority came to tame wilderness, build their own houses and farms and stores, form new groups and civic associations, create a new world. This frontier mentality has permeated our entire society, even down to this day.

The prominence of personal initiative in American culture was identified by Alexis de Tocqueville early on in the life of the country:

The citizen of the United States is taught from infancy to rely upon his own exertions in order to resist the evils and the difficulties of life; he looks upon the social authority with an eye of mistrust and anxiety, and he claims its assistance only when he is unable to do without it. This habit may be traced even in the schools, where the children in their games are wont to submit to rules which they have themselves established, and to punish misdemeanors which they have themselves defined. The same spirit pervades every act of social life. (Tocqueville [1835] 1946)

In today's world this reverence for personal initiative is expressed in the attitude of Americans toward entrepreneurs who start up small businesses to organize their communities to fight an environmental problem. It is probably no accident that the United States is responsible for a very high percentage of new inventions or that the recent electronics revolution started here. Tinkering is built right in.

Not surprisingly, the high value placed on personal initiative in American culture is evident as we help our youngest children to grow and develop. In many countries children follow the lead of the teacher (e.g., teacher, getting a box of blocks down from a cupboard, says, "Suppose you build a castle. John, why don't you put that block here…"). In contrast, good practice in the United States would be to allow or encourage children to experiment with building the tower themselves—learning as much when it falls down as when it rises up. Programs for toddlers emphasize the great importance of playing with objects, of allowing children to manipulate toys in many different ways—no doubt more ways than the teacher would have thought of—and then discussing with the children or elaborating on what they are doing.

In some cultures infants and toddlers are more commonly fed with a spoon by an adult. In the United States, children more frequently are allowed and encouraged to feed themselves by manipulating bits of food with their fingers. Babies are encouraged to crawl, with less restraint than found elsewhere. Adults encourage children to learn, through practice and experience, that they can make things happen.

Floor time and the beginning of equality

Floor time, a term popularized by the infant psychiatrist Stanley Greenspan (Greenspan & Greenspan 1989), is a good characterization of the hundreds of hours parents, caregivers, and early childhood teachers spend on the floor where infants and toddlers typically play. The very act of sitting down on the same level with the crawling baby or toddling child is symbolic of a more equal relationship between adult and child. It levels the playing field. Whether an adult is sitting with feet spread apart and rolling a ball back and forth with a toddler or watching what the child is playing with and talking about it with her, that adult is giving the message, "You are as important as I am. Your interests are my interests."

Floor time is much less common outside the United States. More often adults stand or sit on chairs—or crouch or kneel. In spatial terms they are demonstrating the body language of authority. The relative absence of floor time also leaves children in other countries interacting more with *each other* than with the adults. Here again, by getting down on the floor with our children, we emphasize the value of one-on-one adult-child interaction. Floor time with infants and toddlers is the first step in education toward the deeply held American belief in equality.

Expressiveness

In many parts of the world, infants, carried everywhere by their mothers, have no need to learn to cry lustily to signal their needs. A grunt or snuffle suffices. As they get older, they may have to share a very small space with a large family. In contrast, Western children, and particularly American children, are placed in separate cribs, often in separate rooms. They learn they must use their bodies—in infancy, their voices—as a tool to make things happen. A particularly striking example of this is shown in the following research.

Japanese babies as young as two months cry much less and for a much shorter time on the whole than their American counterparts when receiving a routine immunization shot (Lewis, Ramsey, & Kawakami 1993). This difference is purely behavioral; their levels of cortisol, an indicator of internal distress, are just as high or higher than those of American children the same age. Although there may be some admixture of genetic difference here, the fact is that from the earliest months, American children have a tendency to show their reactions to an averse stimulus.

Self-expression is more highly valued throughout childhood in the United States than in other parts of the world. Here we see a higher level of activity, noisiness, and messiness permitted among infants and toddlers than elsewhere. In U.S. early childhood programs, a few squiggles on a piece of paper may be much admired; whereas, in other countries, the ability to represent a known object is much more strongly encouraged.

Parents' place in the program

In some countries I have noted that child care centers view parents virtually as contaminants. Due to a program's emphasis on cleanliness, parents may be unwelcome in the play area of an infant/toddler center. If allowed in, they must wear smocks and slippers. Children must change their home clothes for clothing provided by the center before entering the room with the other children. Parents are not encouraged to visit. There is very little discussion with them at the beginning or end of the day. The child simply leads two lives, one at home and the other at the center, with little connection between them.

In contrast, in the United States good practice calls for teamwork with parents. Especially in infant/toddler care and education, parents and staff see the need to consult constantly about events in the baby's day—feeding and diapering, degree of fussiness, amount of sleep. In addition, best practice calls for close consultation on toilet learning, discipline, sleep routines, and other issues that may cause tension between adult and child (Lally et al. 1995; Hansen & Kaufmann 1997). Again reflecting American attention to diversity, it is considered the duty of the teacher and caregiver to be familiar with the culture and expectations of the family. Where there might be strong differences between center and family on issues such as corporal punishment, best practice calls for considerable discussion and even negotiation back and forth, finding a place that honors both the expectations of families and the center's policies and philosophy.

What our children will face in this new century

We raise our children from infancy to reflect the values commonly held in our society. But what will these children need as the new century progresses? They will need to

- be always ready to try something new in a world in which the only constant is change, and a premium will be placed on creating new ideas and thinking outside the box;
- be flexible and comfortable with complicated decisions in an increasingly complex society;
- be able to get along with fellow citizens more diverse than ever in ethnicity and culture;
- be very competent with language; and if their families are immigrants, children will need to be as competent in English as in their family's language of origin;
- believe they can make things happen—that they can make a difference in their own lives and the lives of those around them;
- be comfortable speaking out, negotiating, substituting words and logic for violence in persuading others;
- have a profound sense of the importance of equal opportunity for all our citizens and of the dignity and rights of each individual; and
- be gifted parents, maintaining and strengthening the role of family in

American life, working well with services designed to help and support families.

As we know, education begins at birth. Therefore when young children start to learn about differences or express their feelings or have lots of "talk" with a caring adult down on the floor with them; when they are given a chance to move freely, play with toys of their own choosing, manipulating them in ways they choose and trying new ways; when they see their parents valued by their teachers, they are beginning the long journey of becoming adults prepared to do well in the future in the United States. They are being helped to espouse the common values of a diverse nation.

So what's the problem?

How then can there be a problem if we naturally arrange the care of young children in groups in ways that are distinctive to American culture? Why should we not simply continue what we are doing? There seem to be *two* problems.

The first is that "our own" culture includes *many* cultures within it, and not all of us agree about what quality infant/toddler child care should look like. This important problem is being discussed in many places, but is not the subject of *this* article.

Ironically, the second problem comes partly from the very realization—new to many—of the importance of the earliest years, zero to three. (The threat may also be related to the present emphasis on test scores and measurable performance in schools.) Child care programs are now seen by policymakers and the public in general not merely as babysitting for infants and toddlers while their parents work.

Early Head Start, Even Start, state level early intervention programs, and a greatly expanded number of child care programs are trying to provide meaningful learning experiences for children not yet even two years old. This is wonderful when relationships are good, the atmo-

sphere is homelike, not instructional, and the activities are age appropriate. But I also see and read curricula with lesson plans, measurable goals, and suggested teacher-led group activities to achieve them, which are being developed at a great rate. One extreme illustration of the problem that came across my desk recently was part of a center's daily schedule for its toddlers:

10:00 a.m.   *Math and science*
10:30 a.m.   *Diapering*

This distressing move toward pushing lessons on small children is not limited to early childhood programs. New parents are presently bombarded with "smart baby" products, from flash cards to videos teaching the baby to read.

Greatly magnifying this problem is the lack of staff well trained to work with the infant/toddler age group. The demand has burgeoned too fast for the supply, given the small amount of money we devote to the training and pay of our children's earliest teachers. The problem is exacerbated by the low salaries earned by teachers and caregivers of this age group, resulting in turnover rates close to 50% a year and the need to train an entirely new group of teachers.

As a result, I see too many teachers and providers from all walks of life cling to written curricula with lesson plans and lots of group activities. This can be a particular problem with teachers who have taught older children. In part they are urged on by parents, newly sensitized to the importance of stimulation in the early years, who want to know what their babies are learning.

Well-trained or experienced teachers of infants and toddlers or unusually gifted novices can answer parents in general terms. They will know what developmental tasks lie ahead of the children in their care and what kinds of play activities and experiences allow children to address them. (For infants and toddlers, of course, play *is* work.) Over a period of weeks and months, skilled providers see that their children have these experiences but at their own pace, and when they are interested in them (never "We teach colors Monday, shapes Tuesday, Mozart Wednesday"). Skilled, well-trained teachers and providers have a lot of experience in observation and consider ongoing observation essential in making available toys and tasks appropriate for children (see "Curriculum in Head Start" 2000).

Conclusion

The United States is one of the few nations that has invented itself. That invention is based not so much on the history and culture of its people—though the histories of its *peoples* is an important part of it—but rather on a set of ideas as to what people can and should become. As we have seen, this process begins very early, but it's now in danger.

It is distressing in this era of budget surplus that national policymakers argue simply about spending more on Social Security or Medicare or providing further tax relief. Is it too much to ask that they invest in adequate training and pay for those helping to raise our youngest children for life in this land in this new century?

References

Baldwin, J. 1961. The discovery of what it means to be an American. *Nobody knows my name: More notes of a native son*. New York: Dial.

Bredekamp, S., & C. Copple, eds. 1997. *Developmentally appropriate practice in early childhood programs*. Rev. ed. Washington, DC: NAEYC.

Bryant, D.M., & M.A. Graham, eds. 1993. *Implementing early intervention: From research to effective practice*. New York: Guilford.

Curriculum in Head Start. 2000. *Head Start Bulletin* 67 (March).

Discoveries of infancy: Cognitive development and learning. 1992. West Ed, Program for Infant/Toddler Caregivers (PITC). Videocassette. (Available from California Department of Education, Sacramento: 800-995-4099).

Greenspan, S., & N.T. Greenspan. 1989. *The essential partnership: How parents and children can meet the emotional challenges of infancy and childhood*, 19–62. New York: Viking Penguin.

Hansen, K.A., & R.K. Kaufmann. 1997. Families and caregivers together supporting infants and toddlers. In *Creating child-centered programs for infants and toddlers*, ed. E.S. Szanton, 135–58. Washington, DC: Children's Resources International.

Hansen, K.A., R.K. Kaufmann, & S. Saifer. 1996. *Education and the culture of democracy: Early childhood practice*. Washington, DC: Children's Resources International.

Lally, J.R. 1995. The impact of child care policies and practices on infant/toddler identity formation. *Young Children* 51 (1): 58–67.

Lally, J.R., A. Griffin, E. Fenichel, M.M. Segal, E.S. Szanton, & B. Weissbourd. 1995. *Caring for infants and toddlers in groups: Developmentally appropriate practice*. Washington, DC: ZERO TO THREE/The National Center or Infants, Toddlers and Families.

LeVine, R.A., S. Dixon, S. LeVine, A. Richman, P.H. Leiderman, C.H. Keefer, & T.B. Brazelton. 1996. *Child care and culture: Lessons from Africa*. Reprint, New York: Cambridge University Press.

Lewis, C.C. 1995. *Educating hearts and minds: Reflections on Japanese preschool and elementary education*. New York: Cambridge University Press.

Lewis, M., D.S. Ramsay, & K. Kawakami. 1993. Differences between Japanese infants and Caucasian American infants in behavioral and cortisol response to inoculation. *Child Development* 64: 1722–31.

Maccoby, E.E., & C.N. Jacklin. 1974. *The psychology of sex differences*, 303–48. Stanford, CA: Stanford University Press.

O'Brien, M. 1997. *Inclusive child care for infants and toddlers: Meeting individual and special needs*. Baltimore, MD: Brookes.

Tocqueville, A. de. [1835] 1946. *Democracy in America*. Ed. by J.P. Mayer and trans. by G. Lawrence. Reprint, New York: Knopf.

Eleanor Stokes Szanton, Ph.D., is president of Consulting for Infants and Toddlers and lecturer at Johns Hopkins School of Public Health. She was executive director of ZERO TO THREE: National Center for Infants, Toddlers and Families from 1979 to 1993 and is coauthor of Part 3 of Developmentally Appropriate Practice in Early Childhood Programs, *revised edition*.

All They Do Is Play?
Play in Preschool

BY ANGIE DORRELL, M.A.

The preschool director and parent walk into the four-year-old class and see children actively engaged. Allyson is preparing a feast with plastic foods while Katy pretends to feed a baby doll. Collin is concentrating on different colors of bear counters while Kelsey and Courtney busily rearrange the unit blocks. The parent smiles and says, "So when does the educational program begin?" The director and teacher share an understanding look as the director begins to explain.

Sound familiar? Play is extremely important to children, but this importance is not widely understood. Parents need to hear from their child's trusted teacher that building with blocks is a valuable learning experience, otherwise they come to rely on worksheets as benchmarks of their child's learning.

Why Is Play Important?

Children learn by being active participants who explore, experiment, and inquire. Vygotsky believed that during play, children are free to experiment, attempt, and try out possibilities, enabling them to reach above and beyond their usual level of abilities. Play offers children opportunities to master their environment. When children play, they are in command; they use their imagination and power of choice to determine the conditions of play. In an environment where children are allowed to discover independently, at their own pace and in their own unique way, they are more likely to become enthusiastic, inquisitive learners. The following describes the unique learning that takes place in the block, language, creativity, dramatic play, math, and science centers.

Block Center

When children place one block on top of another, they learn basic science concepts such as balance, size, and weight relations. When children make a barn for play animals, they learn to use their imagination and gain self-confidence to try their own ideas. Even clean-up time promotes learning. Important beginning math skills are learned as blocks are sorted and classified.

A good block center has:

- Carpet
- Multicultural people
- Small and large vehicles
- Shelving at child's level
- Animal sets (jungle, farm, zoo, dinosaurs)
- Complete set of wooden unit blocks (at least 340)
- Floor equipment (barn, doll house, play mats)

Additional Learning Opportunities in the Block Center

- **Social Development**: Cooperating, sharing, negotiating, developing patience, and tolerance.
- **Emotional Development**: Gaining self-confidence to try ideas, expressing feelings through role-playing, and feeling a sense of accomplishment and success.
- **Physical Development**: Strengthening fingers and hands by reaching, picking up, stacking, lifting, carrying, and fitting together, and increasing eye-hand coordination.
- **Cognitive Development**: Exploring basic science concepts of shape, size, proportions, reversibility, conservation, and gravity (blocks always fall down, not up); developing prediction and comparison skills; exploring basic math concepts such as larger than and smaller than, measuring, counting, grouping, adding, subtracting, sizing; and problem-solving skills.

• **Language Development**: Developing vocabulary about size, shape, and position.

Language and Circle Time Center

When children listen and talk about a story, they learn to love books, remember a sequence and recognize that there is a beginning, middle, and end to books and stories. When children sing as a group they learn how to participate with others, to hear and repeat rhythms, and extend their memory.

A good language and circle time center has:

• Carpet
• Chart tablet
• Puppets
• Paper and pencils
• Musical instruments
• Shelf for language materials
• Soft furniture for book reading
• Flannel board and flannel sets
• Teaching pictures or magazines
• Letter sets (sandpaper, magnetic, flannel)
• Multicultural books about a variety of topics
• Music and appropriate player (cassette, record player, etc.)
• Book shelf for books at the child's level at all times
• Language games (rhyming, opposites, spelling, bingo, lotto, matching)

Additional Learning Opportunities in the Language and Circle Time Center

• **Social Development**: Cooperating with others, working as part of a group toward a common goal, waiting for a turn, understanding, and developing a positive attitude about others.
• **Emotional Development**: Gaining independence skills and expressing ideas in different ways.
• **Physical Development**: Holding and turning pages and coordinating eye-hand movements.
• **Cognitive Development**: Increasing attention span and ability to focus, building correct concepts of objects, and forming new ideas.
• **Language Development**: Following left to right progression, learning how a book works, developing vocabulary through meaningful experiences, associating the written and spoken word, listening skills, and understanding that printed words have meaning.

Creativity and Art Center

It can be difficult to understand how the mass of lines and colors a child creates is part of the learning process. When children choose and gather paper, scissors, and crayons, they learn decision-making skills such as how to implement their ideas and how to follow through on a task. When children create with paint, they learn to mix colors and use their own ideas while exploring and discovering consequences.

A good creativity and art center has:

• Easel
• Scissors
• Paint brushes
• Washable paints
• Watercolors
• Protective clothing
• Table and child-size chairs
• Clay and playdough
• Washable ink pads and stamps
• Multicultural materials
• Paint cups or other appropriate containers
• Consumables available for daily children's choice such as: crayons, washable markers, different types of paper, collage materials (yarn, tissue, craft sticks, glue)

Additional Learning Opportunities in the Creativity and Art Center

• **Social Development**: Sharing and cooperating with others, valuing and respecting others' work, ideas, and property.
• **Emotional Development**: Expressing ideas and self freely in appropriate ways, stretching imaginations, instilling confidence in the child's vision of the world, and gaining a sense of pride.
• **Physical Development**: Strengthening muscles that will be used in writing as they grasp a crayon or mold with clay.
• **Cognitive Development**: Exploring concepts like color, size, shape, texture, and pattern helps children develop sensory abilities.
• **Language Development**: Learning new vocabulary (sticky, firm, cool, slippery, gushy).

Dramatic Play Center

When children put on dress-up clothes, they learn to express themselves and try out different roles. When children make "dinner" together they learn to cooperate, share, and make friends. A child who has a new sibling at home can express his or her feelings in a safe setting, and a child who is missing his or her Grandma can pretend to visit her.

A good dramatic play center has:

- Doll bed
- Child-size kitchen set
- Paper and pencil
- Pans, pots, cooking utensils
- Small table and chairs
- Plates, cups, silverware
- Nonbreakable mirror
- Multicultural boy and girl dolls and clothing
- Multicultural dress up clothing for boys and girls
- Multicultural food that fits in the plates and pots
- Prop box supplies including: doctor's kit, purses, shoes, hats, bags, menus, paper, pencils, etc.

Additional Learning Opportunities in the Dramatic Play Center

- **Social Development**: Learning to share, making friends, being creative, and understanding others.
- **Emotional Development**: Expressing emotions appropriately and recognizing that they are themselves regardless of how they are dressed or who they pretend to be.
- **Physical Development**: Learning life skills such as turning knobs, buttoning, and zipping.
- **Cognitive Development**: Making decisions and choices, learning problem-solving skills, and exploring new ideas from others.
- **Language Development**: Communicating effectively and appropriately with others, and incorporating print into daily activities.

Math and Manipulatives Center

To many adults, math is a difficult subject. However, if from an early age children have positive hands-on experiences, they learn math concepts in a nonthreatening way and take what they learn from one concept and apply it to the next. When children are investigating sea shells with magnifying glasses, they begin to recognize similarities and differences of objects. When children sort bear counters of different shapes and sizes, they learn to classify.

A good math and manipulatives center has:

- Stacking toys
- Dressing vests
- Counters
- Peg boards and pegs
- Puzzles and puzzle rack
- Sorting bowls or trays
- DUPLOS® (or similar type bricks)
- Lacing sets (beads, cards, etc.)
- Manipulative sets (Bristle Builders®, Flexi-blocks®, Space Links®, etc.)

Additional Learning Opportunities in the Math and Manipulatives Center

- **Social Development**: Taking turns and respecting others.
- **Emotional Development**: Feeling proud and willing to try new activities.
- **Physical Development**: Coordinating eye-hand movements, grasping, stacking, and matching.
- **Cognitive Development**: Learning about size, shape, color, and patterns, grouping, classifying, counting, weighing, measuring, time, temperature, space and volume concepts, observing and describing concrete objects, and one-to-one correspondence.
- **Language Development**: Describing objects, pronouncing new terms, and communicating questions and ideas.

Science and Sensorial Center

In order for children to understand their world, they must have opportunities to explore and question and then actively construct their own knowledge. When children pour water into containers they learn to estimate quantity. When children investigate smelling jars, they learn to use their sense of smell in new ways.

A good science and sensorial center has:

- Balance
- Magnet wands
- Sensory table or tubs
- Nonbreakable magnifying glasses
- Sand and water equipment (sand wheel, sieves, containers, scoops, measuring cups)
- Games (nature lotto, texture dominos, feely box)
- Discovery items (seashells, bird's nests, ant farm, prisms)

Additional Learning in the Science and Sensorial Center

- **Social Development**: Working beside each other at the sensory table encourages social interactions and gaining an understanding of why events happen the way they do.
- **Emotional Development**: Learning appropriate ways to relieve tension.
- **Physical Development**: Pouring and measuring develops eye-hand coordination.
- **Cognitive Development**: Observing, exploring, measuring, comparing, classifying, predicting, discovering, and learning general knowledge concepts such as round, triangular, big, and small.
- **Language Development**: Enhancing curiosity of children and recognizing similarities and differences.

Angie Dorrell, M.A., is director of curriculum for La Petite Academy, one of the nation's largest providers of early childhood education programs. She also serves as a NAEYC accreditation validator and commissioner. Most importantly, she is mother of two daughters, a toddler and preschooler.

From *Earlychildhood News*, March/April 2000, pp. 18-22. © 2000 by *Earlychildhood News*. Reprinted by permission.

10 Signs of a Great Preschool

Is your child learning or just playing? Here's what makes for an excellent early education.

What an adventure awaits your little one as he heads off to preschool—new friends, new experiences, and new kinds of fun. Though you certainly want your child to enjoy himself, he'll also be practicing important skills that will prepare him for kindergarten and beyond.

"Your 3- or 4-year-old will learn the fundamental building blocks of reading, writing, math, and science, as well as how to interact with teachers and classmates," says Barbara Willer, Ph.D., deputy executive director of the National Association for the Education of Young Children (NAEYC), in Washington, D.C. "However," she says, "the overarching goal of any preschool should be to help a child feel good about himself as a learner and to feel comfortable in a school-like setting."

Chances are you chose your child's school carefully and can rest assured that he's in good hands. However, as you look around the classroom, here's what you should see.

By Irene Daria-Wiener

1 The Right Student-Teacher Ratio

There should be one teacher for every seven to ten students and no more than 20 children per classroom, according to the NAEYC. State laws vary, however, and some permit even higher ratios. Choosing a school that follows the NAEYC guidelines will ensure that your child receives enough attention and that her teachers will get to know her as an individual.

2 Daily Circle Time

During this group meeting, children practice important social skills, such as taking turns, listening to each other, and sitting still. They'll also hone their language skills by listening to stories and singing songs. In fact, singing is very important in pre-school. "As kids get older, they can link song words to written words, and that encourages literacy," Dr. Willer says. Songs also help children recognize rhythms and count beats, which enhances their understanding of math.

3 A Language-Rich Environment

Children should be read to every day. The classroom should have plenty of books available, as well as words posted all over the walls: signs labeling objects, weather charts, and posters describing the children's activities. Even preschoolers' artwork can be used to promote literacy; teachers should write the children's dictated descriptions ("Here is my brown dog.") on the bottom of their pictures.

4 An Art Center

This should be stocked with easels, chunky paintbrushes, and other materials, such as crayons and clay. While art—and getting messy—is certainly fun, it also allows children to express their thoughts in a way they might not yet be able to in words. In addition, art helps kids develop fine motor control and a basic understanding of science concepts, such as seeing what happens when colors are mixed and how different media create varying textures. It also gives children a sense of how things change as time passes—paint dries and clay hardens.

5 A Block Corner

Building with large blocks has been shown to help children develop crucial spatial and problem-solving skills. For example, your preschooler will learn that two of the small square blocks equal one of the longer rectangular blocks—a fundamental principle of geometry. Boys tend to gravitate to the block corner more than girls do. To help interest girls, some teachers have found it helpful to place dollhouse furniture in the block corner, because girls like to play house with the buildings that they create.

6 Rotating Chores

Besides developing a sense of responsibility and accomplishment, many chores your child will be asked to help out with in preschool foster math basics. For instance, handing out cups, paper plates, or napkins to each child at snack time introduces the key math concept of one-to-one correspondence.

7 Manipulatives

These items build the fine motor skills that are necessary for writing. In addition, puzzles strengthen spatial skills; sorting and counting buttons or beads help develop early math skills; and Peg-Boards and stringing beads require hand-eye coordination, which is also an important part of learning how to write.

8 A Water Table and a Sand Table

Not only are both of these materials fun, but children can explore so much with them—space, size, weight, force, pressure,

terrific teachers

Of course, no matter how good a school is, your child's experience there will depend on whether he has an engaging and energetic teacher. According to Barbara Willer, Ph.D., deputy executive director of the National Association for the Education of Young Children, teachers should:

• Have a bachelor's degree or a formal credential in early-childhood education. "The research is very clear that a teacher with a degree makes a big difference in the quality of the program," Dr. Willer says.
• Come over and kneel down to talk to the children at their eye level and not call to them from across the classroom.
• Greet your child by name and with a smile each morning.
• Structure the daily curriculum around the children's interests and questions and give kids freedom to choose at least some of the activities in which they participate.
• Keep parents informed of the day's activities and of any issues that their child may be having.

and volume, says Lilian Katz, Ph.D., codirector of the ERIC Clearinghouse on Elementary and Early Childhood Education at the University of Illinois at Urbana-Champaign. "Of course, 3- and 4-year-olds will

understand these concepts only on a very rudimentary level, but when they're older, they'll be able to build on their preschool experience," Dr. Katz says.

9 Physical Activity Every Day

Your child's class will probably go to the playground when the weather is nice. But the school should also have equipment (mats, climbing apparatus, tricycles, or other riding toys) and space for the kids to play actively indoors. "Three- and 4-year-olds are still developing their coordination, and need a chance to practice their basic physical skills," Dr. Katz says.

10 New Materials Introduced Frequently

Some classrooms have an official "discovery table" for displaying items such as autumn leaves or beach glass. "Bringing in new items for the children to explore leads to discussion as well as longer-term projects," Dr. Katz says. For example, an assortment of leaves may prompt a discussion of different types of trees and plants and then inspire the class to plant seeds to see how plants grow, as well as gain an appreciation for the living world around them. "Kids need the chance to wrap their mind around a topic in depth," says Dr. Katz, "and to know that there's something they can come back to and explore the next day."

Article 20

Study: Full-Day Kindergarten Boosts Academic Performance

By Debra Viadero
New Orleans

A study of 17,600 Philadelphia schoolchildren suggests that full-day kindergarten programs may have both academic and financial payoffs.

The study found that, by the time they reached the 3rd and 4th grades, former full-day kindergartners were more than twice as likely as children without any kindergarten experiences—and 26 percent more likely than graduates of half-day programs—to have made it there without having repeated a grade.

Moreover, the researchers calculated, the lower retention rates for graduates of Philadelphia's full-day classes shave close to 19 percent off of the cost of providing them, which in 1999 came to about $2 million for every 1,000 kindergartners.

"A lot of research suggests that how students are doing those first few years is very telling of what they'll do later on," said Andrea del Gaudio Weiss, the lead researcher on the study, which was conducted by the research office of the 208,000-student district. "If we can show we're saving money, that's all to the better."

She presented her report here this month during the annual meeting of the American Educational Research Association, a 23,000-member group based in Washington.

The study's cost-benefit information comes at a critical time for the debt-ridden Philadelphia school system. Taken over by the state of Pennsylvania in December, the district faces a projected budget shortfall of $105 million by 2005. (*See* "Takeover Team Picked in Phila.," *Education Week, April 3, 2002.*) The popularity of full-day kindergarten programs has been growing nationwide—with or without evidence of their economic and educational effectiveness.

Although only eight states and the District of Columbia now require schools to provide full-day kindergarten, nationwide surveys suggest that close to half of 5-year-olds attend them. And parents in some cities, such as Seattle, are even willing to ante up the money for their local public schools to provide them.

In her search for studies on the long-term benefits of the full-day programs, however, Ms. Weiss came across only one other study that tracked former full-day kindergartners through the 3rd grade, and few that focused on the programs' effects for poor, minority students in cities like Philadelphia.

Better Scores, Attendance

For her study, Ms. Weiss gathered data on groups of children who started school two years before the district made the move to all-day kindergarten in the fall of 1995 and two years after. Before the policy change, schools offered a mix of options for 5-year-olds, including full- and half-day programs; some schools provided no kindergarten at all.

Even though the results for the full-day programs were more dramatic, both kinds of kindergarten classes seemed to increase the likelihood that pupils would be promoted to the next grade on time. Compared with pupils who had never been to kindergarten, for example, the half-day graduates had a 70 percent better chance of reaching 3rd grade on schedule.

Among just those students who made it to 3rd grade on time, the full-day graduates were also likely to score higher on standardized reading and math tests, get better grades, and come to school more often, compared with youngsters who hadn't been full-day kindergartners. That was true, the researchers said, even after they adjusted the numbers to account for any differences between the groups in age, gender, and family income.

The former half-day students in that group were likely to score higher on standardized tests in science, however, according to the report.

The academic edge that the full-day kindergartners enjoyed in 3rd grade dissipated a little the following year. Compared with all the students who had made it to 4th grade on time, the former full-day pupils were more likely to have better outcomes that year in just two areas: attendance and science.

But Ms. Weiss, a senior research associate in the district's office of research and evaluation, said the apparent drop-off was not a cause for concern, since the former full-day kindergartners were not lagging behind any group of their peers.

What the study did not show was how teachers of the full-day kindergarten classes used the additional time. Other researchers have pointed out, for example, that some full-day classes offer a double dose of playtime, while others increase the time children spend learning academic material.

"More research is needed," the authors conclude, "to determine whether full-day students' higher long-term achievement is related to greater instruction or to qualitative differences in the curriculum, or to a combination of the two."

The Child-Centered Kindergarten**
A Position Paper

Joan Moyer

The child-centered kindergarten is not new; it has its roots in the 19th century. At that time, the kindergarten was envisioned as a "garden for children" (the literal meaning of the German word "kindergarten"), a place where children could be nurtured and allowed to grow at their own pace. While that image has changed somewhat over the years, the "roots" of sensitivity to children remain. Children's developmental needs have not changed, and so the importance of educating the whole child—recognizing his or her physical, social/emotional, and intellectual growth and development—remains. A change in the kindergarten curriculum, however, was brought about by: 1) societal pressure, 2) misunderstandings about how children learn, 3) aggressive marketing of commercial materials largely inappropriate for kindergarten-age children, 4) a shortage of teachers specifically prepared to work with young children, and 5) the reassignment of trained teachers in areas of declining enrollment.

Since its beginning more than 100 years ago as a professional organization, ACEI has emphasized the importance of the kindergarten years in a child's development. The official position of ACEI concerning kindergarten states: *The Association for Childhood Education International recognizes the importance of kindergarten education and supports high-quality kindergarten programs that provide developmentally, culturally, and linguistically appropriate experiences for children* (Moyer, Egertson, & Isenberg, 1987).

Purpose of Kindergarten

Many of the earliest kindergartens in the United States served the purpose of easing the acculturation of newly arrived immigrant children. Later, the purpose became easing the child's transition from home to the more formal aspects of the elementary school. For some children, the transition purpose continues to be important. The vast majority of children today, however, have experience at preschool and/or child care settings before they attend kindergarten. Nevertheless, many people in and out of education continue to perceive the kindergarten as the initial group experience for children (National Center on Education Statistics, 1984, p. 43).

Unfortunately, many parents and elementary educators do not view experiences in child care or other prekindergarten programs as "real learning." Spodek (1999) reported that many of the programs have shifted their emphasis from spurring kindergartners' development to highlighting specific learning goals. While programs vary in quality (as they do in elementary and secondary schools), children of any age are learning in every waking moment. Education provided for children at any level simply serves to organize their learning into more well-defined paths, governed by the philosophical orientation of program planners and the quality of the program. Although broad variations in children's abilities are evident, all children can learn. Noddings (1992) reminds teachers not to expect all children to bring similar strengths and abilities to the classroom. These variations in abilities, coupled with children's varying ethnic backgrounds and socioeconomic levels, add interest, joy, and challenge to the kindergarten program.

The work of such developmental theorists as Dewey, Piaget, and Vygotsky serves as a foundation for kindergarten practices. The theoretical background is expressed through the integrated curriculum, which also best accommodates the variations in children's understanding of the world around them. Early childhood professionals at all levels are concerned about the methods and content in the majority of kindergarten programs. Despite societal changes, kindergarten remains a place where children need a quality program in order to achieve their full potential.

Program Goals

The need for flexibility in planning programs that serve children and their families is well-documented. Parents need options so that the services they select for their children can meet family needs, as well as the needs of each child. Some parents, however, have misconceptions about the goals of the kindergarten program and, as a result, they focus on such cursory academic skills as counting and reciting the alphabet (Simmons & Brewer, 1985). Many people feel comfortable emphasizing such learning because it is easily measured. Elkind (1996) warns, however, that pushing children into academic areas too soon has a negative effect on learning, and refers to this practice as the "miseducation" of young children.

According to Katz (1985), early childhood educators need to consider children's dispositions, which she defines as "characteristic ways of responding to categories of experience across types of situations. Examples include curiosity, humor, creativity, affability, and quarrelsomeness.... Dispositions are not likely to be acquired through workbook exercises, lessons, or direct instruction" (p. 1).

Some parents, concerned over the demanding nature of the kindergarten curriculum, delay their children's kindergarten entrance. This practice has tended to institutionalize the more demanding and narrowly academic curriculum (Walsh, 1989). While 6-year-olds may be more capable of accomplishing the curricular goals, such programs try to "fit" children to the curriculum, rather than adjusting the curriculum to respond to the nature of the learner. Thus, younger children are more likely to fail.

The activity/experience-centered environment, which is essential if young children are to reach their maximum potential, provides for a far richer and more stimulating environment than one dominated by pencil-and-paper, teacher-directed tasks. A well-designed kindergarten program capitalizes on the interest some children may show in learning academic skills. At the same time, it does not have that same expectation for *all* children; nor does it use up precious time to inculcate skills and knowledge for which children have no immediate use or real understanding. Learning to learn should be the emphasis in the early years (Bloom, 1981).

Program Content

Kindergarten programs must be related to the needs and capacities of the children enrolled in them. In spite of major sociological and technological changes, developmental rates have not accelerated, nor are children more intelligent than they used to be (Elkind, 1986). Only the variety and intensity of early experiences have changed. Most kindergarten children are only 5 years old, and they have the basic needs of this age group, whether or not they have attended preschool or know how to read (Webster, 1984). Young children still need supportive environments, rich in direct experiences that are meaningful to them (Nebraska State Department of Education, 1984). A high-quality kindergarten program provides a strong foundation upon which children can build the skills, knowledge, and attitudes toward schooling necessary for lifelong learning.

Program Implementation

An effective, individually and culturally developmentally appropriate kindergarten program:

- Recognizes and accepts individual differences in children's growth patterns and rates by setting realistic curriculum goals that are appropriate to their developmental levels.

- Educates the whole child—with attention to his or her physical, social/emotional, and intellectual developmental needs and interests.

- Responds to the needs of children as developing, thinking individuals by focusing on the process of learning rather than on disparate skills, content, and products.

- Provides multiple opportunities for learning with concrete, manipulative materials that: 1) are relevant to children's experiential background; and 2) keep them actively engaged in learning and discovering through use of all the senses, leading to more input upon which thought is constructed.

- Provides a variety of activities and materials by incorporating: 1) learning activities that encourage active participation through "hands-on" activity, communication, and dialogue; 2) large blocks of time to pursue interests; 3) time to ask questions and receive answers that develop concepts and ideas for use at varying levels of difficulty and complexity; and 4) time to *reflect upon* and abstract information when encountering viewpoints that are different from one's peers.

- Views play as fundamental to children's learning, growth, and development, enabling them to develop and clarify concepts, roles, and ideas by testing and evaluating them through the use of open-ended materials and role-enactment. Play further enables children to develop fine and gross motor skills, to learn to share with others, to learn to see others' points of view, and to be in control of their thoughts and feelings.

- Provides many opportunities for the use of multicultural and nonsexist experiences, materials, and equipment that enhance children's acceptance of self and others; these experiences
enable children to accept differences and similarities among people, including those who are challenged in some way.

- Embraces the teaching of all content areas, especially when they are presented as integrated experiences that develop and extend concepts, strengthen skills, and provide a solid foundation for learning in language, literacy, math, science, social studies, health, art, and music and movement.

- Allows children to make choices and decisions within the limits of the materials provided, resulting in increased independence, attention, joy in learning, and the feelings of success necessary for growth and development.

- Utilizes appropriate assessment procedures, such as observation techniques and portfolios, to measure learning for all kindergarten children.

Play Is Essential

The pressure for academic achievement, coupled with the mistaken idea that today's children have outgrown the need to play, have led to increased emphasis on "basic skills" in kindergarten. The principal source of development in the early years is play (Vygotsky, 1976); in fact, Catron and Allen (1999) state that the optimal development of young children is made possible through play. When viewed as a learning process, play becomes a vehicle for intellectual growth, and it continues to be the most vital avenue of learning for kindergartners. In contrast, research indicates that academic gains from non-play approaches are not lasting (Schweinhart & Weikert, 1996). Play involves not only use of materials and equipment, but also words and ideas that promote literacy and develop thinking skills, Consequently, in addition to the three R's, play also promotes problem-solving, critical thinking, concept formation, and creativity skills. Social and emotional development also are enhanced through play. Play fosters holistic learning (Isenberg & Jalongo, 1997). "Children integrate everything they know in all domains when they play" (Almy, 2000, p. 10). The classic words of Lawrence Frank (1964) remain as meaningful as ever today:

> A conception of play that recognizes the significance of autonomous, self-directed learning and active exploration and manipulation of the actual world gives a promising approach to the wholesome development of children.... It is a way to translate into the education of children our long-cherished, enduring goal values, a belief in the worth of the individual personalities, and a genuine respect for the dignity and integrity of the child. (p. 73)

Suransky (1983) warns that "eroding the play life of early childhood has severe implications for the children we attempt to 'school' in later years" (p. 29). Froebel believed that in free play children reveal their future minds (cited in Bruce, 1993). It is important to emphasize that critics of the current practice of emphasizing academic work over free play are not advocating an environment that makes fewer demands on children. Almy, Monighan, Scales, and Van Hoorn (1984) state, "Teachers who, drawing on recent research and their own classroom research, justify an important place for play in the early childhood curriculum will not lose sight of their responsibility as instructors.... Teachers have responsibility... for providing the play opportunities in which children can consolidate and make personally meaningful the experiences they have had" (p. 22).

Kindergarten teachers agree with researchers and experts who contend that child-centered activities that provide cognitive challenges, and also facilitate the development of autonomy and social skills, are essential for young children (Spidell Rusher, McGrevin, & Lambiotte, 1992). Wardle (1999, p. 7) writes "... as we [have] seen many of our public funded early childhood programs become downward extensions of public schools, we need to advocate for the children's right to play."

Appropriate Physical Environment

Kindergarten children are active, curious learners who need adequate space, a variety of materials, and large blocks of time in which to try out their ideas. Attention to the arrangement of physical facilities is an integral part of their educational experience. How teachers arrange kindergarten classrooms affects children's interests, level of interaction and involvement, initiative development, skill development, and overall attitude toward schooling and learning. A classroom arrangement that supports learning gives attention to the organization and use of space, the arrangement of materials, and the role of both adults and children in the learning environment.

How space is organized and used influences how comfortable children feel and how they work, contributing to a challenging and satisfactory learning environment. Because children's activity patterns change as they gain new skills and mature, and because spatial organization influences other behaviors, the physical facilities must be flexible enough to change to accommodate the children.

Similarly, the arrangement of learning materials determines their level and use. How well materials are arranged also affects the ideas and connections children can make with the materials.

Although children and teachers occupy the same physical space, their perceptions and use of that space are not the same. Kindergarten teachers must arrange the space from the *kindergartner's* point of view and perspective. In order to build a sense of community, kindergarten classrooms should reflect the children, individually and as a group, as well as the teacher.

The following environmental principles address spatial organization, use of materials, and the role of adults in the kindergarten:

- Rooms should be arranged to accommodate individual, small group, and large group activities.
- Interest areas should be clearly defined; differ in size, shape, and location; and attend to traffic patterns while permitting continuity of activity and reducing distractibility. All spaces should be clearly visible to the teacher.
- Rooms should be arranged to facilitate the activity and movements of children at work by attending to available paths for their use and minimizing the amount of interference.
- Learning materials should be arranged and displayed so that they are inviting to children and suggest multiple possibilities for use; they should be clearly visible and accessible, enabling children to return and replace materials as easily as they can get them. Clear, well-organized materials facilitate children's ability to use and explore them.
- Materials should be changed and combined to increase levels of complexity, thus helping children become more self-directed and increasing their level of involvement.
- Children perceive space they can see, reach, and touch. Teachers can support, stimulate, and maintain children's involvement in learning by providing a variety of raw materials for exploration, tools for manipulation, containers for storage and displays, adequate work spaces, inviting displays at eye level, and appropriate sources of information within the children's reach.

Textbooks and Materials

Considerable discussion in the educational and popular media has focused on the quality of textbooks used in schools. The concerns of early childhood educators, however, appear to have been overlooked in this discussion. Many kindergarten teachers are expected to use commercial texts that present information and activities that are developmentally inappropriate. These materials also may be culturally inappropriate. Many "how to" books for teachers are simply collections of reproducible worksheets that result in a pencil/paper curriculum. Such practices do not reflect what we know about how young children learn. Today's kindergarten programs must reflect developmentally appropriate practices that promote active learning, and should match goals and content to the child's level of understanding (Isenberg & Jalongo, 2000).

The introduction of technology into kindergarten classrooms, while promising (and becoming more common), still requires the teacher to determine appropriate uses of that technology. "Used appropriately, technology can enhance children's cognitive and social abilities" (National Association for the Education for Young Children, 1996, p. 12). Elkind (1996) cautions: "The danger is that the young child's proficiency with the computer may tempt us to ignore what we know about cognitive development.... If we rate a child's intellectual competence by his or her performance on a computer, then we will have lost what we have been working so hard to attain—a broad appreciation of developmentally appropriate practice" (p. 23).

Teachers for Kindergartens

Aside from parents, teachers frequently are the most significant adults in young children's lives. Therefore, quality kindergarten programs must be staffed by caring teachers who have faith in every child's potential to achieve and succeed.

Assigning primary and upper elementary teachers to the kindergarten is a questionable practice—indeed, it is cause for great concern. Many of these teachers have limited understanding of appropriate programs for 5-year-olds, and so they operate under the false assumption that young children learn in the same way that older children do (Association for Childhood Education International et al., 1986). Consequently, they use a "watered-down" primary curriculum, replete with workbooks, textbooks, and one-dimensional tasks that can be readily evaluated.

ACEI advocates developmentally appropriate kindergartens staffed with early childhood teachers who:

- Are knowledgeable in child development, committed to children, and able to plan a curriculum that will promote the full development of each child—enabling teachers to have a profound influence on children's lives.
- Listen thoughtfully to children, extend children's language about ideas and feelings, ask questions that encourage insights and highlight contradictions, and promote and value creative, divergent responses from all children.
- Regularly assess children's interests, needs, and skill levels—enabling them to plan continuous, flexible, and realistic activities for each child.
- Design learning environments that provide for successful daily experiences by matching activities to each child's

developmental level, and by using positive interactions, encouragement, and praise for children's efforts.

- Promote a positive self-image by helping children succeed in a variety of activities and experiences, and by providing techniques to help children establish their own limits. Children's self-esteem affects what they do, say, and think.
- Utilize a variety of instructional approaches, including individual, small group, large group, role-enactment activities, and activity centers—all suited to kindergartners' wide range of ability, interests, and needs.

- Provide varied experiences about which kindergarten children can communicate by: 1) encouraging them to use their own experiences as a basis for developing language activities through individual and small group interactions with peers and adults; 2) arranging for periodic change of materials, equipment, and activities in the environment; and 3) providing experiences for children to use their senses as they interact with people and materials.

Such teachers provide effective interaction with children, as well as encouragement, support, and guidance.

Program Support

Parental involvement is essential if they are to understand the purpose of kindergarten education, assist in achieving kindergarten goals and reinforce those lessons in the home setting. Parents who are unable to participate directly in the classroom can contribute in myriad other ways (Barbour & Barbour, 2000; Isenberg & Jalongo, 1997). Parents can show their support for their children's learning by volunteering in the classroom, exchanging information with teachers, acting as chaperones on field trips, helping with homework, reading to children, discussing the school day with the kindergarten child, informing teachers about home situations that may affect the child's behavior at school, and paying attention to materials sent home. Parents must advocate for child-centered kindergarten programs for their children, in part by informing administrators and school boards of their eagerness to support these programs. Teachers, administrators, and parents must work together as advocates for child-centered kindergarten programs.

Central administrators, supervisors, and building principals who oversee the kindergarten program also must be educated about the developmental needs of kindergarten children and the unique needs of the kindergarten program. As Spidell Rusher, McGrevin, and Lambiotte (1992) state, "Communication among teachers, principals, policymakers, experts in childhood education, and parents is vital" (p. 294). With this knowledge, they can provide the administrative support essential to the success of the kindergarten program, value its uniqueness, and interpret it to the community professionally and with integrity. Elkind (1986) cautions that "the risks of miseducating children are both short- and long-term. In each case, the potential psychological risks of early intervention far outweigh any potential educational gain" (p. 634).

ACEI advocates child-centered kindergarten programs that encourage active experiential learning, are developmentally appropriate, increase independence, and promote joy in learning—staffed by teachers who are professionally prepared to work with young children.

As Lewis (2000) writes, "Perhaps what is needed are super programs that provide balance, giving every child a chance to succeed and to play" (p. 564).

**An earlier version of this paper was published in *Childhood Education* (April 1987), 63(4), pp. 235–242.

References and Other Readings

Almy, M. (2000). What wisdom should we take with us as we enter the new century? *Young Children, 55*(1), 6–10.

Almy, M., Monighan, P., Scales, B., & Van Hoorn, J. (1984). Recent research on play: The teacher's perspective. In L. Katz (Ed.), *Current topics in early childhood education, V* (pp. 1–22). Norwood, NJ: Ablex.

Association for Childhood Education International et al. (1986). Literacy development and pre-first grade: A joint statement of concerns about present practices in pre-first reading instruction and recommendations for improvement. *Childhood Education, 63*, 110–111.

Ballenger, M. (1983). Reading in the kindergarten: Comment. *Childhood Education, 59*, 186–187.

Barbour, C., & Barbour, N. H. (2000). *Families, schools and communities: Building partnerships for educating children*. Upper Saddle River, NJ: Prentice-Hall.

Bloom, B. (1981). *All our children learning*. New York: McGraw-Hill.

Border, G., & Berkley, M. (1992). Educational play: Meeting everyone's needs in mainstreamed classrooms. *Childhood Education, 69*, 38–42.

Bredekamp, S., & Copple, C. (Eds.). (1997). *Developmentally appropriate practice in early childhood programs* (Rev. ed.). Washington, DC: National Association for the Education of Young Children.

Bruce, T. (1993). The role of play in children's lives. *Childhood Education, 69*, 237–238.

Catron, C., & Allen, J. (1999). *Early childhood curriculum*. Upper Saddle River, NJ: Merrill/Prentice-Hall.

Christie, J., & Enz, B. (1993). Providing resources for play. *Childhood Education, 69*, 291–292.

Elkind, D. (1986). *Miseducation: Preschoolers at risk*. New York: Knopf.

Elkind, D. (1996). Young children and technology: A cautionary note. *Young Children, 51*, 22–23.

Frank, L. K. (1964). The role of play in child development. *Childhood Education, 41*, 70–73.

Frost, J., Wortham, S., & Reifel, S. (2000). *Play and child development*. Upper Saddle River, NJ: Merrill/Prentice-Hall.

Isenberg, J., & Jalongo, M. (Eds.). (1997). *Major trends and issues in early childhood education: Challenges, controversies, and insights*. New York: Teachers College Press.

Isenberg, J., & Jalongo, M. (2000). *Creative expression and play in early childhood* (3rd ed.). Upper Saddle River, NJ: Merrill/Prentice-Hall.

Isenberg, J., & Quisenberry, N. L. (1988). Play: A necessity for all children. *Childhood Education, 64*, 138–145.

Katz, L. (1985). Dispositions in early childhood education. *ERIC/EECE Bulletin, 18*(2), 1–3.

Lewis, A. (2000). 'Playing' with equity and early education. *Phi Delta Kappan, 81*(8), 563–564.

Moyer, J., Egertson, H., & Isenberg, J. (1987). The child-centered kindergarten. Position paper of the Association for Childhood Education International. *Childhood Education, 63*, 235–242.

National Association for the Education of Young Children. (1996). Position statement: Technology and young children—ages three through eight. *Young Children, 51*(6), 11–16.

National Center on Education Statistics. (1984). *Digest of education statistics, 1983–84*. Washington, DC: U.S. Government Printing Office.

Nebraska Center on Education Statistics. (1984). *Position statement on kindergarten*, 1–8. Lincoln, NE: Author.

Noddings, N. (1992). *The challenge to care in schools: An alternative approach to education*. New York: Teachers College Press.

Okagaki, L., & Sternberg, R. (1994). Perspectives on kindergarten. *Childhood Education, 71*, 14–19.

Schweinhart, R., & Weikert, D. (1996). *Lasting differences: The High/Scope preschool curriculum comparison study through age 23. Monographs of the High/Scope Educational Research Foundation, No. 12*. Ypsilanti, MI: High/Scope Press.

Simmons, B., & Brewer, J. (1985). When parents of kindergartners ask "why?" *Childhood Education, 61*, 177–184.

Spidell Rusher, A., McGrevin, C., & Lambiotte, J. (1992). Belief systems of early childhood teachers and their principals regarding early childhood education. *Early Childhood Research Journal, 7*, 277–296.

Spodek, B. (1999). The kindergarten. In K. Pachiorek & J. Munro (Eds.), *Sources: Notable selections in early childhood education* (2nd ed.) (pp. 101–111). Guilford, CT: McGraw-Hill.

Stone, S. (1995–96). Integrating play into the curriculum. *Childhood Education, 72*, 104–107.

Suransky, V. (1983). The preschooling of childhood. *Educational Leadership, 40*(6), 27–29.

Swick, K. (1993). *Strengthening parents and families during the early childhood years*. Champaign, IL: Stipes Publishing Company.

Vygotsky, L. (1976). Play and its role in the mental development of the child. In J. Bruner (Ed.), *Play: Its role in development and evolution*. New York: Basic Books.

Walsh, D. (1989). Changes in kindergarten: Why here? Why now? *Early Childhood Research Quarterly, 4*, 377–391.

Wardle, F. (1999). Play as curriculum. *Early Childhood News*, March/April, pp. 6–9.

Wassermann, S. (1992). Serious play in the classroom: How messing around can win you the Nobel Prize. *Childhood Education, 68*, 133–139.

Webster, N. (1984). The 5's and 6's go to school: Revisited. *Childhood Education, 60*, 325–329.

Wing, L. (1995). Play is not the work of the child: Young children's perceptions of work and play. *Early Childhood Research Quarterly, 10*(2), 223–248.

Joan Moyer is Professor, College of Education, Arizona State University, Tempe.

Measuring Results

There's a growing demand to assess the results of early-childhood programs, but what's appropriate?

By David J. Hoff

Somewhere, a 4th grader is gripping a No. 2 pencil in his sweaty palms, about to take a test that might determine his school's accreditation or future funding. At the very least, the results from the child's school will be posted on the Internet or printed in the newspaper.

Somewhere else, a high school senior may be reviewing the algebra she's learned, trying once again to pass an exam that will make or break her attempt to earn a high school diploma.

Meanwhile, a group of 4-year-olds is building a tower with blocks, playing a game, or telling a story to a teacher. Like the standardized or standards-based tests given to their older peers, the young children's play may be used to evaluate the program that they attend, inform parents whether their children are ready to move on to kindergarten, or help the teacher understand what challenges and experiences the pupils need to make the developmental leaps common in their age group.

But the experience will have none of the high pressure of entering a new situation and trying to master a set of skills that dominates testing in the K–12 arena.

The contrast demonstrates that assessment and accountability are completely different in preschools, Head Start, and other early-childhood programs that a majority of children experience before they enter the K–12 system.

Assessments in early-childhood programs must be different from the kinds of tests youngsters take after they're in school, experts say, because young children are especially subject to wide variations in their development. Their skills grow in fits and starts, so an assessment of their academic skills one month could be out of date the next.

Moreover, along with their cognitive skills, preschoolers are also working to develop their motor and social skills, which are best judged by observation rather than a formal assessment.

As state and local policymakers start to demand data that show the impact of their spending on early-childhood programs, assessment experts find themselves searching for ways to obtain that information accurately, fairly, and in a way that's best for children.

"It's very complex," says James H. Squires, a consultant in early-childhood education for the Vermont education department. "What we're grappling with is: How do you do it at all? How can you get meaningful, accurate results without doing damage?"

Some state officials are requiring local programs to evaluate themselves using whatever method they choose. Others specify the kinds of assessment tools to be administered. Still others are collecting statewide data by giving a specific assessment or a combination of them to a sample of children in the state's early-childhood programs.

So far, though, none has come up with a uniform or even widely accepted method for assessing young children.

> ## "There hasn't been something that people could call a standardized way to assess children this age for accountability."
>
> CATHERINE SCOTT-LITTLE
> Senior Program Specialist, Serve

"There hasn't been something that people could call a standardized way to assess children this age for accountability purposes," says Catherine Scott-Little, a senior program specialist for Serve, the Greensboro, N.C., federally financed research laboratory serving the Southeastern states.

The Foundation

As state leaders begin wading into testing young children, most are building their systems around the recommendations of a 1998 report issued by the National Education Goals Panel, a federally subsidized committee of state and federal policymakers.

The panel convened a group of early-childhood experts to define how states and districts should monitor progress to ensure that children enter school ready to learn—the first of the education goals set for the nation that were to be achieved by 2000. At the end of 1999, the goals panel reported that the goal had not been reached.

The 40-page booklet released by the panel in 1998 suggested that early-childhood programs evaluate individual children's skills, starting at age 3, and aggregate them as part of a formal appraisal of the programs. Not until children reach the 3rd grade, the report concluded, should high-stakes assessments be used to hold schools, students, and teachers accountable.

"Before age 8, standardized achievement measures are not sufficiently accurate to be used for high-stakes decisions about individual children and schools," the booklet said.

But early-childhood programs must conduct assessments for other purposes. Under federal special education law, districts and federal programs have been required to screen children who are suspected of having a disability. Head Start programs, for example, must assess children's physical and learning abilities within 45 days of their enrollment.

Such screening "helps to identify children who may be at risk for school failure," says Samuel J. Meisels, the president of the Erikson Institute for Advanced Study of Child Development, a Chicago graduate school. "It can be done simply, inexpensively, and fairly accurately."

According to the Erikson Institute, 15 states and the District of Columbia require diagnostic or developmental screening for children in prekindergarten.

Assessing youngsters to determine the success of the programs in which they're enrolled, however, is new territory for most states, Scott-Little of Serve says.

Of the statewide pre-K programs, "very few have begun to invest in assessment," says Meisels, one of the creators of the Work Sampling System, an assessment instrument that many states use in early-childhood programs and kindergartens.

Getting Started

Even those states in the forefront are just now getting started and searching for the best ways to evaluate children's progress and programs' success.

North Carolina, for example, collected data from 1,034 kindergartners in fall 2000. The study tried to determine, for the first time, how well a variety of early-childhood programs prepared children to enter school.

Researchers gave a representative sample of 10 percent of the state's new kindergartners assessments that gauged an assortment of skills, such as vocabulary, literacy, and social development. The research team selected portions of several different assessment batteries, including the Woodcock Johnson Test of Achievement-Revised Form A and the Social Skills Rating System, because the team couldn't find one product that fit all its needs, according to Kelly Maxwell, who headed the project.

"Some people thought there would be one magic test out there," says Maxwell, a research investigator at the Frank Porter Graham Child Development Center at the University of North Carolina at Chapel Hill. "It didn't work that way."

The study also surveyed parents, teachers, and principals about the school readiness of kindergartners.

In the end, the published report included only general findings and none of the specific score data that are common in accountability systems for the upper grades. For example, the study found that North Carolina's kindergartners "generally knew the names of basic colors," and that they had "demonstrated a wide range of social skills" that "were about as well-developed" as those of kindergartners nationally. Their language and math skills fell below the national averages.

Despite the generalities of the conclusions, the report has made a valuable contribution in the debate over how to improve early-childhood programs in North Carolina. "This is what we know about our children and our schools," Maxwell says. "It sets the stage for a discussion."

Maryland collected information on 1,300 kindergartners using portions of the Work Sampling System. In that system, teachers continually observe their students and note their progress in such areas as language, mathematical thinking, scientific thinking, physical development, and social and personal skills.

Even though scores from the Work Sampling System are based on teacher observations, the results are as reliable as older students' standardized-test scores, according to studies conducted by Meisels and his colleagues at the University of Michigan in Ann Arbor, where until recently he was a professor of education.

In a report published last year, Maryland concluded that about 40 percent of the state's kindergartners entered school "fully ready to do kindergarten work." Half needed "targeted support" so they could succeed in their first year of school, and 10 percent required "considerable support" from their kindergarten teachers.

In particular, the children needed the most help in mathematical and scientific thinking, language development, and social studies.

"I don't think we were surprised by anything," says Trudy V. Collier, the chief of language development and early learning for the Maryland education department. "There's a real need for children to be read to, talked to, and encouraged to participate in conversations."

Last fall, every kindergarten teacher evaluated every student using the same set of Work Sampling System indicators. The state hopes to use the results to continue tracking school readiness.

While the overall results are general, individual student outcomes help teachers design curricula to meet their classes' needs, Collier says. "They begin to establish very early what a child's specific needs and gifts may be," she says.

Other states are taking similar approaches, according to Scott-Little. She led a brainstorming session last fall for officials in the states that are furthest along in assessing early-childhood programs.

Missouri's School Entry Profile collects data from new kindergartners, and the state uses the results to shape policies for early-childhood programs. In Ohio, teachers are collecting data on 4-year-olds' skills so the state can evaluate the early-childhood programs. The process may also help teachers prepare curricula for their classes, Scott-Little says.

Do-It-Yourself Approaches

While some states are coming up with statewide ways of measuring young children's abilities, and the success of programs serving them, others are letting individual programs monitor themselves.

Michigan, for example, has a prekindergarten program serving more than 25,000 youngsters in 1,000 classrooms, but it has only three part-time consultants to evaluate them, according to Lindy Buch, the state's supervisor of curricular, early-childhood, and parenting programs.

The state has chosen to train local program directors to evaluate their own programs, using a tool created by the High/Scope Educational Research Foundation, a leading research and development group on early-childhood programs. In addition, the Ypsilanti, Mich.-based High/Scope is conducting in-depth reviews of randomly chosen programs to give a statewide snapshot of the program's success.

Evaluators score the program on a variety of measures, including the quality and size of the facility, the extent to which the curriculum is tailored for each child, and the amount of time teachers spend evaluating pupils' progress. In Georgia, local officials can choose from one of several approved assessment programs, including the High/Scope evaluation tool.

Meanwhile, school districts in Vermont are conducting school-readiness screenings of prekindergartners, says Squires, the state's early-childhood consultant. But the state is urging districts to conduct the evaluations in a nonstandardized way. Many local programs are inviting children in for a "play based" assessment. They enter a classroom and demonstrate their physical, language, motor, and cognitive skills while they play with toys, create art, and build structures.

"We did not want to create an individual assessment or a group assessment for every child where they were being asked to sit down and perform specific tasks," Squires says.

The federal Head Start program is taking a similar approach to complying with the 1998 law that requires every Head Start center to conduct evaluations based on performance indicators.

While many of the performance indicators are selected by federal administrators, local centers are required to do their own evaluations of children in the areas of language and literacy, mathematics, science, creative arts, social ability, interest in learning, and physical and motor skills.

The instruments they use must be validated for the way they're being applied. For example, a center may not rely on a test intended to individualize curriculum as part of its program evaluation.

Programs were collecting such information in various forms already, whether as part of the disabilities-screening requirement or their own curriculum planning. What's new to Head Start programs is tabulating the data to figure out the overall outcomes of participating children.

"This is—almost in every case—a new idea," says Thomas Schultz, the director of the program-support division of the federal Head Start bureau.

For all the activity aimed at assessing children to ensure that they received the services they needed or to communicate their abilities to parents, he says, "it was rare that programs would use that information at a management level. What we're talking about now is a new strategy."

Kindergarten: Stakes Rising?

While the evaluations conducted throughout early-childhood programs don't carry high stakes for the children involved, the nature of assessment changes once children enter kindergarten because of the nationwide goal to have every child reading at grade level by grade 3.

Still, such assessments are administered to drive instruction rather than reward or penalize the child. Michigan has devised a literacy assessment in which teachers evaluate a child's reading skills starting in kindergarten, with monitoring continuing through 3rd grade.

The one-on-one testing is designed to help teachers formally measure a child's skills and then determine what help he or she needs to take the next steps toward independent reading.

The state plans to expand the program so children in the pre-K program take it, too, says Buch, the Michigan education official.

The New York City public schools started a similar program—called the Early Childhood Literacy Assessment System, or ECLAS—in 1999.

The battery of tests assesses children on a wide range of literacy skills from kindergarten through 2nd grade.

The Early Childhood Literacy Assessment System "gives a complete knowledge of where the kids are and what they need."

CHARLIE SOULE, Associate Education Officer,
New York City Board of Education

"It gives a complete knowledge of where the kids are and what they need for literacy," says Charlie Soule, the city school official who runs the testing program.

Such programs can be great tools for helping children reach the goal of becoming independent readers, according to one reading expert.

In an evaluation of a California reading program, children in schools that conducted regular classroom assessments showed better reading results than those in other schools in the state, says Marilyn J. Adams, a Harvard University research associate specializing in reading.

"The best [an assessment] can do for you is say, 'You need to sit with this child and figure out if he's having trouble with this dimension,'" Adams says. Once teachers do that, they respond with individualized instruction.

"The pressure for results... may force early-childhood programs and administrators to adopt relatively simplistic methods."

SAMUEL J. MEISELS, President, Erikson Institute

But such programs also can eventually become a back door into high-stakes testing, some experts warn. If a child isn't reading well in the 2nd grade, and the teachers know that the pupil will face a state reading test in the 3rd grade, they may be tempted to hold the boy or girl back a grade.

"The literacy assessments," Meisels of the Erikson Institute says, "are only a problem if they are expected to accomplish more than they are intended to do—which, at least in the case of the Michigan profile, is to enhance teaching and learning."

But with the weight of accountability systems looming and a new emphasis on academic skills, early-childhood educators may be inclined to rely on assessments in ways that are unfair to young children, he adds.

"The pressure for results—both in skills and in accountability—may force early-childhood programs and administrators to adopt relatively simplistic methods of teaching and assessing that are not successful for young children," Meisels says.

From *Education Week*, January 10, 2002, pp. 48-52. © 2002 by Education Week. Reprinted by permission.

DIFFERENT APPROACHES TO TEACHING:

Comparing

Three* Preschool Program Models

AMY SUSSNA KLEIN, ED.D.

As early childhood educators, we all have our own philosophies and approaches to education. Our approach to teaching is created from a multitude of resources and probably includes knowledge from early childhood theorists, an understanding of child development, and our experiences with children in different learning environments. Whether you are a new teacher about to embark on an early childhood career or a well-seasoned professional, it is helpful to know what other educators are doing in different types of programs. New approaches to teaching and learning can be adapted within our own environment and information about how your philosophy of education compares or differs from others can be shared with parents considering your program for their children.

- **What is the program's history?**
- **What are its main components?**
- **What is unique about the program?**
- **How can one tell if a school is truly following the model?**

THE MONTESSORI METHOD

Maria Montessori, Italy's first woman physician, opened her first school in 1907. The first Montessori school in the United States opened in 1911, and by 1916 the Montessori method was found in locations across the world.

The use of *natural observation* in a *prepared environment* by an objective teacher led Montessori to consider her method scientific. After Montessori completed her direct study of children, she specified every particular detail of how the school should be operated to ensure accurate replication. The teacher's role in a Montessori school is to observe in order to connect the child with suitable materials (Goffin, 2001).

Two main branches of Montessori method have developed: the Association Montessori Internationale (AMI) and the American Montessori Society (AMS). The Association Montessori Internationale was founded in 1929 by Montessori, herself, to maintain the integrity of her life's work and to ensure that it would be perpetuated after her death. Nancy Rambush attempted to Americanize the Montessori method and founded the American Montessori Society (AMS) in 1960. What is most important to note about the two branches is that both are currently in preschools throughout the United States, and both have excellent programs with credentials for teachers. Also, both AMI and AMS support the use of Montessori materials. These learning materials are "self correcting;" they can only be used by a child in one way, thus avoiding the possibility of the child learning the wrong way to use them.

What Are Montessori's Main Components?
Social

- The link between family and school is important.

- Most Montessori classrooms have multiple age groups, which is intended to give children more opportunity to learn from each other.
- Montessori advocated that children learn best by doing.
- In order to help children focus, the teacher silently demonstrates the use of learning materials to them. Children may then choose to practice on any material they have had a "lesson" about.
- Once children are given the lesson with the material, they may work on it independently, often on a mat that designates their space.

Curriculum

- There is a belief in sensory learning; children learn more by touching, seeing, smelling, tasting, and exploring than by just listening.
- The child's work as a purposeful, ordered activity toward a determined end is highly valued. This applies both to exercises for practical life and language.
- The main materials in the classroom are "didactic." These are materials that involve sensory experiences and are self-correcting. Montessori materials are designed to be aesthetically pleasing, yet sturdy and were developed by Maria Montessori to help children develop organization.

- Evans (1971) summarized the pre-school curriculum in a Montessori program as consisting "… of three broad phases: exercises for practical life, sensory education, and language activities (reading and writing)." (p. 59)

Environmental Set-Up

- Montessori believed that the environment should be prepared by matching the child to the corresponding didactic material.
- The environment should be comfortable for children (e.g., child-sized chairs that are lightweight).
- The environment should be homelike, so child can learn practical life issues. For example, there should be a place for children to practice proper self-help skills, such as handwashing.
- Since Montessori believed beauty helped with concentration, the setting is aesthetically pleasing.
- In the setting, each child is provided a place to keep her own belongings.

What Is Unique About the Program?

The environment is prepared with self-correcting materials for work, not play. The Montessori method seeks to support the child in organization, thus pretend play and opportunities to learn creatively from errors are less likely to be seen in a Montessori classroom. Chattin-McNichols (1992) clarifies how Piaget, often called the "father of constructivism," and Montessori both agreed that children learn from errors, yet the set-up in which errors may occur is controlled differently in the Montessori classroom. The didactic, self-correcting materials assist in controlling error versus an adult correcting the child.

How Can One Tell If a School Is Truly Following the Montessori Method?

The first step to ensure whether a school truly practices the Montessori method is making sure that its teachers are AMI or AMS credentialed. Not every Montessori school has teachers with Montessori training.

Although Montessori schools are sometimes thought of as being elitist institutions for wealthy families, this is not true. There are many charter and public Montessori schools. Nor, despite the fact that Montessori began her work with poor special needs children in Rome, are Montessori schools reserved for low-income children with disabilities.

THE HIGH/SCOPE® APPROACH

High/Scope® was founded in 1970 and emerged from the work Dave Weikart and Connie Kamii did on the Perry Preschool Project. This project, initiated in 1962, involved teachers working with children (three and four years old) a few hours a day at a school, attending staff meetings, and making weekly home visits. The program was developed with the idea that early education could prevent school failure in high school students from some of the poorest areas in Ypsilanti, MI (Kostelnik, 1999). The Perry Preschool Program is one of the few longitudinal studies in the early childhood field and had significant findings. For instance, compared with a matched control group, the children that were part of the Perry Preschool Program had significantly more high school graduates and fewer arrests.

The High/Scope Foundation is an independent, nonprofit research, development, training, and public advocacy organization. The Foundation's principal goals are to promote the learning and development of children worldwide from infancy through adolescence and to support and train educators and parents as they help children learn.

The High/Scope Approach has roots in constructivist theory. Constructivists believe that we learn by mentally and physically interacting with the environment and with others. Although errors may be made during these interactions, they are considered just another part of the learning process.

Although both Constructivism and the Montessori Method involve learning by doing, there are significant differences. In Montessori, for instance, the didactic, self-correcting materials are specifically designed to help prevent errors. Children learn by repetition, instead of by trial and error. The role of pretend play is also different in the two methods. In High/Scope, children's creative exploration is encouraged, and this sometimes leads to pretend play, while in Montessori, "practical life work" that relates to the real world is stressed.

Although Constructivism is a theory of *learning*, as opposed to a theory of *teaching*, High/Scope has exemplified an approach of teaching that supports Constructivist beliefs. Thus, children learn through active involvement with people, materials, events, and ideas.

What Are High/Scope's Main Components?
Social

- One of the fundamental points in the High/Scope approach is that children are encouraged to be active in their learning through supportive adult interactions.
- The High/Scope approach includes times for various grouping experiences in the classroom. There are specific periods in each day for small group times, large group times, and for children to play independently in learning centers through out the classroom.
- Children are encouraged to share their thinking with teachers and peers.
- Social interactions in the classroom community are encouraged. Teachers facilitate work on problem resolution with children as conflicts arise.
- When a child talks, the teachers listen and ask open-ended questions; they seek to ask questions that encourage children to express their thoughts and be creative rather than a "closed" question that would elicit more of a yes/no or simplistic answer.
- Each day the High/Scope teacher observes and records what the children are doing. During the year, teachers complete a High/Scope Child Observation Record from the daily observations they have collected.

Curriculum

- "Key experiences" were designed specifically for this approach. The following is a brief summary of key experiences taken from Kostelnik, Soderman, & Whiren (1999, p. 32). The key experiences for preschool children are:

  -Creative representation
  -Classification
  -Language and literacy
  -Seriation
  -Initiative and social relation
  -Number
  -Movement
  -Space
  -Music
  -Time

- "Plan-do-review" is another major component of the High/Scope framework. Children are encouraged to: 1) **plan** the area, materials, and methods they are going to work with; 2) **do**, actually carry out their plan; and 3) **re-**

view, articulate with the classroom community what they actually did during work time. The review time helps children bring closure to their work and link their actual work to their plan.

- Cleanup time is a natural part of plan-do-review. Children are given a sense of control by cleaning up. Representative labels help children return materials to appropriate places (Roopnarine & Johnson, 1993).
- The High/Scope classroom has a consistent routine. The purpose of the resulting predictability is to help children understand what will happen next and encourage them to have more control in their classroom.

Environmental Set-Up

- The High/Scope® classroom is a materials-rich learning environment. Usually, the locations for classroom materials are labeled to help children learn organizational skills.
- Materials are set-up so that they are easily accessible at a child's level. This helps facilitate children's active exploration.
- Teachers set up the classroom areas purposefully for children to explore and build social relationships, often with well-defined areas for different activities.

How Can One Tell If a School Is Truly Following the High/Scope Approach?

Teachers new to the High/Scope curriculum sometimes find work confusing be-cause they are not sure of their roles (Roopnarine & Johnson, 1993). Sometimes, a list of the key experiences is displayed in the classroom, but then most of the day is spent in teacher-directed activities. This is not what was meant by key experiences! Key experiences in which the children have plenty of time for active exploration in the classroom, is a major component of the High/Scope approach. Furthermore, the teacher is not just passively facilitating while the children play. Rather, teachers in High/Scope classrooms are interactive (though not interruptive of peers playing). Often the role of a High/Scope teacher is to be actively observing and setting up problem solving situations for children.

Plan-do-review was developed to help play become meaningful. There are many ways of implementing the review piece of plan-do-review. One example of successful review is when the children draw a picture of what they worked on. However, it is not usually successful for children to each individually recall during a long large-group time. For example, when children sit for a long period of time through large-group time and each child is asked to say something (sometimes anything). These group times can grow long and the children get restless or drift off.

What Is Unique About High/Scope?

"Key experiences," "plan-do-review," and the High/Scope Child Observation Record are all unique components of the High/Scope framework.

References

Chattin-McNichols, J. (1992). *The Montessori controversy*. New York: Delmar.

Evans, E. (1971). *Contemporary influences in early childhood education*. New York: Holt, Rinehart, and Winston, Inc.

Goffin, S., & Wilson, C. (2001). *Curriculum models and early childhood education appraising the relationships*. New Jersey: Prentice Hall.

Kostelnik, M. Soderman, A., & Whiren, A. (1999). *Developmentally appropriate curriculum best practices in early childhood education*. New Jersey: Prentice Hall.

Roopnarine, J. & Johnson, J. (1993) *Approaches to early childhood education*. NY: Macmillan Publishing Company.

Website Resources
Montessori

www.montessori-ami.org
www.americanmontessorisociety.org

High/Scope®

www.highscope.org

---

*The second installment of this two-part article, which covers Reggio Emilia, is available at
www.earlychildhoodnews.com

Amy Sussna Klein, Ed.D., is President of ASK Education Consulting. She can be reached by email at Askeducation@cs.com.

Examining the Reggio Emilia Approach to Early Childhood Education

Valarie Mercilliott Hewett

INTRODUCTION

Reggio Emilia, a prosperous region in Northern Italy, is the site of one of the most innovative, high-quality, city-run infant-toddler and pre-primary systems in the world (Edwards, Gandini, & Forman, 1993; New, 1990). Italy's nationwide dedication to the welfare and development of its children is evidenced by a 1968 national law instituting funding of public preschools for all children ages three to six years (Gandini, 1993; New, 1990; Walsh & Albrecht, 1996). Since the end of World War II, however, well before the establishment of this national law, the city of Reggio Emilia has been developing an educational system for young children through the collaborative efforts of parents, teachers, and the general community, under the guiding influence of Loris Malaguzzi (Gandini, 1994; Malaguzzi, 1993b; New, 1990).

As part of the city's post-war reconstruction, the first school for young children in Reggio Emilia was built literally by the hands of parents using proceeds gained from the sale of a war tank, three trucks, and six horses left behind by retreating Germans (Gandini, 1993; Malaguzzi, 1993b; Walsh & Albrecht, 1996). The essential role and intimate involvement of parents in their children's education is, to this day, a fundamental element of the Reggio Emilia Approach.

Today, the city of Reggio Emilia finances and runs 22 schools for children ages 3 to 6 years, as well as 13 infant-toddler centers. Forty-seven percent and 35% of children from the two age groups are served, respectively (Edwards, Gandini, & Forman, 1993; Gandini, 1993; Gandini, 1994; New, 1990). "The schools in Reggio Emilia... have grown out of a culture that values children, out of the intense commitment of a group of parents, out of the leadership of a visionary man" (Neugebauer, 1994, p. 67).

Similar to how the Reggio Emilia Approach to educating young children values the "processes of 'unpacking' or defamiliarizing everyday objects and events" (Katz, 1993, p. 23), I intend to unpack the Reggio Emilia Approach by examining several of its key principles. In this article I will explore the Reggio Emilia Approach within the context of its theories regarding (a) the image and role of the learner, (b) the role of the instructor, and (c) the nature of the knowledge to be learned.

THE IMAGE AND ROLE OF THE LEARNER

The Child as Having Rights

Within the Reggio Emilia Approach, the fundamental belief on which the image of the child is constructed is that of the child having rights rather than simply needs (Malaguzzi, 1993a; 1993b; Rinaldi, 1993). According to Loris Malaguzzi (1993b), "If the children had legitimate rights, then they also should have opportunities to develop their intelligence and to be made ready for the success that would not, and should not, escape them" (p. 51). Influenced by this belief, the child is beheld as beautiful, powerful, competent, creative, curious, and full of potential and ambitious desires (Malaguzzi, 1994; Rinaldi, 1993). Her nature, thoughts, and work are taken seriously and respected; therefore, the act of truly listening to the child is emphasized. This romantic view of the child is reminiscent of Friedrich Froebel's notion that a child possesses a "divine essence" (Froebel, 1887, p. 4) in need of only cultivation and protection rather than interference.

The critical belief that the child possesses rights is the foundation on which the Reggio Emilia Approach is built. The eclectic blend of underlying theories which help to inform the Reggio Emilia Approach serves to support and expand this conviction.

The Child as an Active Constructor of Knowledge

The concept of the child having rights, and thereby possessing strength, competence, and potential, informs a view of the child as a protagonist, occupying the primary active role in her education and learning. As a protagonist, the child is understood as having an innate desire to discover, learn, and make sense of the world. Thus, within the Reggio Emilia Approach, the child is viewed not as a target of instruction, but rather as having the active role of an apprentice (Katz, 1993), working alongside others in the discovery and construction of solutions to meaningful questions and problems; learning is not something that is done to the child, but rather something she does (Firlik, 1994). Loris Malaguzzi (1994) summed up this idea when he eloquently described children as being "authors of their own learning" (p. 55).

This focus on "active education" (Malaguzzi, 1993b, p. 53). is influenced greatly by Jean Piaget's writings on constructivism in which he examined how children's active, physical interactions with the environment aid in their construction of knowledge (Malaguzzi, 1993b; Rankin, 1997). According to Piaget (1973). "A student who achieves a certain knowledge through free investigation and spontaneous effort will later be able to retain it" (p. 93).

The Child as a Researcher

Piaget's (1973) reference to children's "investigation" (p. 93) suggests the role of the child as that of a researcher. John Dewey (1966), also one of many theorists from which the Reggio Emilia Approach draws, more plainly stated, "All thinking is research" (p. 148). This idea is consistent with the image and role of the child within the Reggio Emilia schools. "They [children] are natural researchers as they question what they see, hypothesize solutions, predict outcomes, experiment, and reflect on their discoveries" (Staley, 1998, p. 20).

Within the Reggio Emilia Approach, the role of the child as researcher takes place within the context of projects, or "in-depth stud[ies] of a particular topic that one or more children undertake" (Katz & Chard, 1989, p. 2), the primary form of instruction and learning in Reggio Emilia schools. While engaging in a project, children have the opportunity to explore, observe, question, discuss, hypothesize, represent, and then proceed to revisit their initial observations and hypotheses in order to further refine and clarify their understandings, thereby expanding the richness of their thinking (Forman, 1996), and further defining their role as that of a researcher.

The Child as a Social Being

Although the Reggio Emilia Approach draws from Piaget's ideas, it also has sought to expand and overturn many of his theories (Malaguzzi, 1993b; Rankin, 1997). According to Malaguzzi (1993a), "[the Reggio Emilia Approach] has gone beyond Piagetian views of the child as constructing knowledge from within, almost in isolation" (p. 10). Rather, it places a strong emphasis on children's social construction of knowledge through their relationships (Malaguzzi, 1993a) within the context of collaboration, dialogue, conflict, negotiation, and cooperation with peers and adults (Edwards, Gandini, Forman, 1993; Gandini, 1993b).

Within Reggio Emilia schools it is believed that "only as children articulate to others that which they believe to be true do they come face-to-face with errors in their thinking" (Staley, 1998, p. 21). This emphasis on communication and language in learning may be found in the writings of Lev Vygotsky, whose theories have also greatly influenced the development of the Reggio Emilia Approach. Referring to Vygotsky's ideas concerning language, Malaguzzi (1993b) stated, "[Vygotsky] reminds us how thought and language are operative together to form ideas and to make a plan for action" (p. 79). Children's communication through language, any of "the hundred languages of children" (Edwards, et al., 1993, p. 6), is considered essential to bringing meaning to knowledge within the Reggio Emilia Approach.

THE ROLE OF THE INSTRUCTOR

The Teacher as a Collaborator and Co-Learner

Inasmuch as the child within the Reggio Emilia school is viewed as an active and competent protagonist in her learning, the teacher consequently takes on the role of collaborator and co-learner (Edwards, 1993; Gandini, 1997; Rankin, 1992). "In fact, teachers consider themselves to be partners in this process of learning…" (Gandini, 1997, p. 19). Reciprocal exchanges between children and adults throughout the course of constructing knowledge are valued and fostered. The idea that instruction travels in a two-way direction through the collaboration between children and adults is illustrated in Loris Malaguzzi's (1993b) metaphoric description of a Ping-Pong match. Both players, adult and child, are required to make appropriate adjustments in order to allow for and advance optimal growth and learning. A single player would be unable to participate successfully in the game.

The role of the teacher as partner and co-learner is most clearly demonstrated as both child and teacher engage in collaborative learning during the process of working through a project. "…Reggio's overarching educational principle of reciprocity appears again and again as teacher and learner together guide the project" (Rankin, 1992, p. 30). The teacher does not control nor dominate the child or her learning, but rather, demonstrates respect for the child's rights through mutual participation and joint action.

The role of the teacher as collaborator is not understood in respect solely to his relationship with the child, as the teacher's collaborative efforts with colleagues and parents are also considered vital (Albrecht, 1996; Malaguzzi, 1993a). "Our proposition is to consider a triad at the center of education—children, teachers, and families" (Malaguzzi, 1993a, p. 9). Collaboration, from all angles, is a cornerstone of the Reggio Emilia Approach.

The Teacher as a Guide and Facilitator

Although the teacher is a partner with the child in the process of learning, he also serves as guide and facilitator. According to Carolyn Edwards (1993), the teacher's role "centers on provoking occasions of discovery through a kind of alert, inspired facilitation and stimulation of children's dialogue, co-action, and co-construction of knowledge" (p. 154). Within this role, the teacher does not sit back and simply observe a child construct her own knowledge, although at times he may if appropriate; rather, he plays an active role in providing the child with the provocations and tools necessary to achieve her personal goals and advance her mental functioning.

There is a fine line, however, between "provoking occasions of discovery" (Edwards, 1993, p. 154) and imposing ideas. As a partner to the child, the teacher is "inside the learning situation" (Bredekamp, 1993, p. 16) and, therefore, attuned to the child's thought development, goals, and levels of ability and understanding. This insight provides him with the opportunity to ask questions, offer suggestions, or provide information and technical assistance without taking over the learning experience.

The role of the teacher as guide and facilitator is consistent with Vygotsky's theory of the Zone of Proximal Development

(ZPD), within which adults provide scaffolding to assist children in their learning and consequent development (Diaz, Neal, & Amaya-Williams, 1990; Vygotsky, 1978; Wertsch, 1985). Vygotsky (1978) defined the ZPD as "the distance between the actual developmental level as determined by independent problem solving and the level of potential development as determined through problem solving under adult guidance or in collaboration with more capable peers" (p. 86). Referring to the Reggio Emilia Approach, Malaguzzi (1993b) offered a similar description: "We seek a situation in which the child is about to see what the adult already sees. …In such a situation, the adult can and must loan to the children his judgement and knowledge" (p. 80).

The Teacher as a Researcher

The teacher's role of facilitating children's learning according to their interests, questions, curiosity, and current understandings necessitates that he also take on the role of researcher (Edwards, 1993; Malaguzzi, 1994). Through observing and listening to the children, following-up with the collection and analysis of data, the teacher is able to ascertain critical knowledge concerning the children's development and learning, as well as their interests and curiosities, thereby enabling him to "produce strategies that favor children's work or can be utilized by them" (Malaguzzi, 1993b, p. 82).

Connected to the teacher's role of researcher is the substantial component of documentation. As teachers conduct their research they compile a large amount of data including, but not limited to, photographs of the children engaged in learning endeavors, children's artwork in various stages of completion, videos, and transcribed audio recordings of the children's conversations as they engage in collaboration and reciprocal dialogue with peers and adults. In addition to analyzing the data through careful reflection and extensive discussion, the teachers prepare and display them on beautifully arranged panels (Edwards, et al., 1993; Gandini, 1993b). This meticulous documentation of the process and results of children's work serves three primary functions: (1) provides the children with a visual "memory" of what they have done and, thereby encourages a revisiting and expanding of old ideas, or the inspiration and development of new ideas; (2) provides teachers with a tool for research in order to assist them in continuing to improve and expand project ideas, better understand children, and evaluate their own work; and (3) is a way to provide parents with detailed information about what happens in the school and hopefully facilitate their input and involvement in present and future projects (Edwards, et al., 1993; Edwards & Springate, 1993; Gandini, 1993a; Katz & Chard, 1997; Staley, 1998).

The Teacher as a Reflective Practitioner

In order for a teacher within a Reggio Emilia school to successfully carry out his complex role, it is important that he engage in continuous reflection during which he questions that which he and others have previously assumed to be unquestionable (Filippini, 1993; McCarthy, 1995). Just as the schools in Reggio Emilia have, and will continue to, constantly evolve, so too must the teacher.

This notion of intense reflection advocates Maxine Greene's idea that rather than blindly accepting handed-down slogans and beliefs, teachers much participate in the act of "do[ing] philosophy… [in which they] become critically conscious of what is involved in the complex business of teaching and learning" (Greene, 1973, p. 7). According to the social constructivist-influenced philosophy of the Reggio Emilia Approach, this reflection and questioning on the part of the teacher must take place within the context of discussion and collaboration with colleagues, parents, experts within the community, and yes, even the children (Filippini, 1993; Malaguzzi, 1993a).

THE NATURE OF THE KNOWLEDGE TO BE LEARNED

Knowledge as Socially Constructed

Within the Reggio Emilia Approach knowledge is viewed not as a static list of skills and facts to be transmitted from adult to child, as, according to Rinaldi (1993), "the potential of children is stunted when the endpoint of their learning is formulated in advance" (p. 104). Rather, knowledge is perceived as dynamic in that it is constructed within the context of the child-child and child-adult relationships (Malaguzzi, 1993a; Rinaldi, 1993). Communication and the sharing of ideas is believed to bring meaning to knowledge and, in turn, understandings may vary according to the individuals, the group, and the social context.

Social relationships, and the construction of knowledge within, often involve debate, discord, and conflict. In some cultures these emotions are frequently avoided and discouraged, however, in Reggio Emilia conflict is desired and valued as a means to advance higher-level thinking. According to Loris Malaguzzi (1993a), "Even when cognitive conflicts do not produce immediate cognitive growth, they can be advantageous because by producing cognitive dissonance, they can in time produce progress" (p. 12). This idea is clearly influenced by Piaget's (1973) theory outlining the value of cognitive conflict and disequalibrium as means to higher mental functioning.

Multiple Forms of Knowing

Since knowledge is perceived within the Reggio Emilia Approach as socially constructed and, thereby, dynamic, it follows that no ultimate truth may be understood to exist, but rather multiple forms of knowing. This notion is consistent with the constructivist view of knowledge. According to Fosnot (1996), "We as human beings have no access to an objective reality since we are constructing our version of it, while at the same time transforming it and ourselves" (p. 23). Consequently, within the schools of Reggio Emilia, the goal is not to pass information along or replicate thinking, but rather to advance thinking.

Within the Reggio Emilia schools there are no planned curriculums or standards indicating what is to be learned (Malaguzzi, 1993b; Rinaldi, 1993), as "these would push our schools towards teaching without learning" (Malaguzzi, 1993, p. 8). Rather, it is up to the children, in collaboration with teachers and one another, to determine the course of their investigations and learning (Malaguzzi, 1993b).

Just as there are multiple forms of knowing, so too are there multiple ways of expressing, demonstrating, and interpreting knowledge. Within the Reggio Emilia Approach children are encouraged and facilitated as they represent their plans, ideas, and understandings using one or more "languages, or modes of expression" (Edwards, et al., 1993, p. 3) including, but not limited to, sculpture, drawing, painting, dance, drama, writing, and puppetry (New, 1990). In fact, this act in itself is valued as contributing to the advancement of knowledge. "As children compare these various representations, they confront new possibilities and generate new questions that would not have occurred had they used only one medium" (Forman, 1996, p. 172); meaning is enhanced and expanded. Therefore, the use of various expressions of knowledge may be understood as assisting to create and continually unfold multiple forms of knowing.

Knowledge as Whole

While constructing their own knowledge and achieving understanding within the context of reciprocal relationships with peers, teachers, and parents, children within the schools of Reggio Emilia create important connections for themselves. "In Reggio the process of learning involves making connections and relationships between feelings, ideas, words, and actions" (LeeKeenan & Nimmo, 1995, p. 262). Through the course of making these connections, and guided by the belief that learning is a spiraling process in which ideas, opinions, and thoughts must be expressed, revisited, reflected upon, and expressed again, children consolidate their ideas, thoughts, and feelings into meaningful and cohesive wholes.

This view of learning and knowledge is consistent with the Gestalt approach in which the world is believed to be experienced in "meaningful patterns or organized wholes" (Phillips & Soltis, 1998, p. 35). Understanding the world through the detailed examination of isolated bits of information succeeds only in altering the whole and, thereby contravenes true understanding and higher level thinking.

Children's effort to make meaning and create connections is again facilitated by the project-approach utilized within the schools of Reggio Emilia (Katz, 1993). Within the context of projects, "young children learn through meaningful activities in which different subject areas are integrated" (Edwards & Springate, 1995, p. 27). Children are provided opportunities and support as they discover interrelationships, connections, and underlying principles while following their interests and ideas and engaging in authentic tasks.

It is important to note, however, that even though the making of connections in the process of comprehending the whole is of utmost importance within the schools of Reggio Emilia, specific skills and understandings are not neglected; although, they are understood as needing to remain within the context of meaningful activities. According to Malaguzzi (1993b),

We… [are] convinced that it is not an imposition on children or an artificial exercise to work with numbers, quantity, classification, dimensions, forms, measure-

ment, transformation, orientation, conservation and change, or speed and space, because these explorations belong spontaneously to the everyday experiences of living, playing, negotiating, thinking, and speaking by children. (p. 45)

CONCLUSION

The Reggio Emilia Approach to early childhood education draws from the ideas and theories of many great thinkers—including and beyond those referred to within this article. Yet, the fundamental philosophy serving to guide this approach is much more than an eclectic mix of theories. The ideas from which it draws have, for over 30 years, been reflected upon, expanded, and adapted within the context of the unique culture of Reggio Emilia, Italy, thus resulting in the creation of a singular, cohesive theory.

The Reggio Emilia Approach to educating young children is strongly influenced by a unique image of the child and deeply embedded within the surrounding culture. It is not a model nor recipe with a set of guidelines and procedures to be followed, therefore, one cannot and should not attempt to simply import it to another location. Rather, it must be carefully uncovered and redefined according to one's own culture in order to successfully affect practice elsewhere.

REFERENCES

1. Albrecht, K. (1996). Reggio Emilia: Four key ideas. *Texas Child Care, 20* (2), 2–8.
2. Bredekamp, S. (1993). Reflections of Reggio Emilia. *Young Children, 49* (1), 13–18.
3. Dewey, J. (1966). *Democracy and education.* NY: Free Press.
4. Diaz, R. M., Neal, C. J., & Amaya-Williams, M. (1990). The social origins of self-regulation. In L. C. Moll (Ed.), *Vygotsky and education: Instructional implications and applications of sociohistorical psychology* (pp. 127–154). Cambridge, MA: Cambridge University Press.
5. Edwards, C. (1993). Partner, nurturer, and guide: The roles of the Reggio teacher in action. In C. Edwards, L. Gandini, & G. Forman (Eds.), *The hundred languages of children: The Reggio Emilia approach to early childhood education* (pp. 151–169). Norwood, NJ: Ablex.
6. Edwards, C., Gandini, L., & Forman, G. (1993). *The hundred languages of children: The Reggio Emilia approach to early childhood education.* Norwood, NJ: Ablex.
7. Edwards, C. P., & Springate, K. (1993). Inviting children into project work. *Dimensions of Early Childhood, 22* (1), 9–11.
8. Edwards, C. P., & Springate, K. W. (1995). The lion comes out of the stone: Helping young children achieve their creative potential. *Dimensions of Early Childhood, 23* (4), 24–29.
9. Filippini, T. (1993). The role of the pedagogista. In C. Edwards, L. Gandini, & G. Forman (Eds.), *The hundred languages of children: The Reggio Emilia approach to early childhood education* (pp. 113–118). Norwood, NJ: Ablex.
10. Firlik, R. (1994). Promoting development through constructing appropriate environments: Preschools in Reggio Emilia, Italy. *Day Care and Early Education, 22* (1), 12–20.
11. Forman, G. (1996). The project approach in Reggio Emilia. In C. T. Fosnot (Ed.), *Constructivism: Theory, perspectives, and practice* (pp. 172–181). NY: Teachers College Press.

12. Fosnot, C. T. (1996). *Constructivism: Theory, perspectives, and practice.* NY: Teachers College Press.

13. Froebel, F. (1887). *The education of man.* NY: Appleton & Company.

14. Gandini, L. (1993). Fundamentals of the Reggio Emilia approach to early childhood education. *Young Children, 49* (1), 4–8.

15. _____. (1994). Not just anywhere: Making child care centers into "particular" places. *Child Care Information Exchange 3,* 48–51.

16. _____. (1997). Foundations of the Reggio Emilia approach. In J. Hendrick (Ed.), *First steps toward teaching the Reggio way* (pp. 14–25). Upper Saddle River, NJ: Prentice-Hall.

17. Greene, M. (1973). *Teacher as stranger: Educational philosophy for the modern age.* Belmont, CA: Wadsworth.

18. Katz, L. (1993). What can we learn from Reggio Emilia? In C. Edwards, L. Gandini, & G. Forman (Eds.), *The hundred languages of children: The Reggio Emilia approach to early childhood education* (pp. 19–37). Norwood, NJ: Ablex.

19. Katz, L. G., & Chard, S. C. (1989). *Engaging children's minds: the project approach.* Norwood, NJ: Ablex.

20. LeeKeenan, D., & Nimmo, J. (1993). Connections: Using the project approach with 2- and 3-year-olds in a university laboratory school. In C. Edwards, L. Gandini, & G. Forman (Eds.), *The hundred languages of children: The Reggio Emilia approach to early childhood education* (pp. 251–267). Norwood, NJ: Ablex.

21. Malaguzzi, L. (1993a). For an education based on relationships. *Young Children, 49* (1), 9–12.

22. _____. (1993b). History, ideas, and basic philosophy. In C. Edwards, L. Gandini, & G. Forman (Eds.), *The hundred languages of children: The Reggio Emilia approach to early childhood education* (pp. 41–89). Norwood, NJ: Ablex.

23. _____. (1994). Your image of the child: Where teaching begins. *Child Care Information Exchange, 3,* 52–61.

24. McCarthy, J. (1995). Reggio Emilia: What is the message for early childhood education? *Contemporary Education, 66* (33), 139–142.

25. Neugebauer, B. (1994). Unpacking my questions and images: Personal reflections of Reggio Emilia. *Child Care Information Exchange, 3,* 67–70.

26. New, R. (1990). Excellent early education: A city in Italy has it. *Young Children, 45* (6), 4–10.

27. Phillips, D. C., & Soltis, J. F. (1998). *Perspectives on learning.* NY: Teachers College Press.

28. Piaget, J. (1973). *To understand is to invent: The future of education.* NY: Grossman Publishers.

29. Rankin, B. (1997). Education as collaboration: Learning from and building on Dewey, Vygotsky, and Piaget. In J. Hendrick (Ed.), *First steps toward teaching the Reggio way* (pp. 70–83). Upper Saddle River, NJ: Prentice-Hall.

30. Rinaldi, C. (1993). The emergent curriculum and social constructivism. In C. Edwards, L. Gandini, & G. Forman (Eds.), *The hundred languages of children: The Reggio Emilia approach to early childhood education* (p. 101–111). Norwood, NJ: Ablex.

31. Staley, L. (1998). Beginning to implement the Reggio philosophy. *Young Children, 53* (5), 20–25.

32. Vygotsky, L. S. (1978). *Mind in society.* Cambridge, MA: Harvard University Press.

33. Walsh, K., & Albrecht, K. (1996). Reggio Emilia: A view from the classroom. *Texas Child Care, 20* (1), 2–6.

34. Wertsch, J. V. (1985). *Vygotsky and the social formation of mind.* Cambridge, MA: Harvard University Press.

Valarie Mercilliott Hewett is a Doctoral student, Department of Curriculum and Instruction, College of Education, University of Nevada, Reno.

Correspondence should be directed to Valarie Mercilliott Hewett, 728 Plumas St., Reno, NV 89509; e-mail: Vmhewett@unr.edu

I am grateful to Martha Combs, Ed.D. for her advice and support in completing this article.

The Silencing of Recess Bells

Judith Kieff

In approximately 40 percent of American elementary and middle schools, recess or break time bells have been silenced. Recent policies severely limit or eliminate children's opportunities to engage in self-chosen activities such as free play, unstructured and vigorous physical exercise, and informal social interactions during the school day (Alexander, 1999). This growing trend toward restricting children's freedom to interact and play in relatively unsupervised settings is also affecting the United Kingdom and Australia (Blatchford, 1996). Policymakers cite issues related to the use of time in schools and to playground safety as reasons for curtailing such activity. Unfortunately, informal and unstructured break time, commonly called "recess" in American elementary schools, often is eliminated because many teachers, parents, and policymakers underestimate both the immediate benefits of recess as a partner to quality instruction, and the cumulative and deferred benefits of play for children's learning and development.

There is both theoretical and empirical evidence that allowing time for recess or playground activities can yield immediate and long-term benefits for children of all ages, throughout their school careers (Bar-bour, 1996; Blatchford, 1996; Demp-ster, 1988; Johnson, 1996; Pellegrini & Bjorklund, 1996; Pellegrini & Davis, 1993; Pellegrini, Huberty, & Jones, 1995; Pellegrini & Smith, 1993). Therefore, it is important to re-examine those issues related to time and safety while developing policies that are sensitive to the nature of child development and learning. Pairing recess with quality instruction provides an essential feature of the school day that promotes learning across domains.

Issues Related to Time

In this age of accountability and test-driven instruction, "time-on-task" has become a common battle cry of administrators. Indeed, the time-on-task literature (see Brophy & Good, 1974, for a summary) clearly shows that achievement is directly related to the amount of time spent on a related task. Increasing time in the classroom by eliminating recess may, at first glance, appear to be a sound policy that could lead to improved student achievement. Pellegrini and Bjorklund (1996) state that assuming "a positive correspondent between increased work time and increased student learning… is not the same as stating that more intense, break-free hours of instruction will enhance learning" (p. 5).

Children learn more effectively when their efforts are distributed over time rather than concentrated into longer periods (Ebinghaus, 1964; Hunter, 1929). This phenomenon is known as "task spacing" or "distributed effort" (see Dempster, 1988, for a review). Pellegrini and Bjorklund (1996) point out that "the positive effects of distributed effort have specifically addressed the ways in which children learn numerous school-like tasks, such as native and foreign language vocabulary, recall from text, and math facts" (p. 8). Therefore, when recess or break time is paired with quality instruction, the spacing of these activities generally provides an immediate, positive effect on learning.

Further evidence supporting recess as a partner to quality instruction is found in the work of Pellegrini and his colleagues (Pellegrini & Davis, 1993; Pellegrini et al., 1995). These researchers examined how using recess to separate cognitively demanding tasks affected elementary children's ability to pay attention. The results showed that children paid the most attention when their efforts were spaced apart; the effects are even greater for cognitively immature children (see Pellegrini & Bjorklund, 1996, for a summary).

Pellegrini (1991) explains that recess fulfills children's need for novelty.

Children need recess because they are temporarily bored with their immediate classroom environment. When they go outdoors for recess they seek novelty by interacting with different peers in different situations. But, when the novelty of the recess environment begins to wane, they again need to change. At this point, the classroom becomes a novelty and children actually pay closer attention. (p. 40)

Therefore, it is not a good idea to eliminate recess as a way to increase time-on-task. Indeed, what may at first seem a logical and easy strategy aimed at increasing student achievement can actually backfire. Without consistent breaks, children become restless, fidgety, and unfocused. Since breaks between cognitive tasks support learning, and time is an issue in schools because of the mass of material that must be covered, it is important that break time be structured to maximize potential learning. Instead of silencing the recess bell, administrators should make every effort to provide high-quality recess experiences for children.

The Cumulative and Deferred Benefits of Play

High-quality recess experiences are those in which children of all ages have a high degree of choice in their activities. Primary-age children will most likely engage in vigorous outdoor play such as climbing, running, jumping rope, skipping, and bouncing and catching balls, either alone or with one or two favored pals. Older students will most likely engage in cooperatives games and other activities of a highly social nature. Recess may be the only time during the school day that children can interact with others on their own terms. The playful aspects of recess activities, which include choice,

spontaneity, social interaction, creative use of time, and problem solving, provide children not only opportunities to learn, but also a rich context that fosters development across all areas of development. Play gives children a chance to learn, consolidate, and practice skills necessary for further growth and learning (Bateson, 1976; Piaget, 1962; Vygotsky, 1978). Play is valuable for children primarily as a medium for development and learning (Bergen, 1998); therefore, its effects are both cumulative and deferred. Most children regard recess as fun and look forward to it. Yet recess not only provides a break, it also adds to the overall quality of a child's school experience.

Issues Related to Safety

Many policymakers point to concerns about safety when justifying the elimination of recess. Unfortunately, many school playgrounds have fallen into disrepair over the years, posing safety hazards. School budgets are tight, often leaving little funding to replace play equipment. Teachers and administrators may even cancel recess because of some children's behavior. If schools can offer safe playground environments that promote positive interactions, however, children can reap the immediate benefits of recess for learning and the long-term benefits for their general development.

Steps can be taken to develop playground rules and routines that support social development, encourage physical development, and provide a needed break in academic instruction. Consistent supervision is one key aspect to effective recess. Having interesting activities is another. Teachers or paraprofessionals may need special training to supervise playground activities effectively. Parents, community members, senior citizens, or high school or college students can serve as playground volunteers, not to supervise but to teach and engage children in games, help children resolve

conflicts, and help them organize their own play.

Conclusion

At first glance, eliminating recess may seem like a logical and expedient decision, one that adds time to the instructional day. Such a decision is not based on empirical evidence, however. High-quality recess experiences have immediate and deferred positive effects on children's learning and development. Administrators, teachers, and parents should work together to create environments that promote quality recess experiences for students in elementary and middle schools. Let the recess bells ring again, along with the laughter of children on the playground.

References

Alexander, K. K. (1999). Playtime is canceled. *Parents, November,* 114–118.

Barbour, A. C. (1996). Physical competence and peer relationships in 2nd graders: Qualitative case studies from recess play. *Journal of Research in Childhood Education, 11*(1), 35–46.

Bateson, P. P. G. (1976). Rules and reciprocity in behavioral development. In P. P. G. Bateson & R. A. Hinde (Eds.), *Growing points in ethology* (pp. 401–421). London: Cambridge University Press.

Bergen, D. (Ed.). (1998). *Readings from... Play as a medium for learning and development.* Olney, MD: Association for Childhood Education International.

Blatchford, P. (1996). "We did more then": Changes in pupils' perceptions of breaktime (recess) from 7–16 years. *Journal of Research in Childhood Education, 11*(1), 14–24.

Brophy, J., & Good, T. (1974). *Teacher-student relationships.* New York: Holt, Reinhart & Winston.

Dempster, F. N. (1988). The spacing effect. *The American Psychologist, 43,* 627–634.

Ebinghaus, H. (1964). *Memory.* New York: Teachers College Press. (original work published in 1885)

Hunter, W. (1929). Learning III: Experimental studies of learning. In C. Murchison (Ed.), *The foundation of ex-*

perimental psychology (pp. 564–627). Worcester, MA: Clark University Press.

Johnson, J. E. (1996). Playtime revisited: Growing is not necessarily for noses only. *Journal of Research in Childhood Education, 11*(1), 82–88.

Pellegrini, A. D. (1991). Outdoor recess: Is it really necessary? *Principal, 70*(5), 40.

Pellegrini, A. D., & Bjorklund, D. F. (1996). The place of recess in school: Issues in the role of recess in children's education and development, an introduction to the theme issue.

Journal of Research in Childhood Education, 11(1), 5–13.

Pellegrini, A. D., & Davis, P. (1993). Confinement effects on the playground and classroom behavior. *British Journal of Educational Psychology, 63*, 88–95.

Pellegrini, A. D., Huberty, P. D., & Jones, I. (1995). The effect of play deprivation on children's recess and classroom behaviors. *American Educational Research Journal, 32*, 845–862.

Pellegrini, A. D., & Smith, P. K. (1993). School recess: Implications for educa-

tion and development. *Review of Educational Research, 63*, 51–67.

Piaget, J. (1962). *Play, dreams, and imitation.* New York: Norton.

Vygotsky, L. S. (1978). *Mind in society.* Cambridge, MA: Harvard University Press.

Judith Kieff is Associate Professor, Early Childhood Education, University of New Orleans, New Orleans, Louisiana.

UNIT 4

Guiding and Supporting Young Children

Unit Selections

Key Points to Consider

- What do you believe is the most challenging aspect of caring for children?

- From your experiences in classrooms, how have you observed time-out being used?

- Make a list of some of the school-related "stressors" that primary-grade children may experience.

- How should early childhood educators help young children deal with death and grief?

 **Links: www.dushkin.com/online/**
These sites are annotated in the World Wide Web pages.

Child Welfare League of America (CWLA)
http://www.cwla.org
National Network for Family Resiliency
http://www.nnfr.org

Early childhood teaching is all about problem-solving. Just as children work to solve problems, so do their teachers. Every day, teachers make decisions about how to guide children socially and emotionally. In attempting to determine what could be causing a child's emotional distress, teachers must take into account a myriad of factors. They consider physical, social, environmental, and emotional factors, in addition to the surface behavior of a child. Whether it is an individual child's behavior or interpersonal relationships, the pressing problem involves complex issues that require careful reflection and analysis. Even the most mature teachers spend many hours thinking and talking about the best ways to guide young children's behavior: What should I do about the child who is out of bounds? What do I say to parents who want their child punished? Should intrinsic motivation be taught to every child, or are tangible reinforcers appropriate for some? How do I guide a child who has experienced trauma and now acts out violently?

A technique that is traditionally used in early childhood classrooms is time-out, yet its appropriateness has rarely been questioned. In "Guidance & Discipline Strategies for Young Children: Time Out Is Out," Kathy Preuesse presents a clear argument that time-out is actually a punishment strategy. Better guidance strategies than time-out should be considered if the goal is for young children to learn self-control.

As children with special needs are included in early childhood programs, some instruction and discipline methods may need to be changed. The authors of "Reinforcement in Developmentally Appropriate Early Childhood Classrooms" link two approaches that are typically considered incompatible. They believe that behavioral strategies, such as positive reinforcement or tangible reinforcers, can be used appropriately with young children. A set of guidelines for using reinforcers is particularly useful in understanding how behavioral strategies can be used without violating principles of developmentally appropriate practice.

At some point, every early childhood teacher will need to deal with a child who bullies other children in the classroom or on the playground. While it may be easy to identify the bullying behaviors, it is more difficult to understand the reasons behind such aggressive actions. "Bullying Among Children" is an in-depth look at what may be causing some children to bully others and provides teachers with effective strategies for guiding these children.

Helping children cope with stress can be difficult for teachers in these times of upheaval and trauma. Children today—and their teachers—are learning that terrorism is a fact of life. With acts of violence occurring randomly across the nation, teachers must be very alert to the effects of stress on young children. These are times that call for teachers to demonstrate care and concern as they teach children to cope.

In some circumstances, it may be school experiences that lead to symptoms of emotional distress. "Helping Children Cope with Stress in the Classroom Setting" is an honest look at how regular routines, like standardized tests, overly demanding curriculum, or athletic competition, can result in emotional or physical problems. Teachers should be sensitive to children's differing reactions to classroom pressure. Books and discussion can be useful in preparing children for stressful classroom events. "Children and Grief: The Role of the Early Childhood Educator" is an article worth keeping for future reference. Many children experience the death of someone close to them. This article describes young children's stages of grieving and gives suggestions for supporting them as they deal with death.

Determining strategies of guidance and discipline is important work for an early childhood teacher. Because the teacher-child relationship is foundational for emotional well-being and social competence, guidance is more than applying a single set of discipline techniques. Instead of one solitary model of classroom discipline strictly enforced, a broad range of techniques is more appropriate. It is only through careful analysis and reflection that teachers can look at children individually, assessing not only the child but the impact of family cultures as well. Only then can the teacher determine what is appropriate and effective guidance.

Guidance techniques that work

What's the most challenging aspect of caring for children? Many caregivers and teachers say "discipline."

Actually, the word *discipline* is off target. *Guidance* is a more accurate term. As caregivers and teachers, we *guide* children's behavior. We teach them acceptable behavior and guide them to develop self-control. The goal is that children learn to make good decisions about how to act in specific situations.

Here are some tried-and-true guidance techniques that help children achieve that goal.

Focus on "do's" instead of "don'ts."

Listen to how you speak to children. If you hear the words *don't, stop,* or *quit* before your directions to children, try to rephrase your words to tell children what to do instead of what not to do. Telling children what not to do doesn't give them any information on the correct way to behave. Translating your "don'ts" into "do's" give children clear guidance on what you expect.

Don'ts	Do's
• Stop running in the hall.	Walk in the hall, please. You can run when we go outdoors.
• Don't squeeze the kitten.	Pat the kitten gently with your hand flat and loose.
• Quit whining.	Tell me about the problem with words.
• Don't climb on that counter.	In our classroom, feet stay on the floor.

Build confidence.

Help children feel that they are capable, worthwhile, and able to do things. Feeling dignity and confidence enables children to try new things and approach new experiences with confidence. Ridicule, sarcasm, and belittling comments destroy confidence. Guide children with constructive, clear, and supportive words.

Example	Destructive comment	Constructive guidance
• Jenny spills paint.	Can't you do anything right?	It's hard to walk without spilling. Next time put a paper towel under the can to catch the spills.
• Harry has trouble pedaling his tricycle.	If you'd just listen to me.	On the playground, we have gravel, grass, and the path. Decide which is best for riding your trike.
• Four-year-old José has wet his pants.	You are such a baby. Shame on you.	Accidents sometimes happen. Get your dry clothes and go to the bathroom to change. I'll make sure you have time to finish your painting when you get done.
• May's block tower topples.	I told you it wouldn't work.	Constructing tall towers is really hard. What do you think you could do to make your building sturdier?

Change the environment to promote behavior changes.

Wise caregivers look for the causes of misbehavior. Are there squabbles over too few toys? Are children climbing because materials are out of reach? Are children whiny and cranky because meals and naptimes are too late? Consider changes in the environment that can make you less irritated and the children less frustrated.

Example	Old environment	New environment
• Toddler Hannah spills her milk—every day.	Hannah uses a tall, narrow plastic cup.	Hannah uses a heavy, broad-bottomed cup.
• Carlos and Sam fight over blocks.	There are 10 cardboard stacking blocks.	There are 40 blocks in a variety of shapes.
• Milton can't find his shoes.	There is one jumbled shelf unit for children's items.	Each child has a labeled hook and cubby for storing personal items.

Offer choices—and be ready to accept the decision.

Caregivers know that offering choices helps children develop independence. But conflicts can arise when you are unwilling or unable to accept the choice a child makes. In general, it's best to offer two options. If there is no choice, state your expectations simply and concretely.

Example	Invites conflict	Builds independence
• At lunchtime	What do you want to drink? (Too many options, many of which may not be acceptable.)	Would you like milk or water with your sandwich? (Either choice is acceptable.)
• Going outside	It's cold today. Do you want your coat? (Child could say "No.")	Let's get our coats and go for a walk. (No choice.)
• Billy is wandering aimlessly in the classroom.	What do you want to do? (Child could say "Go home," or "Go outside.")	Billy, you look like you need something to do. Would you rather paint at the easel or feed the fish?

Work with children, not against them.

Make sure your expectations are appropriate to the ages and developmental levels of the children in your care. When 3-year-old Alyssa flushes the toilet five times in a row, ask yourself: Is this misbehavior, or is this normal behavior? She may be trying to satisfy her curiosity.

Remember that infants and toddlers learn through their senses—from things that they can hear, taste, touch, smell, and see. Preschoolers follow their curiosity, need hands-on activities, and use their imagination for learning and discovery. You can minimize conflicts with children by anticipating their behaviors and preparing the environment to be safe and ready for exploration. Keep your expectations clear and reasonable—and share them with the children.

Age group	Anticipate	Prepare
• Infants and toddlers	Infants and toddlers explore with their fingers and mouths.	Baby-proof the environment and put dangerous, fragile, and breakable objects out of reach.
• Preschoolers	Preschoolers want to know how things work.	Offer concrete, hands-on activities with real objects that teach children about their world, like magnifying glasses, keys, and magnets.
• School-agers	School-age children can think abstractly and are learning about symbols.	Plan opportunities for pretend play, board games, and word games.

Use mistakes as teaching tools.

Treat mistakes, errors, and accidents as steps to learning—everyone makes them as they try new things. Share some of your mistakes—"Oops, I mixed too much water into the paint. Next time I better measure more carefully." In doing so, you help children know that adults too have accidents and can still learn. Build a learning environment that discourages failure and promotes success.

Example	Encourages failure	Promotes success
• After a water table activity, the floor is slippery and children's clothes are wet.	Fuss about the mess and children's carelessness--without offering solutions.	Anticipate the mess by covering the floor under the table with newspaper, having towels nearby, and providing smocks.
• Yetta has a hard time completing a puzzle or another project.	Make Yetta sit in one place to "finish what you have started."	Accommodate Yetta's needs by letting her finish the puzzle on the floor or stand to paint.
• The toddler room floor is covered with toys, making Ben and Laurie reluctant to practice walking.	Leave the disorder until naptime "since it will just get messy again" and the children can crawl to what they want.	Arrange furniture and materials so that there is always a clear path for new walkers.

Give children limits—and security.

Everyone needs to have boundaries defined. You, for example, rely on speed-limit signs, price tags, and recipes to guide some of your activities. Children need to know limits and, within those limits, need the freedom to practice making appropriate decisions. They need adults to help draw the line between not enough and too much decision-making freedom.

Children also must know behavior limits will be enforced consistently—what's OK today will be OK tomorrow. Look at your own behavior for mixed messages. Did you have children finger paint with pudding yesterday and then get frustrated at lunch today when children smeared the pudding on the table?

Set behavioral limits to reflect the safety of children, the safety and well-being of others, and the protection of community property. Rules that are few, enforceable, and essential give children the freedom and responsibility to make good behavioral choices. Evaluate limits—or rules—regularly. Ask: Is the rule still necessary, or have the children outgrown it? Is the rule for my convenience alone? Does the rule restrict experimentation or keep a child from trying new things? Can the rule be enforced? Make sure you understand the reason for the rule—the children will surely ask for it.

Example	Invites conflict	Offers security and reassurance
• On the playground you monitor 5-year-olds climbing the old oak tree.	No climbing above that branch.	I know you want to go higher. I'll be here if you feel like you're getting into trouble.
• In the classroom you use a timer to remind children to give up a place at a favorite activity.	Because I say so.	We have this rule so that every child has a chance to play with the train. Would you like to read the train book while you wait?
• At naptime you help children settle on their mats.	Go to sleep. Close your eyes right now and quit wiggling.	Sometimes it's hard to sleep. Would you like to choose a book to look at during rest time?

Use logical consequences.

Respond to inappropriate behavior with logical consequences—the natural result of a particular behavior. A logical consequence for an adult, for example, may be a stomach ache after eating spicy food. For a child, a logical consequence may be feeling cold after going outside without a sweater.

This kind of learning goes on all the time. In some cases, we can set up a logical consequence if one doesn't occur naturally. If a 3-year-old spills milk, for example, one logical consequence is to have the child help with cleanup. The consequence is not punishment and it always relates to the original behavior. It's not logical, therefore, to deny time in the art center to a child who spills milk—the two things don't relate to each other.

The consequence must also be reasonable. If a child's behavior poses danger—picking up broken glass or running into the street, for example—stop it immediately. Avoid extremes. If 9-year-old Josh breaks a baseball bat by swinging it against a brick wall, don't say, "You can never play baseball here again." Show children that you trust them to change and learn. "Here's a glove for you to practice catching. You can try batting later this afternoon."

For a logical consequence to be effective, you must respond immediately. Make it clear that it's the behavior—not the child—that is objectionable.

Example	Illogical punishment	Logical consequence
• Benny runs on the playground and knocks Jena over.	Make Benny sit in the sandbox for the rest of outdoor time. (Not related.)	Have Benny help Jena up and walk with her to clean her hands and knees.
• Toddler Mike scribbles on a wall with crayon.	Remove crayons from the classroom for six weeks.	Help Mike scrub off the wall with a soapy rag.
• Laura misuses a book and tears several pages.	Take the book away from Laura and tell her she has ruined it. (Not related.)	Show Laura how to use tape to repair the book.

Set an example.

Children learn by watching you. They observe your interactions with children and other adults and are likely to model their behavior on yours. For example, if you consistently talk to children rudely in a loud voice, you're teaching them that this is the way to treat others. If you tell the director that you are out of glue and then produce a hidden bottle from the closet, you'll have a difficult time convincing children that it's not right to lie.

Instead, show concern for others, work out conflicts, and respect the dignity of others—both adults and children. In this way, you model behaviors children need to learn for their social and emotional success.

Example	Negative role model	Positive role model
• At lunchtime	You watch the children eat their lunch while you have a snack of soda and chips.	You sit with the children and model sound nutritious and social mealtime habits.
• On the playground	You scream across the yard to tell Hank his dad is ready to go home.	You wave to Hank's dad, walk across the yard to tell Hank it's time to leave for the day, and help Hank say goodbye to his friends.
• In the art center	Mirabelle spatters paint on the floor and wall. You tell her that it doesn't matter because the custodian is paid to clean up.	You let Mirabelle get the sponge and help her wipe down the wall and floor. When she's finished you congratulate her for helping make the classroom a pleasant place to work and play.

Tips for handling common behaviors

The child	It may mean the child	So don't	Instead try to
becomes angry.	• does not feel successful with an important task. • has been told *stop, no*, and *don't* too many times. • is being forced to do something. • feels frustrated by too many demands from adults.	• become angry. • allow an out-of-control tantrum.	• remember anger is normal and sometimes appropriate. • evaluate and modify the environment to minimize frustration. • help the child express anger in ways that don't hurt anyone. • provide an outlet for strong emotions.
won't share.	• is too young (under 3 years) to understand sharing. • needs experience and guidance in owning and sharing.	• snatch an object from the child. • scold the child. • say you don't like the child.	• help the child feel more secure. • teach problem-solving skills. • provide duplicate toys and materials.
bites other children.	• is teething. • is using the mouth for learning. • communicates through biting rather than words. • doesn't understand that biting hurts. • feels frustrated but hasn't learned more appropriate coping skills.	• bite the child back. • encourage biting back. • make the child bite soap. • force the child to say, "I'm sorry."	• provide toddlers with alternative and soothing objects to bite. • supervise closely to prevent biting. • help children develop other communication skills. • evaluate and modify schedule, environment, or materials to reduce children's stress. • comfort victims. • teach children that biting hurts. • share information with parents, stressing how typical biting is.
is jealous.	• feels replaced by a new person in the family. • has been unfairly compared with others. • has been treated unfairly.	• shame the child. • ignore the child.	• provide warmth, love, and understanding. • discuss the child's feeling one-on-one. • help children feel competent and successful with tasks. • make available books that deal with jealousy. • ignore the incident.
uses foul language.	• doesn't know any better. • is imitating someone. • is trying something new. • is trying to get your attention. • is letting off steam.	• show shock or embarrassment. • get excited. • over-react. • wash out the child's mouth with soap. • put hot pepper on the child's tongue.	• offer a substitute word. • teach children new, extra-long words. • evaluate and modify materials to be stimulating but not overwhelming.

Tips for handling common behaviors			
The child	**It may mean the child**	**So don't**	**Instead try to**
hurts you or other children.	• is too young to understand the pain. • is inexperienced in social relationships. • is angry. • is frustrated.	• get angry. • hurt the child. • force the child to say, "I'm sorry." • say you don't like the child. • ignore the child.	• attend the hurt person first and involve the child who did the hurt in the comforting. • quietly separate the children. • divert the children's attention. • take away hurting objects —calmly and firmly. • offer different ways to express feelings.
destroys materials.	• is curious about how things work. • does not understand the correct way to use the materials. • has had an accident. • feels excited or angry. • finds the materials too difficult or frustrating.	• scold, yell, or shout. • tell the child "You're bad." • hurt the child.	• teach and model the proper ways to handle materials. • examine fragile items with the child. • remove broken materials from the area. • teach the difference between valued and throw-away items. • involve the child in repair work.
refuses to eat.	• is showing a normal decrease in appetite. • is not hungry. • does not feel well. • dislikes a particular food, flavor, or texture. • is imitating someone. • is trying to be independent. • is trying to get attention.	• make a scene. • reward or bribe the child. • threaten the child. • scold the child. • force the child to eat. • withhold other foods or drink.	• remain calm and casual. • make food interesting and attractive. • introduce new foods a little at a time. • help children learn to serve and feed themselves. • serve small portions. • involve children in food preparation.
demands attention.	• is tired, hungry, or not feeling well. • feels left out, insecure, or unloved. • really likes you and is jealous of the attention you give other children. • hasn't yet learned to play creatively and independently.	• ignore or isolate the child. • shame the child. • scold or punish the child.	• attend to the child's physical needs. • show interest in the child's ideas and discoveries. • offer interesting activities for the child to do with other children. • recognize the child's efforts and successes.

Adapted from "Tips for Handling Common Situations With Children," *Texas Child Care*, Winter 1983.

From *Texas Child Care*, Spring 2002, pp. 10-16. © 2002 by Texas Workforce Commission.

GUIDANCE & DISCIPLINE STRATEGIES FOR YOUNG CHILDREN:

TIME OUT IS OUT

BY KATHY PREUESSE

In a typical early childhood classroom, children engage in a variety of behaviors—some appropriate and some inappropriate. Early childhood teachers need to deal with all behaviors, but of course it is the inappropriate ones that are the subject of so much study! And even more than the inappropriate behaviors themselves, our response to the behaviors is weighed, measured, and quantified by a wide range of early childhood experts. The question remains: how do teachers react to children's behavior, and how does that reaction impact the child in later incidents? Through the years, styles of discipline have changed. "Spare the rod and spoil the child"—the in vogue punishment over perhaps a hundred years—gave way to time out sometime in the late 1970s. And now time out, the "strategy of choice" for 20 years or so, seems to be falling out of favor. What is time out, why has it been so popular, and what strategy will replace it if indeed it is on the way out?

What Is Time Out?

Sheppard and Willoughby (1975) define time out as the "removal of an individual from a situation which contains minimal opportunity for positive reinforcement." According to Schreiber (1999) the intent of time out is to "control and extinguish undesirable behaviors." When you say time out to a classroom teacher, many

times the image evoked is that of a chair in the corner of the classroom where a child is put when she has "misbehaved." The length of time that child needs to "think about what she has done wrong" is many times determined by the child's age. The rule of thumb generally has been one minute per year.

The Use of Time Out as a Discipline Strategy

Time out was originally used in institutional settings with people who had a variety of mental or emotional disorders (Marion, 2001). In that setting, time out might have been used to ensure the safety of other residents by removing a dangerous or disruptive resident from a setting. It might also have been used as a consequence, when a resident refused to comply with requests of the staff. In such a setting, time out was considered a legitimate guidance strategy.

At some point during the 1970s, time out made its way into schools as a discipline technique. As corporal punishment declined, time out arose to fill the void with what seemed as a more caring, humane, and non-violent method. In an early childhood classroom, time out has seemingly been used as a discipline strategy to control and extinguish undesirable behaviors. Well-meaning teachers might use it to cope with non-compliance in young children, or to give a con-

sequence for unsafe behavior. In some situations time out may be viewed as a logical consequence to inappropriate behavior or the loss of self-control (Gartrell, 2001).

How effective is time out in the typical early childhood environment? *Two-and-half-year-old Ben runs over to giggling two-year-old Jack and pushes him. The teacher says, "Ben! I told you not to push Jack! Use your words!" Ben tries again to push Jack. The teacher shouts, "Ben! That is not okay! You need to sit in the time-out chair!" She leads Ben to the chair and sits him down. In the time-out chair, Ben might be thinking, "I'm sitting in the chair... What is that noise?... I'm sitting in the chair... I want my mommy... I'm sitting in the chair." Ben is probably not thinking, "Wow! I guess I'll never push Jack again! I'm really sorry I did that!" Jack might be thinking: "What happened? I was giggling and then I was pushed down!"* (Schreiber, 1999, p. 22).

Should the Use of Time Out be Questioned?

Although many teachers view this technique as discipline, the lost opportunities and deprivation of positive interactions move this technique into the punishment category. The NAEYC Code of Ethical Conduct, P-1.1, states, "Above all, we shall not harm children. We shall not participate in practices that are disrespectful, degrading, dangerous, exploitative, intimidating, psychologically damaging, or physically harmful to children. This principle has precedence over all other in this code." Marion and Swim (2001) point out that "punishment has great potential for doing harm to children because it often serves as a model of negative, hurtful and aggressive measures."

Teachers may view time out as discipline rather than punishment, but children view these strategies as painful. When two-, three- and four-year-old children were asked in a study about time out, they expressed sadness and fear, as well as feeling alone, feeling disliked by the teacher and feeling ignored by peers (Readdick and Chapman, 2000).

Many early childhood experts agree with Readdick and Chapman. For example, Montessori (1964) sees these external controls that reward and punish as an opportunity lost to teach children how to self-regulate (Gartrell, 2001). The removal period can be confusing to the child because he lacks the cognitive ability to understand the process (Katz, 1984; Gartrell, 2001). Schreiber (1999) calls the practice of using time outs "undesirable" for five reasons: 1) external controls overshadow the need to develop internal controls; 2) adult needs are met at the expense of the child's needs; 3) a negative effect can be seen in the child's self-worth and self-confidence; 4) confusion arises over the connection between the action and the consequence; and 5) the lost opportunity for learning. These "undesirable" aspects of time out, along with the others mentioned above, make this strategy developmentally inappropriate. The needs of the child are not met, thus, causing harm to the child.

Guiding Children's Behavior

Time out needs to be revisited under the broader umbrella of guidance. Guidance can be defined as "Everything adults deliberately do and say, either directly or indirectly, to influence children's behavior, with the goal of helping them become well-adjusted, self-directed, productive adults" (Hildebrand and Hearron, p. 4, 1999). Using this definition, it is obvious that teachers have a re-

sponsibility to guide interactions towards a meaningful end. It is through positive actions or techniques that learning takes place. Today many positive techniques are available to early childhood teachers. Let's look at three areas: 1) managing the environment, 2) demonstrating developmentally appropriate practices, and 3) fostering the development of self-regulation in children.

Managing the Environment

Managing the environment must start with safety as the first priority. Consider the child who seems to be always running in the classroom. The teacher says, *"John, stop running before you hurt yourself. I've told you many times that if you run you will have to sit on a chair and slow down."* A positive alternative to this would be to take a look at the environment. Is there sufficient space for large muscle or active play? Instead of changing the child's behavior with negative consequences, add a tunnel for crawling through, steps for walking up and down or change your schedule to provide outdoor play earlier in your morning routine. Schreiber (1999) lists several ways to minimize conflicts such as keeping group sizes small so each child gets more attention and minimize crowding of play spaces to minimize disruptions. Classrooms need personal spaces and social spaces. Personal space refers to an area where children put belongings or spend time when privacy is needed. Social space refers to an area around the child that the child feels is his such as a seat at the art table, or a section of the sand box (Hildebrand & Hearron, 1999). Teachers need to provide enough social spaces in their classrooms so children feel comfortable while playing. Take a look around your room. Is there adequate play space? Consider having 50 percent more play spaces than the number of children present.

Developmentally Appropriate Practices

Developmentally appropriate practices and positive guidance strategies go hand in hand. As teachers, we must make sure

our expectations are in line with the developmental levels of the children.

Giving children choices is one of Eaton's (1997) suggestions for positive guidance techniques. For example, *if a two-year-old is having difficulty coming to the snack table, the teacher can say, "It is time to sit down for snack now Jody. You may sit on the red chair or this blue chair."* Choices allow the child to have control over her environment within the boundaries set by the teacher.

Teaching expected behavior is another positive guidance strategy (Marion & Muza, 1998). As teachers we model behavior continuously. As a toddler teacher, I find myself modeling appropriate behaviors in the house area in my room especially at the beginning of the year. The children love to set the table and serve food. They also love to put everything in their mouths as they play and pretend to eat. In order to keep the toys clean (and out of the sanitizing container), I need to model how to hold the food inches from my mouth and move my lips as if I was eating. I tell them what I am doing and why. I label it by saying, "I'm pretending to eat the spaghetti." They love to watch and then repeat the modeled behavior.

Redirecting behavior takes on many forms—diverting, distracting, substituting (Marion, 1999). Consider having two of some items in your room so that substituting can easily happen such as in this example: *Sydney is playing with a doll when Michael tries to take it away. The teacher redirects by substitution when he hands Michael the second doll and replies, "Michael you may use this doll. Sydney is feeding that doll now."*

Setting limits in a preschool classroom provides boundaries for the children and teacher. Limits are set to assure the safety of children, adults, and materials. They also provide a framework in which trust, respect, equality, and accepting responsibility can flourish. Routines and transition times are ideal opportunities to apply positive guidance strategies. Use phrases such as, "It's time to (wash hands, go outside, rest quietly,)" "It's important to (use soap to remove germs, stay where a teacher can see you)," and "I need you to (wait for me before you go outside, pick up those two blocks)." (Reynolds, 2001).

Using action statements to guide behavior in young children. Telling children what to do, such as "we walk inside," takes the guesswork out of the situation. The child knows exactly what is expected of him. Hildebrand and Hearron (1999) point out that putting the action part of the statement at the beginning of the sentence is an effective method. For example, saying, "Hold on to the railing" is better than, "You might fall off the slide, so be sure to hold on." This allows the important part to be stated before it's too late or the child loses interest in your comments.

Demeo (2001) suggests when using positive guidance strategies a teacher must also take into account the variables that affect compliance. When advocating for behavior change in young children we should:

- Use statements
- Give the child time to respond
- Use a quiet voice, don't give multiple requests
- Describe the behavior we want to see
- Demonstrate and model
- Make more start requests than stop requests (do vs. don't)
- Be at the child's eye level and optimal listening distance of three feet.

Fostering the Development of Self-Regulation in Children

Self-regulation allows children to control their actions. They must develop the ability to know when to act, when to control their impulses and when to search for alternative solutions. This is a learned, ongoing process that can be fostered by teachers who use an integrated approach that considers the whole child and the developmental level of that child. "To support developing impulse control [in toddlers], caregivers can use responsive guidance techniques that emphasize individual control over behavior, provide

simple cause-and-effect reasons for desired behaviors, use suggestions rather than commands, and use language to assist self-control" Bronson (2000, p. 35). When we teach problem-solving skills, we help children take responsibility for their actions, see a situation from another point of view, and develop decision-making skills (Miller, 1984). These internal processes help children think of alternative solutions and possible outcomes. As teachers we can start the thought process by asking children, "How can you…?" or "What could we do to…?" As children develop these skills they will soon generate their own solutions and gain control of their actions.

Conclusion

Time out is out! As early childhood professionals, we must abide by the code of Ethical Conduct laid out by NAEYC, which states that "Above all we shall not harm children." The use of time out as a discipline strategy can harm children and must not be used in our classrooms. It is our responsibility to help "children and adults achieve their full potential in the context of relationships that are based on trust, respect, and positive regard" (NAEYC, 1990). As teachers we influence children daily. We can choose to affect children in positive ways by managing the environment, using developmentally appropriate practices, and fostering self-regulation. An effective teacher uses a mix of several techniques. One strategy may work one day while another may be best another day. It takes forethought and reflection. Positive guidance strategies help children develop into caring, respectful human beings.

References

Bronson, M. (2000). Recognizing and supporting the development of self-regulation in young children. *Young Children,* 55 (2), 33–37.

Demeo, W. (2001). Time-out is out: Developing appropriate alternatives for helping difficult young children develop self-control. Presentation at NAEYC Conference, Anaheim, CA.

Eaton, M. (1997). Positive discipline: Fostering the self-esteem of young children. *Young Children,* 52 (6), 43–46.

Gartrell, D. (2001). Replacing time-out: Part one—using guidance to build an encouraging classroom. *Young Children,* 56 (6), 8–16.

Hildebrand V. & Hearron P. (199). *Guiding young children.* Upper Saddle River, NJ: Prentice-Hall, Inc.

Katz, L. (1984). The professional early childhood teacher. *Young Children,* 39 (5), 3–10.

Marion, M. (1999). *Guidance of young children.* Upper Saddle River, NJ: Prentice-Hall, Inc.

Marion, M. & Muza, R. (1998). Positive discipline: Six strategies for guiding behavior. *Texas Child Care,* 22, (2), 6–11.

Marion, M. & Swim, T. (2001). First of all, do no harm: Relationship between early childhood teacher beliefs about punitive discipline practices and reported use of time out. Manuscript, under review.

Marion, M. (2001). Discussion information.

Miller C. (1984). Building self-control: Discipline for young children. *Young Children,* 39 (6), 15–19.

Montessori, M. (1964). *The Montessori method.* New York: Shocken Books.

NAEYC Code of Ethical Conduct and Statement of Commitment (1990).

Readdick & Chapman, P. (2000). Young children's perceptions of time out. *Journal of Research in Childhood Education,* 15 (1).

Reynolds, E. (2001). *Guiding young children: A problem-solving approach.* Mountain View, CA: Mayfield Publishing Company.

Schreiber, M. (1999). Time-outs for toddlers: Is our goal punishment or education? *Young Children,* 54 (4), 22–25.

Sheppard, W. & Willoughby, R. (1975). *Child behavior: Learning and development.* Chicago: Rand McNally College Publishing Company.

Kathy Preuesse is currently a lab school teacher in the two-year-old toddler class at the Child and Family Study Center at the University of Wisconsin-Stout in Menomonie, WI.

From *Earlychildhood News,* March/April 2002, pp. 12-16. © 2002 by Excelligence Learning Corporation. Reprinted by permission.

Reinforcement in Developmentally Appropriate Early Childhood Classrooms

As greater numbers of children with disabilities participate in early childhood programs, teachers are faced with the challenge of expanding their repertoire of teaching and guidance practices to accommodate the needs of children with diverse abilities and needs.

Tashawna K. Duncan, Kristen M. Kemple, and Tina M. Smith

Each day from 10:30 to 11:00, the children in Mrs. Kitchens's 1st-grade classroom are expected to sit silently in their desks and copy words from the chalkboard into their notebooks. Children who finish early are required to remain silently in their seats. After five minutes has passed, Mrs. Kitchens assesses whether every child in the class has been behaving according to the rules. If they have been, she makes a check mark on the chalkboard and announces, "Good! There's a check." If even one child has violated the rules, she announces "no check." At the end of the week, if 20 or more checks have accrued on the board, the whole group is awarded an extra-long Friday recess period. This longed-for reward is rarely achieved, however.

Five-year-old Rodney has recently joined Mr. Romero's kindergarten class. On his first day in his new class, Rodney punched a classmate and usurped the tricycle the other boy was riding. On Rodney's second day in the class, he shoved a child off a swing and dumped another out of her chair at the snack table. In an effort to deal with Rodney's problematic behavior, Mr. Romero is taking a number of steps, including making sure that Rodney knows the classroom rules and routines, helping Rodney learn language and skills to resolve conflicts, exploring ways to make Rodney feel welcome and a special part of the class, and arranging for a consultation with a special education specialist to see if support services would

be appropriate. Mr. Romero is concerned for the emotional and physical safety of the other children, and he believes that Rodney will have a hard time making friends if his reputation as an aggressor is allowed to solidify. He feels the need to act fast. Deciding that a system of reinforcement, along with other strategies, may help Rodney control his aggressive behavior, Mr. Romero implements a token reinforcement system. Rodney earns a ticket, accompanied by praise, for each 30-minute period during which he does not behave aggressively. At the end of the day, Rodney can trade a specified number of earned tickets for his choice of small toys.

The above examples illustrate two teachers' efforts to use the behavioral strategy of reinforcement—with varying degrees of appropriateness. In Mrs. Kitchens's class, reinforcement is being used as a means to get children to sit still and be quiet in the context of a developmentally inappropriate lesson. In an effort to keep children "on task," Mrs. Kitchens substitutes a control tactic for a meaningful and engaging curriculum. Mr. Romero, on the other hand, is making efforts to identify and address the reasons for Rodney's behavior. Furthermore, he believes that Rodney's behavior is so detrimental to himself and to the other children that additional measures must be used to achieve quick results and restore a sense of psychological safety in the classroom community. Mr. Romero utilizes a variety of strategies in the hopes of creating lasting change in Rodney's behavior.

Inclusion of Children With Special Needs

The trend toward including children with disabilities in early childhood education settings is growing (Wolery & Wilbers, 1994). As greater numbers of children with disabilities participate in early childhood programs, teachers are faced with the challenge of expanding their repertoire of teaching and guidance practices to accommodate the needs of children with diverse abilities and needs. To this end, teachers responsible for the care and education of diverse groups of young children are encouraged to examine their beliefs about their role in promoting children's development and learning, and to explore their understanding of developmentally appropriate practices as outlined by the National Association for the Education of Young Children (NAEYC) (Bredekamp & Copple, 1997).

Historically, early childhood special education has had stronger roots in behavioral psychology and applied behavior analysis than has early childhood education.

Recent federal legislation requires that children be educated in the "least restrictive environment." This means that, to the maximum extent possible, the setting in which children with special needs are educated should be the same as that in which typically developing children are educated, and that specialized services should be provided within the regular classroom (Thomas & Russo, 1995).

Early Childhood Education and Early Childhood Special Education

Most early childhood teachers have little or no training in early childhood special education. Historically, differences have existed between teachers who work with young children with disabilities and teachers who work with typically developing children, including different educational preparation, separate professional organiza-

tions, and reliance on different bodies of research (Wolery & Wilbers, 1994). As both groups of children are increasingly cared for and educated in the same programs, early childhood educators and early childhood special educators are called upon to work in collaboration to ensure that children receive individually appropriate education. This collaborative effort requires that all teachers have familiarity with and respect for the philosophy and practices of both disciplines.

Historically, early childhood special education has had stronger roots in behavioral psychology and applied behavior analysis than has early childhood education. As Wolery and Bredekamp (1994) noted, developmentally appropriate practices (DAP) (as outlined by NAEYC) have their roots primarily in maturational and constructivist perspectives. While current early childhood special education practices also tend to be rooted in constructivist perspectives, the additional influence of cultural transmission perspectives (including behaviorist models of learning) is evident. Given their diverse origins, it should not be surprising that the two disciplines would advocate, on occasion, different practices (Wolery & Bredekamp, 1994). This potential tension is exemplified in an editor's note found in the recent NAEYC publication *Including Children With Special Needs in Early Childhood Programs* (Wolery & Wilbers, 1994). Carol Copple (the series' editor) stated,

> Certainly early childhood educators are well aware of the limits of behaviorism as the sole approach to children's learning and are wary of overreliance on rewards as a motivational technique. From this vantage point, some readers may have a negative first response to some of the techniques described in this chapter. Although we must be aware of the limitations and pitfalls of such methods, I urge readers to keep an open mind about them.... They are not for every situation, but when used appropriately, they often succeed where other methods fail. (Wolery & Wilbers, 1994, p. 119)

The current authors hope that readers will be open to considering the judicious use of methods of reinforcement described in this article. When included as part of a total developmentally appropriate program and used after careful assessment of individual needs, these methods can be important tools for implementing *individually* appropriate practice.

Developmentally Appropriate Practice

In 1987, NAEYC published *Developmentally Appropriate Practice in Early Childhood Programs Serving Children From Birth to Age 8* (Bredekamp, 1987), which was revised and published in 1997 as *Developmentally Appropriate Practice in*

DAP Guidelines:
Developmentally Appropriate Practice for
3- Through 5-Year-Olds: Motivation and Guidance*

Appropriate Practices

Teachers draw on children's curiosity and desire to make sense of their world to motivate them to become involved in interesting learning activities. Teachers use verbal encouragement in ways that are genuine and related to an actual task or behavior, and acknowledge children's work with specific comments like, "I see you drew your older sister bigger than your brother."

In cases of children with special needs, such as those identified on an Individualized Education Plan, those resulting from environmental stress, such as violence, or when a child's aggressive behavior continually threatens others, teachers may develop an individualized behavioral plan based on observation of possible environmental "triggers" and/or other factors associated with the behavior. *This plan includes motivation and intervention strategies that assist and support the child to develop self-control and appropriate social behaviors.* (italics added)

Inappropriate Practices

A preponderance of experiences are either uninteresting and unchallenging, or so difficult and frustrating so as to diminish children's intrinsic motivation to learn. *To obtain children's participation, teachers typically rely on extrinsic rewards (stickers, privileges, etc.) or threats of punishment.* (italics added) Children with special needs or behavioral problems are isolated or punished for failure to meet group expectations rather than being provided with learning experiences at a reasonable level of difficulty.

Teachers constantly and indiscriminately use praise ("What a pretty picture"; "That's nice") so that it becomes meaningless and useless in motivating children. (italics added)

*Guidelines for 6- to 8-year-olds are virtually identical. See Bredekamp & Copple, 1997.

Early Childhood Programs (Bredekamp & Copple, 1997). Many have argued that DAP (see Figure 1) provides an appropriate educational context for the inclusion of young children with disabilities, assuming that the interpretations of DAP guidelines leave room for adaptations and extensions to meet the child's specific needs (Bredekamp, 1993; Carta, 1995; Carta, Atwater, Schwartz, & McConnell, 1993; Carta, Schwartz, Atwater, & McConnell, 1991; Wolery & Bredekamp, 1994; Wolery, Strain, & Bailey, 1992; Wolery, Werts, & Holcombe-Ligon, 1994). For some young children, this may mean the use of behavioral strategies, such as planned programs of systematic reinforcement. In fact, the current DAP guidelines do not identify reinforcement systems as inappropriate practice. Some early childhood educators, however, view many forms of reinforcement as completely unacceptable. If inclusion is to succeed, it may be necessary for teachers to consider using such strategies for particular children in particular circumstances.

While reinforcement through use of stickers, privileges, and praise is *not* identified as developmentally *inappropriate* practice, it does become inappropriate when used in exclusion of other means of promoting children's engagement and motivation, and when used indiscrimi-

nately (for the wrong children, and/or in the wrong situations). Children's active engagement is a guiding principle in both DAP and early childhood special education (Carta et al., 1993). As Carta et al. (1993) have pointed out, however, many young children with disabilities are less likely to engage spontaneously with materials in their environments (Peck, 1985; Weiner & Weiner, 1974). The teacher's active encouragement is needed to help such children become actively involved in learning opportunities. A principal goal of early intervention is to facilitate young children's active engagement with materials, activities, and the social environment through systematic instruction (Wolery et al., 1992). Such instruction may include use of reinforcement as incentives.

Behavioral Strategies in Early Childhood Education

Behavioral theory holds that behaviors acquired and displayed by young children can be attributed almost exclusively to their environment. Several behavioral strategies are employed by early childhood teachers to facilitate children's learning, including the use of praise and external rewards. However, practitioners often fail to identify these strategies in their repertoire and dismiss, out of hand, their use in the classroom. Misunderstandings may exist concerning the appropriate use and potential effectiveness of these strategies for young children. As a result, they are not always well accepted in the early childhood community (Henderick, 1998; Rodd, 1996; see also Strain et al., 1992).

A review of contemporary literature suggests that behavioral strategies are appropriate for creating and maintaining an environment conducive to growth and development (e.g., Peters, Neisworth, & Yawkey, 1985; Schloss & Smith, 1998). Research has demonstrated that behavioral strategies are successful in school settings with various diverse populations, including those with young children (Kazdin, 1994). Furthermore, while many such "best practices" are unrecognized by early childhood professionals, they are grounded in behavioral theory (Strain et al., 1992).

The Use of Positive Reinforcement

Positive reinforcement is perhaps the strategy most palatable to educators who are concerned about the misuse of behavioral strategies. A particular behavior is said to be positively reinforced when the behavior is followed by the presentation of a reward (e.g., praise, stickers) that results in increased frequency of the particular behavior (Schloss & Smith, 1998). For example, Stella has been reluctant to wash her hands before lunch. Mrs. Johnson be-

gins consistently praising Stella when she washes her hands by saying, "Now your hands are nice and clean and ready for lunch!" Stella becomes more likely to wash her hands without protest. In this case, we can say that Stella's handwashing behavior has been positively reinforced.

Most frequently, positive reinforcement strategies are used to teach, maintain, or strengthen a variety of behaviors (Zirpoli, 1995). Although some early childhood teachers may be reluctant to endorse the use of reinforcement, they often unknowingly employ reinforcement strategies every day in their classroom (Henderick, 1998; Wolery, 1994).

Types of Reinforcers

Reinforcers frequently used by teachers generally fall within one of three categories: social, activity, or tangible (see Table 1). These three categories can be viewed along a continuum ranging from least to most intrusive. Social reinforcers are the least intrusive, in that they mimic the natural consequences of positive, prosocial behavior. At the other end of the continuum are tangible reinforcers. Tangible reinforcers involve the introduction of rewards that ordinarily may not be part of the routine. In selecting a reinforcer, the goal is to select the least intrusive reinforcer that is likely to be effective. If reinforcers other than social ones are necessary, teachers should develop a plan to move gradually toward social reinforcers. The following sections describe each category of reinforcers and how they can be used effectively within the context of developmentally appropriate practice.

Table 1

Examples of Social, Activity, and Tangible Reinforcers in the Early Childhood Setting

Social	Activity	Tangible
Praise	Extra playground time	Stickers
Smile	A special recording or tape	Prizes
Hugs	A party	Trinkets
Pat on back	Tablewasher or other desirable privilege	Tokens
Light squeeze on shoulder	Playing with an intriguing new toy	

Intangible- -Tangible

Social reinforcers. Teachers employ social reinforcers when they use interpersonal interactions to reinforce behaviors (Schloss & Smith, 1998). Some commonly used social reinforcers include positive nonverbal behaviors (e.g., smiling) and praise (Alberto & Troutman, 1990; Sulzer-Azaroff & Mayer, 1991). Because they are convenient, practical, and can be highly effective, social reinforcers are the most widely accepted and frequently used type of reinforcer in the early childhood classroom (Sulzer-Azaroff & Mayer, 1991). One means of effectively reinforcing a child's behavior via social reinforcement is by using a "positive personal message" (Gordon, 1974; Kostelnik, Stein, Whiren, & Soderman, 1998). For example, Ms. Tarrant says, "Sally, you put the caps back on the markers. I'm pleased. Now the markers won't get dried up. They'll be fresh and ready when someone else wants to use them." This positive personal message reminds Sally of the rule (put the caps on the markers) at a time when Sally has clear and immediate proof that she is able to follow the rule. The personal message pinpoints a specific desirable behavior, and lets the child know why the behavior is appropriate. When used appropriately, social reinforcers have been shown to enhance children's self-esteem (Sulzer-Azaroff & Mayer, 1991). When used in tandem with less natural (e.g., tangible) reinforcers, social reinforcers have been shown to enhance the power of those less natural reinforcers (Sulzer-Azaroff & Mayer, 1991).

Many early childhood teachers have concerns about the use of tangible reinforcers and believe that they cannot be used appropriately in the early childhood classroom.

Of the various types of social reinforcers, praise is used most frequently and deliberately by teachers (Alberto & Troutman, 1990). In recent years, several articles have been published on the topic of praise (Hitz & Driscoll, 1988; Marshall, 1995; Van der Wilt, 1996). While praise has the potential to enhance children's self-esteem, research has demonstrated that certain kinds of praise may actually lower children's self-confidence, inhibit achievement, and make children reliant on external (as opposed to internal) controls (Kamii, 1984; Stringer & Hurt, 1981, as cited in Hitz & Driscoll, 1988). These authors have drawn distinctions between "effective praise" (sometimes called "encouragement") and "ineffective praise." Effective praise is consistent with commonly held goals of early childhood education: promoting children's positive self-concept, autonomy, self-reliance, and motivation for learning (Hitz & Driscoll, 1988).

Effective praise is specific. Instead of saying, "Justin, what a lovely job you did cleaning up the blocks," Mrs. Constanz says, "Justin, you put each block in its place on the shelf." In this case, Mrs. Constanz leaves judgment about the *quality* of the effort to the child. By pinpointing specific aspects of the child's behavior or product (rather than using vague, general praise), Mrs. Constanz communicates that she has paid attention to, and is genuinely interested in, what the child has done (Hitz & Driscoll, 1988).

Effective praise generally is delivered privately. Public uses of praise, such as, "I like the way Carlos is sitting so quietly," have a variety of disadvantages. Such statements are typically intended to manipulate children into following another child's example. In the example, the message was, "Carlos is doing a better job of sitting than are the rest of you." With time, young children may come to resent this management, and resent a child who is the frequent recipient of such public praise (Chandler, 1981; Gordon, 1974). As an alternative, the teacher could whisper the statement quietly to Carlos, and/or say to the other children, "Think about what you need to do to be ready to listen." As individual children comply, the teacher may quickly acknowledge each child, "Caitlin is ready, Tyler is ready; thank you, Nicholas, Lakeesha, and Ali..." (Marshall, 1995).

Another characteristic of effective praise is that it emphasizes improvement of process, rather than the finished product. As Daryl passes out individual placemats to his classmates, he states their names. Mrs. Thompson says, "Daryl, you are learning more names. You remembered Tom and Peg today." She could have said, "Daryl, you are a great rememberer," but she chose not to, because Daryl knows that he did not remember everyone's name, and tomorrow he may forget some that he knew today. In this example, Mrs. Thompson's praise is specific and is focused on the individual child's improvement.

Activity reinforcers. Teachers employ activity reinforcers when they use access to a pleasurable activity as a reinforcer (Sulzer-Azaroff & Mayer, 1991). Some commonly used and effective activity reinforcers include doing a special project, being a classroom helper, and having extra free-choice time (Sulzer-Azaroff & Mayer, 1991). When using activity reinforcers, teachers create a schedule in which an enjoyable activity follows the behavior they are trying to change or modify (Sulzer-Azaroff & Mayer, 1991). Teachers often use such activity reinforcers unknowingly. Following social reinforcers, activity reinforcers are the most frequently used (Alberto & Troutman, 1990), probably because teachers view them as more convenient and less intrusive than tangible reinforcers (Sulzer-Azaroff & Mayer, 1991). When used appropriately, activity reinforcers can modify a wide variety of be-

Figure 2

Guidelines for Using Reinforcers

Reinforcers are unique to an individual. There are no universal reinforcers. What one child finds reinforcing another child may not. Therefore, teachers must consider each child's interests when selecting appropriate reinforcers.

Reinforcers must be perceived by children as being worth the time and energy it takes to achieve them. In other words, the reinforcer must be more desirable to the child than the behavior the teacher is attempting to modify.

Teacher expectations must be clear to the children. Children must clearly understand what specific behaviors are expected of them and know what is required of them to earn the reinforcer.

Reinforcers must be awarded immediately after the desired behavior. If reinforcers are not awarded immediately, they will not be effective.

Use more natural reinforcers whenever possible. Teachers should first consider the least intrusive reinforcer to modify children's behavior. For example, consider social reinforcers before tangible reinforcers.

Use reinforcers less frequently when children begin to exhibit the desired behavior. Later, after the targeted behavior is modified, teachers can phase out the use of reinforcement.

haviors. The following examples illustrate the appropriate use of activity reinforcers.

> *In Miss Annie's class, a brief playground period is scheduled to follow center clean-up time. Miss Annie reminds the children that the sooner they have the centers cleaned up, the sooner they will be able to enjoy the playground. It appears that the playground time is reinforcing children's quick clean-up behavior: They consistently get the job done with little dawdling.*

> *As part of a total plan to reduce Christopher's habit of using his cupped hands to toss water out of the water table, Mrs. Jackson has told Christopher that each day he plays without throwing water out of the table, he may be table washer after snack time (which Christopher delights in doing). This strategy was implemented following efforts to help Christopher develop appropriate behavior through demonstrations and by redirecting him with water toys chosen specifically to match his interests.*

Tangible reinforcers. Teachers sometimes employ tangible reinforcers, such as stickers and prizes, to strengthen and modify behavior in the early childhood classroom. Tangible reinforcers are most often used to modify and maintain the behavior of children with severe behavior problems (Vaughn, Bos, & Schumm, 1997).

Stacey, who has mild mental retardation, is a member of Miss Hamrick's preschool class. She rarely participates during free-choice activities. Miss Hamrick has tried a variety of strategies to increase Stacey's engagement, including using effective praise, making sure a range of activity options are developmentally appropriate for Stacey, modeling appropriate behaviors, and implementing prompting strategies. None of these strategies appear to work. Aware of Stacey's love of the TV show "Barney," Miss Hamrick decides to award Barney stickers to Stacey when she actively participates. Stacey begins to participate more often in classroom activities.

One major advantage of tangible reinforcers is that they almost always guarantee quick behavioral change (Alberto & Troutman, 1990), even when other strategies (including other types of reinforcers) fail. Although the use of tangible reinforcers can be very effective, their use in early childhood classrooms has been highly controversial. Many early childhood teachers have concerns about the use of tangible reinforcers and believe that they cannot be used appropriately in the early childhood classroom. Such reinforcers often are intrusive, and their effective use requires large amounts of teacher time and commitment.

Given these disadvantages, when using tangible reinforcers teachers should gradually move toward using more intangible, less intrusive reinforcers (Henderick, 1998). Teachers can accomplish this goal by accompanying all tangible reinforcers with social reinforcers (e.g., praise). Later, as children begin to exhibit the desired behavior consistently, the teacher may begin to taper off the use of tangible reinforcers while maintaining the use of social reinforcers. Eventually, the teacher will no longer need to award tangible reinforcers after the desired behavior occurs. In time, the teacher also should be able to fade out the use of social reinforcers, and the children will begin to assume control over their own behaviors.

References

Alberto, P. A., & Troutman, A.C. (1990). *Applied behavior analysis for teachers* (3rd ed.). Columbus, OH: Merrill.

Bredekamp, S. (1987). *Developmentally appropriate practice in early childhood programs serving children from birth through age eight.* Washington, DC: National Association for the Education of Young Children.

Bredekamp, S. (1993). The relationship between early childhood education and early childhood special education: Healthy marriage or family feud? *Topics in Early Childhood Special Education, 13*(3), 258–273.

Bredekamp, S., & Copple, C. (1997). *Developmentally appropriate practice in early childhood programs* (Rev. ed.). Washington, DC: National Association for the Education of Young Children.

Carta, J. (1995). Developmentally appropriate practice: A critical analysis as applied to young children with disabilities. *Focus on Exceptional Children, 27*(8), 1–14.

Carta, J. J., Atwater, J. B., Schwartz, I. S., & McConnell, S. R. (1993). Developmentally appropriate practices and early childhood special education: A reaction to Johnson & McChesney Johnson. *Topics in Special Education, 13,* 243–254.

Carta, J. J., Schwartz, I. S., Atwater, J. B., & McConnell, S. R. (1991). Developmentally appropriate practice: Appraising its usefulness for young children with disabilities. *Topics in Early Childhood Special Education, 11*(1), 1–20

Chandler, T. A. (1981). What's wrong with success and praise? *Arithmetic Teacher, 29*(4), 10–12.

Gordon, T. (1974). *Teacher effectiveness training.* New York: Wyden.

Henderick, J. (1998). *Total learning: Development curriculum for the young child.* Columbus, OH: Merrill.

Hitz, R., & Driscoll, A. (1988). Praise or encouragement? *Young Children, 43*(5), 6–13.

Kamii, C. (1984). The aim of education envisioned by Piaget. *Phi Delta Kappan, 65*(6), 410–415.

Kazdin, A. E. (1994). *Behavior modification in applied settings* (5th ed.). Pacific Grove, CA: Brooks/Cole.

Kostelnik, M. J., Stein, L. C., Whiren, A. P., & Soderman, A. K. (1998). *Guiding children's social development* (2nd ed.). New York: Delmar.

Marshall, H. H. (1995). Beyond "I like the way…" *Young Children, 50*(2), 26–28.

Peters, D., Neisworth, J. T., & Yawkey, T. D. (1985). *Early childhood education: From theory to practice.* Monterey, CA: Brooks/Cole.

Rodd, J. (1996). *Understanding young children's behavior: A guide for early childhood professionals.* New York: Teachers College Press.

Schloss, P. J., & Smith, M. A. (1998). *Applied behavior analyses in the classroom* (Rev. ed.). Boston: Allyn and Bacon.

Strain, P. S., McConnell, S. R., Carta, J. J., Fowler, S. A., Neisworth, J. T., & Wolery, M. (1992). Behaviorism in early intervention. *Topics in Early Childhood Special Education, 12*(1), 121–141.

Sulzer-Azaroff, B., & Mayer, G. R. (1991). *Behavior analysis for lasting change.* New York: Harcourt Brace.

Thomas, S. B., & Russo, C. J. (1995). *Special education law: Issues and implications for the 90's.* Topeka, KS: National Organization on Legal Problems of Education.

Van der Wilt, J. (1996). Beyond stickers and popcorn parties. *Dimensions of Early Childhood, 24*(1), 17–20.

Vaughn, S., Bos, C. S., & Schumm, J. S. (1997). *Teaching mainstreamed, diverse, and at-risk students in the general education classroom.* Boston: Allyn and Bacon.

Wolery, M. (1994). *Including children with special needs in early childhood programs.* Washington, DC: National Association for the Education of Young Children.

Wolery, M., & Bredekamp, S. (1994). Developmentally appropriate practices and young children with disabilities: Contextual issues in the discussion. *Journal of Early Intervention, 18,* 331–341.

Wolery, M., Strain, P. S., & Bailey, D. (1992). Reaching potentials of children with special needs. In S. Bredekamp & T. Rosegrant (Eds.), *Reaching potentials: Appropriate curriculum and assessment for young children. Vol. 1* (pp. 92–111). Washington, DC: National Association for the Education of Young Children.

Wolery, M., Werts, M. G., & Holcombe-Ligon, A. (1994). Current practices with young children who have disabilities: Issues in placement, assessment and instruction. *Focus on Exceptional Children, 26*(6), 1–12.

Wolery, M., & Wilbers, J. S. (1994). Introduction to the inclusion of young children with special needs in early childhood programs. In M. Wolery & J. S. Wilbers (Eds.), *Including children with special needs in early childhood programs* (pp. 1–22). Washington, DC: National Association for the Education of Young Children.

Zirpoli, T. J. (1995). *Understanding and affecting the behavior of young children.* Englewood Cliffs, NJ: Merrill.

Tashawna K. Duncan is a doctoral candidate, Department of Educational Psychology; Kristen M. Kemple is Associate Professor, School of Teaching and Learning; and Tina M. Smith is Assistant Professor, Department of Educational Psychology, University of Florida, Gainesville.

From *Childhood Education,* Summer 2000, pp. 194-199. Reprinted by permission of Tashawna K. Duncan, Kristen M. Kemple, Tina M. Smith, and the Association for Childhood Education International. © 2000 by ACEI.

Bullying Among Children

Most teachers are aware that bullying begins early, yet many appear to believe the myth that children "picking on" or teasing one another is a "normal" part of childhood.

Janis R. Bullock

Six-year-old Sam is barely eating. When asked by his dad what is wrong, he bursts into tears. "The kids at school keep calling me a nerd, and they poke and push me," he sobs.

"There's a kid at school no one likes," 7-year-old Anika shares with her parents. "We all tease her a lot. She is a total dork. I would never invite her to my birthday party."

Bullying is a very old phenomenon; European researchers have studied its effects for decades (Olweus, 1991). Until recently, however, the issue has received less attention from researchers in the United States, perhaps because of the prevailing belief that bullying among children is inevitable. Considering that bullying often is a sign that aggressive or violent behavior is present elsewhere in children's lives—young children may be acting out at school what they have observed and learned in the home—and the fact that bullying among primary school-age children is now recognized as an antecedent to progressively more violent behavior in later grades (Saufler & Gagne, 2000), it behooves teachers to take notice.

Unfortunately, teachers have differing attitudes toward children who bully. Most teachers are aware that bullying begins early, yet many appear to believe the myth that children "picking on" or teasing one another is a "normal" part of childhood. They also may believe that these conflicts are best resolved by the children themselves. Consequently, some teachers do not intervene.

CHARACTERISTICS OF BULLIES AND THEIR VICTIMS

Bullying refers to repeated, unprovoked, harmful actions by one child or children against another. The acts may be physical or psychological. Physical, or direct, bullying includes hitting, kicking, pushing, grabbing toys from other children, and engaging in very rough and intimidating play. Psychological bullying includes name calling, making faces, teasing, taunting, and making threats. Indirect, or less obvious and less visible, bullying includes exclusion and rejection of children from a group (Olweus, 1991).

Children who bully are impulsive, dominate others, and show little empathy. They display what Olweus (1991) defines as an "aggressive personality pattern combined with physical strength" (p. 425). Without intervention, the frequency and severity of the bullying behaviors may increase. Even more disturbing, it appears that the patterns of bullying learned in the early years can set children on a course of violence later in life (Batsche & Knoff, 1994; Baumeister, 2001).

Although a longstanding characterization of children who bully points to their low self-esteem, there is little empirical evidence to support this view. In fact, more recent research (Baumeister, 2001; Bushman & Baumeister, 1998) suggests that an inflated self-esteem increases the odds of aggressive behavior. When a bully's self-regard is seriously threatened by insults or criticisms, for example, his or her response will be more aggressive than normal. Furthermore, bullies often report that they feel powerful and superior, and justified in their actions.

Research on family dynamics suggests that many children already have learned to bully others by preschool age. Many young children who bully lack empathy and problem-solving skills, and learn from their parents to hit back in response to problems (Loeber & Dishion, 1984; Vladimir & Brubach, 2000).

Children who are bullied, on the other hand, are often younger, weaker, and more passive than the bully. They appear anxious, insecure, cautious, sensitive and quiet, and often react by crying and withdrawing. They are often lonely and lack close friendships at school. Without adult intervention, these children are likely to be bullied repeatedly, putting them at-risk for continued social rejection, depression, and impaired self-esteem (Schwartz, Dodge, & Coie, 1994). A smaller subset of these children, known as "provocative victims," have learned to respond aggressively to perceived threats by retaliating not only against the aggressor, but also against others (Olweus, 1993).

INCIDENCES OF BULLYING AMONG CHILDREN

Evidence suggests that, in the United States, the incidence of bullying among children is increasing and becoming a nationwide problem. One out of five children admits to being a bully (Noll & Carter, 1997). In general, boys engage in more physical, direct means of bullying, whereas girls engage in the more psychological and indirect bullying, such as exclusion. Roland (1989) reported that girls may be involved in bullying as much as boys, but are less willing to acknowledge their involvement. In addition, because indirect bullying is often less apparent, girls' bullying may be underestimated. Girls tend to bully less as they get older. The percentage of boys who bully, however, is similar at different age levels (Smith & Sharp, 1994).

Twenty-five to 50 percent of children report being bullied. The great majority of boys are bullied by other boys, while 60 percent of girls report being bullied by boys. Eight percent of children report staying away from school one day per month because they fear being bullied. Forty-three percent of children have a fear of being harassed in the school bathroom (Noll & Carter, 1997). Children report that many incidents of bullying occur in situations that are difficult for the teacher to monitor, such as during playground activity.

THE EFFECTS OF BULLYING ON CHILDREN

To succeed in school, children must perceive their environment as being safe, secure, and comfortable. Yet, for many children, bullying and teasing begins as soon as children first form peer groups. For some children, this is a time when patterns of victimizing and victimization become established. Consequently, the victims perceive school as a threatening place and experience adjustment difficulties, feelings of loneliness, and a desire to avoid school. These feelings may linger even when bullying ceases (Kochenderfer & Ladd, 1996).

Children desire and need interaction with peers, physical activity, and time outdoors. Consequently, they often consider outside recess to be their favorite part of the school day. Sadly, however, many children who are bullied report that problems occur on the playground and view the playground as a lonely, unhappy, and unsafe environment.

If children are fearful or feel intimidated, they cannot learn effectively. They may react by skipping school, avoiding certain areas of the school (the bathroom or the playground), or, in extreme, yet increasingly common, cases, they may bring weapons to school (Noll & Carter, 1997). Olweus (1991) reminds us that "every individual should have the right to be spared oppression and repeated, intentional humiliation in school, as in society at large" (p. 427). As early exposure to bullying can produce both immediate and delayed effects in children's ability to adjust to school, school staff need to intervene as soon as problems are detected.

RECOMMENDATIONS FOR TEACHERS TO SUPPORT CHILDREN

A comprehensive plan to address the problems of bullying and teasing must involve school personnel, teachers, children, and families. Intervention must occur on three levels: school-wide, in specific classrooms, and with individuals.

School-wide Intervention

School personnel must recognize the pervasiveness of bullying and teasing and its detrimental effects on children's development. Inservice training can be developed that outlines a clear policy statement against bullying and intervention strategies for addressing it. The school also can develop a comprehensive plan geared to teach children prosocial behaviors and skills. The children may be involved in the development of such policies and strategies, providing their input on what behavior is appropriate and identifying sanctions against bullies (Lickona, 2000; Olweus, 1997).

School personnel could enlist families' support and involvement by sharing details of the policy through parent-teacher conferences and newsletters. Families need to be aware of the specific sanctions that will be imposed on children who bully, and they need opportunities to offer feedback and suggestions. It is important to encourage parents to talk with their children about bullying. Children who are bullied often believe that their parents are unaware of the situation, and that their concerns are not being addressed or discussed. Children *do* want adults to intervene, however (Gropper & Froschl, 1999). If families are kept informed, they can work as a "team member" with school counselors and teachers to change the school environment.

Additional sources of school-wide support for children who are bullied and teased may be developed, including mentoring programs. Teachers can identify children who need support, and find them a mentor. Children may feel more at ease and less anxious when they have a "buddy," such as an older student, who can help intervene (Noll & Carter, 1997). Counselors at one elementary school selected, trained, and supervised high school students to teach the younger children how to deal with bullying and harassment. After implementation of this program, the teachers observed a decline in reports of harassment (Frieman & Frieman, 2000).

Bullying frequently occurs on the playground (Whitney, Rivers, Smith, & Sharp, 1994), yet many children believe that teachers do little to stop it. Consequently, "play-time... is more of a prison sentence than an opportunity to play and socialize" (Slee, 1995, p. 326). Therefore, school personnel may need to review playground design and space, children's access to these spaces, teacher supervision, and the role of the school in early intervention on the playground (Lambert, 1999). Yard monitors and lunch time supervisors can be trained to watch for signs of bullying. In addition, children can be asked to identify those places where bullying most frequently occurs.

Intervention in Specific Classrooms

Clearly, bullying and hurtful teasing affects children's ability to learn and enjoy play, as well as the teacher's ability to teach. Within the classroom, teachers can begin addressing the problem by creating times for children to talk about their concerns. Interestingly, one study showed that when children ages 5 to 7 years of age were asked about assisting someone who was being bullied, 37 percent replied that it was none of their business to help (Slee & Rigby, 1994).

Teachers can ask children to talk about what makes them feel unsafe or unwelcome in school. The teacher then can make a list of the children's responses, discuss them (e.g., "I don't like it when someone hits me or calls me a name"), and create corresponding rules (e.g., "Hitting and name calling are not allowed in the classroom"). When necessary, the discussions can be continued during class meetings so that the rules can be reviewed, revised, and updated. The teacher can also show children what to do to help themselves or other children, and remind them of the consequences of breaking the rules. Teachers can reduce children's anxiety by setting firm limits on unacceptable behavior (Froschl & Sprung, 1999).

If the bullying continues, teachers may need to make referrals to school counselors who will work with children, either individually or in groups, to talk about concerns, discuss solutions and options, and give suggestions on how to form friendships. Children without close friends are more likely to be victimized and may benefit from specific suggestions for building friendships (e.g., invite a friend to your house, work together on a school project, share a common interest, play a favorite game together).

Certain types of curricula, especially those that provide opportunities for cooperative learning experiences, may make bullying less likely to flourish. Children need to be engaged in worthwhile, authentic learning activities that encourage their interests and abilities (Katz, 1993). When they are intellectually motivated, they are less likely to bully. For example, project work (Katz & Chard, 2000) involves children's in-depth investigations into topics of their own choosing. As they explore events and objects around them in the classroom, in the school yard, in the neighborhood, and in the community, they learn to cooperate, collaborate, and share responsibilities. Project work can be complemented by noncompetitive games, role playing, and dramatization to raise awareness of bullying and increase empathy for those who experience it. Some teachers use children's literature to help create caring and peaceful classrooms (Morris, Taylor, & Wilson, 2000).

Intervention With Individuals

Developing both immediate and long-term strategies for identifying and working with bullies may be necessary. When teachers observe an incident of bullying, they can intervene by asking the bully to consider the consequences of his or her actions and think about how others feel. By talking calmly, yet firmly, to the bully, the teacher can make it clear that such behavior is unacceptable. Teachers can show the bully alternate ways to talk, interact, and negotiate; at the same time, they can encourage victims to assert themselves. By doing so, the teacher is showing the bully and the victim that action is being taken to stop the bullying. Acting promptly can prevent the bullying from escalating.

When interacting with children on a one-on-one basis, teachers should provide encouragement that acknowledges specific attributes, rather than dispensing general praise, approval, or admiration ("I am so glad that you have done a great job; it is wonderful; yours is one of the best projects") that may appear to be contrived. Expressions of specific encouragement ("You seem to be pleased and very interested in your project, and it appears you have worked on it for many days and used many resources to find answers to your questions"), as opposed to general praise, are descriptive, sincere, take place in private, focus on the process, and help children to develop an appreciation for their efforts and work. While developing children's self-esteem is a worthwhile goal, false praise may instead promote narcissism and unrealistic self-regard. Teachers should avoid encouraging children to think highly of themselves when they have not earned it (Baumeister, 2001; Hitz & Driscoll, 1988).

Additional long-term strategies may include encouraging children to resolve their own problems and using peers to mediate between bullies and their targets. Furthermore, teachers can spend time helping children to form ties with peers who can offer protection, support, security, and safety, thus helping to reduce children's exposure to bullying (Kochenderfer & Ladd, 1997; Ladd, Kochenderfer, & Coleman, 1996).

SUMMARY

Bullying and teasing are an unfortunate part of too many children's lives, leading to trouble for both bullies and their victims. Children who are bullied come to believe that school is unsafe and that children are mean. They may develop low self-esteem and experience loneliness. Children who continue to bully will have difficulty developing and maintaining positive relationships. A comprehensive intervention plan that addresses the needs of the school, the classroom, teachers, children, and families can be developed and implemented to ensure that all children learn in a supportive and safe environment.

References

Batsche, G. M., & Knoff, H. M. (1994). Bullies and their victims: Understanding a pervasive problem in the schools. *School Psychology Review, 23*, 165–174.

Baumeister, R. (2001). Violent pride: Do people turn violent because of self-hate, or self-love? *Scientific American, 284*, 96–101.

Bushman, B. J., & Baumeister, R. F. (1998). Threatened egotism, narcissism, self-esteem, and direct and displaced aggression: Does self-love or self-hate lead to violence? *Journal of Personality and Social Psychology, 75*, 219–229.

Frieman, M., & Frieman, B. B. (2000). *Reducing harassment in elementary school classrooms using high school mentors.* (ERIC Document Reproduction Service No. ED 439 797).

Froschl, M., & Sprung, B. (1999). On purpose: Addressing teasing and bullying in early childhood. *Young Children, 54*, 70–72.

Gropper, N., & Froschl, M. (1999). The role of gender in young children's teasing and bullying behavior. Montreal, Canada. (ERIC Document Reproduction Service No. ED 431 162).

Hitz, R., & Driscoll, A. (1988). Praise or encouragement? New insights into praise: Implications for early childhood teachers. *Young Children, 42*, 6–13.

Katz, L. G. (1993). *Distinctions between self-esteem and narcissism: Implications for practice.* Urbana, IL: ERIC Clearinghouse on Elementary and Early Childhood Education.

Katz, L., & Chard, S. (2000). *Engaging children's minds: The project approach* (2nd ed.). Stamford, CT: Ablex.

Kochenderfer, B. J., & Ladd, G. W. (1996). Peer victimization: Cause or consequence of school maladjustment? *Child Development, 67*, 1305–1317.

Kochenderfer, B. J., & Ladd, G. W. (1997). Victimized children's responses to peers' aggression: Behaviors associated with reduced versus continued victimization. *Development and Psychopathology, 9*, 59–73.

Ladd, G. W., Kochenderfer, B. J., & Coleman, C. (1996). Friendship quality as a predictor of young children's early school adjustment. *Child Development, 67*, 1103–1118.

Lambert, E. B. (1999). Do school playgrounds trigger playground bullying? *Canadian Children, 42*, 25–31.

Lickona, T. (2000). Sticks and stones may break my bones AND names WILL hurt me. Thirteen ways to prevent peer cruelty. *Our Children, 26*, 12–14.

Loeber, R., & Dishion, T. J. (1984). Boys who fight at home and school: Family conditions influencing cross-setting consistency. *Journal of Consulting and Clinical Psychology, 52*, 759–768.

Morris, V. G., Taylor, S. I., & Wilson, J. T. (2000). Using children's stories to promote peace in classrooms. *Early Childhood Education Journal, 28*, 41–50.

Noll, K., & Carter, J. (1997). *Taking the bully by the horns.* Reading, PA: Unicorn Press.

Olweus, D. (1991). Bully/victim problems among schoolchildren: Basic facts and effects of a school based intervention program. In D. J. Pepler & K. H. Rubin (Eds.), *The development and treatment of childhood aggression* (pp. 441–448). Hillsdale, NJ: Lawrence Erlbaum.

Olweus, D. (1993). Victimization by peers: Antecedents and long-term outcomes. In K. H. Rubin & J. B. Asendorf (Eds.), *Social withdrawal, inhibition, and shyness in childhood* (pp. 315–341). Hillsdale, NJ: Lawrence Erlbaum.

Olweus, D. (1997). Bully/victim problems in school: Facts and intervention. *European Journal of Psychology of Education, 12*, 495–510.

Roland, E. (1989). Bullying: The Scandinavian research tradition. In D. P. Tattum & D. A. Lane (Eds.), *Bullying in schools* (pp. 21–32). London: Trentham Books.

Saufler, C., & Gagne, C. (2000). *Maine project against bullying. Final report.* Augusta, ME: Maine State Department of Education. (ERIC Document Reproduction Service No. ED 447 911).

Schwartz, D., Dodge, K. A., & Coie, J. D. (1994). The emergence of chronic peer victimization in boys' play groups. *Child Development, 64*, 1755–1772.

Slee, P.T. (1995). Bullying in the playground: The impact of interpersonal violence on Australian children's perceptions of their play environment. *Children's Environments, 12*, 320–327.

Slee, P. T., & Rigby, K. (1994). Peer victimisation at school. *AECA Australian Journal of Early Education, 19*, 3–10.

Smith, P. K., & Sharp, S. (1994). The problem of school bullying. In P. K. Smith & S. Sharp (Eds.), *School bullying* (pp. 1–19). London: Routledge.

Vladimir, N., & Brubach, A. (2000). *Teasing among school-aged children.* (ERIC Document Reproduction Service No. 446 321).

Whitney, I., Rivers, I., Smith, P. K., & Sharp, S. (1994). The Sheffield project: Methodology and findings. In P. K. Smith & S. Sharp (Eds.), *School bullying* (pp. 20–56). London: Routledge.

Janis R. Bullock is Professor, Early Childhood Education, Department of Health and Human Development, Montana State University, Bozeman.

From *Childhood Education*, Spring 2002, pp. 130-133 with permission of the author. © 2002 by the Association for Childhood Education International.

Use the Environment to Prevent Discipline Problems and Support Learning

Nancy Ratcliff

Good teachers are familiar with many ways to address discipline problems in the classroom. When young children exhibit aggressive behaviors, we look for the possible reasons and help children learn appropriate behaviors using behavioral techniques, positive reinforcement, and other supportive strategies.

An organized and well-thought-out classroom and the structure of activities, the daily schedule, routines, and transitions can help prevent discipline problems.

We realize that in some situations there are no easy answers or quick solutions to discipline problems. But two important areas are often overlooked: the physical and programmatic environments. An organized and well-thought-out classroom and the structure of activities, the daily schedule, routines, and transitions can help prevent discipline problems.

Here are eight points that may be familiar to experienced teachers but are worth reviewing from time to time. For quick reference and ongoing assessment, teachers can use the "Checklist for Supporting Positive Behaviors."

The physical environment

1. Design clearly defined activity areas and pathways that minimize crowding.

Research shows that placing young children in relatively small areas may increase aggressive behavior (McGrew 1972). More accidental physical encounters—head bumping and fingers getting stepped on—occur in crowded areas, and children's play and/or creations can be interrupted or accidentally destroyed. Young children often don't see a difference between accidental and intentional actions and respond with aggression (Gump 1975).

Establishing clearly defined learning areas and pathways is relatively easy. Shelving units are the most practical solution—solid barriers and great storage. Stacked milk crates, even sturdy cardboard boxes, also work.

2. Provide adequate space for each interest area.

Consider the nature of the activities that take place in each area. If crowded, the block, dramatic play, and art areas tend to create a higher number of aggressive behaviors. A minimum 10-by-12-square-foot area is best for those areas. In classrooms that do not accommodate areas of this size, teachers need to determine the number of children who can safely work in each area at one time. They should discuss with the children the reasons for any limits; children are more likely to follow rules when they understand the rationale and help set them.

3. Monitor potential problem areas.

Teachers of young children understand the importance of proper supervision throughout the day, yet they can't be everywhere every minute of the day. One effective strategy is to identify the classroom areas in which aggressive behavior occurs most frequently and then carefully monitor those areas during playtime. The block, dramatic play, and woodworking centers typically produce more numerous and intense instances of

Checklist for Supporting Positive Behaviors		
Strategy	**Yes/No**	**Notes**
Physical environment		
1. Design clearly defined areas		
Interest areas		
Group meeting time		
Pathways		
2. Provide adequate space for interest areas		
Set limits of number of children using area		
Discuss rules with children		
3. Monitor potential problem areas		
Blocks		
Dramatic play		
Sand/water play		
Woodworking		
Other		
4. Maintain relaxed, calm, interesting environment		
Engaging activities every day		
Images/words at eye level		
Materials on low, open shelves		
Neatly organized items		
Labeled shelves and containers		
Programmatic environment		
5. Assess structure of activities		
Open-ended activities		
Balance between unstructured/structured activities		
6. Follow age-appropriate schedule		
Alternate active and quiet times		
Group times short		
Group times spread throughout the day		
Children's cues used to assess group time limits		
Adequate choice time		
7. Establish routines		
Consistent yet flexible		
No wait times		
Posted schedule with pictures and words		
8. Plan transitions		
Use consistent signal for end of choice time		
Allow 5 or more minutes for ending activities/cleanup		
Give verbal warning to all children		
Plan and use transitions every day		

aggressive behavior, probably because of the high levels of interaction within these areas (Shapiro 1975; Rubin 1977; Quay, Weaver, & Neal 1986). Positioning an adult within close proximity of these areas ensures quick response, and many situations can be diffused. While intervening, teachers can help children learn to express feelings, solve problems, and resolve conflicts through positive, peaceful means. Once children have had many opportunities to practice these skills, the close proximity of an adult can prevent aggressive behaviors from occurring at all.

4. Maintain a relaxed, calm, and interesting environment.

The physical arrangement of the classroom helps set a tone that states this is a place where children are welcomed and valued. Children are more likely to be helpful and cooperative if they are relaxed and engaged in interesting activities (Eisenberg & Mussen 1989). The classroom should be inviting and attractive. Children's work—words and images—are at their eye level. Materials are easily accessible, organized neatly on low, open shelves, encouraging children to explore all the interest areas. Labels clearly showing where items belong encourage children to replace materials with minimal adult supervision and decrease conflicts during cleanup time.

The progammatic environment

Once the physical aspects of the environment are addressed, teachers must assess the *programmatic environment*. They should look at the structure of activities, the daily schedule, classroom routines, and transitions.

5. Assess the structure of activities offered throughout the day.

The level of structure within a program can contribute to aggressive behaviors in the classroom. Highly structured programs provide limited opportunities for children to develop self-control, engage in cooperative behavior, or make informed decisions. To promote positive social skills, programs must give children

opportunities to engage in many open-ended activities. However, teachers must be aware that, while these activities promote social interaction and prosocial behaviors, they may also create higher levels of assertiveness and aggressive behavior (Huston-Stein, Friedrich-Cofer, & Susman 1977). Teachers must be prepared to effectively deal with conflicts. A program designed with a balance of unstructured and structured activities, in which problem-solving strategies are used to address conflicts, provides the opportunities children need to develop self-control and self-discipline.

6. Follow a schedule appropriate for the age group.

Some young children can easily become overstimulated or bored, which contributes to the potential for aggressive behavior. Teachers should carefully assess the daily schedule to determine if it allows for alternating periods of active and quiet time. Group times should be relatively short and interspersed throughout the day. Teachers can assess the time limit for group times by picking up on clues provided by the children. When children become distracted or "antsy," it is time to wrap up the activity. A beginning point is 10 to 15 minutes for most children ages three to five. The time can be increased as children demonstrate their ability to focus for longer periods of time.

Another important scheduling aspect is planning for choice time. Substantial periods of time, a *minimum* of one hour, should be set aside for children to engage in activities of their own choosing, exploring and learning about their environment (Slaby et al. 1995; Bredekamp & Copple 1997).

7. Establish classroom routines.

An appropriate daily schedule, with consistent routines and well-planned transitions that eliminate wait time, helps create a positive classroom climate. A schedule that is consistent, yet flexible enough to meet the needs and interests of the children, can help reduce aggressive behavior. A visual representation of the schedule—with pictures and words depicting the activities and times—should

be displayed and referred to. Teachers can easily make references to the schedule throughout the day. For example, at the conclusion of storytime, the teacher may point to the appropriate picture on the schedule and ask children what activity happens next.

8. Plan transitions to signal the end to activities.

Although a visual representation of the schedule helps children know the sequence of daily activities, most young children are unable to understand the amount of time allocated for an activity. Therefore, teachers should provide a signal that activities are about to end. This signal gives children the opportunity to end one activity and to prepare for another. For example, "We have time to sing one more song before getting ready to go outside." "It is almost time for lunch. We have time for two more people to share." "Before we start planning for activity time, we need to take the lunch count."

A warning is especially important before the end of choice times so children can complete or store their projects, put away toys and materials, and prepare to move to the next activity in a calm manner. It also demonstrates to the children the teacher's respect for their work and the need to plan ahead (Slaby et al. 1995).

Warning cues and styles vary from teacher to teacher. Good teachers know their children: how much time they need for cleanup and for getting centered before moving on to the next activity. A minimum of five minutes is recommended—more if necessary.

The most effective closing technique is walking around the room, interacting with each child or group of children and reminding them that only five minutes remain for the activity. A timer or musical signal reinforces the message. Sometimes it helps if teachers ask children to acknowledge the fact they have heard the warning and understand that the end of playtime is near. It is also a good idea to be flexible when possible, allowing a child to complete a thoroughly engaging activity while the rest of the group moves on.

Carefully assessing the physical and programmatic environment and taking preventative measures can help alleviate some aggressive behaviors in the classroom. Time, consistency, and the presence of caring adults are the critical components necessary for helping young children develop self-discipline.

References

Bredekamp, S., & C. Copple, eds. 1997. *Developmentally appropriate practice in early childhood programs*. Rev. ed. Washington, DC: NAEYC.

Eisenberg, N., & P.H. Mussen. 1989. *The roots of prosocial behavior in children*. New York: Cambridge University Press.

Gump, P.V. 1975. Ecological psychology and children. In *Review of child development research*, vol. 5, ed. E. M. Hetherington, 75–126. Chicago: University of Chicago Press.

Huston-Stein, A.C., L. Friedrich-Cofer, E. J. Susman. 1977. The relationship of classroom structure to social behavior, imaginative play, and self-regulation of economically disadvantaged children. *Child Development* 48: 908–16.

McGrew, W.C. 1972. Aspects of social development in nursery school children with emphasis on introduction to the group. In *Ethnological studies of child behavior*, ed. N.B. Hones, 129–56, New York: Cambridge University Press.

Quay, L.C., J. H. Weaver, & J. H. Neal, 1986. The effects of play materials on positive and negative social behaviors in preschool boys and girls. *Child Study Journal* 16 (1): 67–76.

Rubin, K.H. 1977. The social and cognitive value of toys and activities. *Canadian Journal of Behavioral Sciences* 9: 382–85.

Shapiro, S. 1975. Some classroom ABC's: Research takes a closer look. *Elementary School Journal* 75: 436–41.

Slaby, R.G., W.C. Roedell, D, Arezzo, & K. Hendrix. 1995. *Early violence prevention: Tools for teachers of young children*. Washington, DC: NAEYC.

Nancy Ratcliff, Ph.D., *is an assistant professor of early childhood education at the University of South Florida in Tampa. Her research focuses on early childhood teacher licensure and preservice teacher portfolio assessment. Nancy taught in public school for 12 years before entering the teacher education field.*

Helping Children Cope With Stress in the Classroom Setting

Stress is part of even the youngest students' lives, making the concept of a carefree childhood nearly obsolete.

Karen Fallin, Charlotte Wallinga, and Mick Coleman

Ten-year-old Sheila lives with her mother and 7-year-old brother in a middle-class neighborhood. Although Sheila usually receives good grades in school she becomes very anxious prior to a big test or project. She has a few friends, but frequently has disagreements with them. In fact, she is considered unpopular and is occasionally taunted at school. At the end of each school day, Sheila and her brother go home to an empty house, where they are usually alone for an hour or two. On the days their mother works late, Sheila and her brother may be alone for up to four hours, and Sheila is responsible for preparing dinner.

Although faced with numerous stressors, Sheila has only a few coping strategies at her disposal, none of which are very effective. For example, Sheila starts fights when she has trouble getting along with her classmates. She uses television as an escape from the pressures of schoolwork or being alone at home. As a result, Sheila usually gets a late start on her assignments, and subsequently stays up past her normal bedtime to complete her work. She becomes tired and irritable, making it difficult for her to pay attention the next day in class or to get along with her peers and teachers.

Like Sheila, many school-age children are subject to school-related stressors such as failing grades, overly demanding classroom environments, athletic requirements, peer relationships, tests, and conflicts with teachers (Jewett, 1997; Romano, 1997; Scherer, 1996; Sears & Milburn, 1990). Stress is part of even the youngest students' lives, making the concept of a carefree childhood nearly obsolete (Large, 1999). Teachers witness many of these stressors and their effects on the classroom. Academic problems, behavioral problems, children's complaints of stomachaches or headaches, and drug use all may be related to excessive levels of stress in children's lives (Omizo, Omizo, & Suzuki, 1988; Ryan-Wenger & Copeland, 1994).

Various theoretical models explain stress and its effects on individuals. None of these models, however, deals explicitly with childhood stress. One popular model, the cognitive-transactional model, does provide a convincing means of describing children's experiences with stress (e.g., Atkins & Krantz, 1993; Ryan-Wenger & Copeland, 1994; Sharrer & Ryan-Wenger, 1991; Sorensen, 1994).

Key Concepts of the Cognitive-Transactional Model

Within the cognitive-transactional model people and their environments are thought to be "engaged in a dynamic, mutually reciprocal, bi-directional relationship" (Lazarus & Folkman, 1984b, p. 289). Environmental stimuli evoke cognitive, affective, and behavioral responses, which then influence the environment. A person's thoughts, emotions, and actions change as a stressful encounter progresses. His or her appraisal of the situation consequently determines the choice of coping actions.

Daily Stressors and Cognitive Appraisal

A stressor is "any event in which environmental demands, internal demands, or both tax or exceed the adaptive resources of an individual, social system, or tissue system" (Monat & Lazarus, 1985, p. 3). Stressors may be divided into major life events (e.g., the death of a parent or the birth of sibling), chronic strain (e.g., living in poverty, ongoing abuse, or chronic illness), and daily stressors (e.g., taking a test or arguing with a sibling) (Haggerty, 1986; Trad & Greenblatt, 1990). This article focuses on daily stressors. Daily stressors are "the irritating, frustrating, distressing demands that to some degree characterize everyday transactions with the environment" (Kanner, Coyne, Schaefer, & Lazarus, 1981, p. 3). For the school-age child, daily stressors may include anxiety about school, conflicts with teachers, competition with peers or siblings, lack of parental interest, personal injury or loss, poor grades, fear of success or failure, and fear of medical visits and procedures (Dickey & Henderson, 1989; Sears & Milburn, 1990). Other stressors reported among school-age children include fear of negative evaluation, parental conflict or loss, unfair punishment, school work, and boredom (Atkins, 1991; Dickey & Henderson, 1989; Kanner, Feldman, Weinberger, & Ford, 1987; Lewis, Siegel, & Lewis, 1984; Spirito, Stark, Grace, & Stamoulis, 1991). The occurrence of daily stressors in childhood appears to be related to adaptational outcomes such as depression, sense of self-worth, and overall health status (Kanner et al., 1987; Siegel & Brown, 1988).

The meaning attached to a stressor varies from child to child, according to individual perceptions (often referred to as cognitive appraisals). Cognitive appraisal is a matter of determining which events are considered stressful and evaluating one's coping resources and options (Folkman, Lazarus, Dunkel-Schetter, DeLongis, & Gruen, 1986; Lazarus & Launier, 1978). Cognitive appraisal, which is influenced by situational factors (Lazarus & Folkman, 1984b), further determines the degree of psychological stress.

Coping Strategies

Coping may be defined as "efforts to master conditions of harm, threat, or challenge when a routine or automatic response is not readily available" (Monat & Lazarus, 1985, p. 5). Coping strategies refer to purposeful, cognitive, and behavioral efforts to manage stress. Some coping strategies may increase the risk of physiological arousal or maladaptation during stressful events, while others improve adaptation and reduce the risks of undesirable outcomes (Monat & Lazarus, 1985; Rutter, 1983). Children's coping strategies are affected by personal and environmental factors such as age, gender, temperament, developmental level, the environmental context in which the stressor occurs, personal resources, prior ways of coping, and personal control (Compas, 1987; Lazarus & Folkman, 1984a; Moos & Schaefer, 1993; Rutter, 1983; Sorensen, 1993).

Children use a variety of coping strategies in response to daily stressors (Beaver, 1997). Some strategies are directed at changing stressors, while others are directed at managing the *emotions* triggered by stressors. Specific examples include thinking about something else, participating in religious activities, expressing emotions, being physically active, and behaving aggressively (Atkins, 1991; Britt, 1995; Dickey & Henderson, 1989; Jewett, 1997; Ryan-Wenger, 1992, 1996). Other coping strategies frequently reported among school-age children include cognitive restructuring, problem solving, emo-

tional regulation, wishful thinking, and submission (Sorensen, 1993; Spirito et al., 1991).

Resources

Children may call upon both psychological and environmental resources, which precede and influence coping (Lazarus & Folkman, 1984b). When a stressful event occurs, children mobilize their resources in response (Lazarus & Folkman, 1984a; Lazarus & Launier, 1978). Resources "are something one draws upon, whether they are readily available to the person (e.g., money, tools, people to help, or relevant skills) or whether they exist as competencies for finding resources that are needed but not available" (Lazarus & Folkman, 1984b, p. 158). Examples of resources that affect coping are health and energy, positive beliefs, problem-solving skills, self-esteem, mastery, social skills, material resources, and social support (Lazarus & Folkman, 1984b; Pearlin & Schooler, 1978). Social support can modify the potentially negative effects of stress by either reducing the stress itself or facilitating an individual's efforts to cope (Monat & Lazarus, 1985).

Children's social support needs may be emotional (e.g., enhancing self-esteem), informational (e.g., giving advice), instrumental (e.g., providing material resources), and/or companionship (e.g., doing fun activities together) (Reid, Landesman, Treder, & Jaccard, 1989). Parents, grandparents, siblings, teachers, and friends often provide this support (Dunn, Slomkowski, & Beardsall, 1994; Furman & Buhrmester, 1985; Wasserstein & La Greca, 1996).

Suggestions for Interventions in the Classroom

Classroom teachers can play a vital role in helping students manage daily stress effectively. Because so many stressors are directly related to the school environment and because stress-related problems affect students' performance in school topics of stress and coping should be considered part of the curriculum. Lessons about stress and coping can be incorporated into various subject areas. For example, biological responses to stress can be taught in science, and skills for coping with stress and for enhancing social support can be taught in health and wellness classes. Children can read and write about stressors in language arts, and can express their feelings about stressors through artwork.

Through ongoing collaborative efforts with the school counselor, nurse, other school personnel and parents, teachers can help children learn to cope effectively with stress. By working together, sharing ideas, and combining resources, these adults will offer the best assistance to students.

Identifying Daily Stressors

Teachers should familiarize themselves with the stressors that commonly affect children, keeping in mind that what is stressful for one child may not be stressful for another child. Identifying stressors in the classroom is the first step teachers can take in helping their students manage stress. Teachers can accomplish this through graffiti boards, group discussions, and behavioral observations.

Graffiti Board. A graffiti board—a bulletin board covered with paper—can be useful for assessing stressors by providing students with an opportunity for self-expression. Label the paper with a title like "Things that are stressful for me," and encourage the children to anonymously describe their stressors. Students will feel some release by writing down their problems, and they will learn what their classmates find stressful. A graffiti board may be used in conjunction with lessons on stress and coping, especially during particularly stressful times of the school year (e.g., before the holidays or prior to important tests). In a similar technique, teachers provide a box in which children can anonymously submit stressors they would like to hear discussed in class. Teachers will gain a general sense of the types of stressors experienced by the students.

Large-group Discussion. An effective classroom dialogue could be generated by using the Feel Bad Scale, a childhood stressor instrument created by Charles Lewis and his colleagues (Lewis, Siegel & Lewis, 1984). Specifically, they recommend children could be asked these questions:

• What makes you feel bad, nervous, or worried?
• How often has this happened in the last [time frame]?
• How did this make you feel?

This questioning technique will likely elicit comparable responses from different children. It can be reassuring for children to know that their peers also find certain events to be stressful.

Some children may not be comfortable sharing their stressors in a group setting. As an alternative, have children submit written responses. Teachers then can lead a group discussion and share the students' stressors without identifying anyone. A fun activity to complement such a group discussion is to have children draw, decorate, and cut out pictures of bugs. On their pictures they can write down the things that "bug" them (i.e., their stressors) (Chenfeld, 1995).

Observations. Teachers can observe students for signs or symptoms of stress, such as regressive behaviors, withdrawal, irritability, inability to concentrate in school, and difficulty getting along with peers (O'Rourke, 1996). Other indicators include recurrent abdominal pain and frequent headaches (Ryan-Wenger & Copeland, 1994). If a teacher finds that a child is demonstrating ongoing stress-related symptoms, it may be useful to document firsthand observations and seek the observations of other school professionals. Communication with the student and parents about the observed behaviors is vital.

Responding to Daily Stressors

Having identified specific stressors, teachers should address those that cause students to feel the worst and that occur most frequently. Teachers may respond by changing stressors or by helping children to appraise stressors more positively. These interventions help shape children's cognitive appraisals of stressors, thus decreasing their stress levels.

Changing Stressors. One way to reduce the severity of stressors is to change or remove them, although this is not always possible. Educators can help a student who complains that he is bored by assignments that are too easy, for example, by providing more difficult assignments. Also, teachers may be able to intervene in peer-related stress by separating children who persistently tease or annoy one another, or who compete with one another. Sheila, the child in the opening example, could benefit from such interventions.

Changing Appraisals. Another way to reduce the severity of stressors is to help change children's perceptions of stressors. Such a process is difficult and may require the child to undergo counseling (Ryan-Wenger, 1990). Within the classroom, teachers could ask the children to role-play their perceptions of various stressful situations. Scenarios of different stressors may be read to children (e.g., "Imagine you have a spelling test the next day, but when you get home from school, you realize you have forgotten to bring your spelling book"). Children state their perceptions of such a situation and describe how it would make them feel (e.g., "My day would be ruined. I would feel like a loser for forgetting my book, and I would worry that my parents would be mad at me. I would not know how I was going to be able to study"). A group could generate alternative ways of perceiving the event (e.g., "It's not that big of a deal. Everybody forgets things. It was an honest mistake. I'm sure I can find a way to study").

Another way to alter children's appraisals of daily events is to help them focus on positive experiences. This may be accomplished by having children brainstorm the people, places, times, and events in their lives that make them happy. The teacher can facilitate the brainstorming session and write down all of the suggestions on a colorful display, which can be decorated with children's illustrations (Chenfeld, 1995).

Identifying and Facilitating Coping Strategies

Children respond to stressors with various coping strategies. Learning to cope effectively with stress may help prevent illness or reduce the chance that the child will behave inappropriately. Changing unsuccessful coping strategies appears to be a practical intervention that can be facilitated by various people. As children will most likely be more successful using techniques they are comfortable with and have had prior experience using, teachers should encourage children to identify effective strategies that they already use, rather than teach them new ones. These strategies may be identified through regular group discussions or as part of a health and wellness curriculum.

Group Discussion. Teachers can ask children the following questions, which were used in the development of the School-agers' Coping Strategies Inventory (SCSI) (Ryan, 1989):

• Think of the last thing that made you feel bad, nervous, or worried. What did you do? What made you feel better?
• When something happens that makes you feel bad, nervous, or worried, what do you usually do that helps you the most?

- What do you do that doesn't help much, but you do it anyway? (p. 114)

Children may be receptive to trying new coping strategies suggested by their classmates. In small groups, children can address a stressful scenario (e.g., "You have to take an important exam today"). Group members will be asked to think of potential coping strategies and to role-play each suggestion. The children should debate the merits of each proposed strategy as a way to encourage consideration of alternative ways to cope with actual stressors.

Teachers can help children evaluate effectiveness of the coping strategies according to two criteria. First, a strategy is effective if it helps a child to feel better (e.g., less bad, nervous, or worried). Conversely, a strategy is ineffective if it does not help a child to feel better, or if it is dangerous or unhealthful (e.g., it involves overeating or alcohol use). Teachers can emphasize the use of cognitive and problem-solving strategies for those stressors under the children's control (e.g., studying to improve bad grades or saying "I'm sorry" to a friend after a fight). For events that are beyond children's control, coping strategies that rely on distraction can be helpful (e.g., thinking about something else, reading, or watching a video). In Sheila's case, however, watching television was not an effective way of coping, as she delayed working on her school assignments.

Using Literature As a Tool. Books can be an excellent medium for teaching children about stressors and coping strategies. One such book that could be used with younger children is *Alexander and the Terrible, Horrible, No Good, Very Bad Day* (Viorst, 1972). After a classroom reading of this book, teachers can have students identify each stressor described in the book and answer the following questions:

- Did Alexander have any choice or control over this stressor?
- What is something Alexander could do to feel better or to change this stressor?
- Could this response be harmful or dangerous to Alexander or to someone else?

The ensuing classroom discussion would not only help children to identify stressors and potential coping strategies, but also teach children how to evaluate the effectiveness of their own coping strategies. Older children could use a similar approach as part of a book report assignment.

Teaching New Strategies. Children who, like Sheila, have a very limited repertoire of coping methods need to be taught new strategies. Relaxation and breathing techniques, positive imagery, and self-talk skills can be addressed in a group setting and will be helpful for those who experience anxiety before a test or an oral report. Other strategies include exercising, writing in a journal, or learning effective studying techniques. Educators may benefit from the wide variety of related books and videos, as well as workshops that teach such coping strategies (e.g., Attwell, 1994). "Children will experience less stress once they gain access to a wider range of strategies and feel more effective in their coping strategies" (Jewett, 1997, p. 173).

Enhancing Available Resources

According to the cognitive-transactional model, children with few available resources—specifically, good health and energy, self-esteem, and social support—are more likely to use ineffective coping strategies and exhibit stress-related behaviors and symptoms. Therefore, enhancing children's available resources may protect children from the most deleterious effects of stress (Smith & Carlson, 1997).

Promoting Health and Energy. To identify students who may not be healthy or energetic, teachers should consider those children who frequently visit the school nurse, are habitually absent due to illness, or regularly appear tired or malnourished. Efforts to enhance children's well-being must be family-centered. Parents may need to be educated about their child's physical and emotional needs (e.g., adequate sleep and proper nutrition) and provided linking information about outside agencies. Classroom lessons can focus on the importance of exercise, proper hygiene, and a well-balanced diet. For a group activity, children could make posters or a bulletin board about things that they do to take care of themselves.

Promoting Self-Esteem. Because of low self-esteem, some children may appear to lack confidence in their abilities to cope effectively with stressors, and consequently may need sessions with the school counselor. Teachers can do their part to raise students' self-esteem by providing children positive feedback about their unique attributes and skills, and by facilitating specific classroom activities. For example, teachers could designate a "person of the day" and ask each student to write down one thing he or she likes about that person. The teacher then compiles all of the comments and presents the chosen student with a paper filled with positive remarks from classmates. This can be done on a daily basis until each student has been the "person of the day."

In another activity, one day each week throughout the school year one child presents a brief autobiography to the class. The students should follow specific guidelines for giving such a presentation, including talking about their family, sharing their interests and talents, and writing down their favorite things. Students could keep structured journals throughout the school year—a process that can help them identify their unique characteristics and strengths. Each day, children would briefly respond to an open-ended statement (e.g., "My favorite subject at school is…," "I'm a good friend because…," "When I grow up I want to be…").

Promoting Social Support. Children who have difficulty getting along well with others often lack social support from family members and peers. To assess children's level of social support, teachers can ask them the following questions (based on Wenz-Gross & Siperstein, 1997):

- Who are the people you feel close to at home? at school? in your neighborhood? in your extended family? Are there other people you feel close to?
- When do you go to other people for support? Who do you most often turn to? How does that person help you?

Important People in Your Life

Certain things in your life can help you deal with stress. One of the most important is having people around who will help you. These people may include family members, friends, classmates, or a scout leader.

Under each heading in the following "web of support," write down the names of people you feel close to and care about.

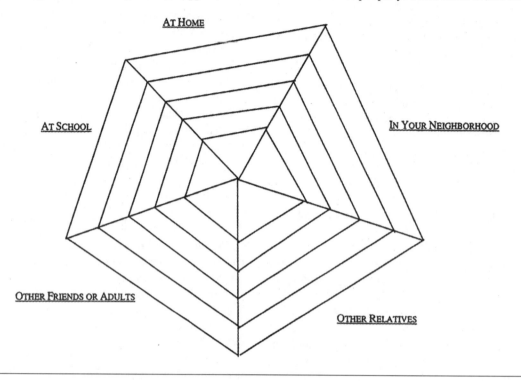

AT HOME

IN YOUR NEIGHBORHOOD

AT SCHOOL

OTHER FRIENDS OR ADULTS

OTHER RELATIVES

Figure 1
Web of Social Support

Children may be more comfortable with written, rather than oral responses. Information sheets (Fallin, 1999) can complement a discussion on social support (see Figure 1).

Children who lack adequate social support at home will need greater support from adults at school. Since peer relationships are such an important component of social support, school personnel should focus on providing opportunities for social skills training. Teachers can promote friendships by encouraging positive interactions among students, providing opportunities for children to socialize at school and promoting teamwork within the classroom setting. A friendship bulletin board is one way to encourage students to evaluate their friendships and create a supportive classroom environment. Choose a theme (e.g., "The only way to have a friend is to be one") and have students draw pictures of activities that friends do together, make a collage of friends' pictures, or write about what qualifies people want in a friend (Jones & Jones, 1990).

Summary of Interventions With Sheila

Sheila's chances for happiness and success in school are hindered by the presence of multiple stressors, her ineffective coping strategies, and inadequate resources. As indicated in

Figure 2, Sheila could benefit from many of the interventions suggested throughout this article. The first step would be to evaluate Sheila's stressors, her existing coping strategies, and available resources. The next step would be to implement specific strategies targeted at: 1) reducing Sheila's stressors or changing her appraisal of stressors, 2) teaching her effective coping strategies, and 3) enhancing her resources.

Conclusion

Classroom teachers, through collaborative efforts with other members of an education team, can be instrumental in helping students manage daily stressors effectively. Using the cognitive-transactional model as a guide, teachers can identify events that children find to be stressful, teach children effective coping strategies, and find creative ways to enhance available resources.

References

Atkins, F. D. (1991). Children's perspective of stress and coping: An integrative review. *Issues in Mental Health Nursing, 12*, 171–178.

Atkins, F. D., & Krantz, S. (1993). Stress and coping among Missouri rural and urban children. *The Journal of Rural Health, 9*, 149–156.

Attwell, A. (1994). *Expanding your child's horizons*. Tempe, AZ: Blue Bird Publishing.

Beaver, B. R. (1997). The role of emotion in children's selection of strategies for coping with daily stresses. *Merrill-Palmer Quarterly, 43*(1), 129–146.

Britt, G. C. (1995). *Children's coping with everyday stressful situations: The role played by religion.* (ERIC Microfiche Document No. ED383432)

Chenfeld, M. B. (1995). *Creative experiences for young children.* Orlando, FL: Harcourt Brace.

Compas, B. E. (1987). Coping with stress during childhood and adolescence. *Psychological Bulletin, 101,* 393–403.

Dickey, J. P., & Henderson, P. (1989). What young children say about stress and coping in school. *Health Education, 20,* 14–17.

Dunn, J., Slomkowski, C., & Beardsall, L. (1994). Sibling relationships from the preschool period through middle childhood and early adolescence. *Developmental Psychology, 30,* 315–324.

Fallin, K. R. (1999). *Stressed out? How to feel better.* Unpublished manuscript, University of Georgia at Athens.

Folkman, S., Lazarus, R. S., Dunkel-Schetter, C., DeLongis, A., & Gruen, R.J. (1986). Dynamics of a stressful encounter: Cognitive appraisal, coping, and encounter outcomes. *Journal of Personality and Social Psychology, 50,* 992–1003.

Furman, W., & Buhrmester, D. (1985). Children's perceptions of the personal relationships in their social networks. *Developmental Psychology, 21,* 1016–1024.

Haggerty, R. J. (1986). Stress and illness in children. *Bulletin of the New York Academy of Medicine, 62,* 707–718.

Jewett, J. (1997). Childhood stress. *Childhood Education, 73,* 172–173.

Jones, V. F., & Jones, L. S. (1990). *Comprehensive classroom management.* Needham Heights, MA: Allyn & Bacon.

Kanner, A. D., Coyne, J. C., Schaefer, C., & Lazarus, R. S. (1981). Comparison of two modes of stress measurement: Daily hassles and uplifts versus major life events. *Journal of Behavioral Medicine, 4,* 1–39.

Kanner, A. D., Feldman, S. S., Weinberger, D. A., & Ford, M. E. (1987). Uplifts, hassles, and adaptational outcomes in early adolescents. *Journal of Early Adolescence, 7,* 371–394.

Large, R. (1999). Easing the strain of students' stress. *NEA Today, 18*(1), 39–41.

Lazarus, R. S., & Folkman, S. (1984a). Coping and adaptation. In W. D. Gentry (Ed.), *The handbook of behavioral medicine* (pp. 282–325). New York: Guilford Press.

Lazarus, R. S., & Folkman, S. (1984b). *Stress, appraisal, and coping.* New York: Springer.

Lazarus, R. S., & Launier, R. (1978). Stress-related transactions between person and environment. In L. A. Pervin & M. Lewis (Eds.), *Perspectives in interactional psychology* (pp. 287–327). New York: Plenum Press.

Lewis, C. E., Siegel, J. M., & Lewis, M. A. (1984). Feeling bad: Exploring sources of distress among pre-adolescent children. *American Journal of Public Health, 74,* 117–122.

Monat, A., & Lazarus, R. S. (Eds.). (1985). *Stress and coping: An anthology* (2nd ed.). New York: Columbia University Press.

Moos, R. H., & Schaefer, J. A. (1993). Coping resources and processes: Current concepts and measures. In L. Goldberger & S. Breznitz (Eds.), *Handbook of stress: Theoretical and clinical aspects* (2nd ed., pp. 234–258). New York: Free Press.

Omizo, M. M., Omizo, S. A., & Suzuki, L. A. (1988). Children and stress: An exploratory study of stressors and symptoms. *The School Counselor, 35,* 267–274.

O'Rourke, K. (1996). *Support groups for children.* Washington, DC: Accelerated Development.

Pearlin, L. I., & Schooler, C. (1978). The structure of coping. *Journal of Health and Social Behavior, 19,* 2–21.

Reid, M., Landesman, S., Treder, R., & Jaccard, J. (1989). "My family and friends": Six- to twelve-year-old children's perceptions of social support. *Child Development, 60,* 896–910.

Romano, J. L. (1997). Stress and coping: A qualitative study of 4th and 5th graders. *Elementary School Guidance and Counseling, 31,* 273–282.

Rutter, M. (1983). Stress, coping, and development: Some issues and some questions. In N. Garmezy & M. Rutter (Eds.), *Stress, coping, and development in children* (pp. 1–41). New York: McGraw-Hill.

Ryan, N. M. (1989). Stress-coping strategies identified from school age children's perspective. *Research in Nursing and Health, 12,* 111–122.

Ryan-Wenger, N. M. (1990). Children's psychosomatic responses to stress. In L. E. Arnold (Ed.), *Stress in children* (pp. 109–138). New York: Wiley.

Ryan-Wenger, N. M. (1992). A taxonomy of children's coping strategies: A step toward theory development. *American Journal of Orthopsychiatry, 62,* 256–263.

Ryan-Wenger, N. M. (1996). Children, coping, and the stress of illness: A synthesis of the research. *Journal of the Society of Pediatric Nurses, 1,* 126–139.

Ryan-Wenger, N. M., & Copeland, S. G. (1994). Coping strategies used by black school-age children from low-income families. *Journal of Pediatric Nursing, 9,* 33–40.

Scherer, M. (1996). On our changing family values: A conversation with David Elkind. *Educational Leadership, 53*(7), 4–9.

Sears, S. J., & Milburn, J. (1990). School-age stress. In L. E. Arnold (Ed.), *Childhood stress* (pp. 224–246). New York: Wiley.

Sharrer, V. W., & Ryan-Wenger, N. M. (1991). Measurements of stress and coping among school-aged children with and without recurrent abdominal pain. *Journal of School Health, 61,* 86–91.

Siegel, J. M., & Brown, J. D. (1988). A prospective study of stressful circumstances, illness symptoms, and depressed mood among adolescents. *Developmental Psychology, 24,* 715–721.

Smith, C., & Carlson, B. E. (1997). Stress, coping, and resilience in children and youth. *Social Service Review, 71,* 231–256.

Sorensen, E. S. (1993). *Children's stress and coping: A family perspective.* New York: Guilford Press.

Sorensen, E. S. (1994). Daily stressors and coping responses: A comparison of rural and suburban children. *Public Health Nursing, 11,* 24–31.

Spirito, A., Stark, L. J., Grace, N., & Stamoulis, D. (1991). Common problems and coping strategies reported in childhood and early adolescence. *Journal of Youth and Adolescence, 20,* 531–544.

Trad, P. V., & Greenblatt, E. (1990). Psychological aspects of child stress: Development and the spectrum of coping responses. In L. E. Arnold (Ed.), *Childhood stress* (pp. 24–49). New York: Wiley.

Viorst, J. (1972). *Alexander and the terrible, horrible, no good, very bad day.* New York: Aladdin Books.

Wasserstein, S. B., & La Greca, A. M. (1996). Can peer support buffer against behavioral consequences of parental discord? *Journal of Clinical Child Psychology, 25,* 177–182.

Wenz-Gross, M., & Siperstein, G. N. (1997). Importance of social support in the adjustment of children with learning problems. *Exceptional Children, 63,* 183–193.

Karen Fallin is a Research Associate, Wilson Consulting. Charlotte Wallinga and Mick Coleman are Associate Professors, Department of Child and Family Development, University of Georgia, Athens.

From *Childhood Education*, Fall 2001, pp. 17–24. © 2001 by the Association for Childhood Education International, Olney, MD. Reprinted by permission of the authors.

CHILDREN AND GRIEF: THE ROLE OF THE EARLY CHILDHOOD EDUCATOR

Andrea Ruth Hopkins

Early childhood educators cannot shield children from learning about death. Children witness death in many different forms, from a neglected houseplant to a favorite pet dying; from a cartoon show character flattened by a steamroller to TV images of exploding airliners and collapsing buildings during the September 11 terrorist attacks. As educators we have no choice about whether or not children receive death education; our only choice is how developmentally appropriate that education will be (Fox 2000).

Perceptions of death and developmental stages

A grieving child's perception of death relates directly to the child's level of cognition. Perceptions of death change as children progress through developmental stages. A clear understanding of these perceptions is essential for educators wishing to respond appropriately and helpfully to a grieving child's unique needs.

Infants and toddlers

Piaget theorized that children birth through age two are in the *sensorimotor stage* of development (Berk & Winsler 1995). During this period they develop a complex behavioral system, with strong attachments to parents and other intimate, dependable caregivers in their lives. Mutual attachment behavior protects the young and vulnerable child from danger. Instinctive behaviors such as smiling, babbling, and crying engage the caregiver in interactions, ensuring that the baby's emotional, physical, and social needs are met (Black 1998). Separation from the primary caregiver is likely to be met with vigorous protestations. The outcomes from a tragic loss are far-reaching, according to researcher Bette Glickfield. In her 1993 study she found the presence of a consistent and emotionally nurturing caregiver during the formative years to be the only reliable predictor of later attachment style in bereaved children (Glickfield 1993).

Preschoolers' Grasp of the Concept of Death

Four subconcepts of death—finality, inevitability, cessation, and causality—are related to the thinking of a child in the preoperational stage. *Finality* refers to the understanding that once a living thing dies, it will never be alive again. Preschool children are unable to comprehend death's permanence. A child may want to write or call the person who died in an effort to continue a physical relationship (Trozzi 1999). For example, after a tragic apartment fire left a young child dead, his classmates discussed the event. One child wasn't sure just who had died. "Carlos comes to breakfast," one of the other children assured him. "I'll show you who he is when he comes to breakfast tomorrow."

The concept of *inevitability* is knowledge that death will occur sometime to every living thing. Preschoolers usually deny the possibility of a personal death. They may see death as something avoidable or an event that happens only to others.

Cessation connotes the realization that there are neither biological nor psychological signs of life present in someone who is dead. The preoperational thinker believes death is a state of reduced functionality, that there are distinctions or degrees of death (Nagy 1948). The cessation of visible aspects of functioning, such as sight, hearing, and motion, is more easily grasped by two- to five-year-old children than is cessation of cognitive functions of feeling, thought, and consciousness.

Causality requires understanding that there are physical or biological reasons death occurs. The abstract thinking necessary to comprehend this makes it the most difficult concept for preschoolers to understand. They may cite external causes for the death rather than biological factors. Children's "magical thinking" may lead them to see unrelated events as a cause or explanation. False assumptions about the cause may include a feeling of responsibility or blame. A child who shouts, "I wish you were dead! I hate you!" to a sibling, friend, or parent will almost certainly feel completely responsible for any accident or tragedy that might befall that person.

Timmy, Who Loved Dinosaurs

Maria Trozzi, director of the Good Grief Program at Boston Medical Center, relates how one teacher dealt with children's need to understand death's permanence (1999). The teacher consulted Trozzi after a child in her first-grade class died from a brain tumor. She had told the children that Timmy died from an illness in his head that had stopped his brain and the rest of his body from working. However, each morning when attendance was taken, the children would say, "You forgot Timmy." Trozzi advised the teacher to ask, "Is Timmy here?" Despite their expectation that he might return, the children replied, "No, Timmy died."

The teacher had considered removing Timmy's desk, because it was a painful reminder to her. Trozzi advised her to leave the desk in place for a while so the class could use it to commemorate Timmy. The teacher asked the class what to do with Timmy's desk.

The children knew Timmy had loved dinosaurs, so they raised money to purchase books about dinosaurs. Inscribed in the front of each book was the message, *To our friend Timmy, who loved dinosaurs.* They placed his desk in a back corner of the classroom, decorated it with dinosaur stickers, and left the books on the desktop. Pillows and a rug finished off Timmy's Corner, a favorite spot for free reading time.

The children in this classroom sent a clear message: Timmy and his time in the classroom were important.

A baby or toddler who loses a parent or other attachment figure needs a stable environment, predictable schedules, and lots of comforting, touching, hugging, and holding by someone who loves her.

For babies younger than six months, the concept of death can be summed up in the phrases "all gone" and "out of sight, out of mind." From six months on a baby is somewhat aware of the absence of an attachment figure and may express limited grief (Papenbrock & Voss 1988) or react to the loss of attention, altered routines, and changes in the environment. Babies and toddlers are sensitive to the stress and emotions of those around them. They may experience temporary delays in motor development as their energy is invested in the process of grieving rather than in new physical or emotional growth (Grief Resource Foundation 1990).

A baby or toddler in the sensorimotor stage who loses a parent or other attachment figure needs a stable environment, predictable schedules, and lots of comforting, touching, hugging, and holding by someone who loves her (Papenbrock & Voss 1988) to help restore some of the security threatened by the loss. When the child is older, the primary caregiver can guide him through an understanding of the earlier loss (Furman 1990).

Talking to Families

Traumatic loss can overwhelm the adults in a family to the point where they may deny, ignore, or overlook their children's feelings (Naierman 1998). Teachers need to take time to talk to parents or other adult family members about problems or changes seen in a grieving child. They can remind them that even small deviations in a routine can be terrifying for children who have experienced loss, and that separation anxiety is a typical reaction for a child experiencing an unfamiliar situation (Farish 1995). Teachers can suggest that parents allow the grieving child to bring an item from home for comfort, or encourage parents to stay longer when bringing in or dropping off the child.

Older toddlers and preschoolers

Piaget's next cognitive stage, *preoperational,* encompasses children ages two to five. The preoperational child's thinking is characterized as magical, egocentric, and causal (Goldman 1998). Preschoolers believe strongly in the power of their wishes, which often leads them to conclude that death is temporary, reversible, or partial. (See "Preschoolers' Grasp of the Concept of Death.") In Maria Nagy's (1948) landmark study of children's conceptions of death, children ages three to five denied death as a natural and final process. They saw death as a departure—a further existence in changed circumstances for the person who died.

Preschoolers tend to respond to death with periods of anger, sadness, anxiety, and angry outbursts. They are also likely to show regressive behaviors and physical disturbances, as mentioned with toddlers (Farish 1995). Appropriate adult responses to a preschooler coping with death include clear communication about the death, reassurance that the child's needs will be met, acceptance of the child's reactions to the death, and plenty of hugging and loving reassurance.

Kindergartners and young schoolagers

Young school-age children from five through nine have reached the *concrete operational stage* of development. They are curious and realistic, and most have mastered some universal concepts, including irreversibility. While they are capable of expressing logical fears and thoughts about death, their understanding of finality can bring on deep emotional reactions (Goldman 1996). They may alternately deny feelings and experience deep anxiety. Fears of further abandonment and intense feelings of loss complicate the grieving process (Christian 1997).

Observable symptoms of and behaviors due to the stress of bereavement vary. Aggressive behaviors and temper tantrums are common in children who feel out of control. Sleep disorders may indicate fear or anxiety. Regression, also common, is an attempt by the grieving child to return to a more secure time in his or her life (Alderman 1989).

A Letter to Parents

Dear Families:

I am writing with sadness to tell you that Rosey, our class rabbit, died yesterday. He died at the Animal Medical Center in the examining room. I was able to be with him, as was the veterinarian from the emergency room. Here are some things we will tell the children.

Rosey died from rabbit pneumonia, which is an infection in the lungs. People cannot get this disease from animals. The veterinarian said it is almost impossible to notice any symptoms of this illness in time to treat it. Rosey suffered no pain or discomfort. When an animal dies at the animal hospital, the doctors and their helpers bury the body. It is sad when pets die—teachers and children feel sad and miss them. Rosey's death may remind them of deaths of loved ones or of pets.

We will tell the children [about Rosey's death] after assembly tomorrow and invite them to participate in a discussion. They will also be invited to help create a Rosey memory book in which they can contribute feelings about the loss of Rosey or happy memories they have of him.

During the upcoming days, some children may speak often of Rosey, while others will be more reticent. Please share your child's response with us. We, of course, will share any school discussions with you, as well as our Rosey memory book.

Warmly,

The Teachers

Source: Reprinted, by permission of the publisher, from E. Winter, "School Bereavement," Educational Leadership, vol. 57, no. 6 (2000).

Children need adult permission to act out, talk about, and interpret their thoughts and feelings about death, a topic adults tend to avoid with young children.

A delayed reaction months after the death is as legitimate as one occurring immediately after the loss (Farish 1995). Reprocessing takes place throughout the bereaved child's development. Years after the death the child will revisit the loss, trying to understand it from the vantage point of his or her current developmental perspective (Perry 1996).

Teachers' role

Three basic responsibilities regarding death education rest with the early childhood educator: to help children feel safe while acknowledging the reality of death, to promote an accepting classroom atmosphere where children's feelings are supported, and to provide developmentally appropriate learning opportunities that allow children to discuss death. Each of these functions plays an important role in developing young children's attitudes and understandings about death.

Helping children feel safe

Helping children feel safe while acknowledging the reality of death requires acceptance of children's views of death as one aspect of their normal curiosity about the everyday world. Teachers need to provide clear, simple facts that a child can comprehend, while avoiding confusing, abstract euphemisms, like equating death with sleep.

In one nursery school, teachers trying to deal effectively with the topic of death drew up some guidelines (Galen 1972). The primary guideline concerns the importance of teachers using the proper perspective. This means accepting preschoolers' views about death as part of their growing curiosity about and understanding of everyday phenomena. Children need adult permission to act out, talk about, and interpret their thoughts and feelings about death, a topic adults tend to avoid with young children.

Early childhood educators can ask themselves two questions before they react with ingrained discomfort to any child's question or comment regarding death:

- How would I treat this action/comment/question if it were not about death?
- What is the child really seeking by his or her action/comment/question? (Galen 1972)

If adults find children's repeated questions about death disconcerting, they should keep in mind that it is very common and completely normal for children to ask the same questions over and over again. This doesn't mean that the answers they give are inadequate, but rather that the children are seeking reassurance and trying to make the information fit their understandings (Cohn 1987). Children gain a sense of control by discussing their fears (Sandstrom 1999).

Creating a supportive classroom

The second function of the early childhood educator in death education is to promote a classroom atmosphere wherein the children's feelings are accepted and supported. The teacher should emphasize to the children through words and actions that there is nothing too sad or too terrible to talk about with a caring adult. Sensitive acknowledgment and support greatly assist children in sorting out their many difficult emotions (Cohn 1987). Teachers must never minimize children's feelings by distracting them or encouraging them to cheer up. The normal process of grieving is necessary if the child is to move on toward understanding a loss and resolving pain.

Educators must acknowledge grief with compassion and support. Providing extra comfort, reassurance, and security in the form of extra hugs, hand holding, and empathic

Teaching about Death through the Life Cycle of Plants

Grief educator Erna Furman strongly advocates providing emotionally neutral opportunities to learn about life and death in the preschool curriculum: "A basic concept of death is best grasped, not when a loved one dies, but in situations of minimal emotional significance, such as with dead insects or worms" (1990, 16). More involved than merely planting seeds in paper cups and watching them grow, her educational goal in using the life cycle of plants is to help young children begin to understand life, growth, death, and generational sequence.

Parent involvement is an integral component of Furman's life cycle curriculum. Parent participation stimulates children's interest and helps them understand—often for the first time—the growth cycle of flowers or vegetables. Parents can support and extend their children's learning at home. When enthusiasm for the life cycle is sparked, entire families may find enjoyment through shared gardening activities, outings to farms, shopping at farmers' markets, or visiting apple orchards.

The key element to the success of the life cycle curriculum, believes Furman, lies in the enthusiasm of the teacher. The teacher must wholeheartedly enjoy and respect the way nature works as well as the way children learn. Furman surmises that one reason her curriculum has been so well received may be that it provides an all-too-rare opportunity to really understand a common experience. It becomes a base of information from which further learning is motivated and, as she states, "engenders hope and trust that more things will, with effort, make sense and bring a feeling of mastery" (Furman 1990, 20).

For example, a teacher might provide props and materials children can use to establish a veterinarian's office. A doctors' kit, stuffed animals, blankets, scales, and pictures of animals create a setting in which children can interact and discuss illness and death in a safe manner. Grieving children can use these props to engage in play that helps them deal with some emotion-laden issues. Teachers observing the play can gain a better perspective of children's progress through their grief "journey" (Greenberg 1996). Clear communication with parents supporting a grieving child's need for these expressions is essential (see "Talking to Families").

Offering developmentally appropriate death education

The third function of the educator's role is to provide developmentally appropriate learning opportunities that discuss death (Crase & Crase 1995). There is great value in teaching young children about death before it enters their lives in an intimate way. Children exposed gradually to small doses of frightening or sad experiences may be able to work through them successfully (Ketchel 1986). Extending this understanding helps prepare children for other more personal losses.

Classroom activities and experiences that can help children understand death in developmentally appropriate ways include something as simple as having live plants in the classroom. Children can help care for the plants, experiencing firsthand that all living things share a need for food, water, and light. (See "Teaching about Death through the Life Cycle of Plants.")

The teacher should emphasize to the children through words and actions that there is nothing too sad or too terrible to talk about with a caring adult.

Live pets reinforce these concepts also. When a classroom pet dies, teachers sometimes respond by shielding children from the death. Rather, this should be used as an opportunity to answer children's questions and reinforce their understanding of the life cycle.

One first-grade classroom learned this lesson during a unit on hatching butterflies. (Hofschield 1991). The first of four butterflies to hatch was born with curled, malformed wings. The first-graders had many concerns and questions about the butterfly. The teacher channeled the children's interest into a focus on disability awareness. The students became very protective of the butterfly, which they named Popcorn. They checked on Popcorn often, verbally encouraging him and feeding him with an eyedropper.

Later that week the children noticed that Popcorn was not moving. The teacher gently lifted him onto a tissue and sat down with the children. She explained that the butterfly had died. Together they talked about the learning and

verbalizations is crucial. These efforts let a child know she is safe and that someone is there to care for her. The classroom structure and limits can bring a welcome feeling of normalcy to a grieving child. Emphasizing familiar routines, playing soothing music, using a calm voice—these strategies offer comfort as well as model coping skills a bereaved child can use (NAEYC 2001). They also show the other children appropriate ways to interact with their bereaved classmate.

Teachers can anticipate children's anger and plan activities that help them express and release anger in healthy ways. Many elements of early childhood classrooms can serve as tension releasers for children dealing with overwhelming emotions. Children can channel physical energy into sensory experiences such as sand and water play or manipulating clay and playdough. Opportunities and materials for emotional expression abound in the dramatic play center, block area, and puppet theater.

Play is an effective means for a child to work through grief. More than a game, acting out death, dying, funerals, and associated feelings can greatly assist children in reducing anxieties. Death play, while not necessarily initiated by the teacher, should be supported rather than discouraged if it occurs spontaneously.

growing they had all experienced because of Popcorn. Some children cried. Later that day, the children buried Popcorn in the school yard, each taking an opportunity to say something about the butterfly.

Reflecting later on the experience, the teacher realized that not only had the children learned scientific knowledge from the butterfly unit, but they also had matured through the group discussions and subsequent individual journal entries in which they wrote about their feelings. In the following weeks the teacher saw the children become more thoughtful toward and accepting of those around them (Hofschield 1991). Perhaps the loss created a shared bond among the children, as well as teaching empathy and tolerance for others.

There is great value in teaching young children about death before it enters their lives in an intimate way.

When the class rabbit died unexpectedly at one school, the teachers saw the opportunity to model mourning and assist children in processing an emotional loss (Winter 2000). The teachers sent a letter home (see "A Letter to Parents") to families in an effort to keep school and home discussions consistent.

Allowing children to watch the decay of something organic, such as a carved pumpkin or a piece of fruit, is another way to help them gain a better understanding of what happens to living organisms after death (Miller 1996). The item, enclosed in a heavy zipper bag or other transparent container, can be examined every few days by the class, and the changes noted. It is important for teachers to emphasize the process of nature, rather than revulsion, when discussing the changes (Miller 1996).

Conclusion

While early childhood educators may wish to protect children from negative or painful experiences, they are also aware that one of their primary tasks is to help children deal with strong emotions in healthy ways. Perhaps at no other time is this responsibility as difficult as when a young child experiences loss through death. An early childhood educator who creates a safe atmosphere for children's concerns, outlets for children's strong emotions, and appropriate life cycle experiences in the classroom can foster resiliency and coping skills that will assist children during an initial loss and help strengthen them for a lifetime.

Resources for helping children understand life and death

Fiction for children ages 3 and up

Anderson, J. 1994. *The key into winter.* New York: Albert Whitman. An allegorical story mixing fantasy and reality. The

march of the seasons is the metaphor for the passages of life. Ages 4–8.

Brown, M. 1995. *The dead bird.* New York: Harper Trophy. A gentle story of a group of children who discover a dead bird and bury it with a simple ceremony. Ages 4–8.

Buscaglia, L. 1983, *The fall of Freddy the Leaf.* New York: Holt, Rinehart, & Winston. Freddy and the other leaves pass through the seasons. This parable helps explain the delicate balance between life and death. Ages 4–10.

Clifton, L. 1983. *Everett Anderson's goodbye.* New York: Henry Holt. Everett has a difficult time dealing with his father's death. Ages 3–8.

DePaola, T. 1973. *Nana Upstairs and Nana Downstairs.* New York: G. P. Putnam's Sons. Little Tomie loves his grandmother and shares many special times with her. Her death leaves him sad and in need of his family's understanding. Ages 3–8.

D'Esopo, K. 1995. Barklay and Eve Series. Westfield, CT: Pratt Resource Center. This series of three books helps children through times of family loss. It aids in cultural awareness in times of grief. The titles include *Together We'll Make It through This, Sitting Shiva,* and *Precious Gifts: Barklay and Eve Explain Organ and Tissue Donation.* Ages 3–8.

Good Cave, A. 1998. *Balloons for Trevor: Understanding death* (Comforting Little Hearts series). St. Louis, MO: Concordia. Interactive pages help parents and children work through issues together. Ages 4–8

Gregory, V. 1992. *Through the Mickle Woods.* Boston: Little, Brown. After his wife's death, a grieving king journeys to an old bear's cave in the middle of the Mickle Woods, where he hears three stories that help him go on living. All ages.

Joslin, M. 1999. *The goodbye boat.* Grand Rapids, MI: Eerdmans. This simple, beautiful story is told with only a handful of words. It represents visually the stages of grief. Baby–Pre-K.

Kirkpatrick, J. 1999. *Barn Kitty.* Santa Fe, NM: Arzo. *Barn Kitty* provides a gentle approach to the subject of death—touching and sure to generate discussion among young children. Ages 4–7.

O'Toole, D. 1998. *Aarvy Aardvark finds hope.* Burnsville, NJ: Mt. Rainbow. This story about animals presents grief, sadness, and eventual resolution after death. Ages 5–8.

Varley, S. 1984. *Badger's parting gifts.* New York: Morrow. After his death, Badger's friends recall their memories of him. All ages.

Nonfiction for children ages 5 to 12

Blackburn, L. 1991. *I know I made it happen: A book about children and guilt.* Omaha, NE: Centering. Sometimes children's magical thinking and guilt make them think they have caused the death of a loved one.

Carney, K. 1995. *Barklay and Eve series.* Westfield, CT: Pratt Resource Center. This series of three books was designed to help children through times of family loss and is written from the perspective of the Jewish religion.

Heegaard, M. 1992. *When someone very special dies.* Minneapolis, MN: Woodland. Young children can use this workbook to help them express their grief.

Mellonie, B., & R. Ingpen. 1987. *Lifetimes: The beautiful way to explain death to children.* New York: Bantam. Life cycles of plants, animals, and people are discussed. The book explains why some lifetimes are shorter.

Mundy, M. 1998. *Sad isn't bad: A good grief guidebook for kids dealing with loss.* St. Meinrad, IN: Abbey. This book affirms that even after loss, the world is still safe and grief eventually lessens.

Nystrom, C. 1992. *What happens when we die?* Chicago, IL: Moody. From a Christian perspective this book answers children's questions about death.

Palmer, P. 1994. *I wish I could hold your hand.* Manassas Park, VA: Impact. This gentle book helps children identify their feelings about loss and assures and comforts them.

Rogers, F. 1982. *When a pet dies.* New York: G. P. Putnam's Sons. This "first experiences" book addresses and affirms questions and feelings children have after the death of a pet. It discusses the importance of memories.

References

Alderman, L. 1989. *Why did daddy die? Helping children cope with the loss of a parent.* New York: Pocket Books.

Berk, L., & A. Winsler. 1995. *Scaffolding children's learning: Vygotsky and early childhood education.* Washington, DC: NAEYC.

Black, D. 1998. Bereavement in childhood. *British Medical Journal* 316 (7135): 93–133.

Christian, L. 1997. Children and death. *Young Children* 52 (4): 7680.

Cohn, J. 1987. The grieving student. *Instructor* (January): 76–78.

Crase, D. R., & D. Crase. 1995. Responding to a bereaved child in the school setting. ERIC ED 394 655.

Farish, J. 1995. *When disaster strikes: Helping young children cope.* Washington, DC: NAEYC.

Fox, S. S. 2000. *Good grief: Helping groups of children when a friend dies.* Boston, MA: New England Association for the Education of Young Children.

Furman, E. 1990. Plant a potato—Learn about life and death. *Young Children* 46 (1): 1520.

Galen, H. 1972. A matter of life and death. *Young Children* 27 (6): 351–56.

Glickfield, B. D. 1993. *Adult attachment and utilization of social provisions as a function of perceived mourning behavior and perceived parental bonding after early parental loss.* Detroit, MI: University of Detroit Mercy.

Goldman, L. 1996. *Breaking the silence: A guide to help children with complicated grief.* Bristol, PA: Taylor & Francis.

Goldman, L. 1998. Helping the grieving child in school. *Healing* 3 (1). Available online: www.kidspeace.org/healingmagazine/issue5/therapist.asp [access date: 7 November 2001].

Greenberg, J. 1996. Seeing children through tragedy: My mother died today—When is she coming back? *Young Children* 51 (6): 76–78.

Grief Resource Foundation. 1990. *Helping young children cope with loss.* Dallas: Author.

Hofschield, K. 1991. The gift of a butterfly. *Young Children* 46 (3): 36.

Ketchel, J. 1986. Helping the young child cope with death. *Day Care and Early Education* (Winter): 24–27.

Miller, K. 1996. *Crisis manual for early childhood teachers.* Beltsville, MD: Gryphon House.

NAEYC. 2001. Helping young children in frightening times. *Young Children* 56 (6): 6–7.

Nagy, M. 1948. The child's theories concerning death. *The Journal of Genetic Psychology* 73: 327.

Naierman, N. 1998. Grieving kids need guidance. *Early Childhood News* (March/April): 50–53.

Papenbrock, P., & R. Voss. 1988. *Children's grief: How to help the child whose parent has died.* Redmond, WA: Media.

Perry, B. 1996. Children and loss. Available online: http://teacher.scholastic.com/professional/bruceperry/childrenloss.htm [access date: 7 November 2001].

Sandstrom, S. 1999. Dear Simba is dead forever. *Young Children* 54 (6): 14–15.

Trozzi, M. 1999. *Talking with children about loss.* New York: Penguin.

Winter, E. 2000. School bereavement. *Educational Leadership* 57 (6).

Andrea Ruth Hopkins, M.Ed., is an early childhood educator with the St. Paul public schools. She teaches both in early childhood family education and in school readiness programs. Andrea is also a volunteer facilitator for the Minnesota Valley Children and Grief Youth Coalition.

UNIT 5
Curricular Issues

Unit Selections

Key Points to Consider

- How can blocks play an integral part in the learning curriculum? Describe the components of effective learning centers.

- What information should teachers be sending to parents about their children's early literacy experiences?

- How can physical activity be enhanced during the early childhood years?

- How can parents best be kept informed about the learning experiences their children have encountered in school?

- What is the appropriate use of technology and computers during the early childhood years? How can science and math learning activities allow for hands-on learning?

 **Links: www.dushkin.com/online/**
These sites are annotated in the World Wide Web pages.

Association for Childhood Education International (ACEI)
http://www.udel.edu/bateman/acei/

California Reading Initiative
http://www.sdcoe.k12.ca.us/score/promising/prreading/prreadin.html

Early Childhood Education Online
http://www.ume.maine.edu/ECEOL-L/

International Reading Association
http://www.reading.org

Kathy Schrock's Guide for Educators
http://www.discoveryschool.com/schrockguide/

Phi Delta Kappa
http://www.pdkintl.org

Reggio Emilia
http://ericps.ed.uiuc.edu/eece/reggio.html

Teachers Helping Teachers
http://www.pacificnet.net/~mandel/

Tech Learning
http://www.techlearning.com

In developing curriculum for young children, teachers and administrators are interested in various strategies and techniques that can further positive educational experience. In the first article, "Learning Centers: Why and How," the reader who is unsure about how to develop appropriate learning centers in his or her classroom is encouraged to give it a try. The children, when given the opportunity, will provide additional suggestions of activities and will continue to contribute to the learning. Teachers can begin developing effective learning centers by collecting a variety of materials that will encourage the children to explore and manipulate as they develop skills for enhancing thinking, socializing, and creativity.

We can learn so much about our current practices with young children by examining our roots. One of the key components of a good learning environment over the years has been the availability of a variety of blocks. Now, more than ever, it is important for teachers to provide an ample supply of blocks in the classroom. Math, creativity, science, social development, and problem solving are all enhanced through blocks. Karen Hewitt provides a historical examination of the use of blocks in early childhood classrooms in "Blocks as a Tool for Learning: Historical and Contemporary Perspectives." Blocks are quite possibly the best play material for young children.

The poor physical condition of young people in America today is cause for great concern. Teachers of young children play a vital role in encouraging a lifelong enjoyment of physical activity. The authors of "Improving Public Health Through Early Childhood Movement Programs" provide suggestions for developing a preschool movement program. Ideas for specific activities are included.

One of the responsibilities of teachers that is often neglected is documenting and communicating the learning going on in the classroom. Teachers get so involved in the day-to-day teaching that they often forget to keep track of what the children are doing and to provide ways for families and administrators to become familiar with the learning opportunities in the classroom. In "Using Documentation Panels to Communicate With Families," the reader can find ideas for educating families about their children's learning. We have a responsibility to keep parents informed, especially since young children cannot provide detailed verbal descriptions of their learning experiences. Actual photographs, drawings, and conversation about works in progress draw the parents into the curriculum.

Young children are eager to delve into curriculum that is compelling. Activities that will allow them to investigate, dig deep, and roll up their sleeves and get involved are the types of learn-

ing experiences that send the message "learning is fun, and I can be successful." What is often presented is watered down, teacher directed, and lacking in true discovery. When we rob children of contributing to the learning process by providing all of the neatly cut papers for them to glue or worksheets for them to complete, we take away their desire to explore and investigate. When their learning is served to them on a platter, they never learn that they can gather information by themselves. Become a facilitator for learning instead of a dispenser of information.

Included are three new articles addressing early literacy, the current hot topic in early childhood education. President George W. Bush has brought the battle over the best way for young children to learn how to read to the attention of parents and educators across the country with his request for $45 million for preschool reading research. What teachers do know about early literacy is the importance of a partnership between the home and school in introducing printed communication to young children. In addition to the article "The Right Way to Read" are "Fostering Language and Literacy in Classrooms and Homes" and "Helping Preschool Children Become Readers: Tips for Parents." All three articles focus on the importance of families in the process.

A number of the articles in unit 5 provide opportunities for the reader to reflect on the authentic learning experiences available for children. How can they investigate, explore, and create while studying a particular area of interest? Make children work for their learning. This unit is full of articles addressing different curriculum areas. Active child involvement leads to enhanced learning. Suggestions for project-based activities in mathematics, science, and technology are also included. Again, the theme runs deep. Hands-on = Minds on!

LEARNING CENTERS: WHY AND HOW

One of the most accepted practices in early childhood education is that classrooms are organized into interest areas or learning centers. Children paint in the art center, work puzzles in the manipulatives center, and look at books in the library center, for example.

Why organize space in this way?

Meeting children's needs

A well-organized and creative classroom reflects children's interests, needs, developmental levels, and learning styles. It invites children to explore and discover. It offers security and safety. And it allows children to develop meaningful relationships with other children and adults.

The key to creating effective environments for young children is to know how they develop. Children grow and develop at unique rates, but almost all follow a predictable sequence of development. For example, an infant is likely to sit unassisted before pulling up to stand. Teachers who understand developmental sequences and can mark developmental milestones—particular skills we expect most children to acquire by a certain age—are likely to prepare the best environments for learning and socializing. We know, for example, that most 10- to 12-month-olds are afraid of strangers, that 18- to 26-month-old toddlers are wobbly walking, and that 5-year-olds are eager to help with chores. This kind of knowledge helps teachers respond to children and can help direct the curriculum and room arrangement.

Goals for every child

Many early childhood educators describe a set of life-long learning skills or universal goals that help prepare children to become cooperative and competent members of society. These include:

- **Self-regulation**—understanding and accepting rules for yourself and the sake of the community.
- **Problem-solving skills**—working to negotiate and resolve conflicts.
- **Initiative**—evaluating a situation and being willing to try to improve it.
- **Trust**—developing honesty and steadfastness in relationships.
- **Independence**—taking responsibility for your own successes and failures.
- **Creativity**—approaching ideas and tasks with initiative, playfulness, and inventive thinking.

Curriculum planning and room arrangement for all ages of children supports these goals. You build trust in infants when you respond promptly to crying and cuddle often. You help toddlers develop self-regulation and independence when you have a low shelf for book storage. And similarly, you support creativity and initiative when you let 4-year-olds plan and dig a corner of the playground for a vegetable garden.

Infants and toddlers

Infants and toddlers learn about their world through their senses—by

Toys and materials for babies

Make sure toys and materials are in good condition, have no sharp or broken parts, and are non-toxic. Check sizes with a choke tube to make sure infants can't swallow or choke on toys. Wash and sanitize all toys after each use.
- mirrors
- musical toys
- chew toys
- busy boards
- balls
- shape sorters
- blocks
- dolls
- books
- mobiles
- wheel toys
- squeeze toys
- rings and chain links that snap or hook together
- household pots, wooden spoons, plastic cups, and cardboard boxes
- nesting blocks, barrels, and bowls

seeing, touching, tasting, hearing, and smelling. Infants and toddlers need to touch, manipulate, and interact with things to know them. To learn, babies need environments that allow—and encourage—the exploration of real materials. Babies build skills when adults respond to them consistently and support their curiosity and developing skills in a safe, supportive way.

The primary activities for infants—diapering, eating, and sleeping—require specific equipment and carefully arranged space. Discovery or exploration zones are additional secure spaces where the youngest children can explore their surroundings. For the youngest infants this might mean a floor blanket with a mirror propped nearby, a mobile to watch, and a hanging cloth ball to kick.

As infants become more mobile, this exploration zone expands. It could include a corner for crawling over pillows and a different area for play with dolls and soft toys. Expand and equip classroom discovery areas to respond to the developmental needs and interests of growing toddlers.

Most toddlers and 2-year-olds depend upon someone else to satisfy their needs, offer support, and entertain. This means they typically play alone or in the presence of another child but with little interaction—unless there is an attractive toy in someone else's hands. Language is limited, so communication is often physical. Toddlers are not yet able to understand the feelings of someone else (empathy) and instead tend to be self-focused.

For a toddler environment to be effective it must be safe and spacious. Because toddlers aren't able to share toys, be sure to provide duplicates of favorite playthings. Use low dividers to help children focus their activities—trains in that corner and housekeeping here. Encourage self-help skills by providing shelves and baskets for toy storage—and encouraging the children to help at cleanup time.

Preschoolers

Three- to 5-year-old children are often described as preschoolers. Preschoolers are active, eager learners. They are constantly exploring, manipulating, and experimenting with the environment to learn more about it. They still rely heavily on their senses but are beginning to think abstractly, to use symbols, and to reason. They learn best when they can use real materials, reflect on what happens, and draw conclusions—what we call "cause and effect."

Preschoolers gradually become less self-centered and begin to understand the viewpoints of others. This allows play to become more cooperative—a key to increased language experiences, problem solving, and experimentation. Increasing physical coordination and strength allows preschoolers to handle new materials, build creatively, and initiate new activities.

Standard materials for the block center

- unit blocks—at least 100
- hollow blocks
- cardboard blocks
- human figures
- animal figures—domestic, farm, and jungle
- vehicles
- measuring tools
- labeled storage shelf

Learning centers

The developmental skills of preschoolers require less space for sleeping, eating, and toileting and more space for play and discovery. Arranging that space in learning centers allows children to play cooperatively and investigate language, roles, materials, and relationships. Learning centers encourage children to work and learn at their own pace, with materials that meet individual needs and levels of development.

Common learning centers include places for art, block play, dramatic play or housekeeping, science and discovery, music, math and manipulatives, a library and listening equipment, and an outdoor play area. In each learning center the aim is to encourage children to work independently in a safe, teacher-monitored atmosphere, on activities that are clear, stimulating, and meaningful.

Space learning centers according to their use. The art center is best placed near a sink, and the library away from water and paint, for example. Consider electricity needs, natural light, floor surfaces (absorbent rug or easy-to-clean vinyl), and storage. Make sure all furniture is child-sized and that materials for the

center are arranged attractively and within children's reach. Try to include math- and literacy-building materials into the activity of each center. For example, post maps and building plans near the block center, encourage children to sign their art work, and supply nature guides and measuring tools in the discovery center. Label learning materials and all areas of the classroom so children will learn to associate written words with information and direction.

Block center

Blocks offer children an opportunity to build representations of structures in their world. There are many kinds of blocks: unit blocks, large hollow blocks, and cardboard blocks made from recycled cardboard boxes. Each kind helps children understand size, spatial relationships, balance, and organization.

For successful construction, unit blocks should relate to each other mathematically—each block is twice as long or wide as the one preceding it in size. A properly built set of unit blocks is not inexpensive, but with proper care will be the most enduring purchase a program can make.

Locate the block center in a corner of the classroom, out of the traffic path, and preferably on a low-pile rug (to absorb sound). Placing the center near the dramatic play center encourages children in the two areas to interact. Place a low, sturdy shelf next to one wall for block storage. Outline each size of block on the shelf with paint or tape to help children evaluate the available materials—and to help with cleanup time. A cardboard box with a jumble of blocks thrown in is not inviting to children and doesn't encourage the proper care of classroom materials.

Encourage increasingly complex constructions by providing an adequate number of blocks, by scheduling long periods of play, and allowing children to leave their structures in place overnight. You may want to help them post a "Building under construction" sign. Tape a building zone on the floor to discourage accidental building collapse.

Set guidelines for safe block play. "Tear down with hands not feet." Kicking down a building is disrespectful of the materials. Limit building height to one a child can see over—"Build to your nose." Encourage children to work together to carry heavy hollow blocks.

Art center materials

- crayons
- markers
- chalk
- colored pencils
- variety of papers
- scissors
- paste
- glue
- collage materials
- brushes
- watercolor paints
- clay
- smocks
- printing stamps
- containers for materials
- display areas
- drying space for finished products
- tempera paints—liquid and dry
- play dough and sculpting tools
- woodworking bench, hammer, nails, and goggles

Art center

The art center supports children's creativity and artistic expression. Typically it contains a standing easel, a tabletop work surface, and non-toxic materials for painting, cutting, drawing, stamping, pasting, and sculpting. A box of beautiful junk—shells, ribbon, cloth scraps, colored wire, textured paper, and wallpaper samples—encourages experimentation and creative expression. Successful, child-centered art centers focus on the process of making art, not on its product. Therefore, it does not contain teacher-made patterns, models, coloring books or sheets, or materials that demand adult direction. Provide containers for different kinds of materials. Make sure children can choose materials from the art shelf, use them, and return the materials to their proper storage space.

Encourage children to investigate, but not destroy, art materials. To be a successful artist, you need to know your materials and how they work. To use scissors, for example, you need to develop small finger muscles and coordination. Help children build these skills by providing numerous opportunities for children to practice with scissors. Similarly, children need to experiment to discover how much water makes watercolor paint runny and pale and how much permits vivid color and paint control. It's this experimentation that teaches children how to be artists.

Help children develop independence and self-reliance by having art smocks available. Buy or make smocks that children can put on and take off without adult assistance. Keep a pile of old newspaper handy for protecting the floor or table during messy art activities. Show how to use a sponge or paper towel to wipe up spills rather than to smear and dribble. Less experienced artists may be confused by too many paint colors and large jugs of glue. Help them out by providing small cups or squeeze bottles for glue and limiting the colors of paint to three. As children master materials they will be able to regulate their choices of materials and methods.

Encourage children to talk about their art by asking questions like, "Tell me about your picture" rather than by making observations that may or may not be accurate. What you see as a yellow car may, in fact, be the artist's interpretation of a submarine. Remember it's the process of art, not the product, that develops skills and confidence. Avoid rushing the art process; give children time to make as many and as elaborate pieces as they want.

To save money in the art center, consider mixing powered tempera yourself rather than buying it already mixed. Make your own modeling and sculpting mixtures as well. Ask parents to donate collage materials, interesting paper, and storage containers.

Dramatic play

The dramatic play center is sometimes called the home center, the

Common dramatic play themes

- florist shop
- restaurant
- post office
- train station
- veterinarian and doctor offices
- barber shop
- astronauts and space exploration
- camping
- farming and ranching
- fire fighting
- business office
- grocery store

housekeeping center, or the home life center. Whatever the name, it is the place where children explore the activities and relationships of the real world. In it children can investigate roles—being a mommy, a doctor, or a construction worker. They build language and communication skills, practice negotiation and problem-solving, and develop literacy skills using menus, lists, messages, cookbooks, or order forms.

Dramatic play centers usually contain child-sized kitchen equipment—stove, refrigerator, and sink (either manufactured from wood or modified from large cardboard boxes), dishes, pot and pans, cooking utensils, mops, brooms, and telephone. Additionally the center usually contains dress-up clothes, dolls, a rocking chair, and standing mirror.

Prop boxes make it easy to expand the home center so that children have opportunities to explore occupations and activities. As you gather materials, remember math and literacy-building props—tickets and pretend money for the train ride or a clipboard, paper, and pencil for bird watchers, for example. Ask parents to help you gather dress-up clothes, tools, and supplies for the prop boxes.

Science center

The science center, sometimes called the discovery center, is a place where children can explore, discover, evaluate, and draw conclusions about materials. Children use their senses to explore both physical and biological

Equipment for the science center

- prisms and color paddles
- magnifiers
- scales
- simple machines
  - —nuts and bolts
  - —pulleys
  - —levers
  - —planes
  - —wheels and axles
- time keepers
  - —egg timer
  - —clock
  - —hourglass
  - —stopwatch
  - —calendar
- flashlights
- gardening supplies
  - —soil
  - —pots
  - —seeds
  - —watering can
  - —trowels
- measuring tools
  - —liquid and dry measuring containers
  - —rulers
  - —tape measures
  - —eye droppers
  - —meter stick
- Pets and supplies
  - —housing
  - —food
  - —cleaning supplies
- paper and pencils for charting
- locks
- magnets and iron filings
- compass
- thermometer
- rocks and shells
- leaves
- compost container
- books and magazines

science. Science is always hands-on and is never magic.

Choose a classroom location that offers natural light. If possible, place the center near an electrical outlet. Some teachers position the science center near the manipulative center so that many materials can be shared. Storage is important because you will rotate some materials and equipment. You do, however, need space for classroom pets, plants, and specifically planned activities.

The sand and water table is an important addition to the science center, though it has uses in almost every area of the classroom. Help keep children healthy by draining and sanitizing the table at the end of every day.

Music

The music center invites children to investigate sound, rhythm, movement, and song. Music appreciation begins early for children—some say before birth. Build on this natural interest with daily activities that include singing, dancing, and playing music. Typical music centers contain rhythm instruments, a record or cassette player, and a box of scarves or ribbon batons for movement activities. A piano, autoharp, or guitar will enrich the center.

The music and movement center is likely to be noisy and active. Place it where the noise and children's movement won't disturb those working in the library and discovery centers, for example. A nearby electrical outlet is important if you want to use recorded music. Store rhythm instruments on a low shelf so children are free to play music throughout the day.

Movement activities can range from singing a finger play or swaying to a recorded tune to dancing and jumping activities that involve the whole body. As you plan movement activities, consider the ways children can use their bodies to make and respond to music.

- **Arm and body movement—** swinging, clapping, reaching, stretching, waving, carrying, patting, bouncing, pounding, punching air, shaking, tugging, twirling, swimming, drooping, and swaying
- **Finger movements—**pinching, tickling, grasping, squeezing, tying, tapping, snapping, rolling, clapping, scratching, and pointing
- **Leg and foot movements—** creeping, kicking, stomping, tip-toeing, tapping heels, spinning, tapping toes, hopping, jumping, leaping, sliding, rolling ankles, bending, and standing on one foot

Rhythm instruments for the music center

- Clicking instruments
  - —rhythm sticks
  - —wood blocks
  - —coconut shells
- Ringing instruments
  - —wrist bells
  - —ankle bells
  - —gong
  - —sleigh bells
  - —jingle sticks
- Rattling instruments
  - —rattles
  - —gourds
  - —tambourines
- Booming instruments
  - —drums
- Scratching instruments
  - —notched rhythm sticks
  - —rhythm board
  - —gourd rasp

Movement activities help children learn directions—up, down, back, forward, above, in a circle, to the side of, in back of, between, and across. They also help reinforce vocabulary as you suggest that children move quietly, loudly, joyfully, heavily, slowly, sadly, or quickly, for example.

Singing in the classroom— whether a cleanup song before lunch or a finger play during a large group time—is an extension of the music center. In general, songs for children have the following characteristics:

- limited vocal range
- simple, meaningful, easy-to-remember words
- clear, steady rhythm
- short length
- subjects that children are familiar with

Teach new songs with your own voice—with or without an instrument—or with a recording. Your singing voice is not important—the song is what children respond to.

Manipulative center

In the manipulative center children discover mathematical concepts by working with shape, size, classifica-

Supplies for the manipulative center

- flannel board and figures
- counting pegs and boards
- geo board and rubber bands
- parquetry tiles
- plastic locking blocks
- number strips
- abacus
- egg cartons and muffin tins
- puzzles
- pretend money
- colored beads
- storage containers
- counting collections
- spinners
- dice
- stacking and nesting containers
- balance scale
- lengths of cord

tion, counting, sequence, and order. These math activities are not limited to a particular center. Instead, math experiences enrich all areas of the classroom: dividing clay, comparing the size of hamsters, setting the table for snack, and weighing the pecans found on the playground. Often, however, teachers do focus on math in the manipulative center. Here children can move, sort, combine, and compare small objects—and see mathematical relationships.

The manipulative center is easy to position in the classroom. It requires only a table and comfortable chairs for the children, and a nearby storage area. Some teachers find that providing carpet squares for manipulatives helps children confine their work, especially when they are working with materials that easily roll off the table. Check school-supply catalogs for ideas of which material to include in the center. Then develop a plan to collect or construct your own materials.

Always introduce activities in the manipulative center. Match the activity with the developmental level of the child, and then expand it as the child develops new skills. For example, stringing beads can be a simple exercise in coordination and preci-

sion—get the bead on the string. Make it a more complex activity by providing a pattern card—red-blue-yellow-red-blue-yellow—and challenge the child to match the color pattern of beads on the string to that on the card.

Managing puzzles for the manipulative center is sometimes a headache. Make organization easier by buying only the sturdiest puzzles. Wooden inlay puzzles are the most durable, but heavy cardboard and plastic inlay puzzles can also last several years with careful use. Invest in a puzzle rack that helps children take puzzles off of the shelf without a spill. Code the backs of puzzle pieces so you can easily identify which piece belongs where. An easy way to do this is to write a symbol or numeral on the back of all the puzzle pieces—all 11 pieces of the balloon puzzle have a star on the back, for example.

Library

The purpose of the library center is to help children become book lovers —eager readers who know where to turn for information and entertainment. The library center frequently includes equipment for listening to books as well as looking at them.

Place the library in a quiet corner of the classroom with good lighting. Make the space inviting by displaying books neatly and providing comfortable chairs or fluffy floor pillows for readers. Some teachers include a table for writing activities in the library center.

Teach children how to care for books. Books are for reading and don't belong scattered on the floor. Show children how to turn pages carefully, and to help you make repairs.

Practice reading books aloud to children. If you're reading to a large group, face the group and hold the book to one side of your face. Make sure all the children can see the pictures. Introduce the book by telling the children the book's title and author: "We're going to read *When Will It Be Spring* by Catherine Walters." Give a one-sentence summary of the book: "It tells about a baby bear who learns how seasons change." Read the book, pausing to answer ques-

tions or to repeat a passage. Allow time to discuss the book after you've finished reading. Ask open-ended questions about a character or action: "Why did Alfie ask his mother about the coming of spring?" Offer other activities to a child who loses interest.

Enlist the aid of parents in helping to maintain the library. Make a list of books you'd like for the classroom and post it for parents to see. Ask families to give books to the class in honor of birthdays and other celebrations. If you want children to be able to listen to a book on tape, ask parents to do the recording. Store the tape with the book—children can listen to the words and "read" along.

Materials for the outdoor classroom

- balls
- hoops
- balance beam
- ropes
- tunnels
- sand and sand toys
- dramatic play props
- ladders
- tires
- art supplies
- blocks
- puzzles
- wheel toys
  —wagons
  —tricycles
  —scooters
- water
  —hose
  —water table or similar tub
  —measuring containers
- garden tools
  —child-sized shovels, rakes, trowels
  —watering cans or hose

Outdoors

The outdoors expands the space for any learning center—yes, it's great to do art or build with blocks on the playground. But the outdoors also Loffers a unique environment for experimentation and discovery—for growing a garden, observing weather, riding wheel toys, and watching cloud movement, for example.

Give children safe opportunities for outdoor play every day. Regularly check to make sure equipment is suitably anchored, that fall zones are well cushioned, and that riding toys are in good repair. Consider dividing the playground into zones or areas designated for swinging and climbing, for wheel toys, for quiet, restful activities, and for gardening. The best playgrounds include shady areas, grass, hard tracks (for riding toys), and provision for water play, digging, rolling, running, and climbing.

Plan outdoor activities and equip playground areas as carefully as you do indoor interest centers.

Resources

Art center

Cherry, Clare. *Creative Art for the Developing Child.* Morristown, N.J.: Fearon Teaching Aids, 1972.

Schirrmacher, Robert. *Art and Creative Development for Young Children.* Albany: Delmar Publishers, 1988.

Block center

Hirsch, Elizabeth. *The Block Book.* Washington, D.C.: National Association for the Education of Young Children, 1974.

MacDonald, Sharon. *Block Play.* Beltsville, Md.: Gryphon House, 2001.

Walker, Lester. *Block Building for Children.* Woodstock, N.Y.: Overlook Press, 1995.

Science and discovery center

Holt, Bess-Gene. *Science with Young Children.* Washington, D.C.: National Association for the Education of Young Children, 1977.

Levenson, Elaine. *Teaching Children About Science.* New York: Prentice Hall, 1985.

Petrash, Carol. *Earthways.* Beltsville, Md.: Gryphon House, 1992.

Williams, Robert A., Elizabeth Sherwood and Robert Rockwell. *More Mudpies to Magnets.* Beltsville, Md.: Gryphon House, 1990.

Rockwell, Robert, Robert Williams, and Elizabeth Sherwood. *Everybody Has a Body.* Beltsville, Md.: Gryphon House, 1992.

Music

Blood-Patterson, Peter, Ed. *Rise Up Singing: 1200 Songs, Words, Chords and Sources.* Bethlehem, Pa.: Sing Out Publications, 1988.

Cherry, Claire. *Creative Movement for the Developing Child.* Morristown, N.J.: Fearon Teaching Aids, 1971.

Math and manipulatives

Copley, Juanita V. *The Young Child and Mathematics.* Washington, D.C.: National Association for the Education of Young Children, 2000.

Baratta-Lorton, Mary. *Workjobs.* Menlo Park, Calif.: Addison Wesley, 1972.

Gilbert, La Britta. *I Can Do It! I Can Do It!* Beltsville, Md.: Gryphon House, 1984.

Moomaw, Sally and Brenda Hieronymus. *More Than Counting.* St. Paul, Minn.: Redleaf Press, 1995.

Library and listening

Armington, David. *The Living Classroom: Writing, Reading, and Beyond.* Washington, D.C.: National Association for the Education of Young Children, 1997.

Jalongo, Mary Renck. *Young Children and Picture Books.* Washington, D.C.: National Association for the Education of Young Children, 1988.

Neuman, Susan, Carol Copple, and Sue Bredekamp. *Learning to Read and Write.* Washington, D.C.: National Association for the Education of Young Children, 2000.

Outdoors

Rivkin, Mary S. *The Great Outdoors.* Washington, D.C.: National Association for the Education of Young Children, 1995.

Rockwell, Robert, Elizabeth Sherwood and Robert Williams. *Hug a Tree.* Beltsville, Md.: Gryphon House, 1983.

Tilgner, Linda. *Let's Grow.* Pownal, Vt.: Storey Communications, 1988.

General environment

Houle, Georgia Bradley. *Learning Centers for Young Children.* West Greenwich, R.I.: Consortium Publishing, 1987.

Isbell, Rebecca and Betty Exelby. *Early Learning Environments that Work.* Beltsville, Md.: Gryphon House, 2001.

From *Texas Child Care*, Spring 2002, pp. 30-42. © 2002 by Texas Workforce Commission.

Blocks As a Tool for Learning: Historical and Contemporary Perspectives

Karen Hewitt

Children have always built, testing their theories about the physical and social world. They stack units, knock them down, enclose spaces, bridge gaps, and repeat and refine ideas—often without the intervention of adults or the introduction of commercial materials.

The natural world provides abundant building material: heavy stones to pile, sticky burdock to connect, green twigs to tie and weave. And children are quick to pick up discarded construction and commerical materials such as wood pieces or boxes. Purchased building blocks and construction sets afford days of open-ended play and learning.

That children's impulse to construct is inherent and connected to learning is an old idea. It can be found in the writings of Plato (429–347 B.c.), Comenius (1592–1670), and Pestalozzi (1746–1827), as well as in the work of modern thinkers such as Jean Piaget (1896–1980).

The importance of play as a recognized mode of learning for young children is clearly reflected in the history of blocks and construction toys. As educators, we should appreciate the central historical and contemporary role of these toys in early childhood education.

COURTESY OF THE AUTHOR
Trade card, late 19th century

Whether blocks were advertised for home use or found their way into the classroom as an educational device, they have always been linked to learning. In *Some Thoughts Concerning Education*, English philosopher John Locke (1693) went against the prevailing trend in childrearing and placed the carrot before the stick: "The chief art is to make all that [children] have to do, sport and play too…. Learning anything they should be taught, might be made as much a recreation to their play, as their play is to their learning."

COURTESY OF THE AUTHOR
Ivory Soap advertisement, early 20th century

Toys now began to be considered influential in a positive way—not as sinful pastimes or baubles, but as a necessity. Locke described what was to become one of the most popular educational block sets—the alphabet blocks—extolling the merits of sweetened learning.

In mid- to late nineteenth century, a small group of European and U.S. manufacturers began producing building toys, often as a sideline to their main woodworking or printing business. The blocks for the commercial market were characterized by three distinct ideas linking learning and play. The first centers on the building unit as a surface for displaying symbols—letters, words, narratives. The second addresses the pure activity of building—constructing with simple, abstract forms. The third focuses on the transmission of a cultural heritage—building a model of an important architectural structure and, through this process, learning architectural styles.

Although the categories often overlap in one block type, it is important to look at each one to understand the pedagogical implications and to consider the discrepancy between what adults want children to do or think they are doing and what children actually do.

Literacy and blocks

The tradition of cladding the surface of blocks with symbols and narratives burgeoned in the mid-nineteenth century and continues today, blending learning and amusement with a mix of symbol, fantasy, and vibrant color. S.L. Hill, one of the first manufacturers of spelling and alphabet blocks, patented his spelling blocks in 1858. Some were thin tablets, which emphasized symbol over structure, while others were cubes, more conducive to building. Hill sold thousands of these sets, and other companies, such as Westcott and Bliss, followed his lead.

COURTESY OF SCHECTER ME SUN LEE, NEW YORK

Wide-Awake Alphabet Blocks, Charles M. Crandall Co., Montrose, Penn., ca. 1870s

Charles Crandall, a manufacturer of furniture and croquet sets, and Jesse Crandall, his brother, produced two unique building toys that resulted from the manufacturing process rather than a priori design. Charles, so the story goes, observed his children building with the thin cutoff pieces of wood used in the manufacture of finger-joint boxes for his croquet sets. Inspired by his children's complex constructions, he began to manufacture his alphabet and construction blocks in 1867, adapting the finger-joint design. In 1881 Jesse Crandall, looking for an efficient way to pack the blocks, began producing nested blocks, a perfect marriage of efficient design and an understanding of children's developmental needs.

COURTESY OF ROBERT HULL FLEMING MUSEUM, BURLINGTON, VT.

Alphabet Blocks and Building Blocks, S.L. Hill Co., Williamsburg, N.Y., ca. 1860

Literacy, in addition to knowing the letters of the alphabet, also meant a familiarity with stories, especially biblical ones. The biblical theme was common to a number of toys in the early and mid-nineteenth century, following the tradition of the popular Noah's Ark.

The design of the Cob House Blocks, produced by the McLoughlin Brothers in 1885, clearly placed the act of building on a par with word construction and the narrative possibilities of storytelling. Adults presumed—or at least hoped—that alphabet and story blocks would lead their children to an understanding of symbol systems, enticing them to learn their *ABC*s, arrange numerals in sequence, read simple words, and follow a narrative order.

For 200 years now, letters and numbers have been neatly painted, stamped, or chromolithographed and silk-screened on blocks, yet children continue to think spatially, piling these blocks, making towers and towns, and often blissfully ignoring the attempt of their elders to inject a dose of literacy.

Blocks as pure form

Playing with forms in space is an activity that has always been valued by artists, architects, and mathematicians as well as young children. These building sets contain unadorned wood forms with a serious intent. Although some sets come with plans or are packaged in a box whose cover indicates some possible building ideas, constructing seems to be the prime focus.

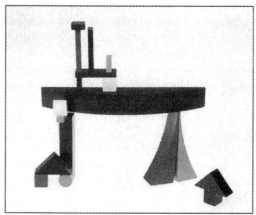

COURTESY OF COLLECTION CENTRE CANADIEN D'ARCHITECTURE/CANADIAN CENTRE FOR ARCHITECTURE, MONTREAL

Bauspiel blocks, Alma Siedhoff-Busher, designer (1923); Kurt Naef, Zeiningen, Switzerland, ca. 1980

The Embossing Company produced numerous sets of plain building blocks, some with the added feature of holes that turned them into construction sets. Dandonah, The Fairy Palace, a German block set based on the architectural designs of Bruno Taut, reflects the modernist interest in form for form's sake. Bauspiel was designed by Alma Siedhoff-Busher in Weimar, Germany, where the Bauhaus marriage of art and industry influenced the world of architecture, design, and education after World War I. These blocks, and the theory behind them, parallel the pedagogy and aesthetics of many of the blocks designed by educators for school use and for the home.

A further extension of the use of pure form is the building sets designed for children to make their own repeatable forms. The child as a constructive worker, learning to be a useful part of the great industrial world, is implicit in these building sets. Also implicit is a strong gender bias, so often portrayed on the covers and advertisements of building toys, sometimes subtly, other times as blatant as The Boy Contractor—"Practical Construction for Boys."

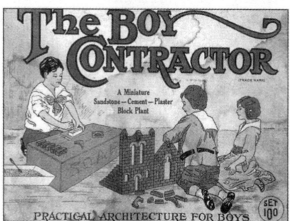

COURTESY OF ROBERT HULL FLEMING MUSEUM, BURLINGTON, VT.

The Boy Contractor, Cruver Manufacturing Co., Chicago, 1919

Blocks as transmitters of culture: Rebuilding architectural history

The idea that children could be taught a range of building types and architectural styles and highlights of architectural history was a dominant focus of blocks designed by the European and American toy market. F. Ad Richter and Company produced thousands of building sets using blocks made of artificial sandstone and linseed oil. Perfectly proportioned and colored in muted tones of red, gray, and blue, these sets were compactly packaged (a lesson in spatial organization) and were accompanied by plan books and scale drawings of real and imagined buildings. They were a great success.

COURTESY OF THE AUTHOR

Anchor Blocks instruction sheet, F. Ad Richter and Co., Germany and New York, 1899

Many block sets depicted buildings from "exotic" countries. The Peking Palace (1870), a fanciful set of German wood blocks with architecture decorations lithographed on paper, encouraged children to rearrange the building into a variety of forms, thus inventing their own versions of a palace.

Sets of village blocks were also common. Some sets contained simple block forms that represented specific buildings, allowing children to create arrangements of nineteenth-century town plans. Other village sets had components that could be combined like a three-dimensional puzzle to build a church or other familiar architectural structure. Although children most likely built many other wildly imaginative structures, at least their parents were reassured that they were being both constructive and religious—a winning combination for learning in the 1880s.

New building toys emerging in the early twentieth century encouraged children to represent more modern architectural forms. For example, the Bilt E-Z The Boy Builder construction set paralleled the curtain wall of the new modern skyscraper. Building toys were declared a necessity for every home. Newspapers and magazines and, later, television advertised an abundant variety of educational building blocks, and parents purchased them in ever-increasing quantity.

Learning materials in the classroom

During the late nineteenth century when the McLoughlin Brothers were pumping out their charming nested blocks, children faced primary classrooms devoid of visual stimulation and, certainly, of objects of play. Although some nineteenth-century rural schoolteachers used the natural environment as part of their lessons—picking flowers, making baskets from reeds, collecting birds' nests—most teachers stuck to the slate board and seat work.

But a revolution in the education of very young children was brewing, a revolution that emphasized the importance of building/construction materials in the learning process. This began with Friedrich Froebel (who was certainly influenced by Johann Pestalozzi's hands-on learning approach), followed by Maria Montessori, Caroline Pratt, and Patty Smith Hill, and continued into the 1950s with George Cuisenaire and into today with computers and Seymour Papert. Although many theorists study the play behavior of children, only a few go on to design play/learning material and to write passionately about its use.

Froebel Gifts 5 and 6, Milton Bradley Co., Springfield, Mass., 1869

The materials designed by Froebel, Montessori, and Pratt were austere and monochromatic, emphasizing the structural relationships between the units. In contrast, the alphabet and picture blocks manufactured by Jesse Crandall, S. L. Hill, and R. Bliss were decorated with colorful images, following Locke's idea of mixing pleasure with learning.

If Froebel (1782–1852) is the father of kindergarten, then perhaps his Gifts and Occupations are the mother of

manipulatives. Before Froebel, geometric blocks/toys were used as simple building materials or as drawing models. Froebel's series of Gifts and Occupations were designed as part of a systematic method for children to learn through play.

Based on the construction and transformation of forms, the materials were presented in a strictly determined sequence. Children began with solid shapes—the sphere, the cylinder, and the cube—moved to the flat plane and the line, and finally returned to three-dimensional construction with points and lines using peas or waxed pellets and sticks. Children would build three basic forms with the blocks: "forms of life" (representing objects from the world—houses, furniture, trees), "forms of knowledge" (giving physical substance to abstract ideas—number and geometry); and "forms of beauty" (creating imaginative designs, mainly based on symmetry, for aesthetic appreciation).

Although Froebel's work ([1826] 1887) was based on highly abstract ideas, symbolized by blocks and other three-dimensional materials, the fact that children were given physical objects to play with as the basis for learning revolutionized early childhood education.

The kindergarten movement, which started in Germany in the 1840s, quickly spread to the United States through the efforts of educators who had observed the Froebelian kindergartens in action. Milton Bradley, an enterprising lithographer, began in 1869 to manufacture the Gifts and Occupations for the American school market.

But by the 1890s the Froebelian materials and methods were under attack by kindergarten reformers. They criticized the formal, sequential use of the gifts, the lack of what they considered self-determined purpose in the child's play, the small size of the items, and the emphasis on sedentary activities.

Cooperative building with Patty Smith Hill blocks, ca. 1930

In 1905 Patty Smith Hill, a faculty member of Teachers College/Columbia University, questioned the lack of free play and proceeded to make modifications to the blocks.

Recognition of the child's need for large-motor activity and the child as a social being led to the design of larger blocks.

The Hill Blocks, first manufactured by the Schoenhut Company in Philadelphia, continued to be made in modified form into the 1950s. They consisted of a series of blocks, square pillars, and metal rods that secured the pieces. Because of their size and weight, the blocks necessitated the involvement and cooperation of several children to construct a building.

It is clear why John Dewey was in sympathy with the work of Patty Smith Hill: "The [Hill] kindergarten, as a laboratory of democratic citizenship, was in keeping with Dewey's pragmatic policy of expanding the school's social responsibility" (Weber 1979, 31). Children worked together as "a miniature community, an embryonic society" (Dewey 1899, 41) as they explored and represented the world they knew—their home, their neighborhood, and the larger community.

In 1913 Caroline Pratt, an educator who had received woodworking training in Sweden, developed unit system blocks for her experimental classroom at Harley House and at the City and Country School that she helped found in New York City. She designed "do-withs," wood figures of family and community workers, to accompany the unit blocks. Pratt's designs, and her pioneering work on the use of blocks ([1948] 1990) as a social, intellectual, and aesthetic learning tool, still resonate today.

Harriet Johnson, in her *Children in the Nursery School* ([1928] 1972), documented the block work of children 14 months to three years old at The Nursery School, a project of the Bureau of Educational Experiments, organized in New York City in 1917 by Harriet Johnson, Caroline Pratt, and Lucy Sprague Mitchell. The City and Country School and Bank Street School for Children still carry on this strong block-building tradition.) This classic book presents a richly detailed discussion of children using blocks in a natural setting.

At the Casa dei Bambini in Italy, Maria Montessori (1870–1952) originated a series of blocks called "didactic materials" based on the systematic training of the senses as a way for children to understand the world. She observed that children between the ages of two and six go through a period in which they are interested in the placement of objects.

Montessori's sensorial materials, used on small mats, were designed to isolate a specific attribute such as height, length, width, depth, or color. For example, the Pink Tower builds up incrementally from large to small. The resulting structure is taken down and rebuilt over and over again until the child tires of the process.

In *Spontaneous Activity in Education*, Montessori wrote, "Our sensorial material, in fact, analyses and represents the attributes of things: dimensions, forms, colors, smoothness or roughness of surface, weight, temperature, flavor, noise, and sounds. It is the qualities of the object, not the objects themselves, which are important,

COURTESY OF ROBERT HULL FLEMING MUSEUM, BURLINGTON, VT.

Pink Tower, Maria Montessori, designer (ca. 1908); Nienhuis Montessori USA, Mountain View, Calif., 1985

although these qualities, isolated one from the other, are themselves represented by objects" ([1917] 1971, 203).

The materials designed by Montessori were precisely crafted and either painted with a single color or left natural. With little alteration, they are still being made for Montessori classrooms today.

COURTESY OF GUMMY LUMP (WWW.GUMMYLUMP.COM)

Unit Blocks

The blocks of Hill, Pratt, and Montessori were based in great part on the observation and knowledge of children's natural interests. Children's interaction with open-ended materials has been observed and studied by several developmental psychologists, beginning with G. Stanley Hall in the 1890s, by Arnold Gesell at the Yale Clinic in the 1930s, in clinical settings, and by Piaget with his own children. Teachers, informed by these studies and the work of early progressive educators, rallied together and tried to influence the selection of classroom materials and to change the prevailing methods of pedagogy.

Unit blocks can be found today in most preschools, nursery schools, and some kindergartens. More infrequently they are found in the early grades, where they are usually in the guise of math manipulatives; the floor blocks, literally and figuratively, have been elevated to the table, assuming an academic aura.

This math emphasis began in the late 1950s as a reaction to the former Soviet Union's launch of Sputnik, with the U.S. government declaring that schools needed to improve the teaching of math and science. The initiative led to the development of a wide variety of manipulatives and supporting educational guides, derived in part from the work of Froebel, Montessori, and Pratt—for example, Cuisenaire Rods, the Stern Apparatus, Dienes Logiblocs, Unifix Cubes, and the Lowenfeld Poleidoblocs.

The richness of block building was funneled into one specific area of knowledge: mathematical thinking. "The variety of shapes and sizes in Poleidoblocs G and A enables children through construction and experiment to discover the basic structure of mathematics. The range of shapes gives wide opportunities for discovering and establishing equivalencies in length, height, area, and volume, making tangible, and therefore real, what children have so far learned only symbolically (Educational Supply Association 1971, 28). But the originators of the new manipulatives also encouraged free play and exploration.

Electronic blocks

Computers, though seemingly not blocklike at all, have entered the block market. Gryphon Bricks, a CD-Rom developed in 1996 by Gryphon Software Company, is one of several software programs that allow children to "construct" on the computer.

Advertisements and articles extol the advantages of virtual computer blocks over physical blocks for the classroom teacher since they are "neat," "convenient," and "easy to manage"—not a convincing pedagogical argument. Although the computer has vast possibilities as a "manipulative," it is not a substitute for building in three dimensions.

The most complex and far-reaching work combining blocks and computers is occurring at the MIT Media Laboratory. Over the last 10 years, researchers there have developed a group of digital manipulatives (for example, LEGO MindStorms programmable bricks).

We believe that these new manipulatives can combine the best of the physical and the digital worlds, drawing on children's passions and intuitions about physical objects, but extending

those objects to allow new types of explorations. In this way, digital manipulatives are starkly different from traditional use of computers in education, which tend to draw children away from the physical-world interactions. (Resnick et al. 2000, 2)

MindStorms is aimed at children beyond preschool, but the underlying idea is common to all block building: "Learners are particularly likely to make new ideas when they are actively engaged in making some type of external artifact—be it a robot, a poem, a sandcastle, or a computer program—which they can reflect upon and share with others" (Kafai & Resnick 1996, 1).

Educators, developmental psychologists, designers, and manufacturers have helped develop and promote the educational value of blocks and open-ended play. Yet, except as math manipulatives, blocks are still rarely seen in classrooms beyond kindergarten. Even in many early childhood classrooms today, their full potential as learning tools is not considered.

The destructive/deconstructive activity characteristic of block play, an integral part of this activity, makes some adults uncomfortable. However, as in all learning, we cannot understand until we take apart, examine, and rebuild. Children need an environment with open-ended materials and teachers who understand, encourage, build on, and even participate in this basic and complex mode of learning. This means having enough

- classroom space devoted to block play;
- time set aside for serious and ongoing play with blocks;
- focus on block work as evidenced by teachers' interaction with children through observation, documentation, revisiting structures, and sometimes participating in the play process; and
- time for teachers to share observations with colleagues and understand how children's block play connects with the development of literacy, physical knowledge, and mathematical thinking.

Blocks have been with us for a long time—and the activity of building even longer. The rich potential of blocks as a learning tool for young children to invent and represent ideas is still a challenge for teachers today.

References

Dewey, J. 1899. *The school and society.* Reprinted in *Dewey on education,* ed. M.S. Dworkin (New York: Teachers College Press, 1959). Out of print.

Educational Supply Association. 1971. *Educational Supply Association Limited.* Harlow, Essex, UK: Author.

Froebel, F. [1826] 1887. *The education of man.* Trans. WN. Hailmann. New York: Appleton.

Johnson, H. [1928] 1972. *Children in the nursery.* New York: Bank Street College of Education.

Kafai, Y, & M. Resnick, eds. 1996. *Constructionism in practice. Designing, thinking, and learning in a digital world.* Mahwah, NJ: Erlbaum.

Locke, J. 1693. *Some thoughts concerning education.* Text available online at www.socsci.kun.nl/ped/whp/histeduc/locke/index.html. See sections 63, 74.

Montessori, M. [1917] 1971. *Spontaneous activity in education.* Trans. F. Simmonds. Cambridge, MA: Robert Bentley.

Pratt, C. [1948] 1990. *I learn from children.* New York: Harper & Row, Perennial.

Resnick, M., M. Eisenberg, R. Berg, D. Mikhak, & D. Willow. 2000. Manuscript. Learning with digital manipulatives: New frameworks to help elementary-school students explore "advanced" mathematical and scientific concepts. Available online at www.media.mit.edu/papers/mres/digital-manip/.

Weber, E. 1979. Play materials in the curriculum of early childhood. In *Educational toys in America. 1800 to the present,* eds. K. Hewitt & L. Roomet. Burlington, VT: Robert Hull Fleming Museum.

For further reading

Exhibition catalogs from the Canadian Centre for Architecture, Montreal, Quebec:
Building in boxes. Architectural toys from the CCA. 1990.
Potential architecture: Construction toys from the CCA collection. 1991.
Toys that teach. 1992.
Toys in the modernist tradition. 1993.
Dream houses, toy homes. 1995. Toy town. 1998.
Toy town. 1998

Brosterman, N. 1997. *Inventing kindergarten. Nineteenth century children.* New York: Abrams.

Cartwright, S. 1988. Play can be the building blocks of learning. *Young Children* 43 (5): 44–47.

Cartwright, S. 1990. Learning with large blocks. *Young Children* 45 (3): 38–41.

Cartwright, S. 1995. Block play: Experiences in cooperative learning and living. *Child Care Information Exchange* (May): 30–41.

Charney, R., M.K. Clayton, & C. Wood. 1990. *Bringing blocks back to the classroom.* Greenfield, MA: Northeast Foundation for Children.

Clements, D. 1999. Young children and technology. In *Dialogue on early childhood science, mathematics, and technology education.* Washington, DC: American Association for the Advancement of Science. Available online at www.project2o6l.org/newsinfo/earlychild/experience/clements.htm.

Cuffaro, H.K. 1986. The development of block building. In *Building block art,* ed. P.H. Sperr. Philadelphia: Please Touch Museum.

Cuffaro, H.K. 1995. Block building: Opportunities for learning. *Child Care Information Exchange* (May): 36–38.

Cuffaro, H.K. 1995. *Experimenting with the world: John Dewey and the early childhood classroom.* New York: Teachers College Press.

Forman, G.E. 1982. A search for the origins of equivalence concepts through microanalysis of block-play. In *Action and thought. From sensorimotor schemes to symbolic operations,* ed. G.E. Forman. New York: Academic.

Guanella, F. 1934. Blockbuilding activities of young children. *Archives of Psychology* 174: 1–92.

Gura, P., ed. 1992. *Exploring learning. Young children and block play.* New York: Paul Chapman.

Hewitt, K. 1998. The building toy/the toy building: Symbol, structure, and style. In *Toying with architecture: The building toy in the arena of play.* Katonah, NY: Katonah Museum of Art.

Hirsch, E.S., ed. 1996. *The block book.* 3d ed. Washington, DC: NAEYC.

Papert, S. [1980] 1999. *MindStorms: Children, computers, and powerful ideas.* 2d ed. New York: Basic.

Reifel, S. 1984. Block construction: Children's developmental landmarks in representation of space. *Young Children* 40 (1): 61–67.

Reifel, S., & P.M. Greenfield. 1982. Structural development in symbolic medium: The representational use of block construction. In *Action and thought: From sensorimotor schemes to symbolic operations,* ed. G.E. Forman. New York: Academic.

Reifel, S., & J. Yeatman. 1991. Action, talk, and thought in the block corner: Developmental trends. In *Play and the social context of development in early care and education,* eds. B. Scales, M. Almy, A. Nicolopoulou, & S. Ervin-Tripp. New York: Teachers College Press.

Stritzel, K. 1995. Block play is for ALL children. *Child Care Information Exchange* (May): 42–47.

From *Young Children,* January 2001, pp. 85-91 with permission of the author, Karen Hewitt. © 2001 by the National Association for the Education of Young Children. Reprinted by permission.

Improving Public Health Through Early Childhood Movement Programs

Clersida Garcia, Luis Garcia, Jerald Floyd, and John Lawson

Early childhood is a unique period of life, a time when children are developing physically, emotionally, intellectually, and socially. Providing a movement development program at this early age enables children to acquire fundamental motor skills and the feeling of competence in movement. Once in place, these skills serve as the foundation for building more complex motor skills later in life. Early development of competence in movement has the potential to create a healthy habit of physical activity participation.

While learning motor skills is rewarding in itself, it also has significant health benefits. Research has demonstrated that virtually all individuals will benefit from regular physical activity. The Surgeon General's report on physical activity and health concluded that moderate physical activity can substantially reduce the risk of developing or dying from heart disease, diabetes, colon cancer, and high blood pressure (U.S. Dept. of Health and Human Services, 1996). If more Americans were physically active, our health care expenses would be reduced and the quality of our lives would improve.

Common sense suggests that happy and successful experiences early in life predispose people to enjoy physical activity. If that is true, school administrators, early childhood educators, motor development specialists, and physical educators have a tremendous opportunity to influence the health of the next generation by providing movement program opportunities to young children.

This article discusses how movement programs can help young children develop fundamental movement patterns and healthy, active lifestyles while learning cognitive and psychosocial concepts. In addition, it describes specific techniques and approaches that educators can use to promote physical activity.

These techniques can give children positive, developmentally appropriate experiences with the ABCs of movement skills, thereby inspiring continued participation in and enjoyment of physical activity.

Public Health Goals for Physical Activity

In January 2000, the U.S. Department of Health and Human Services (USDHHS) launched Healthy People 2010, a comprehensive, nationwide health promotion and disease prevention agenda, which calls for Americans to increase their daily physical activity (USDHHS, 2000). Looking at the current level of physical activity, there is reason for great concern.

A significant portion of the United States population is sedentary. Forty percent of the adult population reported that they engaged in no leisure-time physical activity, while children and adolescents reported that they ride a bicycle on 2.4 percent of all trips two miles or less (USDHHS, 2000). As a result of our lack of exercise, too many of us are at risk for cardiovascular disease and other diseases. The problem is made worse by our being overweight and eating unhealthy diets. According to the National Center for Chronic Disease Prevention and Health Promotion (NCCDPHP, 2000), the percentage of overweight and obese children has more than doubled between 1980 and 1994, with 10 percent to 15 percent of children and adolescents being overweight. Sixty percent of five-to-ten-year-old obese children already have at least one risk factor for cardiovascular disease, and 25 percent of obese children have two or more risk factors (NCCDPHP, 2000). Young people are at particular risk for becoming sedentary as they grow older (President's Council on

Figure 1. Developmentally Appropriate Activity

In this self-paced activity, a child throws different kinds, sizes, and weights of balls while learning to place the throwing arm and stepping leg in position.

Figure 2. Integrating Other Domains

While playing "Pretending to Be Grownup People," these "firefighters" will earn play money for completing their job (negotiating obstacles) and then use the money to buy healthy food.

Figure 3. Meaningful Activity

Activities need to have a purpose that children understand. "Feeding the Animals" was a favorite.

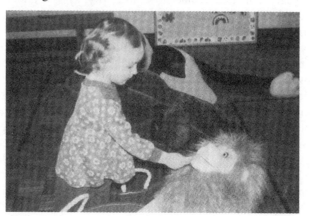

Figure 4. Hand-Eye Coordination

In another purposeful activity, "Going to Fish," children practice hand-eye coordination to connect their magnetic hook to the fish in the lake.

Figure 5. Agenda-Setting Activity

Children explore different means of transporting blood (blue bean bags represent deoxygenated blood; red bean bags represent oxygenated blood) to various body parts.

Figure 6. Creative Spontaneity

Children throw objects across a "river." Soon after, they spontaneously began to jump over the river. Activities that allow such creative spontaneity will engage children's interest longer.

Physical Fitness and Sports, 2001). Even among children aged three to four years, those who are less active tend to remain less active after the age of three than most of their peers (Pate, Baranowski, Dowda, & Trost, 1996). Viewed together, these statistics are quite alarming. Therefore, encouraging moderate and vigorous physical activity among youths seems essential.

Why are people inactive? No one knows the answers for sure. However, Barnett and Merriman (1991) have identified three misconceptions about early physical activity and motor skill development that may be partly responsible for the pattern of physical inactivity and the health problems our youth and adult populations are experiencing today.

Misconception #1: Children are "naturally" predisposed to vigorous activity. Various studies suggest that this is a false assumption and support early intervention. Cardiovascular disease has been detected among young children (NCCDPHP, 2000; Newman, Freedman, & Berenson, 1986). Furthermore, cardiovascular disease risk factors in children are increasing and have been tracked from childhood into adulthood (Nicklas, Webber, Johnson, Srinivasan, & Berenson, 1995). Today's youths are more sedentary than any previous generation. Nader, et al. (1995) found that young girls and boys between the ages of four and seven years showed similar deficiencies in physical activity at home. Not surprisingly, more children than ever have risk factors for cardiovascular and other diseases. High-tech toys and technological recreation often worsen these trends, encouraging children to sit for hours in front of the television or the computer screen rather than using their bodies. To counteract these influences, children need to be encouraged, instructed, and exposed to physical activity in order to develop the habits and dispositions to be physically active for life.

Misconception #2: Children "naturally" develop the fundamental motor skills they need through undirected play. Systematic observation of children demonstrates that they do not naturally develop fundamental motor skills. Many children never develop certain mature patterns of fundamental motor skills; as a result, they perform poorly as they get older. Furthermore, these early failures can damage the child's self-esteem, leading to statements like "I can't dance," or "I can't throw." A vicious circle may start, in which young people feel embarrassed. They know that they can't move efficiently; they feel awkward, uncoordinated, and inhibited, and therefore learn to avoid movement. Movement is no longer associated with joyful self-expression, but with failure and humiliation.

Longitudinal studies on the development of throwing (Garcia & Garcia, in press) found that this fundamental skill does not automatically mature. Most young children in this study began to perform at a mature stage of throwing after a year and a half of instruction and more than 400 trials. In other words, children need instruction, encouragement, and a lot of practice to achieve mature stages of this skill.

Misconception #3: Movement programs take away time and resources from other, more important educational activities. In fact, children's domains do not develop in isolation from one another. Cognitive, affective, social, and motor skills are interdependent. They should also be integrated in our movement curriculum designs and teaching practices. Movement pro-

Figure 7. Designing Equipment for Success

This child uses a suitable paddle: wide, light, and with a small grip. The balloon is set on a ring so it will stay in place before being hit.

All photos courtesy of the authors

grams can be more effective if they include activities that enhance cognitive, affective, and social development. At the same time, activities that develop those other domains have greater impact when they include movement and movement-related concepts (e.g., see Block, 2001; Block & Campbell, 2001). As we will suggest below, a developmental curriculum of movement activities includes all domains of development.

In conclusion, the misconceptions about physical activity and motor skill development in early childhood have had serious adverse effects on our youth and adult populations. The unique developmental opportunity offered by early childhood movement experiences is crucial to the overall health status of our youth and adult populations. We need to pay greater attention to the development of movement skills and to patterns of activity during the early childhood years. Once children develop sedentary habits, they are not likely to become more physically active as they grow to adulthood.

Designing and Developing the Preschool Movement Program

We know from common observation that there are at least two keys to developing successful movement programs: (1) allowing children to have fun with the activity, and (2) teaching children the fundamental motor skills. When children have fun with movement, they develop favorable attitudes toward it (Henderson, Glancy, & Little, 1999). An educational approach built on enjoyment helps to ensure that children will view physical activity positively, and thus will be predisposed to engage in it.

Figure 8. The Effect of Actions

Children kick plastic bottles toward targets. They said they liked the sounds the bottles made when kicked and the sounds of the bottles hitting the targets or the wall.

But having fun isn't enough. Many children have fun on the playground but never develop the basic skills they need. Thus, another key to a successful program is to teach children those basic motor skills using a developmentally and instructionally appropriate approach.

How do we design a successful early-childhood movement program? Garcia (1994) demonstrated that such programs are based on three principles:

1. Activities must be developmentally appropriate. Children's activities should accommodate a variety of individual characteristics and needs, including overall developmental status, previous movement experiences, fitness and skill level, body size, interests, and motivations. Children must be interested in the activities and have a choice—there is a great risk of destroying a positive attitude by forcing or pressuring children into performing activities they are not ready to try, or in contexts that make them uncomfortable.

Development programs provide the opportunity for active learning—learning through motion, through play, and through guided discovery. An example of this approach appears in figure 1, which shows children throwing objects of different kinds, sizes, and weights at a variety of targets. The children are allowed to make choices of distance, targets, and equipment. They pace their own activity while the teacher focuses on the opposition of the throwing arm to the stepping leg.

2. Activities should integrate and reinforce other developmental domains besides the physical domain. Physical, emotional, social and cognitive development are interrelated. Learning in one domain affects the others, and children are always striving to make connections between domains (National Association for Sport and Physical Education, 1994). Physical activities can be planned to engage children's imagination, their capacity for thinking and planning, and their ability to empathize and cooperate.

In figure 2, children are using different locomotor skills in a gamelike situation called "Pretending to be Grownup People," in which an obstacle course challenge becomes their 'job." After they are paid for finishing their job, they go to the grocery store to buy food. In the store they use the food pyramid to make healthy choices to place in a table setting. Afterwards, the instructor talks with the children about their choices and helps them to identify the foods found in the pyramid. This is an exciting game with a lot of pretending and physical activity, and its similarity to life events enables children to transfer and relate the information to their real life.

3. Activities should have contextual reinforcement. A well-planned movement curriculum can fill children with enthusiasm for physical activity, but those children must receive encouragement to use their physical skills elsewhere—in the home, in other classes, and among their peers. Teachers and program administrators can help to make sure their students receive that kind of encouragement by communicating with other teachers, parents, and the community at large. They can also include incentives for children to use their skills outside of class as a part of their curriculum.

Activities should occur in environments similar to those that children experience daily. By building associations between those environments and pleasurable physical activities, teachers increase the likelihood that children will continue to engage in movement on their own.

Research has shown that children continue to participate in physical activity when movement activities are meaningful to the children themselves (Garcia, 1994). The movements must have a purpose that children can understand. For instance, when asked which of several activities they liked best, children typically responded that they liked "feeding the animals" (figure 3). This was an activity in which they moved back and forth using different locomotor skills to get food and feed stuffed animals. They also liked it "when the activity kept going," as it did in the grocery store activity, in which they bought one food item and set the table each time. Both of these are activities in which the children repeatedly go around obstacle courses.

Obstacle courses are a favorite of children, especially when the course provides personal excitement, such as crawling through a "tunnel." Other examples of "purposeful" activities include "delivering mail," "visiting the zoo," and "going to fish" (figure 4). Children perform locomotor activities and utilize arm and leg strength to get into the lake before "going to fish." During the fishing action (connecting the end of the fish pole to the magnet on the fish), children practice hand-eye coordination skills. These activities include locomotor activities that relate to things the children can do in the course of their daily life outside school. All these activities have strong associations across the developmental spectrum, from physical to cognitive.

In addition, Garcia (1994) has shown that children continue to participate when activities include prompts or situations that allow them to develop their own agenda. Such situations typically lead to discoveries or exercise of the imagination. One agenda-setting activity (figure 5) allowed children to explore different ways of transporting blood (beanbags) to different body parts and organs.

Several pictures of the body parts were posted for guidance and motivation. All children were willing to move around to bring blood to all the body parts. Another activity provided children with pieces of small equipment (ropes, ribbons, hoops) and encouraged them to use those items in creative forms of activity.

Teachers facilitated and guided the children, posing questions and appropriate challenges. Children responded with a variety of movements. After the activity, children's typical comments included: "I played with the rope, and pretended it was a snake," "I used the rope as my choo-choo train," and "I like to turn it over my head." Another agenda-setting activity asked children to imagine that they were throwing things over a "river." Soon, children were jumping into the imaginary river, just as they might if they really were playing on a riverbank. When movement activities allow for creative spontaneity and adaptation of this kind, children remain engaged in them longer (figure 6).

Garcia (1994) found that children continue activities when they experience success in the task at hand. Success is more likely if physical activities are designed and equipment is adjusted to correspond with children's individual skill levels. In figure 7, the size and weight of the ball and racquet conform with the child's individual skill level and success rate.

When success rates are high, children try their best virtually every time. When asked why they repeated certain actions many times, children's responses included: "I like when I hit the clown and he goes down and goes up again—it's funny;" "I like kicking the shaker bottles," and "I like the sound they make" (figure 8). They like to see the impact of their actions. This reinforces the notion that children like to exert control over the situation. When they are able to influence the situation, children tend to balance their challenges and successes in ways that keep them engaged and ensure a positive experience.

By applying the principles illustrated in this section, movement education programs can help children master fundamental motor skills. Equally important, they can help children develop positive associations with activity that will predispose them favorably toward physical activity in other areas of their lives. These are prerequisites of a lifetime of healthful and joyful physical activity.

References

Barnett, B. & Merriman, W. (1991). Misconceptions in motor developments. *Strategies, 5*(3), 5–7.

Block, B. A. (2001). Literacy through movement: An organizational approach. *Journal of Physical Education, Recreation & Dance, 72*(1), 39–48.

Block, B. A., & Campbell, E. F. (2001). Reinforcing literacy through movement for children with hearing disabilities. *Journal of Physical Education, Recreation & Dance, 72*(7), 30–36.

Garcia, C. (1994). Motivating fundamental motor skills learning in preschool children. *Journal of Sport and Exercise Psychology, 16*(Suppl. 94), S55.

Garcia, C., & Garcia, L. (in press). Examining developmental changes in throwing: A close up look. *Motor Development Research & Reviews.*

Henderson, K., Glancy, M., & Little, S. (1999). Putting the fun into physical activity. *Journal of Physical Education, Recreation & Dance, 70*(8), 43–45, 49.

Nader, P. R., Sallis, J. F., Broyles, S. L., McKenzie, T. L., Berry, C. C., Davis, T. B., Zive, M. M., Elder, J. P., & FrankSpohrer, C. C. (1995). Ethnic and gender trends for cardiovascular risk behaviors in Anglo and Mexican-American children, ages four to seven. *Journal of Health Education, 26*(2, Suppl.), S27–35.

National Association for Sport and Physical Education. (1994). Developmentally appropriate practices in movement programs for young children. Reston, VA: Author.

National Center for Chronic Disease Prevention and Health Promotion. (2000). Preventing obesity among children. *Chronic disease notes and reports, 13*(1), 1–4.

Newman, W. O., Freedman, D. S., & Berenson, G. (1986). Regulation of serum lipoprotein levels and systolic blood pressure to early atherosclerosis. The Bogalusa Heart Study. *New England Journal of Medicine, 314*, 138–144.

Nicklas, T. A., Webber, L. S., Johnson, C. C., Srinivasan, S. R., & Berenson, G. S., (1995). Foundations for health promotion with youth: A review of observations from the Bogalusa Heart Study. *Journal of Health Education, 26*(2, Suppl.), S18–26.

Pate, R. R., Baranowski, T., Dowda, M., & Trost, S. G., (1996). Tracking of physical activity in young children. *Medicine and Science in Sports and Exercise, 28*(1), 92–96.

President's Council on Physical Fitness and Sports. (2001). Healthy people 2010: Physical activity and fitness. *Research Digest*, Series 3, No. 13.

U.S. Department of Health and Human Services. (2000). *Healthy People 2010*. Washington, DC: Author.

U.S. Department of Health and Human Services. (1996). *Physical activity and health: A report of the Surgeon General.* Atlanta, GA: Centers for Disease Control and Prevention.

Clersida Garcia is an associate professor, Luis Garcia is an assistant professor, and Jerald Floyd is a professor emeritus of the Department of Kinesiology & Physical Education at Northern Illinois University, DeKalb, IL, 60115. John Lawson is an assistant professor of communications at Robert Morris College, Pittsburgh, PA, 15108.

Reprinted with permission from the January 2002 issue of *Journal of Physical Education, Recreation & Dance*, pp. 27-31, 53, a publication of the American Alliance for Health, Physical Education, Recreation and Dance, 1900 Association Dr., Reston, VA 20191, www.aapherd.org.

Using Documentation Panels To Communicate With Families

Teachers have always faced the challenges of developing communication between the home and the school, as well as of conveying their understanding about how children learn.

Judith Brown-DuPaul, Tracy Keyes, and Laura Segatti

Upon arriving at her son's classroom one afternoon, a mother noticed several other parents and children clustered around a table. The table contained a large, three-sided board filled with photographs, simple text, and some children's artwork. As the mother approached the group, she heard excitement in the voices of the children: "Oh look! That's when we tried to rub all the trees with crayons." "See, I'm in the picture where we put all the tree parts into piles on trays." Finally, her son saw her and pulled her toward the large board. He said, "Look, Mom! The teacher finished the big board on all the stuff we did with trees!"

The large board that caused all of the excitement in the classroom is called a documentation panel. Such panels showcase class photographs and children's artwork and dictation, which are linked with educational captions, information from books and journals, and curriculum webs. Traditionally, many early childhood programs have used bulletin boards to display art projects and class photographs for parents to enjoy. One of the main differences between such displays and documentation panels is that the panels are a communicative tool (Tarini, 1997).

When teachers pair these materials with clear captions about the knowledge children are constructing, parents begin to develop an understanding of how children learn. For example, by linking art samples to captions describing color mixing, problem-solving, and creativity, teachers can help parents to understand the benefits of a hands-on, open ended curriculum. The panel mentioned in the above vignette showed how, through many child-initiated and planned experiences, the class had been studying trees. The [panel], Science for Young Children, show[ed] the documentation panel teachers created to share with families some of the activities and learning

that had occurred during this tree project. The panel emphasized that learning occurs during everyday learning experiences, such as rubbing a tree with crayons and classifying all of the parts of trees.

Benefits of Documentation Panels

Teachers have always faced the challenges of developing communication between the home and the school, as well as of conveying their understanding about how children learn. Documentation panels are a unique way to highlight classroom learning; teachers can use them to communicate with families about a myriad of concepts and issues. The panels can effectively document learning in classrooms with students of all ages, from infancy through elementary school.

The web in Figure 1 details some common foci for panels. While many teachers choose to create panels about certain curriculum areas or projects, the specific topics will vary depending on the age of the children, that particular class's interests, parental questions or concerns, and the message that the teacher wants to communicate.

Teachers traditionally have communicated their educational philosophies to families through parent workshops or newsletters. These methods have their drawbacks, however. The barriers that limit attendance at parent meetings have been well-chronicled (Foster, 1994; Kieff & Wellhousen, 2000). Newsletters may be discarded or not read thoroughly; and those that are only written in English distance parents for whom English is not their home language (National Association for the Education of Young Children, 1996).

Documentation panels, because of their interactive format, and because they draw parents into the classroom,

Construction of Documentation Panels

Make a decision on what you want to communicate

Projects or themes
Special events
Specific curriculum areas
Learning environments
Skill acquisition
Child development

Collected materials for the panel

Children's actual work or photocopies
Observation notes/anecdotal records
Information and quotes from books and journals
Curriculum webs
Quotes and dictation from children and teachers
Photographs
  —various sizes (enlarge or shrink on a photocopier)
  —color, or black-and-white

Select the best items that represent the idea or theme of your panel

Write an educational caption for each piece
Use a type size large enough to be read from a distance

Layout of panel

Determine where the panel will be displayed (on a table or wall?)
Select type of panel: poster board (best for wall) or three-sided board

Title the panel
Select a strong image as the focal point on the panel
Aesthetics are important
  —Matte work and photographs
  —Use colored paper to support, not detract from, the images
  —Less is best; too many items will distract the viewer
  —Remember that people tend to look at things from left to right and top to bottom
Use the following Guiding Questions to check for changes:
  —Does the panel convey your intended message?
  —How many different kinds of documentation do you see?
  —What can you add now?
Will this panel entice children and families to view it?
Ask someone to give you feedback on the layout before attaching pieces to the panel
Attach the items to the panel with glue or double-sided tape

Display

Place the panel in a location where families and children may easily view it, such as the entryway into the classroom or near children's cubbies.

(Adapted from *Spreading the News* by Carter and Curtis, 1996)

Table 1

are much more effective than newsletters. Parents are particularly attracted by the visual appeal of the panels, as well as of children's photographs and work samples. Furthermore, as the vignette from the beginning of the article illustrated, children will often prompt parents to look at the panels. Together, the adult and the child may discuss an art experience, classroom project, or field trip that is highlighted on the panel (Saltz, 1997).

Families who linger in the center reap additional benefits. They have the opportunity to observe teacher-child interactions, ask the teacher questions, offer feedback about curriculum or development, and meet other families. Family-school partnerships are strengthened when families are encouraged to spend more time in the classroom and offered more information about their children's education (McBridge, 1999). Hence, viewing the panels in the classroom opens and supports homeschool communication more readily than does reading a newsletter at home.

Some researchers hypothesize that parents become more involved as their awareness of classroom learning grows (Carter & Curtis, 1996; Katz, 1994). After viewing panels, parents may feel more comfortable volunteering or offering suggestions for future projects. Family members also may choose to extend some of the learning experiences or projects at home. This "search for common ground" between the home and school environment may lead to more successful family involvement programs (Coleman & Wallinga, 2000, p. 209).

Using Panels To Convey Educational Philosophy

Because information must be conveyed succinctly, documentation panels help teachers to clarify their understanding of how children learn. Carter and Curtis (1996) emphasize that "collecting stories of children's activities and broadcasting them through documentation displays offers a method and a motivation to pay closer attention to the value of children's play" (p. 17). This reflection should influence teachers' planning and help them to articulate their philosophy to families. This process is especially important in those circumstances when parents question the value of play or of emergent curriculum (Breign-Allen & Dillon, 1997) and, consequently, pressure teachers for tangible evidence of children's learning, such as dittos or worksheets. Documentation panels provide evidence that children are engaged in active learning.

Figure 1

When parents see the panels, they may stop asking, "How could she be here for four hours and 'do nothing'?" or "All he ever does is play… when are you going to teach him something?"

Integrating Visual and Written Knowledge

Documentation panels educate parents through two distinct modes of information. One is visual knowledge, such as photographs of children building with blocks; the other is a written explanation. An example of written knowledge is a caption that describes the benefits of block play ("It stimulates children's creativity, teaches them cooperative problem-solving methods, and helps them learn about gravity, physics, classification, and shapes"). By exploring these concepts in more than one way, parents may develop a better understanding of the teacher's preferred teaching philosophy.

Photographs and visual aids are especially meaningful in centers with multilingual populations. Captions could be printed in more than one language, to provide a way

for everyone to participate in their children's learning experiences.

Constructing Documentation Panels

Some guidance is in order to ensure that the documentation panels are educational and are not simply attractive bulletin boards (see Table 1 for ideas.) Initially, teachers need to decide what—through photographs, work samples, observation notes, and children's dictation—they hope to communicate to parents. Supporting information, such as curriculum webs or quotes from academic sources, can then be integrated with descriptive captions.

Paying attention to aesthetics will give the panel a professional, attractive appearance. The colors and materials need to catch the viewer's eye, yet should not detract from the purpose of the panel. Some consideration also should be given to achieving a balance of children's artwork, photographs, and text. See Carter and Curtis (1996) for specific recommendations on designing panels. As culminating step, teachers need to take time to ask themselves guiding questions (see Table 1) to ensure that the documentation panels are as engaging and instructional as they are attractive.

Displaying Documentation Panels

These family education tools can be used in numerous ways. Panels may be posters mounted on walls, or they may be three-sided, free-standing boards used alone or with three-dimensional objects (Helm, Beneke, & Sternheimer, 1988a, 1988b). In some centers, panels are displayed for extended periods of time. Panels dealing with developmental issues provide an ongoing source of information for families. Panels can help prospective families or parents who are new to the center learn more about its philosophy. Some panels may be displayed for shorter time periods, or may be added to throughout the year.

To maximize exposure, centers often display panels in high traffic areas near the cubbies or in the hallways. When home visits are an option, teachers may bring small portable boards with them to foster home-school communication.

Panels provide a professional centerpiece for a parent meeting, and offer information for any family members who could not attend an event or workshop. Hand-outs may help teachers highlight key points from the panels.

Conclusion

A documentation panel is an innovative way to "document with our pens and camera the learning process of our children and adults" (Carter & Curtis, 1996, p. 8). The panels provide an opportunity for parents to become more fully aware of what occurs in their child's learning environment. For staff, creating the panels becomes part of the documentation of children's learning, a process that may lead to more activities that are attuned to each child's interests and skill levels. Finally, the panels promote parent-teacher partnerships by providing a springboard for discussion of best practices, projects or themes, classroom experiences, curriculum, and child development.

References

Breig-Allen, C., & Dillon, J. U. (1997). Implementing the process of change in a public school setting. In J. Hendrick (Ed.), *First steps toward teaching the Reggio way* (pp. 126–40). Columbus, OH: Merrill.

Carter, M., & Curtis, D. (1996). *Spreading the news.* St.Paul, MN: Red Leaf Press.

Coleman, M., & Wallinga, C. (2000). Connecting families and classrooms using family involvement webs. *Childhood Education, 76,* 209–214.

Foster, S. (1994). Successful parent meetings. *Young Children, 50,* 78–80.

Helm, J. H., Beneke, S., & Steinheimer, K. (1998a). *Windows on learning: Documenting young children's work.* New York: Teachers College Press.

Helm, J. H., Beneke, S., & Steinheimer, K. (1998b). *Teacher materials for documenting young children's work: Windows on learning.* New York: Teachers College Press.

Katz, L. (1994). Images from the world: Study seminar on the experience of the municipal infant-toddler centers and preprimary schools of Reggio Emilia, Italy. In L. Katz & B. Cesarone (Eds.), *Reflections on the Reggio Emilia approach* (pp. 7–19). Urbana, IL: ERIC/EECE.

Kieff, J., & Wellhousen, K. (2000). Planning family involvement in early childhood programs. *Young Children, 55,* 18–25.

McBride, S. (1999). Research in review: Family-centered practices. *Young Children, 54,* 62–68.

National Association for the Education of Young Children. (1996). NAEYC Position Statement: Responding to linguistic and cultural diversity—Recommendations for effective early childhood education. *Young Children, 51,* 4–12.

Saltz, R. (1997). The Reggio Emilia influence at the University of Michigan-Dearborn Child Development Center: Challenges and change. In J. Hendrick (Ed.), *First steps toward teaching the Reggio way* (pp. 167–180). Columbus, OH: Merrill.

Tarini, E. (1997). Reflections on a year in Reggio Emilia: Key concepts in rethinking and learning the Reggio way. In J. Hendrick (Ed.), *First steps toward teaching the Reggio way* (pp. 56–69). Columbus, OH: Merrill.

Judith Brown-DuPaul is Adjunct Faculty, Teacher Education Programs, Lehigh-Carbon Community College, Schnecksville, Pennsylvania. Tracy Keyes is Assistant Professor, Elementary Education, Kutztown University, Kutztown, Pennsylvania. Laura Segatti is Assistant Professor, Teacher Education Programs, Lehigh-Carbon Community College.

Correspondence regarding this article should be addressed to Judith Brown-DuPaul, Teacher Education Programs, Lehigh-Carbon Community College, 4525 Education Park Drive, Schnecksville, PA 18078-2598.

From *Childhood Education*, Summer 2001, pp. 209-213 with permission of the authors, Judith Brown-DuPaul, Tracy Keyes, and Laura Segatti. © 2001 by the Association for Childhood Education International.

The Right Way to Read

In the old days, preschoolers had no more pressing business than to learn how to play. New research shows that they benefit from instruction in words and sounds.

BY BARBARA KANTROWITZ AND PAT WINGERT

WHEN YOU WALK THROUGH THE brightly colored door of the Roseville Cooperative Preschool in northern California, you're entering a magical, pint-size world where 3- and 4-year-olds are masters of the universe. At the science table, they use magnifying glasses to explore piles of flowers, cacti and shells. In the smock-optional art area, budding da Vincis often smear blotches of red, blue and yellow directly on the table. (It's wiped off with a damp cloth when the next artist steps up.) There are ropes for climbing and two loft areas: one carpeted and filled with books and a dollhouse, and the other with a clear Plexiglas floor, perfect for keeping an eye on the activities below. There are no letters or numbers on the walls to distract from this focused play. The only rule, says director and founder Bev Bos, is that the kids

are in control. "I tell other teachers, 'Forget about kindergarten, first grade, second grade'," she says. "We should be focusing on where children are right now."

THE NEW THINKING: Without early, explicit instruction in the relationship between letters and sounds, a significant number of young children may be at risk for serious reading problems throughout their lives

Sounds like an idyllic preschool learning environment, right? Wrong, according to a growing number of early-education researchers. Until quite recently, Bev Bos's

philosophy was the standard at preschools around the country, and there are still lots of teachers who passionately defend the idea that they should be helping kids feel secure and learn to play well with others, not learn the three Rs. But researchers now say the old approach ignores mounting evidence that many preschoolers need explicit instruction in the basics of literacy—the stuff most of us started to learn in first grade, how words fall on a page and the specific sounds and letters that make up words. New brain research shows that reading is part of a complex continuum that begins with baby talk and scribbles, and culminates in a child with a rich vocabulary and knowledge of the world. While some children acquire the literacy skills they need by osmosis, through their everyday experiences, many don't. Most at risk are children of poverty, who are twice as likely to have serious trouble reading. But studies have also shown that at least 20 percent of middle-class children have reading disabilities and that early intervention could save many of them from a lifetime of playing catch-up.

Earlier this month the increasingly fractious schoolyard brawl—between old-style educators who fear kids will be pushed to read and the new guard who fear they won't be pushed enough—became even more heated when President George W. Bush rolled out his early-childhood-education plan. Bush put himself squarely in the early-reading camp when he proposed retraining all 50,000 Head Start teachers in the most effective ways to provide explicit instruction in the alphabet, letter sounds and writing—whether through responsive reading to kids, early writing experiences or carefully designed group projects. He also wants Head Start to use a detailed literacy-screening test and asked for an unprecedented $45 million for preschool-reading research. Bush's domestic-policy adviser, Margaret Spellings, says preschool teachers shouldn't be afraid of these changes. "This is not about putting little kids in desks at age 3," Spellings says. "This is about doing things right from the beginning of life. It's the social-emotional *plus* the cognitive."

HEAD START'S WAY:
Youngsters growing up in low-income neighborhoods are the most likely to have reading problems, but they may also need extra help with social-emotional development and health care

That hasn't reassured many preschool teachers, nor the National Head Start Association, which has vigorously attacked the Bush plan. "There's far more to children's development than just reading," says Cynthia Cummings, executive director of Community Parents Inc., a Head Start program in the Bedford-Stuyvesant section of Brooklyn. "We have children who come in who are not potty trained, who don't know how to sit down in a chair, who have difficulty following a routine, who may have some other types of delays that will affect their language. You have to address those." This holistic approach could get a boost this week, when

Sen. Ted Kennedy, a longtime supporter of Head Start, is expected to introduce legislation that would create a comprehensive early child-care system, with reading readiness—the main focus of the Bush plan—as just one component.

Both sides in this debate agree that young children learn best when their five senses are engaged, when teachers and parents provide hands-on ways to master important language skills. But teachers like Bev Bos worry that making the ABCs a top priority will mean "drill and kill" instead of rich language experiences. "I'm afraid kids won't have any childhood," Bos says. Preliteracy advocates admit there's a danger that the new ideas will be incorrectly implemented. They say teacher training will help, and they stress that in the most effective preliteracy programs, there is no "reading hour" or all-group instruction, no teacher with a pointer at the head of the class. The goal isn't to get all kids actually decoding words at 4 or 5—though some may be ready to do that—but rather to expose them to the basics. The kids think they're just having fun when they play word games with blocks, although their teachers know better.

At the Children's Village Child Care Center in Philadelphia, nearly 200 children, many from non-English-speaking homes, spend much of their day engaged in activities specifically designed to develop pre-reading skills. There are lots of alphabet puzzles and games, as well as reading and writing areas full of books, crayons, pencils and paper. The school's library includes bilingual Chinese-English children's books because many of the parents are Chinese immigrants. "We want to encourage parents to read to the children, no matter what the language," says director Mary Graham.

One morning last week, Miranda Tan, who just turned 5, worked with her teacher, Norma Bell, on her "phonics writing book." In it, she practices what is often called invented spelling—writing down words as they sound rather than as they are actually spelled. Early-reading proponents say it would be more accurate to describe this practice as "phonics writing," to get across the message that it's an exercise in phonemics (the way letters represent sounds) rather than true spelling. Miranda's book is titled "My Big Sister," and the first page offers a drawing of a girl with a blue face, pink hair and a brown dress. Underneath, written in shaky print, is "c e s my sistr kli." Bell reads it back to her and then writes, "This is my sister Kelly" underneath Miranda's sentence.

Early-literacy advocates say this kind of detailed instruction is especially important for the kids in the poorest neighborhoods who have the least exposure to books and sophisticated use of language. In one study, researchers found that children of poverty start school with a vocabulary of only about 10,000 words, compared with 40,000 for kids from middle-class homes. Bush has said that statistics like these prompted him to target poor kids, especially Head Start participants. As the governor and First Lady of Texas, Bush and his wife, Laura, were impressed by the success of the preliteracy curriculum at the Margaret Cone Head Start Center in Dallas. Until a few years ago, more than a quarter of the children coming into the program at the age of 4 scored in the bottom 1 percent of a national preschool test. Even more troubling, the same group had even lower scores after a year at the Cone Center, despite special funding from Texas Instruments that gave them access to high-quality health care, often cited as a factor in school success.

THE OLD THINKING: Many
preschool teachers were taught that they should concentrate on helping kids feel confident and learn to get along with other children. More academic work could wait until first grade.

All that changed when the Cone Center adopted a curriculum developed at Southern Methodist University. Every child now wears a name tag, a visual and personal reminder of their link to the world of print around them. Teachers spend time with kids in small groups talking about word sounds and letter names. Children are encouraged to talk in sentences, use new words and stick to proper English. When the new curriculum was introduced, some Cone teachers were dubious. "I didn't think it would go over," says Vina Dawson, a Head Start teacher for more than 13 years. The emphasis on literacy was the exact opposite of all the child-development training she has received. But, Dawson says, "the test scores prove it works." By the end of third grade, 55 percent of the children who attended both Cone and a local elementary with a strong literacy emphasis were reading at grade level, compared with 5 percent in the control group.

Getting a Jump on Literacy

Reading doesn't just happen automatically for every youngster. And while the jury's still out on how young is too young to get started, here are 10 things parents can do to get the ball rolling:

1 Talk with your kids: **Children pick up quickly on the sounds and rhythms of language. Keep the banter going. It will help them grasp the rudiments of conversation.** • Provide a running commentary on both your activities and your child's. • Follow up on what your child says. • Recite rhymes, repeating your child's favorites.

2 Read with them every day: **Reading to kids boosts their knowledge and vocabulary. It introduces them to the mechanics of literacy—like turning pages and reading from left to right.** • Pick a regular reading time when stories can be enjoyed at a relaxed, unhurried pace. • Take books along on errands. • Make sure Mom's not doing all the work. Boys who associate reading with women might dismiss it as a "girl thing."

3 Choose your books wisely: **Find books on subjects that interest them—they'll enjoy reading more.** • Get them involved in choosing their books. • Find books related to current events in their lives, such as on starting school or about a recent vacation destination.

4 Surround your child with books: **Children love having familiar stories nearby that they can go back to again and again.**

• You can find cheap, used books at yard sales, thrift stores and library sales. • Consider subscribing to a children's magazine. This way your child has something to look forward to in the mail every month. • Make sure they see you reading.

5 Slow down and enjoy reading aloud: **Don't just drone along. Kids pick up on boredom and lose interest quickly. Add some drama to your voice, act out different characters and put yourself into the story.** • Pose questions about the story, and follow up on theirs. • Pause here and there so kids have time to take things in.

6 Read stories over and over: **It takes a long time for kids to take it all in, and they love familiar stories where they know what's coming next.** • Tape yourself reading your child's favorite stories so kids can hear them when they want.

7 Foster their awareness of letters and print: **Point out familiar letters in their everyday lives, such as the "S" in "Sesame Street."** • Buy them plastic letters to play with or make some. • Write their names on possessions like lunchboxes. • Give them writing supplies when they play games like house or hospital.

8 Surround them with writing tools: **All kids like having a varied supply at their disposal.** • Provide them with different kinds of papers, as well as markers, crayons and pens. • Encourage kids to tell you stories, write them down, then read them back to them.

9 Don't pressure them: **Nagging your kids about what they read may turn them off to reading in general.** • Comic books and sports magazines are better than no reading material at all. • Agree to take turns in choosing their bedtime stories. • Ask your librarian for books that are both entertaining and educational.

10 Show your appreciation: **Nothing encourages good reading habits like positive reinforcement.** • Display your child's writing in prominent places, such as the refrigerator door. • Don't jump on every mistake a child makes while reading aloud, especially if it doesn't change the gist of the story. • Talk with your kids about what they are reading and writing in school.

SOURCES: NATIONAL ASSOCIATION FOR THE EDUCATION OF YOUNG CHILDREN, INTERNATIONAL READING ASSOCIATION. TEXT BY JOSH ULICK.

Results like that are dramatic, but early-reading advocates say that literacy training can work just as well on kids who aren't poor. Many researchers believe that significant numbers of middle-class children could avoid being labeled learning-disabled if they got early help with language and letters. Teachers are already being encouraged to seek consultations with speech therapists for kids who are slow to talk, since language problems can be a precursor to reading difficulties. Following the example of Texas, a number of states are also considering screening preschoolers and kindergartners for early signs of dyslexia so problems can be treated early. That could save districts money and give more resources to kids with severe learning problems that aren't so easily remedied.

The new literacy-rich curriculum could use projects to teach kids multiple skills. That's the central concept at the Early Childhood Education Center in Oglesby,

Ill., two hours southwest of downtown Chicago. A typical project gives 3- to 5-year-olds the task of researching pizza. They begin by asking questions posted on the classroom walls. What is the crust made of? What is the shovel for putting the pizza in the oven? Are there other ways to get pizza besides from a pizza place? They get answers by visiting local pizza parlors and making and decorating their own pies. In the process, they measure ingredients, chart their progress and write about their experiences. "We aren't 'teaching reading'," says Sallee Beneke, the director, "but we are teaching the precursors to reading by encouraging children to understand that things we draw and write about can be useful for communication."

The fight over what's best for the pizza makers and the finger painters won't be resolved quickly. But some major change seems inevitable. Even Bos is always looking for creative ways to use language. One morning last week she played the autoharp in the indoor play area as youngsters hopped around and made up their own lyrics. Then she read them a book one mother had brought in, "Piggie Pie," with no clear ending. Bos encouraged the kids to pick their own conclusion. Would the witch eat the wolf for lunch or just make him a burger? As usual, there were no easy answers.

With NADINE JOSEPH *and*
KAREN SPRINGEN

Fostering Language and Literacy in Classrooms and Homes

David K. Dickinson and Patton O. Tabors

We based our study on the theoretical assumption that rich language experiences during the preschool years play an important role in ensuring that children are able to read with comprehension when they reach middle school.

Early childhood educators should be delighted. Bolstered by the accumulating research on the importance of early literacy, policymakers are beginning to craft policies with the potential to benefit young children. Researchers with long-standing interest in early literacy now hold major posts in the U.S. Department of Education, and new funding initiatives are being launched to fuel research and expanded services. The Head Start Bureau, which has begun to require programs to track the growth of individual children, has greatly expanded efforts to support children's intellectual growth, giving literacy special attention. States also are focusing new attention on early literacy.

However, we must be aware that heightened visibility brings risks. The new emphasis on accountability will put added pressure on teachers to raise children's scores on assessments. To meet this challenge and take advantage of the current climate, now is the time for early childhood educators to ensure that programs are of the highest quality. Staff at all levels must have a basic understanding of what early literacy is and an awareness of the experiences that support its development. Without such understanding there is a danger that programs will be mandated to address literacy skills in ways that neglect what we know about how children construct literacy. And well-meaning teachers may be tempted to return to heavy-handed didactic instructional methods that have been discouraged for years. Of particular concern is the possibility that early literacy efforts will take a single-minded focus on print-related dimensions and fail to recognize that *oral language* is the foundation of early literacy.

This article discusses how early childhood programs can make a different through classroom-based experiences and by efforts of preschool staff to help parents communicate with their children in ways that build the language skills critical to early literacy. We do not discuss developing phonemic awareness or knowledge of the alphabet and other print-based activities in the classroom, not because they are of less importance, but because we wish to highlight the importance of oral language. In the rush to embrace literacy in early childhood settings, we fear that oral language may be overlooked.

Thinking about early literacy

In 1987 we (that is, the authors, Catherine Snow, and many others) began the Home-School Study of Language and Literacy Development, an intensive examination of how parents and teachers support the development of language skills in young children from families with low incomes. Children living in poverty are less likely to become successful readers and writers—yet many *are* successful. What makes the difference? We wanted to identify the strengths in homes and in preschool programs that can build strong language and literacy foundations, so that we can ultimately make these strengths part of all children's lives. To accomplish this goal, we followed children from preschool through seventh grade (and, more recently, into high school).

Here we briefly summarize some of the key findings of the language and literacy development of 74 of the children during the preschool time period (Dickinson & Tabors 2001). Their families were eligible for Head Start, but about half used state vouchers to attend private programs. They lived in eastern Massachusetts, and all families reported that they used English in the home. We based our study on the theoretical assumption that rich language experiences during the preschool years play an important role in ensuring that children are able to read with comprehension when they reach middle school (Snow & Dickinson 1991). This hypothesis is supported by the findings of other researchers that children's language and literacy skills in kindergarten are strongly related to later academic success (Snow et al. 1991; Cunningham & Stanovich 1997; Whitehurst & Lonigan 1998).

Face-to-face talk relies on gestures such as pointing to objects, intonation, and the speakers' shared experience.

To capture the rich details of home and classroom life, we audiotaped conversations in both classrooms and homes and interviewed mothers and teachers about their experiences with the children (see Dickinson & Tabors 2001 for details). From this information we sought to identify the kinds of interactions and experiences that made a difference in children's later literacy skills. To see what effect these preschool interactions and experiences had on literacy development, we administered a battery of language and early literacy tasks to the children on a yearly basis, beginning in kindergarten. We assessed the children's ability to understand words, their ability to produce narratives, and their emergent literacy skills, including letter knowledge, early reading and writing, and phonemic awareness.

The language skills needed to build the foundation of reading and writing fall into different clusters (Snow & Dickinson 1991). Some skills are required to carry on informal conversations with friends and relatives. What's typical of these interactions is that people understand the meaning of the interaction largely because the ongoing activity makes clear what they are talking about. For example, you probably would be baffled if you were simply to read a transcript of talk that occurred during peekaboo or the feeding of a baby. Face-to-face talk relies on gestures such as pointing to objects, intonation, and the speakers' shared experience.

Another cluster of language skills is needed when people must make sense of words without all these immediate supports. They need to understand language apart from the face-to-face contexts where it is produced. For such occasions people need skill in constructing extended discourse that conveys new information that is not available from what one can see and hear. Later academic work, including comprehension of most texts, requires these abilities. We expected that certain experiences would build the specialized kinds of language skills that children need to become literate. Indeed, our analyses of homes and classrooms revealed three dimensions of children's experiences during the preschool and kindergarten years that are related to later literacy success:

- **Exposure to *varied vocabulary*.** Knowing the "right word" is vital if one is to communicate information clearly. Large vocabularies have long been known to be linked to reading success

(e.g., Anderson & Freebody 1981); they also are a signal that children are building the content knowledge about the world that is so critical to later reading (Neuman 2001).

- **Opportunities to be part of conversations that use *extended discourse*.** Extended discourse is talk that requires participants to develop understandings beyond the here and now and that requires the use of several sentences to build a linguistic structure, such as in explanations, narratives, or pretend talk.

- *Home and classroom environments* **that are cognitively and linguistically stimulating.** Children are most likely to experience conversation that include comprehensible and interesting extended discourse and are rich with vocabulary when their parents are able to obtain and read good books and when their teachers provide classrooms with a curriculum that is varied and stimulating.

The adults used techniques like definitions and synonyms, inference and comparison, the child's prior experience, or the semantic, social, or physical context to help the children understand what the new words meant.

We now will discuss each of these dimensions, describing what we found in the homes and the preschool classrooms that the 74 children attended. We spotlight one child in the study, a boy named Casey, who had both a very supportive family and a very supportive classroom environment.

Varied vocabulary

Opportunities to hear and use a variety of new and interesting words in conversations with adults were especially important to children in our study. These conversations happened at home and in preschool classrooms.

At home

For the Home-School Study we recorded the children in conversation with their mothers during book readings and toy play sessions and with their mothers and other members of their families during mealtimes. In all three conversational contexts we found the adults using new and interesting words with the children. Even more important, we found that the adults used techniques like definitions and synonyms, inference and comparison, the child's prior experience, or the semantic, social, or physical context to help the children understand what the new words meant (Tabors, Beals, & Weizman 2001).

Some families used these techniques more than others—Casey's family, for example, used more new and interesting words than the average for the whole group. How often new words were used also made a difference. On average, children whose families used more new words understood more words and had better emergent literacy skills later in kindergarten.

Teachers who use interesting and varied words may help to create a vocabulary-rich environment—a classroom in which children are exposed to and encouraged to use varied words.

In the classroom

We taped child and teacher conversations in the classrooms during free play, group times (Dickinson 2001b), book reading (Dickinson 2001a), and mealtime (Cote 2001). Across all these settings, children benefited from conversations that included more varied vocabulary. Interestingly, what mattered was not just the variety of words that the teachers used, but also the variety of words that the children used as they spoke with the teachers. We studied only one or two children in each classroom, so this finding suggests that their language growth was bolstered by input from teachers as well as from other children. We speculate that teachers who use interesting and varied words may help to create a vocabulary-rich environment—a classroom in which children are exposed to and encouraged to use varied words.

Extended discourse

Extended discourse is an important contributor to children's language and literacy development. Adults can extend or draw out their talk with children, enriching the conversation and helping children go beyond the here and now. Again, both home and preschool may be settings for this discourse.

At home

In looking at the transcripts of the conversations we recorded with parents and children reading books together, playing with toys, and during mealtimes, we found that each of these settings provided opportunities for extended talk that helped the children recognize and use these types of talk later in school. To see what we mean by extended discourse, let's listen as Casey's mother reads a book about elephants. This mother doesn't just read the book with her child; she also discusses it at length with him, helping him understand the information and tying it to his personal experience.

Mother: [reading] "African elephants have a dip in their backs. They also have ridges on their trunks, which end

in two points. Asian elephants have smoother trunks that end in just one point." See the dip in his back?

Casey: I know why he's different. He has them [pointing to tusks], and he doesn't.

Mother: He has tusks. Well, this is a female. [reading] "Asian elephants often live in forests and swamps. This Asian cow elephant lives in Nepal, a small country north of India."

Casey: Ma! In India?

Mother: Yeah, do you know somebody from there? Deepack? Your friend? Yeah. [reading] "African elephants live in the plains as well as forests. This African elephant lives in the open grassland. It flaps its huge ears to help keep cool in the hot African sunshine." Because it's very hot in Africa. (Dickinson & Tabors 2001, 39)

Casey's mother is using what we call *non-immediate talk*—that is, she gives Casey information beyond what is immediately available from the book. This type of conversation is an important preparation for talk about books at school (De Temple 2001).

Other types of extended discourse we found in the transcripts were fantasy talk during toy play (Katz 2001) and explanations and narratives during mealtimes (Beals 2001). The important thing about all of these forms of extended discourse is that they occurred during normal conversations in everyday activities. Some families used these types of talk more often than others, and their children were better at telling a narrative in kindergarten than were children who had less exposure to extended conversations.

Free play, or choice time, is the ideal opportunity for children to engage in pretend talk, a type of extended discourse that predicts stronger language and literacy development.

In the classroom

Free play, or choice time, is the ideal opportunity for children to engage in pretend talk, a type of extended discourse that predicts stronger language and literacy development. Ann Greenbaum's skilled conversations demonstrate some of the features of teachers' extended discourse that are especially powerful supports for children's oral language. In her exchange about sharks, she built on and extended the children's comments and used varied words ("You must be very brave and daring men to go down there").

Another important but more subtle feature of Ann's knack for conversation is her ability to fine-tune the balance between talking and listening to the children. In looking at the ratio of teacher-to-child talk, we found that children did better on our language and literacy assessments when preschool teachers talked less during free play. This finding may reflect the fact that teachers are better attuned to children when they listen more. It also might point to the benefit of allowing children to put their ideas into words.

We also examined teacher-child talk during group meetings and large-group book reading. During group meeting times we found that the percentage of all talk that provided children with information or engaged them in thoughtful discussions was predictive of later development. Similarly, during book reading sessions, conversations encouraging children to think about the story were beneficial. The following is a conversation that occurred as the teacher read a book in which a child finds a dinosaur and brings it home. The poor dinosaur is overwhelmed by loud noises. Here we see the teacher using extended discourse to encourage the children to analyze the dinosaur's reaction and to recognize the emotion of fear.

Teacher: How do you think Dandy feels, Susan?
Susan: Bad.
Teacher: Why?
Susan: Everybody take a look at the picture.
Teacher: I think he not only feels sad, he feels very—
Children: Happy.
Teacher: I don't think so. What did Dandy do when the truck came?
Todd: Shook.
Teacher: He was scared—he shook. And what did he do when the airplanes zoomed overhead? And when the train roared by? Did Dandy like loud noises?
Children: No!
Teacher: How is Dandy going to feel with all this?
Children: Bad. Sad.
Teacher: Not only sad. What else?
Children: Mad!
James: Scared!
Teacher: You got it, James! He's going to be very scared! (Dickinson & Tabors 2001, 190–91)

There was an interesting difference between the kind of discourse that was most beneficial in the two settings. During free play, relaxed back-and-forth exchanges with limited amounts of teacher talk proved helpful, but teacher efforts during group times to keep individual children talking detracted from the group experience. This result may show that when teachers engage in excessively long interactions with one child, the other children "tune out."

Environments that support oral language

Visits to the children's homes and classroom occurred only once a year during the study because of the large amount of language data that we collected each visit. Although we were able to collect a great deal of information about the types of talk used in these contexts on those particular days, we realized that we couldn't know how often such conversations occurred in normal home life or during the typical preschool day. For these reasons, we interviewed mothers and teachers to help us understand how supportive the overall environment was for the children's language and literacy development.

In the home

We used the mothers' answers to a cluster of questions to see how the home environment supported children's language and literacy development. Questions included:

- How often do you read to your child?
- Does anyone else read to your child and how often?
- How many children's books do you own?
- Do you get books from the library or bookstore?
- Do you read anything else with your child?

We found a lot of variation on this measure of home support for literacy. Not surprisingly, Casey's mother scored the highest in the entire sample on the answers to these questions. Casey was hearing many books and other materials read to him by a lot of different people. His family was buying books in addition to getting them from the library. How did this low-income family, and others with high support for literacy, manage to buy books? Many of the mothers mentioned that they always asked relatives to give their children books on special occasions and that they were always on the lookout for books at tag sales.

Of course, having the books is only the first step in the process. It is also necessary to have willing readers who use the books for enjoyment and to expand the children's knowledge of the world. In this study the children whose mothers reported high support for literacy at home scored well in kindergarten on all three measures of early literacy (receptive vocabulary, narrative production, and emergent literacy).

In the classroom

We interviewed the preschool teachers to discover how they typically organize their classroom day and to learn what they saw as their primary educational goals. We also observed the classroom environments to learn about the curriculum.

We found differences in the pedagogical emphasis of teachers. Some valued social and emotional development highly, others stressed academic growth, and some placed high values on both (Smith 2001). Our conversations revealed how the teachers allocated their classroom time. One of the striking things we found was the large variation in the amount of time teachers reported setting aside for book reading. When the children in our study were four years old, somewhat more than 25% of the teachers reported planning for more than 51 minutes of book reading a week, whereas about 17% reported planning for reading 15 minutes or less per week.

When we looked at what teachers told us about their pedagogical beliefs and their ways of organizing time, we did not find much consistency between belief and practice. We also did not find much evidence that teachers' beliefs were related to children's growth. This set of findings suggests that many preschool teachers may lack well-articulated systems of belief that link understanding of the nature of language and literacy development with notions of effective classroom practices.

Other dimensions of the classroom environment did relate to children's later language and literacy development. One such dimension, the quality of the curriculum, was exemplified in Casey's classroom. For example, after the firefighters demonstrated their equipment to the class and introduced new words and concepts, the teacher extended that experience. We also found that children's later development was more positive if the classroom had a writing center and the teacher planned times for small-group activities.

Our data strongly indicate that it is the nature of the teacher-child relationship that makes the biggest difference in early literacy.

Our measures of the classroom environment were far less potent predictors of later language and literacy than our measures of teacher-child interaction. Our data strongly indicate that it is the nature of the teacher-child relationship and the kinds of conversations that they have that makes the biggest difference to early language and literacy development.

Oral language/literacy support at home and school: The long-term benefits

We were interested in what effects different home and preschool environments, and various combinations of home and preschool environments, had on these children's kindergarten skills and on their more long-term academic achievements. To chart children's growth we individually assessed our children in kindergarten, using tasks that tapped language skills (receptive vocabulary, story understanding and production) and early literacy knowledge (letter knowledge, environmental print "reading," writing, phonemic awareness). Each year we continued to test children, and when they were in elementary school we began to use standardized reading tests.

How important was the home environment in comparison to the school environment—and vice versa? And how much could we predict about these children's later accomplishments based on what we knew about their abilities in kindergarten?

Apparently, the level of language and literacy skill that the children had acquired by the end of their kindergarten year provided a strong basis for the acquisition of literacy and vocabulary skills in the later elementary years.

Let's start with the last question. What we found was that the scores that the kindergartners achieved on the measures (receptive vocabulary, narrative production, and emergent literacy) were *highly predictive* of their scores on reading comprehension and receptive vocabulary in fourth and in seventh grade. Apparently the level of language and literacy skills that the children had acquired by the end of their kindergarten year provided a strong basis for the acquisition of literacy and vocabulary skills in the later elementary years. Although this is perhaps not entirely surprising, it does confirm that for this group of children early learning set the stage for later literacy acquisition in school.

If kindergarten skills are so important, we need to know the relative contributions of home and preschool to children's kindergarten skills. When we looked at each of the three kindergarten measures one at a time, we found that the significant predictors of narrative production were home environmental variables, while home and preschool environment variables were both significant in explaining children's scores in receptive vocabulary and emergent literacy. For these reasons, it was extremely important that we had collected data on interactions and experiences from both the home and the classroom.

For Casey, who came from a supportive home and attended a preschool where language development was a main goal, the combined interactions and experiences provided him with strong scores in both understanding words and emergent literacy in kindergarten, in comparison with the other children in the study.

But not all of the children in the study came from environments as supportive as Casey's. What about them? What if a child from a home with lots of rich talk and exposure to books attends a preschool that does not support emergent literacy? Or what about the child who gets little support for language and literacy development at home, but attends a high-quality preschool with a wonderful language- and literacy-rich environment? Can either of these environments compensate for the other?

Using the data from the Home-School Study, we developed analyses to look at these hypothetical situations—the high-home/low-preschool language and literacy environment combination and the low-home/high preschool language and literacy environment combination. What we found is that, while a child with a high-home/low-preschool combination would score *below* the mean for the sample on all three measures of kindergarten abilities, a child with a low-home/high-preschool mix would score *above* the mean. The implication is that excellent preschools can compensate for homes that have well-below-average language and literacy support—at least as reflected in the children's kindergarten skills (Dickinson & Tabors 2001, 326).

Based on our results, we strongly believe that the early childhood period is key to getting children off to a strong start in language and literacy. Our research suggests that policymakers' attention to literacy skills must include attention to building early foundations in rich oral language, both at home and in preschool. Everyday activities can develop varied vocabulary, engage children in complex uses of language that go beyond the here and now, and surround children with environments that support language and literacy development. For this to happen, we must help all preschool teachers understand the major role they play in supporting children's long-term development. These teachers must deepen the knowhow required to constantly extend children's oral language while they also encourage phonemic awareness and writing skills. Rather than adding an extra burden, this attention to language development is likely to create livelier, more enjoyable experiences for both teachers and children. Finally, teachers also must actively reach out to families, building on their strengths while guiding them toward the kinds of home language and literacy activities that will help their children achieve the educational success that families desire for their children. With these early language experiences, children will be far more likely to acquire the specific reading and writing skills needed for school success.

References

Anderson, R. C., & P. Freebody. 1981. Vocabulary knowledge. In *Comprehension and teaching: Research reviews*, ed. J. T. Guthrie, 77–116. Newark: DE: International Reading Association.

Beals, D. E. 2001. Eating and reading: Links between family conversations with preschoolers and later language and literacy. In *Beginning literacy with language: Young children learning at home and school*, eds. D. K. Dickinson & P. O. Tabors, 75–92. Baltimore: Paul H. Brookes.

Cote, L. R. 2001. Language opportunities during mealtimes in preschool classrooms. In *Beginning literacy with language: Young children learning at home and school*, eds. D. K. Dickinson & P. O. Tabors, 205–21. Baltimore: Paul H. Brookes.

Cunningham, A. E., & K. E. Stanovich. 1997. Early reading acquisition and its relation to reading experience and ability 10 years later. *Developmental Psychology* 33 (6): 934–45.

De Temple, J. M. 2001. Parents and children reading books together. In *Beginning literacy with language: Young children learning at home and school*, eds. D. K. Dickinson & P. O. Tabors, 31–51. Baltimore: Paul H. Brookes.

Dickinson, D. K. 2001a. Book reading in preschool classrooms: Is recommended practice common? In *Beginning literacy with language: Young*

children learning at home and school, eds. D. K. Dickinson & P. O. Tabors, 175–203. Baltimore: Paul H. Brookes.

Dickinson, D. K. 2001b. Large-group and free-play times: Conversational settings supporting language and literacy development. In *Beginning literacy with language: Young children learning at home and school*, eds. D. K. Dickinson & P. O. Tabors, 223–55. Baltimore: Paul H. Brookes.

Dickinson, D. K., & P. O. Tabors, eds. 2001. *Beginning literacy with language: Young children learning at home and school*. Baltimore: Paul H. Brookes.

Katz, J. R. 2001. Playing at home: The talk of pretend play. In *Beginning literacy with language: Young children learning at home and school*, eds. D. K. Dickinson & P. O. Tabors, 53–73. Baltimore: Paul H. Brookes.

Neuman, S. B. 2001. Essay Book Review: The role of knowledge in early literacy. *Reading Research Quarterly* 36 (4): 468–75.

Roach, K. A., & C. E. Snow. 2000. *What predicts fourth grade reading comprehension?* Paper presented at the annual conference of the American Education Research Association, New Orleans, April.

Smith, M. W. 2001. Children's experiences in preschool. In *Beginning literacy with language: Young children learning at home and school*, eds. D. K. Dickinson & P. O. Tabors, 149–74. Baltimore: Paul H. Brookes.

Snow, C. E., & D. K. Dickinson. 1991. Skills that aren't basic in a new conception of literacy. In *Literate systems and individual lives: Perspectives on literacy and schooling*, eds. A. Purves & E. Jennings. Albany: State University of New York (SUNY) Press.

Snow, C. E., W. S. Barnes, J. Chandler, I. F. Goodman, & L. Hemphill. 1991. *Unfulfilled expectations: Home and school influences on literacy*. Cambridge, MA: Harvard University Press.

Tabors, P. O., D. E. Beals, & Z. O. Weizman 2001. "You know what oxygen is?" Learning new words at home. In *Beginning literacy with language: Young children learning at home and school*, eds. D. K. Dickinson & P. O. Tabors, 93–110. Baltimore: Paul H. Brookes.

Whitehurst, G. J., & C. J. Lonigan. 1998. Child development and emergent literacy. *Child Development* 68: 848–72.

David K. Dickinson, Ed.D., is a senior research scientist in the Center for Children and Families at the Education Development Center, Inc., in Newton, Massachusetts, and an affiliate with CIERA (Center for the Improvement of Early Reading Achievement), based at the University of Michigan. David directed the aspects of the Home-School Study that dealt with classrooms and is now developing and studying professional development efforts that build on language and literacy in the classroom.

Patton O. Tabors, Ed.D., a research associate at the Harvard Graduate School of Education since 1987, has been involved in research related to language and literacy acquisition of both young English-speaking and second-language-learning children. She is author of *One Child, Two Languages: A guide for Preschool Educators of Children Learning English as a Second Language* and coeditor of *Beginning Literacy with Language: Young Children Learning at Home and School.*

Portions of this article were excerpted from D. K. Dickinson and P. O. Tabors, eds., *Beginning Literacy with Language: Young Children Learning at Home and School* (Baltimore: Paul H. Brookes, 2001).

Helping Preschool Children Become Readers: Tips for Parents

by Dr. Ann S. Epstein, Director, Early Childhood Division

Parents and other family members lay the foundation for reading and writing long before children enter school. To help preschoolers begin to develop these skills at home, parents need to provide two things:

- **Experiences with language—** having conversations, playing games with language and sounds
- **Experiences with print**—reading to children, giving children tools for reading and writing.

Learning to read and write should be pleasurable; it does not require tedious drills or forced memorization. When learning is fun, children develop good attitudes toward schooling as they master valuable skills. Below are 12 things parents can do to make learning enjoyable and meaningful. These ideas build on children's natural desire to communicate and can easily be included in family routines.

1. Have daily conversations with children.

Listening and speaking are the foundation of reading and writing. When parents converse with children, they should listen patiently, even if it means waiting for children to form their thoughts and words. Adult patience creates a climate in which children feel free to talk.

Children like to talk about themselves, their interests, and their feelings. If parents talk about the things children care about, children will be eager and natural speakers. There are many things parents can do with their children to encourage conversation, for example:

- Looking at pictures in the family photo album and talking about the people and celebrations
- Joining children's pretend play, letting the child be the leader
- Providing materials and sharing the child's favorite activities, such as drawing, building with blocks, racing toy cars, or baking cookies
- Attending sporting events, going for walks, digging in the yard, marking a snow fort, or collecting bugs

To help the conversation along, parents can make encouraging comments ("I see you made a red circle") and repeat the child's remarks ("You're happy because Kyla invited you to her party"). An occasional open-ended question is fine, especially to seek information ("What are you going to serve at your 'tea party'?"). However, too many questions tend to stifle conversation.

Conversation sets the stage for having fun with language. Singing songs, telling stories, reciting rhymes, and moving to rhythmic chants all help children develop *phonological awareness—the ability to perceive the sounds of language.* For example, the repeated words in "Row, Row, Row Your Boat" help make children aware of the sounds that make up these words. Nursery rhymes like "Eensy, Weensy Spider" call attention to words with the same ending sound, as does encouraging children to make up new endings to familiar rhymes: "Jack be nimble, Jack be red, Jack jump over the _____."

---

12 things you can do to help your preschooler become a reader

1. Have daily conversations with your child.
2. Keep lots of print and writing materials in your home.
3. Set up a reading and writing space for your child.
4. Let your child see you read and write.
5. Read with your child every day.
6. Point out reading and writing in everyday activities.
7. Make a message board.
8. Encourage your child to "read."
9. Display your child's writing.
10. Make a bank or file of words your child likes to write.
11. Go to the library with your child.
12. Use television and technology wisely.

When parents point out the individual sounds in words, they promote *phonemic awareness. A phoneme is the smallest unit of sound in the lan-*

guage. It can be the sound made by a single letter, such as /s/, or a letter combination, such as /sh/. *Phonemic awareness is knowing that words are made up of sequences of these individual sounds. Phonics, the next step in learning to read, is knowing sound-letter relationships.* For example, a parent might say "*Mommy* and *muffin*… those both start with the /m/ sound, that's the letter *m*." If a child asks how to spell *dog*, a parent can say, "It starts with the sound /d/, and the letter *d* looks like this." Parents and children can also play games with alliteration, that is, with words that start with the same sound. For example, a parent can put three objects that start with the /b/ sound in a bag (such as a ball, block, and barrette) and the child can find something else that begins with *b* to put in the bag. Guessing games are also fun: "I'm thinking of something in the refrigerator that starts with the /g/ sound—gggg. What do you think it is?"

2. Keep lots of printed materials and writing materials in the home.

Homes should be filled with interesting things to read, including illustrated storybooks, nonfiction books, homemade books, magazines, photo albums, newspapers, catalogs, seed packets, greeting cards, flyers, takeout menus, manuals, junk mail, maps, and so on. Children, like adults, need variety.

Parents should also keep on hand many different types of writing materials, including crayons, markers, chalk, pens and pencils, paper in different sizes and colors, stationery, stamps and ink pads, wooden and plastic letters for tracing and copying. Tools for making books, such as tape, scissors, staplers, a hole punch, and string, will also encourage writing.

Reading and writing supplies do not need to be expensive. Parents can reuse and recycle materials or buy children's books at yard sales, resale shops, and used-book sales at the library. They can also add their own printing around the house, such as labels for things the child uses every day ("toy box" or "dishes"). Reading and writing materials should be placed where children can easily see

and reach them, for examples, on low shelves or in baskets and crates.

3. Set up a reading and writing space for children.

To convey the importance of reading and writing, parents can set up a special space for these activities. It may be a quiet place or somewhere close to the center of action, whatever is most inviting for the child and will keep his or her attention. This space should include materials that belong to the child alone and do not have to be shared with adults or other children in the household. This will encourage the child to think of the area as his or her own play or work space. Parents can offer the child a choice of spending quiet time in this special area instead of taking a nap. Or, they can set aside another regular time each day when the child can choose to go to this area.

4. Let children observe parents reading and writing.

Young children imitate their parents, so modeling reading and writing at home is very important. When parents pick up a newspaper or book instead of turning on the television, they send a powerful message about the pleasure as well as the usefulness of reading. At the dinner table, parents can briefly describe something interesting they have read, or mention some reading and writing they did at work that day. Children should see their parents writing, whether they are paying bills or writing an e-mail message to a friend. If a child wants to know something, a parent might say, "Let's look that up in the dictionary [or in the encyclopedia or on the Internet]." This shows children that written sources provide information and that answering questions can be an adventure.

5. Read with children every day.

Parents should set aside a regular time each day to read with their children. This might be at bedtime, after school, early in the morning—whatever works in the family schedule. They should read in a comfortable place, without a lot of distractions, where they can snuggle or sit side by side with their child. Children should

be able to see and touch the book while parents read to them.

Reading with children will be most beneficial if parents follow these simple techniques:

- **Be familiar with the book.** If the book is new, parents should try to read it themselves beforehand.
- **Read slowly but naturally.** Pronouncing the words carefully helps to build children's vocabulary.
- **Read with interest.** An expressive voice shows interest and engages the child.
- **Use different voices.** This helps children differentiate the characters and their qualities.
- **Use a finger to follow the words.** This shows the connection between spoken and written words. Children will learn to associate sounds with specific letters and letter combinations.
- **Stop reading to talk about the book.** Children want to talk about the pictures, story, and characters. If a book is familiar, they might predict what will happen next or imagine different events and endings.
- **Extend the reading.** Reading is enriched when children represent the events or characters through drawing and play-acting. Other ideas include visiting places and doing things that appear in the book or making up stories and games that build on the book's ideas.

There should be a variety of books to choose from and the child should make the choice, even if it is often the same book. Repetition helps children understand the forms of written language and begin to recognize familiar words and letters. Here are some guidelines to help parents choose storybooks for their young child's library:

- **Illustrations.** Are the drawings, paintings, or photographs visually pleasing? Do the people represent a variety of races, ages, and abilities?
- **Story line.** Is it written in the language the child speaks? Will the activities and messages make sense to the child? Will it encourage discussion?

- **Child interest.** Will the child be curious about the characters and what happens to them? Will the child look at the book alone, even when an adult is not available for reading?
- **Adult interest.** Is it a book the parent wants to read and talk about with the child? Is the parent prepared to answer whatever questions the child may have about the book?

6. Call children's attention to reading and writing in everyday activities.

Children are curious about the daily activities adults view as commonplace. Their natural interest provides many opportunities for parents to call attention to reading and writing. These opportunities include making grocery lists and finding matching coupons; pointing out letters and words on signs and buildings while riding in the car or taking a walk; looking up addresses and phone numbers before going places or making calls; reading maps; reading team names and scores aloud at sporting events; looking at the weather report in the newspaper; reading menus at restaurants or making up menus at home; writing and illustrating children's favorite recipes; labeling pictures in the family photo album; writing thank-you notes; reading the television guide and making a list of the shows the family will watch; writing and mailing fan letters to children's favorite performers and athletes.

7. Make a message board.

A message board lets children know the family's plans for the day. This can be especially important on weekends, when routines may vary. The message board can be a dry-erase board, a chalkboard, or just a pad of paper. The board should be hung at the child's eye level for easy visibility and so the child can add his or her own messages. Each day, the parent and child can draw a few simple pictures and label them with easy words. For example, a picture of a swing on one line and a grocery cart with the word *store* on the next line would indicate they were going to the

playground and then the supermarket. Parents should encourage children to predict what will happen based on the picture and word messages. At the same time they are learning to read, children are learning about sequences, an important concept in math.

8. Encourage children to "read."

Young children "read" in many ways. Before they read actual words, children pretend to read. They follow the pictures in a familiar book, tell the story from memory, or make up their own narrative. With lots of exposure to books, they come to understand basic print concepts, such as turning pages from front to back, reading from top to bottom, and following lines from left to right. Parents can promote children's early reading in several ways. They can encourage young children to read to them, to other family members, even to dolls and stuffed animals. As children begin to write, parents can ask them to read their words. If a child asks the parent to take dictation, either the parent or child can read back the words. It is important for parents to write down the child's exact words. This establishes the direct connection between spoken and written language.

9. Display children's writing.

Parents should display all the different forms of children's writing, including scribble letters and words based on word sounds (for example, *bg* for *big.*). They can also take photos of and display temporary writing (for example, made with sticks in the mud or sand on a tray). Writing should be mounted at the child's eye level so it can be easily seen. It can be attached with tape, pins, clips, or any other household fasteners. Display surfaces include the refrigerator, a wall, a bulletin board, a bookcase, the side of a dresser, the front of a kitchen cabinet; sticky notes can be stuck to the computer, papers hung from a mobile, and so on. If other family members comment on the writing, children will have a sense of its importance and of their accomplishment.

10. Make a word bank or word file.

A word bank is an illustrated dictionary or file of words a child uses in talking, reading, and writing. It organizes the words that are important to the child. A word bank can be created with an old recipe box and index cards, or with a loose-leaf notebook. Each word is put on a separate card or page, written in large and clear letters. Next to the word, the parent or child draws a picture that illustrates it. The cards or pages are then placed in alphabetical order. A word bank should be kept in a place where the child can easily reach it and look up words on his or her own. Whenever the child asks for help writing or spelling a word, the parent can refer the child to the existing list or help the child add a new entry to the word bank.

11. Take children to the library.

Libraries offer books and other reading materials, usually at no cost. Parents should find out where the nearest public library is located or if it sends a bookmobile to their neighborhood. Their child's preschool or day care center may also have a lending library. Library visits should occur frequently, preferably on a regular schedule (for example, every Saturday after soccer practice). A child should have his or her own library card and a tote bag to carry and store books.

Children can check out books, magazines, cassette tapes, and CDs with stories, information, poems and songs. They should pick the items that interest them. Parents can point out something they think is interesting, but in the end the child should make the choice. Children should also be the judge of whether a book is too easy or too hard. Reading or re-reading easy books can build a child's confidence. On the other hand, if a difficult book is interesting enough, the child may be up to the challenge of reading it. If a book is boring or *too* difficult, a child will simply set it aside and pick up something of greater interest.

Many libraries also have regular story hours and other events for young children. Sometimes they have exhibits, for example, an art show by a local artist. Looking at the exhibit together and talking about it is another good way for parents to help develop their child's language skills.

12. Use television and technology wisely.

Young children learn best by doing, not by watching. Television and computers can play a part in early learning but should not replace active exploration and social interaction. Viewing should be limited to one or two programs a day. Parents should look for shows that help develop the intellectual and social skills children need when they enter school, and they should watch and talk about these programs with their child. If the family has a computer, parents should buy software designed for young children. Drawing and writing programs that allow children to create and read their own pictures, words, and stories are more interesting and promote a wider range of skills than programs limited to memorization and practice.

Finally, parents should remember that they are not alone in helping their child along the path to literacy. They can talk to their child's teacher, the librarian, and other parents. They can share the books and activities their family enjoys and get others' ideas on how to support children's learning at home. With a parent's encouragement, a child will enter school ready to learn how to read and write. With a parent's example, a child will become an adult who reads for information and pleasure.

From *High/Scope ReSource*, Summer 2002, pp. 4-6. © 2002 by High/Scope Press.

Children Are Born Mathematicians:
Promoting the Construction of Early Mathematical Concepts in Children under Five

Eugene Geist

Children are mathematicians from the day they are born. They are constructing knowledge constantly as they interact mentally, physically, and socially with their environment and with other people. Young children may not be able to add or subtract, but their relationships with people and their interactions with a stimulating environment set the stage for the development of mathematical concepts (Sinclair et al. 1989). There is even some evidence that the ability to comprehend some mathematical concepts may be innate (Starkey & Cooper 1980; Wynn 1995; Koechlin, Dehaene, & Mehler 1997).

Innate ability to acquire mathematics

Perhaps, just as Chomsky (1999) has shown strong evidence for an innate *language acquisition device* that provides humans with a framework for learning language, there is a *mathematics acquisition device* that provides a framework for mathematical concepts. If such a mathematics acquisition device were present, we would expect children to naturally acquire mathematical concepts without direct teaching, to follow a standard sequence of gradual development, and most important, to show evidence of construction of mathematical concepts from a very early age. With careful examination of infants, toddlers, and preschoolers, one can see evidence for all of these criteria.

Emergent mathematical understanding

Perhaps it is time to begin looking at the construction of mathematical concepts the same way we look at literacy development—as emergent. The idea that literacy learning begins the day that children are born is widely accepted in the early childhood field. Children learn language by listening and by eventually speaking and writing. This language learning is aided by an innate language acquisition device that acts as a foundation for grammatical development and language learning (Chomsky 1999). Reading to infants, toddlers, and preschoolers is known to be an early positive step toward literacy success because it promotes and supports learning to read and write by immersing children in language and giving them an opportunity to interact with it (Ferreiro & Teberosky 1982).

> It is time to begin looking at the construction of mathematical concepts the same way we look at literacy development— as emergent.

Mathematical learning can be viewed in a similar way. Children begin to construct the foundations for future mathematical concepts during the first few months of life.

Before children can add or even count, they must construct ideas about mathematics that cannot be directly taught. Ideas that will support formal mathematics later in life include order and sequence, seriation, and classification.

The seemingly simple idea that a number represents a specific quantity actually involves a complex relationship that children must construct. Quantification is the basis for formal mathematics, and it is a synthesis of order (the basic understanding that objects are counted in a specific sequence and each object is counted only once). Seriation is the ability to place an object or group of objects in a logical series based on a property of the object or objects. Classification is the ability to group like objects in sets by a specific characteristic. This synthesis takes place by children interacting with objects and putting them in many different types of relationships.

A child constructing math concepts

An example of a child not yet capable of this synthesis, but beginning the process of constructing math understanding, is the three-year-old with whom I shared the following interactions. The girl's parents had asked her to say her numbers for me and she correctly counted to 20 with no errors. I then pulled out 20 pennies that I had in my pocket. I asked her if she could figure out a way to make sure we both got the same number of pennies. She looked at the pile of pennies, split the pile down the middle, slid a handful over to me, and took the rest. My pile contained 12 pennies and hers contained 8. I asked her how she knew we had the same amount, and she attempted to count the pennies in front of me by pointing at the pile saying, "One, two, three, four, five, six, seven." However, she did not have an understanding of the importance of order, and therefore counted some pennies twice and missed some completely. I then asked her to count her pennies, and she counted 10. When I again asked her if we both had the same amount, she made another quick visual inventory and replied "yes."

I then lined up eight pennies in a row and asked her to make a row with as many pennies as I had laid out. She took the rest of the pennies (12) and made a row below mine. I again asked her if there were the same number of pennies in each row. She counted her row and replied, "Yes. See—one, two, three, four, five, six, seven, eight, nine, ten." I asked her to count mine, and she came up with eight. I asked her again if they had the same number, and she again replied "yes."

This child was not yet able to coordinate order, classification, and seriation and therefore could not compare the penny quantities. Children as young as two may be able to count to 10 or even 20, but if they do not link their counting to quantification it is no different from memorizing their ABCs or a list of names like Bob, Joe, and Sara.

Because she did not understand that the numbers she recited each represented a specific quantity, this child could not perceive a numerical relationship between the two sets of objects.

This three-year-old used visual cues to estimate the sameness and difference of the sets instead of using number. Her logic and problem-solving ability were still perceptually bound. However, as she continually interacted with the objects and with other children and adults, she would come to realize the limits of her method and begin to construct new ways of reaching a solution. This type of confusion, or what Piaget called *disequilibrium* (Piaget & Inhelder [1964] 1969), is what leads a child to make further constructions and to strengthen her understanding of mathematical concepts.

The development of more complex understanding

Eight months later I had an opportunity to interact with this girl again. We repeated the game with the pennies. This time when I asked her to divide the pennies, she used a one-to-one correspondence method. She gave me a penny and then one to herself until all the pennies were distributed. When I asked her how she knew we had the same number, she counted each penny only once and in a specific order to get the correct answer.

I collected all the pennies in one pile, then showed the girl one more penny and added it to the pile. I asked her if she saw what I had done, and she said, "Yes, you added one more penny!" I then asked her to figure out a way to divide the pennies and make sure we both got the same number. She used the same method of one-to-one correspondence she had used previously. I asked her if we had the same number of pennies and she replied "yes." When I asked her to count them, and it turned out that I had one more penny, she was quite perplexed. She could not figure out how that had happened.

The child had made significant progress in her understanding of basic mathematical concepts. Her method of dividing the pennies was no longer visual. She used number concepts to solve her problem. However, her understanding of quantification was still weak and broke down when strongly challenged. Again, we see the disequilibrium that will lead the child to search for better ways of solving a problem. Through the process the child will construct new mathematical understanding.

Even very young children construct math knowledge

Children even younger than three years of age can use their developing understanding of order, seriation, and classification and their natural problem-solving ability. I observed an 18-month-old child playing in a large pit filled with different-colored balls. The child dropped one ball, then a second ball, and then a third ball over the side of the pit. The child then went to the opposite side of the pit and dropped two balls. He returned to the first side, reexamined the grouping of balls, then moved again to the second side and dropped another ball over the side to make the second grouping a set of three.

This may seem unimpressive by adult standards, but for an 18-month-old child, the coordination and comparison of threes on opposite sides of a structure is evidence of making a mathematical relationship. It is not yet a numerical relationship because the child is using visual perception to make the judgment of same or different. However, the coordination of dropping three balls each time is evidence of an understanding of more and less and basic equality. The child may not be developmentally ready for counting and quantification, but this simple task shows that children as young as 18 months can understand some rudimentary mathematical relationships.

Teachers of infants and toddlers need to be aware of these actions and abilities and help provide activities to encourage construction of mathematical concepts. Activities that provide children with concrete experiences manipulating objects and interacting with other children and adults, such as distributing snacks or sorting items by color or size, promote this type of construction.

Promoting emergent math

Although these basic mathematical concepts cannot and should not be directly taught, educators of young children need to emphasize and encourage children's interaction with their environment as a means of promoting and encouraging emergent math concepts. Children's logical and mathematical thinking develops by being exercised and stimulated. Teachers who encourage children to put objects into all kinds of relationships are promoting children's emergent understanding of mathematics.

Before children can add or even count, they must construct ideas about mathematics that cannot be directly taught.

Making sure that children from birth through age four have a stimulating environment and opportunities to explore many different kinds of relationships can support their emerging understanding of mathematics. Teachers in infant, toddler, and preschool programs can do a number of things, like offering objects to compare, using rhythm activities and music, modeling mathematical behavior, and incorporating math into everyday activities to facilitate the emergent mathematical learning within every child. The basic framework for math cannot be directly taught but can be easily promoted in the classroom.

Birth to two

Infants and toddlers explore their environments using their senses. Piaget and Inhelder ([1964] 1969) called this time the sensorimotor stage because children explore and learn about their environments through motor activity and by touching, seeing, tasting, and hearing. It may not seem that any mathematical construction is going on during this time. However, children begin to perceive relationships between and among objects as they begin to construct ways to classify, seriate, compare, and order objects. Classification begins with a child's ability to match objects and evolves into a system of organizing objects into groups with similar characteristics. Classification is an important foundation for future mathematical concepts such as comparing sets of numbers and quantification.

Rhythm and music. Rhythm and music activities and materials are excellent for promoting emergent mathematics. Using bongo drums with infants and toddlers can help children experience mathematics. Teacher and child take turns repeating each other's beats; the teacher beats the drum twice, and the child beats the drum twice. If the child takes the lead, the teacher echoes the child's playing. This helps support the child's understanding of a one-to-one correspondence. It also demonstrates a matching relationship, which helps refine the child's ability to classify.

Using synthesizers with automatic beat generators is another good way to promote math through music. Let children play notes on the keyboard along with the generated beat. These synthesizers come with headphones so children can play whatever they feel like and not bother other children in the classroom.

I observed one teacher encouraging her children to organize a marching band using the musical instruments and items in the room. The children decided how to march. One child even insisted that he say "one, two, one, two" as they marched. The children for the most part coordinated their beat as they marched through the hall of the center, outside, and back to their room with one child saying "one, two" the whole time to keep them all together.

Using numbers, counting, and quantification in everyday activities. Even children under the age of two can be exposed to math during everyday tasks and activities such as snack time or circle time. Any opportunity to count should be taken advantage of to help the children understand one-to-one correspondence of quantity. Teachers should count and use math whenever possible and even ask children questions about simple mathematical relationships. This type of interaction helps children to recognize the importance of numbers and promotes construction of emergent mathematics. Even children of this age can understand the concept of more. Asking children to compare groups of objects or quantities encourages the development of *more, less,* and *the same* concept.

Although children in this group have not yet constructed an understanding of number, this is no reason not to use math around them. Just as reading to infants and toddlers helps them develop literacy skills, using math around children helps them construct number concepts.

Blocks and shapes. Children who are surrounded with interesting objects are naturally led to make relation-

ships between those objects. Determining whether objects are the same or different, matching, and classifying all require a child to focus on a certain quality of the object in order to make the comparison. The more frequently children make comparisons, the more complex their comparisons become. The simple act of adding an increasing variety of colored balls or blocks to the child's choices can facilitate more and more complex mathematical relationships. These activities support the concepts of seriation and classification.

Shapes can be used to show matching relationships. In infant and toddler rooms there should be an abundance of different-shaped blocks and tiles for children to match and compare. Because their mathematical development is still in its early stages, infants and toddlers naturally look for exact matches. This is the level of classification that they can handle. Infants and toddlers cannot see something as the same and different at the same time.

I observed a teacher working with a 12-month-old. They were examining a group of blue and yellow triangle blocks. The child gave a yellow triangle to the teacher and then picked up another yellow triangle and gave it to the teacher. The teacher then picked up a blue triangle and showed it to the child. The child grasped it and threw it back in the pile, found another yellow triangle and gave it to the teacher. To the child, the yellow and blue triangles are not matches because they are different colors.

Construction using cardboard boxes can also help children make relationships. In my experience, infants and toddlers love to play with cardboard boxes. Boxes of all sizes can be made available for the children to stack and arrange to make structures. Larger boxes can have doors or holes in them for the children to crawl in and out. These boxes can be put together in a variety of ways, and each combination or sequence is another relationship that the child has made. In the process of arranging the boxes, children have discussions and social interactions that also promote the making of new social relationships.

As children develop their matching and classifying skills, they will be able to see more complex relationships. But to construct these concepts, children need time and interaction with objects and other people. Even if children are "prewired" for math, they still have to construct the concepts piece by piece. Children slowly construct formal mathematics understanding step by step, over the infant, toddler, and preschool years. This is why it is so vitally important to offer children as young as a few months old opportunities to match, classify, and compare.

Three- and four-year-olds

As children begin to move out of their sensorimotor stage of development and into what Piaget and Inhelder ([1964] 1969) called the preoperational stage, the big change is that children are able to think representationally and begin to acquire a certain degree of abstract thinking. Due to these abilities, children can think about objects that are not right in front of them, and they can begin to make connections between current and previous experiences. Children of this age can make much more complex relationships between objects. This is important for emerging mathematical concepts because it is during this time that the mental structures allowing a child to understand quantity are constructed.

The concepts of seriation, classification, and order take on a new dimension as children begin to understand more abstract relationships. Three- and four-year-olds can make comparisons to objects that are not present or events that took place in the past. This allows children to synthesize order, seriation, and classification to construct abstract mental structures that will support quantification and formal mathematics.

Children begin to make mental mathematical relationships that build on and refine the idea of *more* into "one more" or "two more." This refinement eventually leads to the child's being able to understand that three is one more than two and two more than one. This is the core idea behind quantification.

Manipulatives.   An easy way to promote math to three- and four-year-olds is simply to ask children to use mathematical concepts in their activities. If a child is using blocks, a teacher can ask, "How many blocks do you have?" or "How many more do you need?" Children are willing and even excited to count objects and make mathematical relationships if the teacher encourages them.

A four-year-old child was making a chain out of different-colored plastic links. I asked him how long he was trying to make the chain. He did not respond, so I tried a more direct question, "How many links do you have so far?" He put on the next link and then proceeded to count each link. There were eight. After he put on another link, I asked again, "How many do you have now?" He went back to the beginning and counted each link again and got an answer of nine. When he again added a link, I asked him a more leading question: "You had nine and you put one more on. How many do you have now?" Again the child counted all the links until he got the answer of 10. After that I did not have to ask him again. Each time he put on a new link, he would count all the links. He eventually made a chain with 27 links.

After 15 links this child's counting became erratic. Sometimes he counted carefully and got the correct answer, and other times he missed some links in his counting. For example, after correctly counting 26 and adding one more, the boy counted again and missed a few. After completing the counting he triumphantly announced, "Fifteen!" The fact that he now had fewer than before did not seem to trouble him. Although he made mistakes and showed an incomplete understanding of number concepts, he was getting closer to using mathematics in a conventional manner. His actions were like those of children who move from drawing squiggles to writing words in the process of learning to write conventionally.

Everyday activities.   Just as with the infants and toddlers, everyday activities such as snack and circle times can be used with three- and four-year-olds to promote the use of math. Dividing up snack, counting plates, and other activities can be assigned to children. They then have to use their own mathematical problem-solving ability to figure out the best way to perform the tasks. A child who is assigned to put out the plates for his table of five may do it by going to the stack of plates, getting one plate and placing it in front of one child, then going back to the plates to get another plate for the next child, and so on until everyone has a plate. Eventually the child will realize that he can count the children, then go to the plates, count out five plates, and distribute them accordingly. Allowing the child to use her own method of solving a problem such as this allows emergent understanding of math to develop in a child-centered developmental pattern.

Everyday activities such as snack and circle times can be used to promote the use of math.

Assigning two children to figure out how to solve an everyday problem as described above promotes problem solving even more. The children can discuss, plan, and even debate the best way to solve the problem. This give-and-take will push both children to construct new ways of seeing the problem (Kamii & Lewis 1990; Kamii 1991). In an argument, the children must clearly communicate their ideas to another person and at the same time evaluate the other person's ideas. In the process, both children examine and perhaps modify their own ideas.

Whenever a decision needs to be made in which children can have input, voting allows the teacher to use math in an integrated way. Not only does it offer an opportunity to count, but to compare numbers as well. Children can be asked to vote on which book to read first. The teacher asks the children to vote for one book. As the teacher counts the hands, she encourages the children to count with her. If the vote is six to five, the teacher can ask the children which book has won.

The project approach

The project approach to early childhood education allows children to explore their world and construct knowledge through genuine interaction with their environment. Lilian Katz (1989) states that young children should have activities that engage their minds fully in the quest for knowledge, understanding, and skill. When engaging in the project approach, children are not just gathering knowledge from a worksheet, structured activity, or teacher but are actively making decisions about not only what to learn, but also how and where to learn it. Through this method, children construct problem-solving techniques, research methods, and questioning strategies.

When children work on projects, a number of opportunities arise for them to use math. In a recent project on construction and transportation, children had an opportunity to use measurement to help them build a truck. They measured how long, tall, and wide they wanted it and then transferred their numbers to the cardboard they were using to make their truck. Their measurements were not accurate, and they did not really understand the concept of using a measuring tape. Still, these activities were at the beginning on the continuum of math learning, just as writing scribbles is a beginning step in literacy learning.

Questioning strategies, activities, and simple games offer a great opportunity for teachers to help children construct basic mathematical concepts.

The children also learned about blueprints, and when they made their own the teacher asked them how many windows they wanted in their house, how many bathrooms, and how many rooms in total. They discussed the layout of the house, which rooms would have windows, and how the rooms were located in the house. The children had to plan, count, use number, and measure to complete the activity.

Conclusion

There are many easy things that teachers can do to encourage the emerging mathematician in every child. Questioning strategies, activities, and simple games offer a great opportunity for teachers to help children construct basic mathematical concepts. An active, stimulating environment and a teacher who is willing to see the child's ability to construct mathematical concepts are invaluable to a child's construction of mathematics.

If we are to view the development of mathematics as emergent, we must understand that construction of mathematical concepts begins the day a child is born. Children construct the basic concepts of mathematics such as quantification, seriation, order, and classification without much interference or direct teaching from adults. The understanding of these concepts is not something that *can* be taught to children; they must construct it for themselves. The role of the teacher is to facilitate learning by offering infants, toddlers, and preschoolers opportunities and materials to promote their construction of mathematical thinking.

References

Chomsky, N. 1999. On the nature, use, and acquisition of language. In *Handbook of child language acquisition*, eds. W.C. Ritchie & T.K. Bhatia, 33–54. San Diego, CA: Academic Press. (Note: This reprinted chapter originally appeared in 1987, Special Issue [11] *Sophia Linguistica*.)

Ferreiro, E., & A. Teberosky. 1982. *Literacy before schooling*. Exeter, NH: Heinemann.

Katz, L.G. 1989. *Engaging children's minds: The project approach*. Norwood, NJ: Ablex.

Kamii, C., & B.A. Lewis. 1990. Research into practice. Constructivist learning and teaching. *Arithmetic teacher* 38 (1): 34–35.

Kamii, C., & others. 1991. Reform in primary mathematics education: A constructivist view. *Educational Horizons* 70 (1): 19–26.

Koechlin, E., S. Dehaene, & J. Mehler. 1997. Numerical transformations in five-month-old human infants. *Mathematical Cognition* 3 (2): 89–104.

Piaget, J., & B. Inhelder. [1964] 1969. *The early growth of logic in the child: Classification and seriation*. New York: Norton.

Sinclair, H., M. Stambak, I. Lezine, & S. Rayna. 1989. *Infants and objects: The creativity of cognitive development*. San Diego, CA: Academic Press.

Starkey, P., & R.G. Cooper, Jr. 1980. Perception of numbers by human infants. *Science* 210 (4473): 1033–35.

Wynn, K. 1995. Origins of numerical knowledge. *Mathematical Cognition* 1 (1): 35–60.

Eugene Geist, Ph.D., is an assistant professor of child and family studies at Ohio University in Athens. His research is focused on understanding how young children develop mathematical concepts and discovering the best ways to facilitate construction of mathematical knowledge in the early childhood years.

SALTING THE OATS: USING INQUIRY-BASED SCIENCE TO ENGAGE LEARNERS AT RISK

Paddy Lynch

In a recent conversation about good writing, my third graders and I agreed that a well-written piece "hooks" us as readers at the beginning and "wows" us in some way at the end. Just as quality literature captivates the reader, quality instruction does the same for the learner by creating an atmosphere of curiosity, presenting challenges and anomalies that pique student interest. Increasingly, though, I find an abundance of children in my class who are hard to "hook" and even harder to "wow."

Teachers and students are under increased pressure to produce test scores that demonstrate at least a year's growth. Students who perform poorly face retention if they don't measure up, so school systems are scrambling for ways to improve student achievement in reading, writing, and math. As a result, a curricular hierarchy is being created that emphasizes the teaching of reading, writing, and math in isolation, and often excludes content area subjects, such as science and social studies. Low-performing students are pulled from their regular classes for one-on-one tutorial sessions, restricting their exposure to group discussions and activities that encourage higher-order thinking skills. In an attempt to "fix" what is "wrong" with at-risk children, are we inadvertently denying them opportunities to demonstrate their potential?

Barbara Means and Michael Knapps (1991) recognized a trend in education to bring at-risk students "up to snuff" academically. However, as they examined how schools attempted to meet the needs of these children, they concluded that "the most widely accepted prescription for compensatory education sought to remedy students' deficiencies by teaching 'the basics' through curricula organized around discrete skills taught in a linear sequence—much like the academic programs these students had previously encountered in their regular classrooms" (Clarizio, Mehrens, & Hapkiewicz, 1994, p. 180). The authors suggested a reshaping of remedial curricula based on the following guidelines:

- Focus on complex, meaningful problems.
- Embed basic skills instruction within the context of more global tasks.
- Make connections with students' out-of-school experiences and cultures.
- Model powerful thinking strategies.
- Encourage multiple approaches to academic tasks.
- Provide scaffolding to enable students to accomplish complex tasks.
- Make dialogue the central medium for teaching and learning.

These six guidelines would eventually provide the framework for the instructional design of my work with at-risk students.

Stepping Out of the Box

I teach in a year-round school where our academic year begins in July, we hold classes for nine weeks, then are off for three-week inter-sessions. Remediation for at-risk students occurs throughout the year during these inter-sessions. In the past, remediation consisted of five, half-day classes that ran concurrently with enrichment classes (open to all students) during the first week of each inter-session. Enrichment classes were designed with lots of hands-on activities and little, if any, pencil-and-paper work. Students who attended enrichment wanted to be there—those who came to remediation often did not. Although remediation teachers typically used games and computer-related activities to reinforce basic skills, the format remained a thinly veiled session of "skill-and-drill." Even changing the name from "remediation" to "mastery" classes didn't fool anyone. It seemed to me that we had fallen into the rut of compensatory education described by Means and Knapp, offering a slightly different version of what the students had failed at in the first place.

Context. That's what was missing in our remediation classes—a context, a purpose for learning. I suspected that the only purpose students might see in attending remediation was to shorten their vacation and reinforce their feeling of academic inadequacy. As a result, not only did these children have academic struggles to overcome, many harbored bad attitudes towards school as well. By creating a context for learning that would "hook" students emotionally and intellectually, I suspected that whatever walls students had built up against learning might begin to crumble. The hook for my remediation classes, I decided, would be science.

I approached my principal with some trepidation because what I had in mind did not target skills in isolation. Instead, I offered to design and teach two sessions of remediation in which reading, writing, and math were imbedded within the context of science. They were tools to be used in learning about something of interest to the children. He conceded that the idea had merit, and gave me permission to implement it for the December and March inter-sessions.

I knew my classes had to begin with lots of materials to manipulate. Not only would concrete activities reinforce scientific concepts, they would be the "hook" to cultivate curiosity and build confidence as well. I felt my remediation students could all be successful with the science process skills upon which these activities were based. Every child would be able to observe, predict, and classify successfully, and with help, they could learn to use numbers, measure, and communicate their findings. Some immediate success was essential for these children in order to create an atmosphere in which they could safely take risks.

As I explored ways in which I could make science come alive for my students, I encountered an article entitled, "Hands-on and First-Hand Experiences in the Context of Reading and Language Arts," by Valerie Bang-Jensen. (Bang-Jensen, 1995). I was intrigued. I had always used the terms "first-hand" and "hands-on" interchangeably. This article helped me see that there was a significant difference. Bang-Jensen believes children must have first-hand experiences with manipulatives—in other words, opportunities to explore, observe, ask questions, and make connections between what they know about the objects at hand and what seems new. Only after that initial experience of "messing around" with materials

would students be prepared for the "hands-on" use of manipulatives—to conduct formal scientific investigations or demonstrate their knowledge of concepts. My students would need time to simply play with materials first before I expected them to use those materials in specific ways.

Putting Faces on the Label "At-Risk"

It is so easy to lump students together under a label like "at-risk." I wanted to resist the temptation to refer to my children as a collective "they," so in order to learn something about each of them, I created surveys to find out how the children perceived themselves as learners, and how their parents and teachers perceived them. The results showed that, as a group, the ten boys and four girls with whom I would work were outgoing, creative, and active children. Reading-related difficulties, such as comprehension of written problems and directions, were the single most significant area of concern. I decided that during the inter-session, frequent discussions and whole-group shared reading would become daily rituals designed to provide the support my children needed to understand content and written directions.

Rock and Roll

Since the weather here in the mountains can be unpredictable in December, I wanted to find a theme that the children and I could explore indoors rather than out. Roller coasters came to mind. We could explore gravity, friction, velocity, and motion, and use cardboard tubes of various sizes to create roller coasters of our own by the end of the week. Thinking back on the six guidelines for revised compensatory curriculum, this theme would allow me to make a connection with the students' out-of-school experiences, since most of them would have ridden on a coaster or at least knew what they were like. Learning about, designing, and then building a roller coaster provided the complex, meaningful problem which lent itself beautifully to integrating reading, writing, and math.

Amazon.com and I became very good friends as I scoured the Internet for resources and ideas that would be appropriate for the class. Signs were plastered all over school pleading for cardboard paper tubes, which soon came pouring in by the bagful. I felt like Templeton the rat from *Charlotte's Web*, scavenging for anything I could get to make my class material-rich and engaging to my students.

For the first 20 minutes of each class, students would have the opportunity to explore six different centers. Each of these contained simple written directions and materials to manipulate that demonstrated concepts with which we would formally experiment later. Students were encouraged to visit all six centers, but were ultimately free to choose where they spent that time first thing in the morning. Sorting cardboard tubes for construction, working with stopwatches, and experiments with friction, gravity, and slope gave students the chance to do something they considered fun and easy. The success students experienced in this "first-hand" time helped put them at ease with themselves and with each other.

As the children began to discover that this remediation class was going to be different, I realized how careful I had to be in introducing the inevitable written tasks related to our topic. Any sign of written work and these kids were ready to bolt. So we talked. We'd experiment a little, then stop and talk. Go back to the experiment, mess around some more, then talk again.

My line of questioning was carefully worded in order to stretch their thinking or challenge them to observe more carefully. "Why do you think...?" "What would happen if...?" "Try that again and see what happens when..." became standard questioning procedure. I understood the need to make dialogue the primary medium for teaching and learning, but I didn't realize how many ways it benefited my students. Not only was it easier for them to talk about what they had done before writing about it, the discussion itself was adding to their knowledge base. With guidance, they were able to create working definitions of newly explored scientific concepts. Having that firm, first-hand foundation made reading about science so much easier for them because they already understood what they were reading about.

Discussion also provided a wonderful opportunity to showcase each student's insights. Instead of looking to me for answers, they began to realize they could learn a great deal from each other. The "smart" kids they depended on in the regular classroom weren't around, so these "at-risk" children became the experts. A "wow" experience if there ever was one!...

Although I believed in the effectiveness of inquiry-based remediation, I wasn't quite sure how it would work, so I planned in excruciating detail for the December session. Lesson plans were revised on a daily basis. As I reflected on that first class, a framework began to emerge that I would use to develop the March session, which focused on water. I came to recognize several crucial elements of successful classroom experiences:

- Daily first-hand experiences with materials we would use to explore scientific concepts

- Whole-group conversations about what students had discovered, then direct instruction to focus student attention on a specific concept

- Individual/small group experiments interspersed with whole-group discussions to share insights and profile student strengths

- Development of working definitions and oral articulation of how things work

- Shared reading of information which underscored the scientific principles students had explored and discussed

- Recording/demonstrating/using what was learned through a variety of tasks involving the written word, drawings, and numbers

A Second Experience

A few balmy days during March allowed us to do some of our activities outside. I filled a 20-gallon tub full of water, and we set about exploring standard liquid measurement. We made it "rain" inside our classroom, created condensation on our windows, explored the three states of matter, then built and acted out the behavior of water molecules in ice, liquid water, and water vapor.

We investigated the stream on our school property, collected samples of the critters who lived there, and graphed the results. No matter what scientific concept we were exploring, we always began with the tactile and the kinesthetic, and then we talked and talked. Only after I believed the students had internalized the concept did we read, write, and do math based on the subject we were studying.

Insights and Observations

"Is it time to go already? Ah, man!"

"This is just like enrichment!"

"Mrs. Lynch, can we do that whole thing again?" In looking back over my revised remediation experience, do I think my students made gains in reading, writing, and math? Absolutely. However, these children are years behind their peers, academically speaking, and anyone who thinks five half-day sessions three times a year will significantly increase test scores is naive. Changes, however, did occur. The content-based, first-hand science program "hooked" these reluctant learners in ways that helped them take academic risks they had previously avoided.

Since I was charged with remediating academic weaknesses in my students, I needed to know if this remediation approach had improved the academic as well as the emotional life of these children. I took notes and some photographs during the course of the week, wrote personal observations in my journal, and tried to step back from the flurry of activity to observe what and how the children were doing. As I sifted through the documentation, questions began to surface. Was there evidence that students were fully engaged in inquiry activities? Were students able to demonstrate their understanding of scientific concepts? Did students demonstrate higher-order thinking? Upon examination of student work and my notes and observations, I could respond with a resounding "yes"! Although there are many examples that demonstrate the successes of my children, the experience of one child in particular stands out. Let me introduce you to Jessica.

Jessica was 20 minutes late to our first class in December. When she entered the room, there was a scowl on her face, and her first words to me after I had greeted her were, "My mom says I don't have to come back if this class is boring!" Fair enough, I thought. She remained aloof and distant from the rest of the class, observant but reluctant to join in. When it came time to write about the day's experiences, she whined that she couldn't think and didn't know what to write.

The next day, Jessica entered the room promptly and more willing to participate than the day before. I could see by the look on her face that she was beginning to enjoy herself. By our third day together, she was really hooked. In her review of the day, she wrote in her learning log, "Scienice is the funiest thing. Scienice is good for your brain." At the end of our first week together, I asked the children to talk about their experiences with this "new" kind of remediation. They immediately compared it to the "fun" enrichment classes that were going on around us, as I had hoped they would. In talking about their successes, Jessica offered, "When you make a mistake, you always learn something. You learn what you did wrong, and then you won't make it again." What incredible insight, coming from a child whose many academic mistakes had landed her in an extra week of school. I only hoped that the confidence reflected in this statement would last.

I didn't see much of Jessica when school began in January because she was not in my regular classroom. But when we came together again in March, the first thing she did was give me a big hug. In her hands, was her new favorite book, *The Big Book of Why*. I heard not a peep of complaint about writing from her this time. Later in the week, I overheard her explaining the results of an experiment to a classmate, using vocabulary we had learned in December. "I'm good at science," she said. The next day, she reported that she had replicated one of our experiments at home. As we worked in our learning logs, Jessica was intent on her task, self-correcting and rereading as she worked. These were "baby steps" to be sure, but for a child for whom any academic task was an obstacle, the progress I saw in Jessica made me proud....

Personal Lessons and Conclusions

Looking back on this wonderful experience with at-risk children, I realized that I was like them in more ways than I cared to admit. Although I was excited about doing something different and hooked on the idea that inquiry-based science could work in remediation, I was afraid of the risk I was taking, of the uncertainty of its outcome, and of the changes I knew I would have to make in myself. By becoming a learner along with my students, I experienced first-hand the insecurity they lived with day after day. I felt as if I were turning my instructional practice inside-out in order to make something fresh from what was old and stale. It was hard work. I had to fight every day to remind myself that process, not product, was the goal, and that change and progress come slowly and in their own time. I learned to look for inspiration and "teachable moments" in the most unlikely places, to be patient, and to look beyond the appearance of a thing to its potential. Just like my students, I had to learn that sometimes even my frustrations could lead to opportunities if I would allow them.

There's an old, familiar expression that says you can lead a horse to water, but you can't make him drink. You can, however, salt his oats. That's what I think science inquiry does for remedial education. It flavors the learning process with an authenticity that is hard for children to resist. It's time-consuming, material-intensive, and messy, but for my third-grade students, it was worth every bit of effort.

Pass the saltshaker again, will you, please?

References

Bang-Jensen, V. (1995). Hands-on and first-hand experiences in the context of reading and language arts. *Language Arts, 72,* 352–358.

Clarizio, H., Mehrens, W., & Hapkiewicz, W. (1994). *Contemporary issues in educational psychology.* Burr Ridge, IL: McGraw-Hill.

Means, B., & Knapp, M. (1991). Cognitive approaches to teaching advanced skills to educationally disadvantaged students. *Phi Delta Kappan, 73,* 282–289.

Paddy Lynch, third-grade teacher, Hendersonville Elementary School, Hendersonville, North Carolina

YOUNG CHILDREN & TECHNOLOGY

BY DOUGLAS CLEMENTS

Computers are increasingly present in early childhood education settings. Toward the end of the 1980s, only one-fourth of licensed preschools had computers. Today almost every preschool has a computer, with the ratio of computers to students changing from 1:125 in 1984 to 1:22 in 1990 to 1:10 in 1997. This last ratio matches the minimum ratio that is favorable to social interaction (Clements and Nastasi 1993; Coley et al. 1997). During the last 13 years, perspectives on the principle of developmental appropriateness have become more sophisticated. Researchers have extended these perspectives to include such dimensions as cultural paradigms and multiple intelligences (Bowman and Beyer 1994; Spodek and Brown 1993).

Research on young children and technology similarly has moved beyond simple questions to consider the implications of these changing perspectives for the use of technology in early childhood education. For example, we no longer need to ask whether the use of technology is "developmentally appropriate." Very young children have shown comfort and confidence in using software. They can follow pictorial directions and use situational and visual cues to understand and think about their activity (Clements and Nastasi 1993). Typing on the keyboard does not seem to cause them any trouble; if anything, it is a source of pride.

With the increasing availability of hardware and software adaptations, children with physical and emotional disabilities can also use the computer with ease. Besides enhancing their mobility and sense of control, computers can help improve their self-esteem. One totally mute four-year-old with diagnoses of retardation and autism began to echo words for the first time while working at a computer (Schery and O'Connor 1992). However, such access is not always equitable across our society. For example, children attending low-income and high-minority schools have less access to most types of technology (Coley et al. 1997).

Research has also moved beyond the simple question of whether computers can help young children learn. They can. What we need to understand is how best to aid learning, what types of learning we should facilitate, and how to serve the needs of diverse populations. In some innovative projects, computers are more than tools for bringing efficiency to traditional approaches. Instead, they open new and unforeseen avenues for learning. They allow children to interact with vast amounts of information from within their classrooms and homes. They tie children from across the world together (Riel 1994).

Not every use of technology, however, is appropriate or beneficial. The design of the curriculum and social setting are critical. This paper reviews the research in three broad areas: social interaction, teaching with computers, and curriculum and computers. Finally, it describes a new project that illustrates innovative, technology-based curriculum for early childhood education.

SOCIAL INTERACTION

An early concern, that computers will isolate children, was alleviated by research. In contrast, computers serve as *catalysts* for social interaction. The findings are wide-ranging and impressive. Children at the computer spent nine times as much time talking to peers while on the computer than while doing puzzles (Muller and Perlmutter 1985). Researchers observe that 95 percent of children's talking during Logo work is related to their work (Genishi et al. 1985). (Logo is a computer programming language designed to promote learning. Even young children can use it to direct the movements of an on-screen "turtle.") Children prefer to work with a friend rather than alone. They foster new friendships in the presence of the computer. There is greater and more spontaneous peer teaching and helping when children are using computers (Clements and Nastasi 1992).

The software they use affects children's social interactions. For example, open-ended programs such as Logo foster collaboration. Drill-and-practice software, on the other hand, can encourage turn-taking but also competition. Similarly, video games with aggressive content can engender competitiveness and aggression in children. Used differently, however, computers can have the opposite effect (Clements and Nastasi 1992). In one study, a computer simulation of the playhouse from the animated t.v. series *The Smurfs* attenuated the themes of territoriality and aggression that emerged with a real playhouse version of the Smurf environment (Forman 1986).

The physical environment also affects children's interactions (Davidson and Wright 1994). Placing two seats in front of the computer and one at the side for the teacher can encourage positive social interaction. Placing computers close to each other can facilitate the sharing of ideas among children. Centrally located computers invite other children to pause and participate in the computer activity. Such an arrangement also helps to keep teacher participation at an optimum level. Teachers are nearby to provide supervision and assistance as needed, but they are not constantly so close as to inhibit the children (Clements 1991).

TEACHING WITH COMPUTERS

The computer offers unique advantages in teaching. Opportunities to aid learning are addressed in the following section. Technology also offers unique ways to assess children. Observing the child at the computer provides teachers with a "window into a child's thinking process" (Weir et al. 1982). Research has also warned us not to curtail observations after a few months. Sometimes, beneficial effects appear only after a year. Ongoing observations also help us chart children's learning progress (Cochran-Smith et al 1988).

Differences in learning styles are more readily visible at the computer, where children have the freedom to follow diverse paths towards a goal (Wright 1994). This flexibility is particularly valuable with special children, as the computer seems to reveal their hidden strengths. Different advantages emerge for other groups of children. For example, researchers have found differences in Logo programming between African-American and Caucasian children. The visual nature of Logo purportedly was suited to the thinking style of African-American children's thinking style (Emihovich and Miller 1988).

Gender differences also emerge when children engage in programming. In one study, a post-test-only assessment seemed to indicate that boys performed better. However, assessment of the children's interactions revealed that the boys took greater risks and thereby reached the goal. In comparison, girls were more keen on accuracy; they meticulously planned and re-

flected on every step (Yelland 1994). Again, the implication for teaching is the need for consistent, long-term observation.

Yet another opportunity offered us by technology is to become pioneers ourselves. Because we know our children best, we can best create the program that will help them. Frustrated by the lack of good computer software, Tom Snyder started using the computer to support his classroom simulations of history. Mike Gralish, a first-grade teacher, used several computer devices and programs to link the base-10 blocks and the number system for his children. Today, both of these gentlemen are leading educational innovators (Riel 1994).

To be innovators and to keep up with the growing changes in technology, teachers need in-service training. Research has established that less than 10 hours of training can have a negative impact (Ryan 1993). Others have emphasized the importance of hands-on experience and warned against brief exposure to a variety of software programs, encouraging an in-depth knowledge of one program (Wright 1994).

CURRICULUM AND COMPUTERS

The computer also offers unique opportunities for learning through exploration, creative problem solving, and self-guided instruction. Realizing this potential demands a simultaneous focus on curriculum and technology innovations (Hohmann 1994). Effectively integrating technology into the curriculum demands effort, time, commitment, and, sometimes, even a change in one's beliefs.

We begin with several overarching issues. What type of computer software should be used? Drill-and-practice software leads to gains in certain rote skills. However, it has not been as effective in improving the conceptual skills of children (Clements and Nastasi 1993). Discovery-based software that encourages and allows ample room for free exploration is more valuable in this regard. However, research has shown that children work best with this type of software when they are assigned to open-ended projects rather than asked merely to "free explore" (Lemerise 1993). They spend more time and actively search for diverse ways to solve the task. The group of children who were allowed to free explore grew disinterested quite soon.

Another concern was that computers would replace other early childhood activities. Research shows that computer activities yield the best results when coupled with suitable off-computer activities. For example, children who are exposed to developmental software alone—the on-computer group—show gains in intelligence, non-verbal skills, long-term memory, and manual dexterity. Those who also worked with supplemental activities, in comparison—the off-computer group—gained in all of these areas and improved their scores in verbal, problem-solving, and conceptual skills (Haugland 1992). In addition, these children spent the least amount of time using the computers. A control group that used drill-and-practice software spent three times as long on the computer but showed less than half of the gains that the on- and off-computer groups did. Given these capabilities of the computer, how has it affected children's learning?

In mathematics specifically, the computer can provide practice on arithmetic processes and foster deeper conceptual thinking. Drill-and-practice software can help young children develop competence in counting and sorting (Clements and Nastasi 1993). However, it is questionable if the exclusive use of such drill-and-practice software would subscribe to the vision of the National Council of Teachers of Mathematics (NCTM) (1989): Children should be "mathematically literate" in a world where the use of mathematics is becoming more and more pervasive. NCTM recommends that we "create a coherent vision of what it means to be mathematically literate both in a world that relies on calculators and computers to carry out mathematical procedures and in a world where mathematics is rapidly growing and is extensively being applied in diverse fields" (National Council of Teachers of Mathematics 1989). This vision *de*-emphasizes rote practice on isolated facts. It emphasizes discussing and solving problems in geometry, number sense, and patterns with the help of manipulatives and computers.

For example, using software programs that allow the creation of pictures with geometric shapes, children have demonstrated growing knowledge and competence in working with concepts such as symmetry, patterns, and spatial order. Tammy overlaid two overlapping triangles on one square and colored select parts of this figure to create a third triangle that did not exist in the program! Not only did this preschooler exhibit an awareness of how she had made this figure, but she also showed awareness of the challenge it would be to others (Wright 1994). Using a graphics program with three primary colors, young children combined these colors to create three secondary colors (Wright 1994). Such complex combinatorial abilities are often thought to be out of the reach of young children. The computer experience led the children to explorations that expanded their boundaries.

Young children can also explore simple "turtle geometry." They direct the movements of a robot or screen "turtle" to draw different shapes. One group of five-year-olds was constructing rectangles. "I wonder if I can tilt one," mused one boy. He turned the turtle with a simple mathematical command, "L 1" (turn left one unit), drew the first side, then was unsure about what to do next. He finally figured out that he must use the same turn command as before. He hesitated again. "How far now? Oh, it *must* be the same as its partner!" He easily completed his rectangle. The instructions he should give the turtle at *this new heading* were, at first, not obvious. He analyzed the situation and reflected on the properties of a rectangle. Perhaps most important, he posed the problem for himself (Clements and Battista 1992).

This boy had walked rectangular paths, drawn rectangles with pencils, and built them on geo-boards and pegboards. What did the computer experience *add*? It helped him *link* his previous experiences to more explicit mathematical ideas. It helped him *connect* visual shapes with abstract numbers. It encouraged him to *wonder* about mathematics and pose problems in an environment in which he could create, experiment, and receive feedback about his own ideas.

Such discoveries happen frequently. One preschooler made the discovery that reversing the turtle's orientation and moving it backwards had the same effect as merely moving it forwards. The significance the child attached to this discovery and his overt awareness of it was striking. Although the child had done this previously with toy cars, Logo helped him abstract a new and exciting idea (Tan 1985).

BUILDING BLOCKS©: AN INNOVATIVE TECHNOLOGY-BASED CURRICULUM

At present, Julie Sarama and I are developing innovative pre-K to grade 2 curriculum materials. The project, "Building Blocks—Foundations for Mathematical Thinking, Pre-Kindergarten to Grade 2: Research-based Materials Development," is funded by a grant from the National Science Foundation. It is designed to enable all young children to build solid content knowledge and develop higher-order thinking. The program's design is based on current theory and research and represents a state-of-the-art technology curriculum for young children in the area of mathematics. It is discussed in this paper in that light. The reader might notice that our description does not begin with a listing of its technologically sophisticated elements, including multimedia features. This strategy is deliberate. We emphasize the art and science of teaching and learning, in contrast to many early childhood software programs, which use technologically advanced bells and whistles to disguise ordinary activities.

The design of a state-of-the-art curriculum must begin with audience considerations. The demographics of this age range imply that materials should be designed for home, daycare, and classroom environments and for children who have various backgrounds, interests, and ability levels. To reach this broad audience, the curriculum materials will be progressively layered: Users will be able to "dig deeper" into them to reach increasingly rich, but demanding, pedagogical and mathematical levels. The materials should not rely on technology alone. They should integrate three types of media: computers, manipulatives (and everyday objects), and print.

The project's basic educational approach is finding the mathematics in children's activities and developing mathematics from them. We focus on helping children extend and find mathematics in their everyday activities, from building blocks to art to songs to puzzles. Thus, we will design activities based on children's experiences and interests, with an emphasis on supporting the development of mathematical activity. This process emphasizes representation: using mathematical objects and actions that relate to children's everyday activities. Our materials will embody these actions-on-objects in a way that mirrors the theory of and research on children's *cognitive building blocks*—creating, copying, uniting, and dis-embedding both units and composite units.

Perhaps the most important aspect of the project's material design is our model for the design process. Curriculum and software design can and should have an explicit theoretical and empirical foundation, beyond its genesis in someone's intuitive grasp of children's learning. It should also interact with the ongoing development of theory and research, reaching toward the ideal of testing a theory by testing the software and the curriculum in which it is embedded. In this model, one conducts research at multiple aggregate levels, making the research relevant to educators in many positions. We have cognitive models with sufficient explanatory power to permit the design to grow co-jointly with the refinement of these cognitive models (Biddlecomb 1994; Clements and Sarama 1995; Fuson 1992; Hennessy 1995).

The phases of our nine-step design process model follow.

1. Draft curriculum goals.
2. Build an explicit model of children's knowledge and learning in the goal domain.
3. Create an initial design.
4. Investigate components.
5. Assess prototypes and curriculum.
6. Conduct pilot tests.
7. Conduct field tests in multiple settings.
8. Recurse.
9. Publish and disseminate.

These phases include a close interaction between materials development and a variety of research methodologies, from clinical interviews to teaching experiments to ethnographic participant observation.

A new technology permits the reflective consideration of objects, actions, and activities, which can help developers re-conceptualize the nature and content of mathematics that might be learned. The developer can also conceive new designs by reflecting on how software might provide tools that enhance students' actions and imagination or that suggest an encapsulation of a process or obstacles that force students to grapple with an important idea or issue. Finally, the flexibility of computer technologies allows the creation of a vision less hampered by the limitations of traditional materials and pedagogical approaches (cf. Confrey, in press). For example, computer-based communication can extend the model for mathematical learning beyond the classroom. Computers can allow representations and actions not possible with other media. The materials in *Building Blocks* will not only ensure that computerized actions-on-objects mirror the goal concepts and procedures, but also that they are embedded in tasks and developmentally appropriate settings (e.g., narratives, fantasy worlds, building projects).

The materials will emphasize the development of basic *mathematical building blocks*—ways of knowing the world mathematically. These building blocks will be organized into two areas: (1) spatial and geometric competencies and concepts; and (2) numeric and quantitative concepts, based on the considerable research in that domain. Three mathematical subthemes will be woven through both main areas: (1) patterns and functions; (2) data; and (3) discrete mathematics (e.g., classifying, sorting, sequencing). Most important will be the synthesis of these domains, each to the benefit of the other. The building blocks of the structure are not elementary school topics "pushed down" to younger ages; they are developmentally appropriate domains, that is, topics that are meaningful and interesting to children. Access to topics such as large numbers or geometric ideas such as depth, however, are not restricted. In fact, research indicates that these concepts are both interesting and accessible to young children.

By presenting concrete ideas in a symbolic medium, for example, the computer can help bridge these two concepts for young children. But are these manipulatives still "concrete" on the *computer* screen? One has to examine what concrete means. Sensory characteristics do not adequately define it (Clements and McMillen 1996; Wilensky 1991). First, it cannot be assumed that children's conceptions of the manipulatives are similar to those of adults (Clements and McMillen 1996). Second, physical actions with certain manipulatives may suggest different mental actions than those we wish students to learn. For example, researchers found a mismatch among students using the number line to perform addition. When adding five and four, the students located the number 5, counted "one, two, three, four" and read the answer. This action did not help them solve the problem mentally, for to do so they have to count "six, seven, eight, nine" and at the same time count the counts—6 is 1, 7 is 2, and so on. These actions are quite different (Gravemeijer 1991).

Thus, manipulatives do not always carry the meaning of the mathematical idea. Students must use these manipulatives in the context of well-planned activities and ultimately reflect on their actions in order to grasp the idea. Later, we expect them to have a "concrete" understanding that goes beyond these physical manipulatives.

It appears that there are different ways to define *concrete* (Clements and McMillen 1996). We define sensory-concrete knowledge as that in which students must use sensory material to make sense of an idea. For example, at early stages, children cannot count, add, or subtract meaningfully unless they have actual objects to aid in those functions. They build integrated-concrete knowledge as they learn. Such knowledge is connected in special ways. (The root of the word *concrete* is "to grow together.") What gives sidewalk concrete its strength is the combination of separate particles in an interconnected mass. What gives integrated-concrete thinking its strength is the combination of many separate ideas in an interconnected structure of knowledge (Clements and McMillen 1996).

For example, computer programs may allow children to manipulate on-screen "building blocks." These blocks are not physically concrete. However, no base-10 blocks "contain" place-value ideas (Kamii 1986). Students must build these ideas from working with the blocks and thinking about their actions. Furthermore, research indicates that physical base-10 blocks can be so clumsy and the manipulations so disconnected from each other that students see only the trees (manipulations of many pieces) and miss the forest (place-value ideas). Computer blocks can be more manageable and "clean" (Thompson and Thompson 1990). Students can break computer base-10 blocks into single blocks, or glue these blocks together to form 10s. These actions are more in line with the mental actions that we want students to learn: They are children's cognitive building blocks.

One essential cognitive "building block" of place value is children's ability to count by 10 from any number, thus constructing composite units of 10 (Steffe and Meinster 1997). The computer helps students make sense of their activity and the numbers by linking the blocks to symbols. For example, the number represented by the base-10 blocks is usually linked dynamically to the students' actions with the blocks, automatically changing the number spoken and displayed by the computer when the student changes the blocks. As a simple example, a child who has 16 single blocks might glue 10 together and then repeatedly duplicate this "10." In counting along with the computer, "26, 36, 46," and so on, the child constructs composite units of 10.

Computers encourage students to make their knowledge explicit, which helps them build integrated-concrete knowledge. Specific theoretically and empirically grounded advantages of using computer manipulatives follow (Clements and McMillen 1996).

- They provide a manageable, clean manipulative.
- They offer flexibility.
- They can change arrangement or representation.
- They can store, and later retrieve, configurations.
- They record and replay students' actions.
- They link the concrete and the symbolic with feedback.
- They dynamically link multiple representations.
- They change the very nature of the manipulative.
- They link the specific to the general.
- They encourage problem posing and conjecturing.
- They provide a framework for problem solving, focus attention, and increase motivation.
- They encourage and facilitate complete and precise explanations.

Of course, multimedia and other computer capabilities should, and will, be used when they serve educational purposes. Features such as animation, music, surprise elements, and especially consistent interaction get and hold children's interest (Escobedo and Evans 1997). They can also aid learning, if they are designed to support and be consistent with the pedagogical goals. In addition, access to technology is an important equity issue. Much of our material will be available on the Internet.

In summary, the *Building Blocks* project is designed to combine the art and science of teaching and learning with the science of technology, with the latter serving the former. Such synthesis of curriculum and technology development as a scientific enterprise with mathematics education research will reduce the separation of research and practice in mathematics and technology education. Materials based on research can then be produced, and research can be based on effective and ecologically sound learning situations. Moreover, these results will be immediately applicable by practitioners (parents, teachers, and teacher educators); administrators and policy makers; and curriculum and software developers.

FINAL WORDS

One can use technology to teach the same old stuff in the same way. Integrated computer activities can increase achievement. Children who use practice software 10 minutes per day increase their scores on achievement tests. However, if the gadgets are computers, the same old teaching becomes incredibly more expensive and biased towards its dullest parts, namely the kind of rote learning in which measurable results can be obtained by treating the children like pigeons in a Skinner box.... I believe with Dewey, Montessori, and Piaget that children learn by doing and by thinking about what they do. And so the fundamental ingredients of educational innovation must be better things to do and better ways to think about oneself doing these things. (Papert 1980).

We believe, with Papert, that computers can be a rich source of these ingredients. We believe that having children use computers in new ways—to solve problems, manipulate mathematical objects, create, draw, and write simple computer programs—can be a catalyst for positive school change.

References

Biddlecomb, B.D. (1994). Theory-based development of computer microworlds. *Journal of Research in Childhood Education*, 8(2): 87–98.

Bowman, B.T., and Beyer, E.R. (1994). Thoughts on technology and early childhood education. In *Young children: Active learners in a technological age*, eds. J.L. Wright and D.D. Shade, 19–30. Washington, DC: National Association for the Education of Young Children.

Clements, D.H. (1991). Current technology and the early childhood curriculum. In *Yearbook in early childhood education, Volume 2: Issues in early childhood curriculum*, eds. B. Spodek and O.N. Saracho, 106–131. New York: Teachers College Press.

Clements, D.H., and Battista, M.T. (1992). *The development of a Logo-based elementary school geometry curriculum (Final Report)*. NSF Grant No.: MDR–8651668. Buffalo, NY/Kent, OH: State University of New York at Buffalo/Kent State University.

Clements, D.H., and McMillen, S. (1996). Rethinking "concrete" manipulatives. *Teaching Children Mathematics*, 2(5): 270–279.

Clements, D.H., and Nastasi, B.K. (1992). Computers and early childhood education. In *Advances in school psychology: Preschool and early childhood treatment directions*, eds. M. Gettinger, S.N. Elliott, and T.R. Kratochwill, 187–246. Hillsdale, NJ: Lawrence Erlbaum Associates.

Clements, D.H., and Nastasi, B.K. (1993). Electronic media and early childhood education. In *Handbook of research on the education of young children*, ed. B. Spodek, 251–275. New York: Macmillan.

Clements, D.H., and Sarama, J. (1995). Design of a Logo environment for elementary geometry. *Journal of Mathematical Behavior*, 14: 381–398.

Cochran-Smith, M., Kahn, J., and Paris, C.L. (1988). When word processors come into the classroom. In *Writing with computers in the early grades*, eds. J.L. Hoot and S.B. Silvern, 43–74. New York: Teachers College Press.

Coley, R.J., Cradler, J., and Engel, P.K. (1997). *Computers and classrooms: The status of technology in U.S. schools*. Princeton, NJ: Educational Testing Service.

Confrey, J. (in press). Designing mathematics education: The role of new technologies. In *Education & technology: Reflections on a decade of experience in classrooms*, ed. C. Fisher San Francisco: Jossey-Bass and Apple Corp.

Davidson, J., and Wright, J.L. (1994). The potential of the microcomputer in the early childhood classroom. In *Young children: Active learners in a technological age*, eds. J.L. Wright and D.D. Shade, 77–91. Washington, DC: National Association for the Education of Young Children.

Emihovich, C., and Miller, G.E. (1988). Effects of Logo and CAI on black first graders' achievement, reflectivity, and self-esteem. *The Elementary School Journal*, 88: 473–487.

Escobedo, T.H., and Evans, S. (1997). *A comparison of child-tested early childhood education software with professional ratings*. Paper presented at the meeting of the American Educational Research Association, Chicago, IL, March 1997.

Forman, G. (1986). Computer graphics as a medium for enhancing reflective thinking in young children. In *Thinking*, eds. J. Bishop, J. Lochhead, and D.N. Perkins, 131–137. Hillsdale, NJ: Lawrence Erlbaum Associates.

Fuson, K.C. (1992). Research on whole number addition and subtraction. In *Handbook of research on mathematics teaching and learning*, ed. D.A. Grouws, 243–275. New York: Macmillan.

Genishi, C., McCollum, P., and Strand, E.B. (1985). Research currents: The interactional richness of children's computer use. *Language Arts*, 62(5): 526–532.

Gravemeijer, K.P.E. (1991). An instruction-theoretical reflection on the use of manipulatives. In *Realistic mathematics education in primary school*, ed. L. Streefland, 57–76. Utrecht, The Netherlands: Freudenthal Institute, Utrecht University.

Haugland, S.W. (1992). Effects of computer software on preschool children's developmental gains. *Journal of Computing in Childhood Education*, 3(1): 15–30.

Hennessy, S. (1995). Design of a computer-augmented curriculum for mechanics. *International Journal of Science Education*, 17(1): 75–92.

Hohmann, C. (1994). Staff development practices for integrating technology in early childhood education programs. In *Young children: Active learners in a technological age*, eds. J.L. Wright and D.D. Shade, 104. Washington, DC: National Association for the Education of Young Children.

Kamii, C. (1986). Place value: An explanation of its difficulty and educational implications for the primary grades. Journal of Research in Childhood Education, 1: 75–86.

Lemerise, T. (1993). Piaget, Vygotsky, & Logo. *The Computing Teacher*, 24–28.

Muller, A.A., and Perlmutter, M. (1985). Preschool children's problem-solving interactions at computers and jigsaw puzzles. *Journal of Applied Developmental Psychology*, 6: 173–186.

National Council of Teachers of Mathematics. (1989). *Curriculum and evaluation standards for school mathematics*. Reston, VA: Author.

Papert, S. (1980). Teaching children thinking: Teaching children to be mathematicians vs. teaching about mathematics. In *The computer in the school: Tutor, tool, tutee*, ed. R. Taylor, 161–196. New York: Teachers College Press.

Riel, M. (1994). Educational change in a technology-rich environment. *Journal of Research on Computing in Education*, 26(4): 452–474.

Ryan, A.W. (1993). The impact of teacher training on achievement effects of microcomputer use in elementary schools: A meta-analysis. In *Rethinking the roles of technology in education*, eds. N. Estes and M. Thomas, 770–772. Cambridge, MA: Massachusetts Institute of Technology.

Schery, T.K., and O'Connor, L.C. (1992). The effectiveness of school-based computer language intervention with severely handicapped children. *Language, Speech, and Hearing Services in Schools*, 23: 43–47.

Spodek, B., and Brown, P.C. (1993). Curriculum alternatives in early childhood education: A historical perspective. In *Handbook of research on the education of young children*, ed. B. Spodek, 91–104. New York: Macmillan.

Steffe, J., and Meinster, B. (1997). *Integrated computer activities to build science skills. (Df-Computer Application Series)*. Cincinnati, OH: South-Western Publishing.

Tan, L.E. (1985). Computers in pre-school education. *Early Child Development and Care*, 19: 319–336.

Thompson, P.W., and Thompson, A.G. (1990). *Salient aspects of experience with concrete manipulatives*. Mexico City: International Group for the Psychology of Mathematics Education.

Weir, S., Russell, S.J., and Valente, J.A. (1982). Logo: An approach to educating disabled children. *BYTE*, 7: 342–360.

Wilensky, U. (1991). Abstract mediations on the concrete and concrete implications for mathematics education. In *Constructionism*, eds. I. Harel and S. Papert, 193–199. Norwood, NJ: Ablex.

Wright, J.L. (1994). Listen to the children: Observing young children's discoveries with the microcomputer. In *Young children: Active learners in a technological age*, eds. J.L. Wright and D.D. Shade, 3–17. Washington, DC: National Association for the Education of Young Children.

Yelland, N. (1994). The strategies and interactions of young children in Logo tasks. *Journal of Computer Assisted Learning*, 10: 33–49.

Douglas Clements is a professor in the department of learning and instruction in the graduate school of education at the SUNY-Buffalo.

From *Earlychildhood News*, November/December 2001, pp. 36-43. © 2001 by Douglas Clements.

UNIT 6
Trends

Unit Selections

Key Points to Consider

- If America were to "design a preschool system the way we built our Interstate highway system," how would it be structured?

- How could the current standards movement in education threaten young children and how they are taught?

- It has been proven that smaller class sizes improve the quality of education for K–3 children. Can you think of any negative consequences of reducing class sizes?

- Is there any problem with the belief that "all children can learn"?

 **Links: www.dushkin.com/online/**
These sites are annotated in the World Wide Web pages.

Awesome Library for Teachers
   http://www.neat-schoolhouse.org/teacher.html
Future of Children
   http://www.futureofchildren.org
National Institute on the Education of At-Risk Students
   http://www.cfda.gov/public/viewprog.asp?progid=1062
Prospects: The Congressionally Mandated Study of Educational Growth and Opportunity
   http://www.ed.gov/pubs/Prospects/index.html

We begin this unit on trends in early childhood education with an article on the need for high-quality, free, universal preschool. Both the title of the article—"The 'Failure' of Head Start"—and its content are provocative. According to the author, our nation has become satisfied with income-based programs like Head Start when we ought to be creating a system of child care and education for all families. Even though many states have placed a priority on preschool education, very few have created a system that provides affordable access for substantial numbers of families.

Accountability is another trend that continues in this decade and is encroaching more and more into early childhood. "Accountability Shovedown: Resisting the Standards Movement in Early Childhood Education" is one educator's perspective on the disadvantages of accountability when applied indiscriminately to early childhood education. For standards to apply reasonably to young children, they must emphasize learning, not performance; diversity, not sameness; and individuals, not groups. Standards must also allow for teachers to use professional judgment and not place them in the role of technicians.

One trend to watch for across America is the move in some states to reduce class size in primary grades. California has led the way in lowering the number of children in K–3 classrooms, with largely rewarding results. The standardized test scores of these children are slightly better than those of children in larger classes. However, not all results have been positive. "Class-Size Reduction in California" highlights the consequences of statewide legislation and offers advice to other states that are entering into reduction moves.

The cost of class-size reform is high, as are many of the accountability measures that have been enacted by school districts across America. How priorities are set and how resources are allocated-these are the issues discussed in "Putting Money Where It Matters." Every decision made to increase the quality of early childhood education costs money. If schools want to continue making choices based on quality, they must rethink their use of

resources. The author of this important policy article leads us to consider five significant ways to realign spending and staffing with quality reforms.

"'All Children Can Learn': Facts and Fallacies" is the type of reading that must be done slowly and thoughtfully. The authors offer reasons for their skepticism with the central tenet of the effective schools movement-that children's learning will improve if schools adopt a certain set of effective practices. Their premise is that children in America do not have equal opportunity to learn or succeed. If disadvantaged children do not receive the resource-rich support they need, inequality in the nation's schools will continue. This provocative article deserves a careful read.

"In Early Childhood Education and Care: Quality Counts" is an executive summary of what states are undertaking in early childhood education. The report is provided in this unit as an overview—showing that most states are interested in early learning and more of them are supplementing federal programs and paying for full-day kindergarten. Another positive indicator is that more states are defining quality in terms of instruction and program accreditation, in addition to traditional health and safety indicators. One of the paradoxes of the accountability trend is that states are paying more attention to early childhood education because of heightened emphasis on academic performance in the elementary years.

The 'Failure' of Head Start

By John Merrow

Head Start has failed. The federal preschool program for 4-year-olds was supposed to "level the playing field" for poor children, and it has not done that.

Educationally and linguistically, poor children are behind from the beginning. Parents with professional jobs speak about 2,100 words an hour to toddlers; those in poverty only about 600. Not surprisingly, a 5-year-old child from a low-income home has a 5,000-word vocabulary, while a middle-class child already knows 20,000 words.

One reason for its failure was the misguided practice at some Head Start centers, where teaching the alphabet was actually banned, in favor of teaching social skills. But the dominant reason for the persistent gap is the fervor with which middle- and upper-middle-class parents embrace preschool.

These parents enroll their own children in preschool because they know that 3- and 4-year-olds are ready and eager to learn. Seventy-six per cent of 4-year-olds from households with an annual income of more than $50,000 are enrolled. The National Center for Education Statistics reports that twice as many 3- to 5-year-olds from families with incomes above $75,000 are enrolled, compared with children whose parents make $10,000 a year.

By contrast, fewer than half of children whose families fall below the poverty line attend preschool, not because their parents don't want them to, but because we haven't created enough Head Start programs. To serve all the eligible children, we'd need twice as many as we have. Once again, we're talking the talk when it comes to helping poor children, but not walking the walk. And, largely for that reason, the gap will not only not disappear, it will grow.

We ought to be embarrassed about our approach to preschool. Most industrialized countries provide free, high-quality preschool for 3-, 4-, and 5-year-olds, regardless of family income. Almost all 4-year-olds in England, Luxembourg, and the Netherlands go to public school; 70 percent of German, Danish, and Greek 4- year- olds go to public school; and over 90 percent of 4- and 5-year-olds in Italy and Spain are in public school.

We're the opposite: a patchwork nonsystem with weakly trained, poorly paid staff members. The quality ranges from excellent to abysmal, the tuition from $15,000 to zero, the teachers' salaries from $45,000 a year with benefits to as low as $8 or $9 per hour, with no benefits.

I've just spent seven weeks driving around Europe, visiting lots of small towns and villages. Every small town I visited in France had a sign, prominently placed, pointing the way to the local école maternelle, the town's preschool. Had I stopped to look, I would have found every 3- and 4- year- old from the village at the school.

A few months earlier, I visited three écoles maternelles in very different neighborhoods in Paris. The school serving poor children was virtually identical to those serving middle-class and upper- middle-class children. All three schools were staffed with well-trained, well- paid teachers, because all école maternelle teachers must have master's degrees, and all are paid at the same rate as elementary school teachers. Today in France, 100 percent of children ages 3 through 5 attend preschool, most in public programs.

In the United States, preschool is a seller's market, and even well-off parents have to endure "preschool panic," because there's not enough quality to go around. One of the families in our forthcoming PBS documentary on the subject moved from New York City to France while we were filming. The parents had been forced to choose between career opportunities for themselves and a decent preschool for their sons. Today, while both parents are struggling to develop their careers in France, their children are in sound educational programs.

Today preschool is on a lot of state agendas. According to the Child Care Action Campaign, 42 states now have some form of "preschool initiative." However, that phrase encompasses everything from legislative proposals to real programs, and only Georgia, New York, Oklahoma, and the District of Columbia have genuine programs that provide free preschool for a substantial number of children.

Georgia is at the head of the preschool class. Its program currently serves more than 63,000 4-year-olds. In toto, 70 percent of Georgia's 4-year-olds are now in some form of publicly subsidized preschool. The Georgia program is the brainchild of former Gov. Zell Miller, now a U.S. senator, who believes that "preschool is more important than the 12th grade in high school." Georgia requires districts to offer prekindergarten and pays the bill—$240 million a year—with money from its lottery and with federal Head Start funds. New York and Oklahoma are leaving it up to school districts to decide whether they will provide such services, with the state paying the bills. But states are hard-pressed for funds these days, and so, for example, New York's legislature has put up less than half the money needed to establish programs across the state.

Creating high-quality programs is proving to be difficult. No state is starting from scratch, of course, which means that any new program must be grafted on to what exists. And what exists is a hodgepodge of programs: Some are run for profit, some are staffed with trained, well-paid teachers, some are storefront operations where a TV set is the caregiver, and so on. Some Head Start programs are excellent, but others are woeful. One evaluation of Head Start found that some children began knowing just one letter of the alphabet, A, and left nine months later without having learned B.

President Bush says he wants to change that, but his proposal is flawed. To improve literacy skills, he plans to give 2,500 Head Start teachers four days of training in early-literacy instructional techniques, after which they are supposed to pass on what they learned to the other 47,000 Head Start teachers. Critical reaction was immediate. A spokesman for U.S. Rep. George Miller, D- Calif., told reporters, "The idea that you would be able to create reading specialists among Head Start teachers with four days of training is absurd."

Moreover, the president's budget won't allow Head Start to grow, even though the program misses more than half of eligible children.

I BELIEVE THAT WE'RE OPERATING FROM THE WRONG PREMISE. Instead of relying on income-based programs like Head Start that are supposed to help the poor, we ought to be creating a system that would be good enough for the well-off. Create something that's good enough for those with money, but make it available to everyone. Design a preschool system the way we built our Interstate highway system. We didn't create separate highways for rich and poor. Instead, we built an Interstate system that was good enough for people behind the wheel of a Cadillac or a Lexus, a Corvette or a Mercedes, and there were no complaints from those driving a Chevy or a Ford.

We know that good preschools have long-term benefits for children, and we ought to recognize that as a nation.

Creating universal, free, high-quality preschool will be difficult, complicated, and costly: By one estimate, it would cost $30 billion a year to run programs just for those 3- and 4-year-olds from families making less that $30,000 a year. For all 3- and 4-year-olds, "The cost could easily be $100 billion," according to Ron Haskins of the Brookings Institution. However, we know that good preschools have long-term benefits for children, and we ought to recognize that as a nation.

It took 50 years for the United States to be able to compete as a peer in soccer's World Cup with Italy, Mexico, Portugal, France, Germany, Sweden, and other long-established powers. We cannot afford to take that long to catch up in the world of preschool education.

John Merrow's documentary "The Promise of Preschool" appeared on PBS. He is the author of Choosing Excellence *(Scarecrow Press, 2001) and an education correspondent for "The NewsHour with Jim Lehrer."*

From *Education Week on the Web,* September 25, 2002. © 2002 by Education Week on the Web.

Accountability Shovedown: Resisting the Standards Movement in Early Childhood Education

Mr. Hatch sees the proliferation of standards for early childhood settings as "accountability shovedown" that threatens the integrity of early childhood professionals and the quality of educational experiences for young children.

BY J. AMOS HATCH

DURING THE 1980s, early childhood educators waged a battle to resist attempts to require more and more of young children at younger and younger ages. This movement to push expectations from the primary grades down into kindergarten and preschool programs was characterized as "curriculum shovedown" by the mainstream early childhood educators, who argued that young children were not developmentally ready for the academic emphasis of such an approach. David Elkind, an articulate spokesperson for the early childhood community, argued that young children were being "miseducated" in settings where they were experiencing stress from academic pressure for no apparent benefit. In *The Hurried Child* and *Miseducation: Preschoolers at Risk,* Elkind provided powerful indictments of curriculum shovedown and related attempts to make children grow up faster.[1]

My view is that the standards movement—so pervasive across educational settings today—is threatening children in early childhood in the same ways as the curriculum shovedown movement did in the 1980s. The point of attack has changed from curriculum to outcomes, but the consequences for young children may be the same. Standards for such federal programs as Head Start are already in place, and the discourse in many states and across the early childhood field assumes the inevitability of standards.[2] After all, who could be against standards?

Who would have the nerve to say that standards are not important? Who would try to build an argument toward the conclusion that standards are somehow bad? Not I, certainly. I am all for standards in early childhood education, unless they fail to pass muster in the 10 areas discussed below.

1. *Pressure on children.* I support standards for early childhood programs—except when the implementation of those standards puts children as young as 3 and 4 at risk of feeling pressured in the classroom environment. Elkind noted that young children experience significant and sometimes debilitating stress when they are expected to perform at academic levels for which they are not ready. Further, he argued that waiting until they are ready puts children at no real academic disadvantage in the long run.[3]

It is axiomatic in early childhood that children develop at different rates. Some young children will be ready to meet the challenges of the new expectations associated with the standards movement; many will not. Holding all children to the same standard guarantees that some will face failure. And just setting up a situation in which failure is possible creates stress for even the most capable child, who might be wondering if he or she is achieving "high enough or fast enough."[4] Getting children to do more sooner sounds like a logical way to cure the ills of education. But ask someone who has comforted a child who cries because she cannot distinguish between a 3 and a 5 or who has coaxed a child to keep trying when he refuses to demonstrate (once again) his inability to match the letters with the sounds. Those who know young children understand that putting them under stress is an unacceptable by-product of accountability efforts designed to achieve dubious educational advantages.

2. *Pressure on teachers.* I see standards as vitally important in early childhood education—unless they are used in ways that put pressure on teachers to abandon their mission of teaching young children in favor of teaching a core set of competencies. The pressure to accelerate achievement gets translated to teachers as "Do a better job of getting your kids up to the standards—or else." If meeting the standards is what is valued in the school where they teach and if student performance provides the basis for how they are evaluated, teachers will feel pressured to meet the standards and to raise student performance. On its face, that kind of pressure may not seem so bad. Indeed, standards are set up to demand more of schools and teachers based on the belief that "demands will result in behavior that conforms to them."[5]

But pressuring early childhood professionals with demands and threats may work against the best interests of teachers and the children they serve. By training and disposition, teachers of young children are concerned with understanding and teaching the whole child. Teachers are motivated to know children's individual capacities and needs and to do whatever is necessary to develop those capacities and meet those needs, whether they are emotional, social, physical, or cognitive. It causes genuine anxiety when other domains of children's development are ignored or put at risk because of an overemphasis on something as narrowly defined as academic standards. In addition, early childhood teachers feel some anxiety when they see themselves as the agents of stress in their students' lives. When they are forced to implement standards-driven programs that focus on academic outcomes and put pressure on young children, teachers experience conflicts between what they believe to be best for their students and the accomplishment of what is required by their programs.[6]

Pressuring teachers to abandon practices that recognize the complexity of children's development is wrong. Demanding that they undertake practices that may ultimately harm children's chances for success in school and life is foolish.

3. *Narrowing of experiences.* I think standards are fine—except in cases where moving to a standards-based curriculum reduces a rich set of experiences to a narrow sequence of lessons. The consequences of implementing standards with older students are clear enough—when standards are in place, the curriculum is reduced to an emphasis on the content on which children, teachers, and schools will be assessed.[7] This narrow emphasis on easily measured objectives seriously limits what is being learned in elementary, middle, and high schools, and critics are not even convinced that the content on which the narrowed curriculum focuses is necessarily the right stuff.[8] Narrowing the preschool curriculum to accommodate standards such as those being promulgated by Head Start and promoted by the Bush Administration[9] not only limits the scope of what is

learned but will also take the life out of young children's initial experiences in classrooms.

The best early childhood programs are those that give children opportunities to explore meaningful content in meaningful ways. Skills and concepts—the same ones found in the standards-based approaches—are learned, but they are learned in the context of meaningful activity. Such programs are characterized by a sense of joyful discovery. Substituting a narrow, skills-based approach for a dynamic, child-responsive curriculum will rob young children of the joy of discovering how much they can learn and just how fulfilling school experiences can be.

4. *Accountability as punishment.* I believe standards are the centerpiece of reform in early childhood education—unless children, teachers, and programs are systematically identified as deficient in an effort to make them accountable. The logic of the accountability movement is based on the premise that students and teachers will not work hard unless they are afraid of the consequences of being found to be below the standard. What happens to 3- and 4-year-old children who are found to be below the standard? Kohn describes what happens in the primary grades:

> Skills develop rapidly and differentially in young children, which means that expecting everyone of the same age to have acquired a given set of capabilities creates unrealistic expectations, leads to one-size-fits-all (which is to say, bad) teaching, and guarantees that some children will be defined as failures at the very beginning of their time in school.[10]

It's wrong to label a 7-year-old second-grader a failure; it's criminal to do it to a 4-year-old preschooler. Using the threat of failure as a tool to motivate young children and their teachers is an absurd notion that characterizes a system designed to "punish rather than improve."[11] That some children will fail to meet a standard is inevitable.[12] That many who fail will come from groups that have historically been shortchanged by the system is highly likely.[13] While it may be politically expedient to join the call for tougher standards, systematically labeling large populations of our youngest students as failures is a price we should never agree to pay.

5. *Teacher deprofessionalization.* I am a proponent of early childhood standards—as long as teachers are not stripped of their roles as professional decision makers. Across the education landscape, the movement toward standards is a movement away from teacher responsibility and agency. As curricula, teaching strategies, outcomes, and evaluation techniques are standardized, teachers' opportunities to make decisions based on their professional judgment are systematically reduced. The implementation of standards-based programs signals students, parents, and society at large that teachers are not to be trusted or respected and that technical/managerial control is what is needed to fix problems that teachers helped create.[14]

For the past five years, I have been working with colleagues in Australia studying how early childhood teachers use child observation in their teaching. One of the striking findings from our work is that teachers in the United States and Australia have reduced their use of child observation as a strategy for shaping curriculum and increased their use of observation as a device for monitoring student progress. Instead of studying children in an effort to better meet their needs and improve their learning opportunities, teachers are now filling out checklists so that they can chart the achievement of a narrow set of competencies. We (and the teachers we have interviewed) see this as evidence of teacher deprofessionalization in the areas of assessment and curriculum development.[15] Early childhood assessment appears to be becoming a form of "product control, closely tied to industrialization and the creation of an end product."[16] Early childhood teachers appear to be becoming what Jonathan Kozol calls "technicians of proficiency" whose task it is to monitor children's progress through a hierarchy of prescribed outcomes.[17] Something important is lost when the work of teachers is downgraded from professional to technical status.

6. *Performance over learning.* I support the standards movement—unless it teaches young children to value the attainment of certain objectives over their ability to learn. Why do children think they are in school? What do we teach them about why they are there? Systems set up on the premise that there are certain standards that everyone must attain teach students that meeting those standards is the reason they are in school. Children learn that doing the work that's put in front of them at a level that will get them by is the stuff of schooling.

In such a system, performance goals dominate learning goals. School tasks have no intrinsic value; they are only means to achieve the extrinsic rewards or avoid the punishments built into the system. Carol Dweck has contrasted performance goals and learning goals.[18] When learning goals are what's important, children are taught that learning itself has inherent value and that the reason they are in school is to learn. It's clear enough that performance-goal structures drive education from elementary through graduate school,[19] but preschools are just beginning to form their conceptions of what school is for and where they fit in. The goal in high-quality early childhood programs is to help students see themselves as able learners and see learning as an exciting adventure that has meaning and importance in their immediate experience. On the effects of standards, Eisner summaries, "In our desire to improve our schools, education has become a casualty."[20] If we continue down the road to standards-based reform in early childhood education, *learning* will be a casualty.

7. *Individual devaluation.* I like the idea of standards in early childhood education—except when their use encourages us to ignore the individual strengths and needs of young children. Susan Ohanian describes those who advocate standards as the cure-all for the ills of school and society as *standardistos,* who try to force their will on others in the form of one-size-fits-all curriculum plans. She argues that such an approach assumes that knowledge is pure and unrelated to the knowledge-seeker, so education can be prepackaged and delivered without regard for the individual needs and interests of the learners.[21] I agree with Ohanian and others who see standards-based approaches as systems that operate as if individual differences do not exist.[22] What is even more troubling for children is that accountability systems operate as if individual differences *should not* exist; that is, if you don't fit the mold, there's something wrong with you.[23]

Such thinking turns contemporary best practices for teaching young children upside down. Knowing what individual children are like and providing the educational experiences they need are the cornerstones of sound early childhood programming. Anyone who has spent 30 minutes in a classroom full of 4- and 5-year-olds can tell you that children bring striking differences to their school experience. Imposing common standards on all students ignores individual differences, limiting the development of the most talented and jeopardizing the learning opportunities of those who need the most help and support.[24] In early childhood education, we should continue to have high standards for ourselves and for our students. But we should avoid implementing one-size-fits-all standards that devalue the uniqueness of the children we serve.

8. *Sameness versus diversity.* Standards seem like a good way to improve early childhood education—except in those instances where family and cultural differences are out of place because programs emphasize sameness. I am not surprised—but I am disappointed—that a tone of cultural elitism runs throughout the standards-for-accountability argument. It's clear that those who are making decisions about what should be taught are those who represent the dominant elite in our society. It's easy for those with cultural power to reach consensus about which knowledge is of the most worth: it's the knowledge they already have.[25] So small groups of privileged individuals are deciding what goes into children's heads based on an artificial consensus that may "underrepresent, misrepresent, or exclude groups of voices from the community."[26]

Children who are already excluded from access to the resources and supports of the mainstream will be further marginalized with the imposition of standards-based reform. They will be expected to perform at prescribed levels on prescribed tasks based on the false assumption that equal opportunities to learn exist.[27] In a model driven by an obsession with sameness, diversity becomes a problem, and children from diverse groups are likely to become casualties simply because of their differences. As a field, early childhood education has not been perfect in its attempts to recognize and celebrate the strengths that diversity brings to educational settings, but early childhood educators are well ahead of most segments of society. Moving to standards-based models that promote sameness and punish diversity is the wrong way to go if we are to continue to improve the life changes of every child in our society.

9. *Who benefits?* I will speak up for standards in my field—unless it is difficult to make a compelling case that young children actually benefit from this movement. There is little empirical evidence of a causal link between standard setting and enhanced student learning.[28] But even if we buy into the idea that young children's performance on academic tasks could be improved, it is reasonable to ask if those gains are worth the cost of the unintended consequences I have enumerated here. A number of respected researchers, educators, and social critics say the costs are too high.[29] So if students don't actually learn more or must pay dearly for improved performance on a nar-

rowly defined set of arbitrary standards, who benefits from the mania to implement standards?

Michael Apple calls the standards movement "reform on the cheap."[30] He and others point out that politicians and other individuals who use their power to influence educational change seek out simple and inexpensive strategies that give the appearance of providing solutions.[31] Politicians make political hay by offering quick fixes that put responsibility on others for their success. When the poorly thought out and inadequately funded reform strategies are unsuccessful, those in power are quick to blame educators, families, and children.

The standards movement is just such a strategy. It provides an opportunity for those in power to "get tough" with students and educators, spending small amounts of money developing outcomes without investing the large sums it would take to achieve significant change. If the standards are not met, you can be sure the victims, not the politicians, will be blamed. It's hard to see how our youngest and least powerful citizens will benefit from standards in early childhood education.

10. *Corporate mentality.* I am aboard the standards bandwagon—unless it means that the forces driving corporate America are being applied in early childhood classrooms. It amazes me that business executives and their political cronies are deciding how children ought to be educated. It makes my head spin to think that the "bottom line" mentality of giant corporations like IBM is having a profound influence on the lives of untold numbers of 3-, 4-, and 5-year-old children. Young children are not PCs to be efficiently assembled according to a set of profit-driven standards. Teachers are not "blue suits" who either meet corporate quotas or are fired. Education is not a commodity to be produced, marketed, and sold. Classrooms are not marketplaces where beating the competition at any cost is all that counts.[32]

It says something profound about what matters in our nation that folks who have committed their lives to caring for and educating young children are being told what to do by individuals whose expertise lies in running large companies or winning political elections. In spite of the rhetoric of those who have the media's attention, early childhood education has a long history of standard setting and accountability.[33] What's different is that our standards presume that young children are complex human beings who learn best when they are guided, nurtured, and cared for, not lifeless commodities that must meet standards of production. Our accountability comes from an ethical commitment to do what is right for every child, not from measuring productivity according to an arbitrary set of narrowly defined outcomes.

ACCOUNTABILITY SHOVEDOWN

In sum, I see the proliferation of standards for early childhood settings as "accountability shovedown" that threatens the integrity of early childhood professionals and the quality of educational experiences for young children. In spite of the seemingly unassailable logic of the standards movement, I believe educators and others interested in the well-being of our

youngest citizens ought to mount a resistance movement to accountability shovedown that parallels the curriculum battles of 20 years ago. Elkind is publishing a new edition of *The Hurried Child.* The field needs to challenge aggressively the appropriateness of standards-based approaches to reforming early childhood education.

I don't see such resistance as a mindless defense of the status quo. Knowledge about how young children develop and learn is expanding rapidly, and the field is opening up to new thinking and expanding its perspective on what is appropriate in early childhood classrooms. I count this as forward movement, designed to improve the experiences of young children and maximize their chances for a rich, full life in school and beyond. Standards-based approaches represent backward movement, designed to force early childhood programs into molds that don't work with older students and are downright harmful for young children.

Kohn characterizes the dominant philosophy for fixing schools as a return to the methods of the past, only using them "harder, longer, stronger, louder, meaner."[34] This article constitutes a plea to resist adding "earlier" to the list. Let's continue to improve the quality of early childhood programs, but let's not do it by forcing children and teachers to suffer the consequences of implementing standards-based reform.

Notes

1. David Elkind, *The Hurried Child* (Reading, Mass.: Addison-Wesley, 1981); and *Miseducation: Preschoolers at Risk* (New York: Knopf, 1987).

2. Lawrence J. Schweinhart, "Assessing the Outcomes of Head Start: Where Is the Early Childhood Field Going?," *High/Scope Resource,* vol. 20, 2001, pp. 1, 9–11.

3. David Elkind, "Educating the Very Young," *NEA Today,* January 1988, p. 23.

4. Elkind, *The Hurried Child,* p. xii.

5. John Kordalewski, *Standards in the Classroom: How Teachers and Students Negotiate Learning* (New York: Teachers College Press, 2000), p. 5.

6. J. Amos Hatch and Evelyn B. Freeman, "Kindergarten Philosophies and Practices: Perspectives of Teachers, Principals, and Supervisors," *Early Childhood Research Quarterly,* vol. 3, 1988, pp. 158–59.

7. Elliot W. Eisner, "What Does It Mean to Say a School Is Doing Well?," *Phi Delta Kappan,* January 2001, pp. 368–69; and Robert L. Linn, "Assessments and Accountability," *Educational Researcher,* March 2000, p. 8.

8. John Goodlad, quoted in John Merrow, "Undermining Standards," *Phi Delta Kappan,* May 2001, p. 656; Alfie Kohn, "Fighting the Tests: Turning Frustration into Action," *Young Children,* vol. 56, 2001, p. 19; and Donald B. Gratz, "High Standards for Whom?," *Phi Delta Kappan,* May 2000, p. 687.

9. See Jacques Steinberg, "Bush's Plan to Push Reading in Head Start Stirs Debate," *New York Times,* 10 February 2001.

10. Kohn, p. 19.

11. Gratz, p. 685.

12. Linn, p. 11.

13. Anita Perna Bohn and Christine E. Sleeter, "Multicultural Education and the Standards Movement," *Phi Delta Kappan,* October 2000, p. 156; and Gratz, p. 682.

14. Gunilla Dahlberg, Peter Moss, and Alan Pence, *Beyond Quality in Early Childhood Education and Care: Postmodern Perspectives* (London: Falmer Press, 1999), p. 2; Bohn and Sleeter, p. 158; and Merrow, p. 655.

15. Susan Grieshaber, Gail Halliwell, J. Amos Hatch, and Kerryann Walsh, "Child Observation as Teachers' Work in Contemporary Australian Early Childhood Programs," *International Journal of Early Years Education,* vol. 8, 2000, pp. 50–53; and J. Amos Hatch, Susan Grieshaber, Gail Halliwell, and Kerryann Walsh, "Child Observation in Australia and the U.S.: A Cross-National Analysis," *Early Child Development and Care,* vol. 169, 2001, pp. 39–56.

16. Gaile S. Cannella, *Deconstructing Early Childhood Education: Social Justice and Revolution* (New York: Peter Lang, 1997), p. 103.

17. Jonathan Kozol, Foreword to Deborah Meier, ed., *Will Standards Save Public Education?* (Boston: Beacon Press, 2000), p. xii.

18. Carol S. Dweck, "Motivational Processes Affecting Learning," *American Psychologist,* vol. 41, 1986, pp. 1040–48.

19. Alfie Kohn, *The Schools Our Children Deserve: Moving Beyond Traditional Classrooms and "Tougher Standards"* (Boston: Houghton Mifflin, 1999), p. 26; and Eisner, p. 369.

20. Eisner, p. 370.

21. Susan Ohanian, *One Size Fits Few: The Folly of Educational Standards* (Portsmouth, N.H.: Heinemann, 1999), pp. 3, 14.

22. Ohanian, pp. 17–29; Kohn, "Fighting the Tests," p. 19; and Marion Brady, "The Standards Juggernaut," *Phi Delta Kappan,* May 2000, p. 650.

23. Rex Knowles and Trudy Knowles, "Accountability for What?," *Phi Delta Kappan,* January 2001, p. 392.

24. William E. Coffman, "A King over Egypt, Which Knew Not Joseph," *Educational Measurement: Issues and Practices,* Summer 1993, p. 8.

25. Brady, p. 649; Alan C. Jones, "Welcome to Standardsville," *Phi Delta Kappan,* February 2001, p. 463; and Lisa Delpit, *Other People's Children* (New York: New Press, 1995), p. 24.

26. Pamela A. Moss and Aaron Schutz, "Educational Standards, Assessment, and the Search for Consensus," *American Educational Research Journal,* vol. 38, 2001, p. 65.

27. Bohn and Sleeter, p. 157; and Kohn, *The Schools Our Children Deserve,* p. 55.

28. Bill Nave, Edward Miech, and Frederick Mosteller, "A Lapse in Standards: Linking Standards-Based Reform with Student Achievement," *Phi Delta Kappan,* October 2000, p. 128; and Gratz, pp. 683–84.

29. See, for example, Linn, p. 14; Ohanian, p. 23; and Michael W. Apple, *Cultural Politics and Education* (New York: Teachers College Press, 1996).

30. Apple, p. 157.

31. Gratz, pp. 683–84; Ohanian, p. 32; and Merrow, p. 657.

32. Brady, p. 651; Eisner, p. 370; and Kohn, *The Schools Our Children Deserve,* pp. 15–16.

33. Marilou Hyson, "Reclaiming Our Words," *Young Children,* vol. 56, 2001, pp. 53–54.

34. Kohn, *The Schools Our Children Deserve,* p. 16.

J. AMOS HATCH is a professor in the College of Education, University of Tennessee, Knoxville.

From *Phi Delta Kappan,* February 2002, pp. 457-462. © 2002 by J. Amos Hatch. Reprinted by permission.

Class-Size Reduction In California

A Story of Hope, Promise, and Unintended Consequences

The overall impact of class-size reduction in California will not be known for a few more years. Nevertheless, much has been learned in the first three years that can inform the national conversation on the topic, the authors point out.

BY BRIAN STECHER, GEORGE BOHRNSTEDT, MICHAEL KIRST,
JOAN McROBBIE, AND TRISH WILLIAMS

IN JULY 1996, the California legislature passed S.B. 1777, an education reform initiative that committed more than $1 billion a year to a class-size reduction (CSR) program of unprecedented magnitude. The measure—though voluntary—provided a powerful financial incentive for school districts to reduce the number of students in K-3 classes. This financial incentive, coupled with strong public support, catalyzed school districts to implement CSR with astonishing speed. By the time students started school in the fall of 1996— just six weeks after the measure's passage—the vast majority of California's school districts had already begun to shrink their first-grade classes from a statewide average of nearly 30 students to a new maximum of 20. By the end of the third year, 98.5% of eligible school districts and 92% of eligible K-3 students were participating in CSR.

Shortly after S.B. 1777 was signed into law, representatives from a group of research and policy organizations in California met to discuss the importance of planning for an evaluation of the new law's impact. This group, called the CSR Re-

search Consortium, was headed by the American Institutes for Research (AIR) and RAND; it also included Policy Analysis for California Education (PACE), WestEd, and EdSource. The authors of this article are the leaders of the CSR Research Consortium, but many other researchers from the five institutions contributed directly to the project.[1]

The speed and enthusiasm with which California implemented CSR underscored a shared optimism on the part of legislators, educators, and parents that smaller classes would quickly improve the quality of education and lead the state's K-3 students to achieve higher scores on standardized tests. To some extent, this optimism has been rewarded: evaluations after the second and third years of CSR in California confirm that students enrolled in smaller classes do perform slightly better on standardized tests than students in larger classes. Educators hope these gains will increase as the program matures and students have longer exposure to smaller classes.

However, these small gains have had large costs. Indeed, class-size reform in California has had a profound unantici-

pated consequence: in its first three years, CSR exacerbated existing inequities within the state's education system. The teacher work force increased by 38% in just two years, causing a drop in teacher qualifications that disproportionately affected school districts already struggling with overcrowding, poverty, and language barriers. The overall costs to implement CSR were also considerably higher for these school districts.

To be sure, the program is young, and its full effects—positive and negative— may not be realized for several more years. However, as class-size reduction programs gain momentum across the nation, educators and legislators would be well advised to learn from California's experience and keep equity foremost in their minds when planning their own programs. This article reviews the history and status of CSR in California, reports results from comprehensive evaluations of the program's first three years, and derives a short set of lessons from the state's experience. These lessons are intended to help inform the debate about class size in other states and in the nation as a whole.

Class-Size Reduction in the U.S.

The strong political support for CSR in California was based on the belief that reducing class size would produce significant improvement in student achievement. This belief, in turn, was based on the positive results of a class-size reduction experiment in Tennessee, the Student/Teacher Achievement Ratio, or STAR, program. Students who participated in reduced-size classes in the STAR program during the primary grades made statistically significant achievement gains in all subject areas tested. The achievement gains were equal for boys and girls. Also important from the perspective of some California legislators, the achievement gains were largest for minority students and students attending inner-city schools.[2]

STAR's success has inspired many states and the federal government to support policies to cut the size of primary-grade classes. In addition to California and Tennessee, Indiana, Nevada, North Carolina, Texas, Virginia, and Wisconsin have implemented class-size reduction initiatives. At least 18 other states are also reported to be involved in or considering some type of class-size reduction program.[3]

The federal government is also investing heavily in class-size reduction. In fiscal year 1999, Congress appropriated $1.2 billion to help school districts hire new teachers in order to drive down the size of primary-grade classes to 18 students or fewer. Congress appropriated an additional $1.3 billion for class-size reduction in fiscal year 2000. Federal class-size reduction assistance is targeted to districts with the highest concentrations of children in poverty as well as to those with the highest overall enrollments. Consequently, large urban school districts have received a significant portion of the federal funds. Within these districts, funds to hire teachers are generally targeted to schools with the greatest need or with the largest classes. The federal policy was designed specifically to avoid creating further inequity in the education system.[4]

Enacting CSR in California

By 1996 a 10-year decline in student achievement in California had reached the point of alarm—classrooms were overcrowded as a result of a 12% increase in K-12 enrollment over the previous five years; qualified teachers were in short supply; and minority students, low-income students, and those whose native language was not English (designated "EL" for "English Learner" students) were falling steadily behind. Public confidence in the state's education system was further eroded by the results of the 1994 National Assessment of Educational Progress (NAEP) reading assessment, in which California's fourth-graders tied for last place out of the 39 participating states.

At the same time, the California economy was booming, and the legislature found itself with a rare budget surplus. Because state law requires that a fixed percentage of surplus revenues be spent on the public schools, the legislature had substantial funds to invest to reverse the educational decline. Then-Gov. Pete Wilson and the legislature agreed to spend up to $1.5 billion a year to reduce K-3 class size. CSR is a voluntary program, but it provides an almost irresistible financial incentive for school districts to participate. In 1996–97, the first year of the program, districts were reimbursed a flat rate of $650 for each child in a reduced-size class. In 1997–98, the per-student rate was raised to $800, and it was increased to $832 for the third year of the program. During the first year of the program, the state also provided $200 million to help overcrowded school districts install portable classrooms (up to $25,000 per classroom), and in the second year it reallocated any "unused" CSR funds for additional facilities grants.

Although California's confidence in class-size reduction was based in large measure on Tennessee's STAR program, CSR and STAR are vastly different programs. STAR was a controlled experiment, albeit a large one involving more than 12,000 students during the course of its four-year intervention. CSR, by contrast, is a statewide program, not a controlled experiment. It is also being implemented on a vastly larger scale—1.8 million California K-3 students were in reduced classes by the end of the initiative's third year. The scale of CSR reform posed unique problems. In particular, many California schools confronted a profound shortage of qualified teachers and adequate teaching facilities. By contrast, all the teachers in the Tennessee experiment were fully qualified. In addition, the curriculum in Tennessee was standardized, while California's curriculum standards were still in development when CSR was implemented. Furthermore, California is culturally diverse in ways that Tennessee is not. While nearly all students in the Tennessee experiment spoke English, almost one-third of California's students live in households in which primarily other languages are spoken.

From its earliest meetings, the CSR Consortium agreed that the evaluation of California's program needed to be comprehensive. The group proposed to consider the effect of reduced class size on student achievement, but it also resolved to examine the impact of the reform on all aspects of the education system. The Consortium believed—correctly, as it turns out—that some of the most important effects of CSR might not relate directly to student achievement.

Effects of CSR: Anticipated Gains and Unanticipated Losses

The Consortium has now completed two evaluations of California's CSR reform, the first covering the first two years of the program (1996–97 and 1997–98), and the second covering the third year (1998–99).[5] The data suggest that CSR is having positive effects on parent attitudes and student achievement. However, the gains to date have come at a substantial cost in terms of equity. School districts serving most of the state's historically disadvantaged students—those who are minorities, those from low-income families, and EL students—have received fewer benefits and may even have been hurt by CSR. These districts found it more expensive to implement CSR, they saw a disproportionate decline in their average teacher qualifications, and they were forced to take more facilities and resources from other programs to create additional classroom space.

Winners and losers in the race to implement CSR. As mentioned above, California's CSR program was implemented very quickly. However, not all school districts were positioned to respond with equal speed. Urban districts—which have high percentages of low-income, minority, and EL students—were significantly slower to implement CSR than suburban and rural districts. Schools in urban districts were already dealing with shortages of space, teachers, and financial resources, all of which contributed to delays in implementing the program. CSR exacerbated these problems. Because funding was linked to the speed of implementation, districts that were slower to reduce class size received proportionally less CSR revenue from the state.

FIGURE 1.

Percentage of Fully Credentialed K-3 Teachers in Schools with Different Proportions of Low-Income Students*

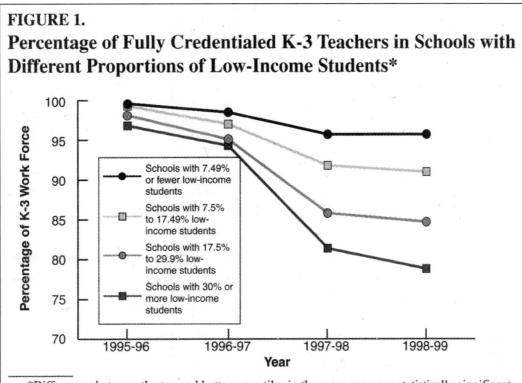

*Differences between the top and bottom quartiles in the same years are statistically significant at the .01 level.

Source: CSR Research Consortium analysis of California Department of Education, CBEDS-PAIF (California Basic Educational Data System-Professional Assignment Information Form) data.

While all districts earned the same amount of revenue for each student in a reduced-size class, districts with smaller classes and more available space prior to CSR needed fewer new teachers and less additional space to implement it, so their overall costs were lower. In the first year of CSR, a majority of superintendents in the state reported that CSR funds were inadequate to cover the cost of implementation. Even after per-pupil funding was increased, more than 40% of superintendents still reported fiscal shortfalls. Districts serving the greatest number of low-income, minority, or EL students were more likely than others to report that the cost to implement CSR was greater than the revenues generated by the initiative. Districts also found that the cost of installing portable classrooms was usually greater than the allocation provided by the state.

Small gains in test scores, individual instruction, and parent/teacher communication. Data from the first three years of CSR do provide some cause for optimism. Test scores have improved for students in smaller classes, teachers say that they are spending more time teaching students and less time disciplining them,

and parents and teachers report having more contact with one another. It is possible that these positive results will increase as CSR matures and teachers learn how best to take advantage of smaller classes, thereby further increasing student achievement.

Third-grade students enrolled in reduced-size classes performed better on the Stanford Achievement Test (SAT-9) than did students in regular classes. This was true both after the second year of CSR, when third-grade students had little or no prior exposure to reduced classes, and after the third year, when third-grade students had been in smaller classes for one or two years. These small achievement gains persisted after students moved to larger fourth-grade classes. However, unlike the case of Tennessee, achievement gains were similar among all students in reduced-size classes, regardless of their family income, fluency in English, or minority status. In other words, there is no evidence that class-size reduction in California is serving, as it did in Tennessee, to close the achievement gap between poor, minority children and others. Furthermore, the test-score improvements made by California students were only a fraction of those

achieved by students in Tennessee's STAR program.

However, teachers of reduced-size classes were optimistic about the effects of CSR in their classrooms. They reported devoting more time to instructing small groups and to working with individual students on mathematics and language arts lessons than did teachers whose classes were not reduced in size. They also provided comparatively more extended attention to poor readers, and they were more positive about their ability to assess and meet student needs and to provide students with quick feedback and individual attention. Teachers of reduced-size classes also reported spending less time disciplining disruptive students. Still, classroom instruction in small classes was generally no different from that in larger classes; regardless of class size, teachers covered about the same number of mathematics and language arts topics, devoted about the same amount of time to each major curriculum element, and used similar teaching strategies.

Parents of children in reduced-size classes echoed the teachers' optimism. These parents rated all aspects of educational quality higher than did parents of children in non-reduced-size classes. Parents of students in smaller classes also reported having more contact with teachers and higher overall satisfaction with schools.

Unanticipated consequences for the most vulnerable districts. CSR's negative effects are more dramatic than its modest gains, and school districts that were already struggling have been hit the hardest. The most devastating consequences have been sharp declines in the average educational level, experience, and credentials of teachers. CSR caused the K-3 teacher work force to grow by at least 25,000 during its first three years, forcing school districts to compete for qualified teachers not only with one another but also with other sectors in the booming state economy. Consequently, a smaller proportion of California's current K-3 teachers have full credentials, education beyond a bachelor's degree, or three or more years' teaching experience.

More disturbing, the decline in teacher qualifications has been greater for elementary schools serving minority, low-income, or EL students. As Figure 1 shows, elementary schools serving the fewest low-income students saw the proportion of fully credentialed K-3 teachers drop 2% from 1995–96 to 1998–99, while schools serving the most low-income students experienced a 16% drop. In the third year of California's CSR program, the rapid decrease in qualified teachers slowed for schools with fewer low-income students but continued for schools with more low-income students. Although better-qualified teachers are not automatically more effective—some teachers on emergency permits may be very hard-working and creative and may produce higher achievement among their students—the uneven distribution of teacher qualifications is hard to justify on any ground.

The speed and scope of CSR implementation challenged district and school administrators to balance existing needs with new demands. Prior to CSR implementation, a small percentage of schools were already taking space that had been dedicated to other activities and converting it to classroom space. This intensified with the implementation of CSR. By 1997–98, more than one-quarter of schools had taken space away from special education, child-care, and music and art programs, and more than one-fifth had converted library space and computer labs. Because schools serving higher proportions of low-income, minority, and EL students were experienc-

ing overcrowding and facility constraints prior to the CSR reforms, those schools suffered a disproportionate blow as they scrambled to find space in which to house new, smaller classes.

CSR also affected the education of special-needs and EL students. As the CSR program grew, many teachers switched from teaching these two groups of students to teaching in regular K-3 classes; in 1997–98 alone, about 1,000 teachers moved out of these programs and into general education classes. Although the proportion of teachers certified to work with bilingual students has increased since CSR began, schools serving more EL students have received proportionately fewer of these specially trained teachers.

Interpreting the Results: Lessons for the Nation

California's CSR program is still young. The small achievement gains evident during the program's first three years may increase as students spend more time in smaller classes and as new teachers gain more experience. No other state has implemented a class-size reduction reform on this scale, and statewide gains—even small ones—are cause for optimism. Additional time and experience are needed before the cumulative effects of reduced-size classes can be measured and a reasonable standard of success established.

Teachers in reduced-size classes did not vastly alter their teaching.

However, other states hoping to implement class-size reduction can learn from California's experience, particularly from the unanticipated consequences of CSR. The overarching lesson is this: when planning for class-size reduction, policy makers and their education advisors should keep a keen eye on the issue of maintaining equity within the education system. Administrators, superintendents, teachers, and other educators should also consider three additional lessons to help maximize the benefits of CSR: the first is aimed at formulating effective policies, the second at improving teaching strategies, and the

third at ensuring that there will be enough qualified teachers.

1. *Design a more thoughtful policy.* As discussed above, several elements of California's CSR reform contributed to its unanticipated consequences. In their race to implement CSR, state legislators unwittingly rewarded the school districts that could implement it fastest—those that were already among the most advantaged. Other states could avoid this pitfall by designing programs that begin slowly. An ideal program would build enough time into the planning process to adequately assess the capacity of schools statewide to increase classroom space. In California, large urban school districts not only received a smaller proportion of state funds for CSR because they found implementation difficult, but they also ended up with the largest proportion of unqualified teachers. In retrospect, the program would have had a more equitable effect if it had

- relied on a cost-based formula for allocating funds,
- targeted funds first to districts with the neediest students,
- included a long-range plan for helping school districts cope with facilities shortages, and
- been rolled out with a staged and controlled implementation.

2. *Learn how to get the most out of smaller classes.* While there is a strong perception that more learning goes on in smaller classrooms, little is known about why smaller classes might be better learning environments. Teachers in California's reduced-size classes did not dramatically alter their teaching strategies or the amount of content they covered, although they did spend more individual time with students, including individual conferences of five minutes or more with students who were having reading problems. Teachers in reduced-size classes also spent less time managing disruptive behavior. Our study design did not link teachers with students; thus we were unable to determine directly if the teacher behaviors we observed corresponded to higher achievement for a teacher's own students. Educators and researchers need to learn more about why class-size reduction works in order to maximize the benefits of this reform through targeted staff development and teacher training. Currently, teachers in smaller classes have an unprecedented opportunity to develop more effective classroom prac-

tices and to contribute to the research base on this subject. Researchers need to continue to develop a theoretical perspective that may help to explain the classroom processes that uniquely apply in smaller classes and affect student achievement.

3. *Attend to issues of teacher supply and teacher professional development.* Before class-size reform begins, states should think about how implementation will change the balance of teacher supply and demand. The key questions are how many additional teachers will be needed to cover reduced-size classes and what is the capacity of the state's higher education institutions to train new teachers. Although most states have a reserve supply of credentialed teachers who are not currently working in schools, California found that its CSR program quickly exhausted this supply. A more thoughtful policy would estimate changes in the demand for teachers and take actions to increase the supply before shortfalls occur. Teacher-training institutions can increase their capacity to prepare new teachers to match the anticipated increase in demand created by CSR. States might also consider reforming their credentialing requirements to create alternative paths to certification for experienced professionals from other fields. In addition, incentive programs can be created to help recruit and retain effective teachers for underperforming schools to counteract the inequities in teacher qualifications that occurred in California.

In addition, administrators at the school, district, and state levels should develop programs to help new and inexperienced teachers succeed. There is a need for more mentoring programs aimed at helping new teachers deal with day-to-day problems, as well as formal workshops designed to broaden their general knowledge

about teaching. Universities will also be called on to provide new forms of training and support to help class-size reduction programs work. The most successful inservice training programs in California are those that provide immediate, problem-specific, and personal support on a continuing basis.

The overall impact of CSR in California will not be known for a few more years. Nevertheless, much has been learned in the first three years that can inform the national conversation about class-size reduction. In fact, early results from the CSR Consortium's evaluation in California played an important role in crafting the federal class-size reduction policy that is currently in effect. Other states can learn from the California experience, as well. Smaller classes do seem to have positive effects on student achievement, and they definitely increase the amount of individual contact between students and teachers. In these ways, CSR has the potential to improve education. Yet the reform also places large demands on schools for extra facilities and additional staff. Unless great care is taken to design and implement CSR reforms thoughtfully, these added demands can fall unevenly on rich and poor districts, leading to greater inequities and undermining the reform's potential.

Notes

1. Contributors to the research include Dominic Brewer, Elizabeth Burr, Delia Burroughs, Lisa Carlos, Tammi Chun, Eric Derghazarian, Marian Eaton, Gerald Hayward, Mette Huberman, Tessa Kaganoff, Victor Kuo, Roger Levine, Daniel McCaffrey, Tor Ormseth, Thomas Par-

rish, Robert Reichardt, Cathleen Stasz, Carol Studier, Jackie Teague, George Vernez, and Edward Wiley. Rachel Hart was instrumental in the development of this article.

2. Jeremy Finn and Charles Achilles, "Tennessee's Class Size Study: Findings, Implications, Misconceptions," *Educational Evaluation and Policy Analysis*, vol. 21, 1999, pp. 97–109.

3. Class-Size Reduction Program home page, U.S. Department of Education, www.ed.gov/offices/OESE/ClassSize/index.html.

4. U.S. Department of Education, "The Class-Size Reduction Program: Boosting Student Achievement in Schools Across the Nation," September 2000, available online at www.ed.gov/offices/OESE/ClassSize/reports.html.

5. George Bohrnstedt and Brian Stecher, eds., *Class Size Reduction in California: Early Evaluation Findings, 1996–1998* (Sacramento: California Department of Education, 1999); and Brian Stecher and George Bohrnstedt, eds., *Class Size Reduction in California: The 1998–1999 Evaluation Findings* (Sacramento: California Department of Education, 2000).

BRIAN STECHER is senior social scientist at the RAND Corporation, Santa Monica, Calif.; GEORGE BOHRNSTEDT is senior vice president for research at the American Institutes for Research, Palo Alto, Calif.; MICHAEL KIRST is a professor of education at Stanford University, Stanford, Calif.; JOAN McROBBIE is senior policy associate at WestEd, San Francisco; and TRISH WILLIAMS is executive director of EdSource, Palo Alto.

"Class-Size Reduction in California," Brian Stecher, George Bohrnstedt, Michael Kirst, Joan McRobbie, and Trish Williams, *Phi Delta Kappan*, May 2001, pp. 670-674. © 2001 by Phi Delta Kappa International. Reprinted by permission of the authors.

Putting Money Where It Matters

In this age of accountability, school and district leaders must set priorities and make tough decisions about how they allocate funds and staff.

Karen Hawley Miles

The focus in the United States on creating accountable, standards-based education is pushing districts and schools to more clearly define their goals and priorities for student learning. Districts and states make headlines with bold proclamations about the importance of academic achievement for all students. But the gap between rhetoric and reality threatens hopes for improvement. While teachers scramble to help students meet more ambitious academic targets, school and district spending patterns and organization structures have changed little in the past three decades (Miles, 1997a). No matter what school leaders and communities say is important, the way schools and districts use their dollars, organize their staff, and structure their time dictates the results.

> **While teachers scramble to help students meet more ambitious academic targets, school and district spending patterns and organization structures have changed little.**

As public institutions, schools and districts try to do everything for everyone—and do it all without making enemies. New dollars come to schools in small increments over time usu-

ally tied to specific purposes. We add new priorities and programs on top of the old. Instead of restructuring and integrating school and district organizations, we create specialties and departments to meet newly defined needs. Schools and districts now spend significantly more to educate each pupil than ever before (Snyder & Hoffman, 1999). Taking advantage of these resources to meet higher academic standards requires a political will and singleness of purpose that is difficult to sustain in public schools. Such action also demands an attention to organizational and budget details that does not come naturally to many educators and policymakers.

> **If the district declares that all students will read by 3rd grade, then staff, dollars, and time should support more effective literacy teaching.**

If we hope to meet our seemingly unreachable goals, districts and schools must define priorities for student performance, make choices about how to organize to meet them, and then move the dollars and people to match those commitments. If school leaders give priority to improving academic achievement, for example, then the district staff and budget should shift to support that

goal. If the district declares that all students will read by 3rd grade, then staff, dollars, and time should support more effective literacy teaching. Districts and schools should expect to give up some long-standing and useful programs to support these choices.

Matching Dollars to Priorities

For the past 10 years, I have helped districts and schools rethink their use of resources to support their reform efforts. In partnership with New American Schools and with support from Pew Charitable Trusts, I have worked with four large urban districts to analyze their district and school spending and then consider ways to reallocate dollars. My colleagues and I have discovered that, in many cases, the dollars needed for reform efforts are there, but they are tied up in existing staff, programs, and practices. We have found that schools need help shifting their use of resources to take advantage of what they already have and that districts often lag behind schools in changing their own spending and organization structures. To support schools in raising student performance, most districts need to realign spending and staffing in at least five ways.

Restructure salaries to attract and retain high-quality teachers. It is no secret that U.S. teaching salaries lag behind those of other professions.

The discrepancy is especially great for two types of teachers needed in schools: high-performing students from top colleges who have many other career options and teachers trained in math and science (Mohrman, Mohrman, & Odden, 1995). The earnings gap grows wider over a teaching career (Conley & Odden, 1995). Maximum teaching salaries fall well below those in other professions, meaning that the most talented individuals sacrifice much higher potential earnings if they remain in teaching. Districts need to reconsider their practice of paying all teachers the same regardless of subject area. In addition, they must find ways to restructure teacher salaries and responsibilities to provide the most talented, productive teachers with the opportunity to earn more competitive salaries during their careers.

Increasing salaries significantly without bankrupting districts means taking a hard look at the way salary dollars are spent. Since the 1920s, virtually all districts have used a salary structure that applies to every teacher regardless of grade or subject. Teachers can move up the salary ladder either by logging more years of teaching or accumulating education credits. Most districts increase salaries far more for experience than they do for education (Miles, 1997b). Boston Public Schools, for example, spent 36 percent of its 1998–99 salary budget to buy years of experience (29 percent) and education credits (7 percent).

For this investment to make sense for students, both teaching experience and accumulated credits would have to be clearly linked to student achievement. But research shows that after the first five years, the quality of teaching does not automatically improve with either course credits or years of teaching (Hanushek, 1994; Murnane, 1996). Experience and coursework have value, but neither is a fail-safe investment without coaching, hard work, and systems that reward and encourage good teaching. Many districts are currently experimenting with increasing teacher salaries on the basis of more direct measures of teaching quality. Most of these plans give bonuses to teachers who meet certain

criteria or student performance targets. These extra dollars are nice symbols, but the plans that have the most promise for significantly raising teacher salary levels redirect existing salary dollars even as they seek to add more.

Redirect district staff and spending from compliance efforts to provide schools with integrated support and accountability. Using standards to measure school performance changes the role of the district office. If schools do not have to report student performance, schools and districts are only held accountable for whether they do as they are told and keep children safe. As a result, curriculum offices issue guidebooks and sometimes check whether they are used, and districts create departments to monitor whether dollars from each funding source are spent as stipulated.

When schools become accountable for student learning, the district role must shift to helping schools measure student learning and supporting the changes in teaching and organization that best support improvement. Most districts need to focus more on four purposes: defining standards and targets, supporting schools and teachers, creating accountability, and restructuring school organizations.

Supporting these four goals is often possible by reallocating existing resources. In many large districts, the traditional compliance focus has resulted in a structure that spreads resources thinly across many schools and priorities. For example, one district was surprised to find that it devoted nine experts to supervising services across 30 schools. Each expert was responsible for making sure that schools met program requirements in one specific area, such as special education, Title I, bilingual education, literacy, or technology. Because these nine individuals focused on only one issue in multiple schools, they could conduct only superficial reviews of effectiveness, and they certainly couldn't provide support to underperforming schools. Even though the district devoted $24,000 in salaries and benefits to each school, the schools barely felt an impact. Instead, the schools needed deeper, integrated school support in

specific areas where improvement was most needed.

Shift more resources to teaching literacy in grades K–3. Research consistently shows that smaller group sizes matter most in early grades when students learn to read (Wenglinsky, 2001). It also shows that when students don't learn to read by 3rd grade, they continue to fall farther behind in school and are more likely to be assigned to costly special education programs and to drop out of school. Research suggests concrete ways to improve reading achievement:

- Class size reduction in grades pre-K–2 can make an important, lasting difference in student achievement.
- Small reductions in class size make little difference; only when class sizes get down to 15–17 students does achievement increase predictably.
- Even smaller group sizes, including one-on-one instruction, are crucial for developing readers, especially those from disadvantaged homes.
- If teachers don't change their classroom practice to take advantage of class size reductions, they can't expect improved student performance.

To incorporate these lessons, both districts and schools need to shift their use of existing resources. U.S. school districts average one teacher for every 17 students—with the ratio much higher in many urban districts—and one adult for every nine students. Yet, elementary school class size averages in the mid-20s (Miles, 1997a; Snyder & Hoffman, 1999). Most districts allocate more staff and dollars per pupil to high schools than to elementary schools.

To focus resources where they matter most, districts need to look first at how much they spend at the elementary school level compared to the high school level. Next, they need to invest to ensure that teachers have access to powerful professional development in teaching literacy. Third, they must actively support school-level changes that shift resources toward literacy instruction.

> **Districts will need to be prepared to defend school leaders who abandon popular, but outmoded or less important, programs and staff positions to support literacy efforts.**

This active support of school-level changes in the use of resources creates special challenges for districts. For example, many schools have found ways to create small reading groups for part of the day by making group sizes larger at other times of the day. Others have reconsidered the role of each teacher, support person, and instructional aide to ensure that they support the focus on literacy. In some schools, this may mean changing the role of physical education, art, and music teachers or making these class sizes larger. It may mean hiring a highly trained literacy specialist instead of a traditional librarian. And redirecting resources toward literacy will mean integrating bilingual, Title I, and special education teachers more fully into a schoolwide literacy strategy. Schools need help making these shifts, which require changes in district policy, contract language, and staff allocation practices. Districts also need to be prepared to defend school leaders who abandon popular, but outmoded or less important, programs and staff positions to support literacy efforts.

Invest strategically in professional development for teachers. To take advantage of smaller class sizes and to improve literacy instruction, districts need to offer teachers high-quality professional development. The assertion that districts invest only a small percentage of their budgets in professional development has become a cliché among education reformers. Although some districts may need to invest more money, the priority, for many, will be to refocus existing efforts to create more effective professional development and more useful teacher time. Research shows that professional development that responds to school-level student performance priorities, focuses on instruction, and provides coaching for individual teachers and teams over time can have a powerful impact on

teacher practice. But professional development doesn't follow this model in most districts. And providing teachers with more professional time and intensive coaching support can seem expensive to districts that use a few traditional workshops as their "training."

In a detailed analysis of four large urban district budgets, we found that districts spend more than they think on professional development (Miles & Hornbeck, 2000). In these four districts, spending on professional development from all sources ranged 2–4 percent of the district budget. These figures are much larger than those districts traditionally report and manage. For example, one district reported $460,000 spent on strategic professional development, but the district actually spent nearly 20 times this amount when professional development efforts by all departments and sources were included. Worse, our analysis showed that professional development spending is often divided among many fragmented, sometimes conflicting, programs managed by different departments. Spending to support improved academic instruction represented only a fraction of total dollars in these districts, and the amount aimed at literacy instruction was even smaller. Harnessing these dollars requires district and school leaders to challenge the status quo and to abandon worthwhile initiatives in order to support more integrated models of professional development.

Reduce spending on nonacademic teaching staff in secondary schools. The traditional comprehensive high school often employs more teaching staff in nonacademic subjects than it does in English, math, science, and history. Traditional high schools devote only about half of each student's school day to courses covering academic skills, resulting in more than half the high school resources being aimed at goals that are not measured by the state and district standards. This allocation of resources also means that class sizes for the core subjects are usually 30 students or more, with teachers responsible for a total of more than 125 students.

But changing the balance of staff to make a meaningful difference in

student loads and academic time would require some high schools to double the number of academic staff. And shifting more resources toward academic subjects means reducing staff in other areas and challenging the structure—or even the existence—of such cherished programs as band and athletics. Given the number of the changes and their sometimes painful nature, it is unreasonable and impractical to expect principals or school-based decision-making groups to make them on their own. Until districts take steps to change the mix of staff, many high schools will make marginal improvements at best.

Making Choices

Organizing resources to act on urgent priorities, such as teaching all students to read in urban schools, requires leaders to take politically difficult stands. Union, district, and school board leaders need courage and strong community support to say:

- Even though all subjects are important, literacy is most important.
- Even though all teachers are important, those who bring deep subject knowledge and can integrate across disciplines or programs are worth more.
- Even though band, sports, and other electives can be a crucial part of a balanced education, the community must find new ways to pay for and provide them.
- Even though student readiness and social health provide a base for student learning, schools cannot be held accountable for providing all services to students, and they aren't staffed to do so.
- Even though investments in teacher professional development and technology may mean an extra student in your class, we can't build and sustain excellent schools without more of such investments.

Ensuring Adequate Funding

Regardless of overall spending levels, district and community leaders need to articulate priorities and direct spending to support them. But they must also ensure that schools have enough money to begin these tasks. There is no one way to define how much money is enough, but a few test questions can help put district spending in perspective: How does spending per pupil in your district compare to spending in other districts with similar student populations? How do teacher salary levels compare? How does the community's tax rate compare to the tax rates in similar districts?

If the community is underinvesting in education, leaders need to make the case for increased spending. But a community may be more likely to support increases in spending if citizens see that leaders have clear priorities and are willing to make difficult choices to ensure that new dollars get to the heart of improving student achievement.

References

Conley, S., & Odden, A. (1995). Linking teacher compensation to teacher career development: A strategic examination. *Educational Evaluation and Policy Analysis, 17*, 253–269.

Hanushek, E. A. (1994). *Making schools work: Improving performance and controlling costs*. Washington, DC: Brookings Institution.

Miles, K. H. (1997a). Finding the dollars to pay for 21st century schools: Taking advantage of the times. *School Business Affairs, 63*(6), 38–42.

Miles, K. H. (1997b). *Spending more on the edges: Public school spending from 1967 to 1991*. Ann Arbor, MI: UMI Press.

Miles, K. H., & Hornbeck, M. J. (2000). *Reinvesting in teaching: District spending on professional development*. Arlington, VA: New American Schools.

Mohrman, A., Mohrman, S. A., & Odden, A. (1995). Aligning teacher compensation with systemic school reform: Skill-based pay and group-based performance rewards. *Educational Evaluation and Policy Analysis, 18*, 51–71.

Murnane, R. J. (1996). Staffing the nation's schools with skilled teachers. In E. A. Hanushek & D. W. Jorgenson (Eds.), *Improving America's schools: The role of incentives* (pp. 243–260). Washington, DC: National Academy Press.

Snyder, T. D., & Hoffman, C. M. (1999). *Digest of education statistics 1999*. Washington, DC: National Center for Education Statistics, Office of Educational Research and Improvement, U.S. Department of Education.

Wenglinsky, H. (2001, June). The effect of class size on achievement [Memorandum]. Available: www.ets.org/search97egi/s97_cgi

Karen Hawley Miles is president of Education Resource Management Strategies, 3705 Euclid Ave., Dallas, Texas 75205; karenhmiles@cs.com.

'All Children Can Learn':

Facts and Fallacies

BY M. DONALD THOMAS AND WILLIAM L. BAINBRIDGE

A FEW decades ago, leaders in the field of school reform introduced the concept of "effective schools" as a way to identify what works best in educating children and to provide models for struggling schools to use for improvement. The effective schools movement is frequently attributed to the work of the late Ronald Edmonds. In a speech delivered to the National Conference of the Teacher Corps in 1978, Edmonds defined the five characteristics consistently evident in effective schools: strong leadership, clear emphasis on learning, positive school climate, regular and appropriate monitoring of student progress, and high expectations for students and staff.[1] From these straightforward principles, an entire belief system has evolved that offers a variety of solutions that are designed to improve schools.

However, the effective schools movement, like most other reform efforts, has developed philosophical and political schisms along its major fault line: the central tenet that children's learning can be improved if schools adopt effective practices. At its heart, this belief is positive, useful, and practical—but it does engender strong opinions and political reactions.

The initial understanding that school practices and policies can make a difference, even for children from homes in which parents have few educational or financial resources, has now been translated into the popular mantra "all children can learn." This phrase sometimes confuses the public and deters the possibility of substantially helping disadvantaged children obtain a high-quality, resource-rich education. In our view, because of the simplistic acceptance of this phrase at face value, the effective schools movement as currently promoted is contaminated with a series of fallacies and a number of unintended consequences. We offer the following ideas as a starting point for further, in-depth discussions that can lead to more thoughtful school policies.

The Fallacies

When we look at many of the potentially harmful policies and practices being implemented in schools today, we can only assume that they have been inspired by the following fallacies, which do not bear careful scrutiny:

- the fallacy that all children can learn—at the same level and in the same amount of time;
- the fallacy of the principal as sole instructional leader;
- the fallacy of setting standards on the basis of exceptions; and
- the fallacy of uniform standards for all children.

The fallacy that all children can learn—at the same level and in the same amount of time. All children *can* learn, at some level, and most children, as Ronald Edmonds stated, can learn the basic curriculum if sufficient resources are provided. The fallacy, however, is the belief that all children can learn the *same curriculum, in the same amount of time, and at the same level.* The problem with such an unexamined belief is that it may be used to deny differential financial support for those who come to school with environmental disadvantages. Not all children have high-quality nutrition, stimulating homes, and extensive learning opportunities prior to entering school.

Research in cognitive brain development shows that formation of synaptic contacts in the human cerebral cortex occurs between birth and age 10,[2] and most of the brain gets built within a few years after birth. Environment matters greatly in brain development. The period of early childhood is critical in brain development, and those who have high-protein diets and lots of sensory stimulation tend to have more synaptic connections. Brains that do not get enough protein and stimulation in their environments lose connections, and some potential neural pathways are shut down.[3] These facts help to explain what educators have long observed: children from impoverished environments, in which they do not receive good nutrition and stimulating experiences, generally achieve at lower levels than children from more enriching environments.

This concrete evidence should be enough to convince us that we should concentrate on improving the lives of children before they come to school and not simply proclaim that "all children can learn" without enacting proper public policy to provide economic opportunity for families, health care for all children, and parenting education for young mothers.

If we as a society can summon the courage and will to do these things, then maybe all children can learn at higher levels and the gap between low-income and more privileged children can really be narrowed.

The fallacy of the principal as sole instructional leader. Promoting the principal as the sole instructional leader may demean teachers. The principal may be a leader, but accountability for effective instruction belongs to *teachers*. Principals should understand instruction, and they can support it in many ways (for example, by hiring excellent teachers and by promoting effective professional development for them), but they do not teach the curriculum.

If teachers cannot teach effectively, then principals must carry out their major accountability duty—evaluating employees and dismissing ineffective ones. This is the most effective way that principals can improve instruction.

Principals have many responsibilities for managing the school: introducing best practices, implementing policies, protecting the ethics of the profession, staying within budget, and promoting a belief system in support of public education, to name just a few. Principals have more than enough to do without taking over responsibilities that belong to teachers.

The fallacy of setting standards on the basis of exceptions. Often, proponents of the effective schools philosophy cite a student who rose out of poverty or a school in which low-income children achieve at unusually high levels. These exceptions are then used to tell the world that all children can "pull themselves up by their bootstraps" or that all schools can reproduce the results achieved by the one cited.

Certainly, examples of success can provide lessons and models if they are considered thoughtfully. However, we must be careful that this kind of thinking does not lead to standards that are set on the basis of exceptions. Such standards imply that all children can achieve at high levels if they choose to do so—one child did it; so can others. No additional help is needed!

The hard truth is that exceptions occur under special circumstances that cannot usually be replicated or that may be partially replicated only if sufficient resources are available.

The fallacy of uniform standards for all children. Of all the fallacies being promoted, this is probably the most bizarre. Decades of history and mountains of research indicate that childhood development is unique for each individual. The idea that children and schools should be evaluated by a uniform criterion—usually a test score—has the potential to do untold damage.

Uniformity of measurement leaves out human judgment—the most critical element in decision making. Those who promote uniform standards (often state legislatures) promote a false system of evaluation that will probably disappear as rapidly as it has been established.

Although it is difficult to accept and even more difficult to admit, children in the United States do not have equal opportunities to learn, nor do they have equal opportunities to succeed. In time, with enough effort and money and solid social policies, the achievement gaps between the advantaged and disadvantaged can narrow. Until then, however, it is unfair to treat all children and all schools "equally" by setting standards that are not equitable. The assumption that all can meet these standards—without our providing educationally disadvantaged children with the extra support they need to achieve at high levels—perpetuates injustice.

As Edmund Burke stated, "The equal treatment of unequals is the greatest injustice of all." This statement has been inscribed on our national documents and should be chiseled into the hearts of all school personnel and those who enact education policy.

Unintended Consequences

Next, let us discuss the unintended consequences of the simplistic "all children can learn" approach. These include:

- establishing accountability based on state-developed tests;
- downplaying the need for early intervention for children who live under conditions of poverty; and
- using punishment as a motivator to improve schools.

Establishing accountability based on state-developed tests. The belief that "all children can learn" has spawned a movement of testing as the basis for student promotion, student graduation, evaluation of school personnel, and state and federal funding. Our experience with state-developed criterion-referenced tests leads us to the conclusion that most of these tests are either too simple or too difficult. In either case, they are inappropriate measures of school effectiveness. Not one study in the school literature can correlate a test score with either student success or teacher effectiveness. Tests created at the state level and imposed on schools may appear to be "politically correct," but their educational value is highly questionable.

As Linda McNeil points out, forcing arbitrary punitive standards on schools undermines both teaching and learning and results in "growing inequality between the content and quality of education provided to white middle-class children and that provided to children in poor and minority schools."[4] In Texas, for example, McNeil found that, even though scores on the state-mandated Texas Assessment of Academic Skills were going up in many disadvantaged schools, teachers reported that students' ability to use the skills that had been drilled into them for the test was actually declining. In fact, she claims, "this system of testing is restratifying education by race and class."[5]

Downplaying the need for early intervention for children who live under conditions of poverty. The "all children can learn" mentality is dangerous because it may lead us to assume that all children can meet the same standards no matter how well or ill prepared they are to start school. This assumption in turn excuses us from addressing the need for better early childhood programs. To claim that "all children can learn" without recognizing that some children start school on a very unequal footing burdens our schools and teachers with daunting and perhaps insurmountable barriers.

An enormous amount of time, effort, and money must be spent to "reclaim" and "remediate" children whose skills lag behind those of their more advantaged peers. Yet there is a widespread attitude that, if students and teachers cannot overcome the obstacles created by poverty and poor nutrition in the short amount of time available in the average school year, they have "failed." This pressure is especially strong when children and their teachers are expected to achieve some arbitrary standard established by a state-mandated proficiency test.

The result of this attitude is that students rarely catch up, and teachers become demoralized. Sadly, this is the current situation in many of our nation's public schools. Even more alarming is the tendency of the news media to leave an impression that gaps in performance among student groups are related to skin color or ethnicity.[6]

Public policy in the U.S. is not as child-friendly as it is in many other countries, such as Sweden, Canada, Japan, or Israel. What is needed most to help children is for politicians to make good on their promise that "all children will be ready to learn" by the time they start school. Enacting public policy that establishes educational programs for very young children should be the major strategy for helping children achieve at higher levels and reducing the achievement gap between children of high and low socioeconomic status. Early intervention stimulates cognitive development, improves sensory development, and increases motivation to learn. It offers the best chance for all children to be ready to learn when they begin kindergarten. Providing good early childhood education is a big and costly responsibility, but this strategy is just, extremely cost-effective in the long run, and a measure of the character of a nation.

Using punishment as a motivator to improve our schools. Frederick Herzberg is dead, and with him the sensible notion that punishment never motivates nor serves as an effective way to improve our schools.[7] The punishment mentality spawns takeover laws, zero-tolerance policies, threats to administrators of losing their jobs, and decreased funding for those schools whose students most need additional support. Whatever happened to "due process of law" and "positive reinforcement"?

Herzberg, Maslow—wherever you are—we need you now more than ever!

Time for Change

If Edmonds were still with us, we believe he would be appalled at what has happened to the effective schools movement. Unfortunately, what began as a no-

ble process to help low-income children achieve at higher levels has become an educational albatross that punishes both teachers and students and declares that schools are ineffective when all children do not learn at arbitrary levels predetermined by individuals external to the schools.

The thinking behind a simplistic interpretation of "all children can learn" suggests that there is no need for adequate resources and child-friendly public policy. Assuming that all children can reach the same high standards through the heroic efforts of educators, without major changes in education and social policy, is similar to assuming that doctors can make all children healthy even though many do not receive adequate home care and appropriate nutrition.

We fervently hope that all children will be treated as individuals, achieving at various levels appropriate to their development, and that they will not be treated as learning at the same level at the same time—all marching to the arbitrary beat of a state proficiency test. It would be much better for all of us to accept differences and provide sufficient resources so that each boy and girl has an opportunity to achieve at the maximum level congruent to whatever gifts or limitations each may have.

The time has come for educators to reexamine the slogan that "all children can

learn." Let's return to the basic research and stress the facts instead of the fallacies that have hurt so many of our teachers, schools, and children.

Notes

1. See Ronald R. Edmonds, "Some Schools Work and More Can," *Social Policy*, March/April 1979, pp. 23–32; and idem, "Making Public Schools More Effective," *Social Policy*, September/October 1981, pp. 56–60.

2. Peter R. Huttenlocher and Arun S. Dabholkar, "Regional Differences in Synaptogenesis in Human Cerebral Cortex," *Journal of Comparative Neurology*, vol. 387, 1997, pp. 167–78.

3. John T. Bruer, "Neural Connections—Some You Use, Some You Lose," *Phi Delta Kappan*, December 1999, pp. 264–77.

4. Linda M. McNeil, "Creating New Inequalities: Contradictions of Reform," *Phi Delta Kappan*, June 2000, p. 730.

5. Ibid., p. 731.

6. William L. Bainbridge, "Is the Test Score Gap Really Color-Based?," *School Administrator*, August 2000, p. 50.

7. Frederick Herzberg, *The Managerial Choice: To Be Efficient and to Be Human* (Salt Lake City: Olympus Press, 1982).

In Early-Childhood Education and Care: Quality Counts

State interest in early learning is growing, but large gaps in access and quality remain.

Most Americans think education begins at age 5—with kindergarten.

But children are learning from the moment they're born. And for millions of youngsters, the reality is that their early learning is a joint enterprise between parents and early-childhood educators.

Today, 11.9 million children younger than 5 in the United States—or about six in 10—spend part of their waking hours in the care of people other than their parents: relatives, caregivers operating out of their homes, workers in child-care centers, Head Start staff members, and teachers in state-financed prekindergartens among them. The quality of the early care and education that young children receive in such settings sets the tenor of their days and lays the building blocks for future academic success.

Studies conclude that early-childhood education makes a difference. Young children exposed to high-quality settings exhibit better language and mathematics skills, better cognitive and social skills, and better relationships with classmates than do children in lower-quality care. Evaluations of well-run early-learning programs also have found that children in those environments were less likely to drop out of school, repeat grades, need special education, or get into future trouble with the law than similar children who did not have such exposure.

Quality Counts 2002: Building Blocks for Success examines what states are doing to provide early-learning experiences for young children; to ensure that those experiences are of high quality; to prepare and pay early-childhood educators adequately;

and to measure the results of early-childhood programs. The report also examines states' commitment to kindergarten, the transition point into the formal public education system. The report is based on the premise that when it comes to early learning, quality counts, just as it does in K–12 education.

Increasingly, states are getting that message. Today, every state subsidizes kindergarten in at least some districts or for a portion of the school day, according to a survey conducted by *Education Week* for *Quality Counts.* Twenty-five states pay for kindergarten for the full school day, at least in districts that opt to offer such services. So does the District of Columbia.

But nine states—Alaska, Colorado, Idaho, Michigan, New Hampshire, New Jersey, New York, North Dakota, and Pennsylvania—still do not require districts to offer kindergarten.

Thirty-nine states and the District of Columbia provide state-financed prekindergarten for at least some of their 3- to 5-year-olds, up from about 10 in 1980. Annual state spending for such programs now exceeds $1.9 billion.

In 2000, 21 states and the District of Columbia supplemented federal aid to serve additional children through Head Start, one of the nation's largest preschool programs for disadvantaged 3- to 5-year-olds. Thirty-one states underwrite one or more programs for infants and toddlers, up from 24 in 1998.

In addition, every state helps at least some low-income families buy child care through a combination of state and federal

money under the Child Care and Development Fund block grant and Temporary Assistance for Needy Families. Twenty-six states, the District of Columbia, and the federal government also help families pay for child care through tax credits or deductions. But only 10 states made the credits refundable in the 2001 tax year so that the lowest-income families could benefit.

Despite federal and state efforts, access to high-quality early-childhood education remains out of the reach of many families. None of the federal programs reaches more than a fraction of the newborns to 5-year-olds who could benefit from such services. And states' financial commitment to early-childhood education varies widely, as do eligibility requirements and the number of children who actually receive services.

Most states focus their prekindergarten efforts on the neediest youngsters. Twenty-six target children from low-income families; 15 of those also look at other risk factors, such as having a teenage parent. And nine states leave it up to local districts to determine which risk factors they will consider.

Only three states—Georgia, New York, and Oklahoma—and the District of Columbia are phasing in prekindergarten for any 4-year-old whose parent wants it, regardless of income.

Similarly, although all states provide child-care subsidies for at least some poor families, wide variations exist in the income limits that families must meet to qualify, the actual dollar amount of the subsidies, and the percentage of eligible children served.

Families with low incomes, particularly the working poor, have the least access to high-quality early-childhood services.

Traditionally, "quality" in early-childhood education has meant ensuring that children are cared for in a safe and nurturing environment. State licensing standards commonly address group size, the number of children per caregiver, and such physical features as the height of playground equipment. Licensing standards rarely, if ever, address the learning aspects of early care and education.

Even those minimal protections often fail to safeguard children adequately. In many states, certain settings are exempt from licensure entirely: family child-care homes that serve a small number of children, preschools that operate only a few hours a day, or sites run by religious organizations.

New research about the importance of early learning, however, has led some states to describe the quality of instruction that should occur in preschool settings, at least for programs that receive state money. While almost all states have standards for students in elementary school, only 19 states and the District of Columbia lay out specific expectations for kindergartners. Fifteen states and the District have specific standards for prekindergarten. Five more states are working on such standards. Only six states—California, Connecticut, Georgia, Maryland, Michigan, and Washington—require preschool programs to adhere to the standards. In addition, seven states require their state-financed prekindergartens to satisfy federal Head Start standards.

States also are mounting efforts to improve the quality of early-childhood programs. Seven require their prekindergarten programs to earn accreditation from the National Association for the Education of Young Children. Twenty-six states and the District of Columbia offer tiered reimbursement rates that provide higher child-care subsidies to providers that earn national accreditation or meet other quality criteria.

But states still have a long way to go to ensure that those who work with young children are well-educated and well-compensated.

As a nation, the United States pays about as much to parking-lot attendants and dry-cleaning workers as it does to early-childhood educators, according to data from the federal Bureau of Labor Statistics. The average annual salary of child-care workers in 1999 was $15,430. Preschool teachers, who typically work with 3- to 5-year-olds, had annual salaries of $19,610, less than half what the average elementary school teacher earned.

Not surprisingly, given those numbers, turnover among early-childhood workers is high, and education requirements are minimal. Every state, for example, requires kindergarten teachers to have at least a bachelor's degree and a certificate in elementary or early-childhood education. But only 20 states and the District of Columbia require teachers in state-financed prekindergartens to meet similar requirements. In 30 states, teachers in child-care centers can begin work without having any preservice training.

Recently, states and the federal government have begun to get more serious about the preparation of early-childhood educators.

Congress has ordered that by 2003, 50 percent of a Head Start program's teachers must have an associate's degree in early-childhood education. A growing number of states also have initiatives either to help providers acquire more education or to supplement their wages. The TEACH Early Childhood Project, which began in North Carolina in 1990, provides scholarships to child-care workers to attend school and bonuses or raises from their employers when they complete their programs of study. Seventeen additional states have since adopted the program. Nine states have programs to improve the compensation of early-childhood educators.

States' growing investments in the early years, and their concerns about school readiness, also have led them to revisit the question of how to measure the success or failure of their early-childhood initiatives. Today, 17 states mandate readiness testing of kindergartners as a first step in identifying children with special needs or to help plan instruction. Six states use kindergarten testing to gauge school readiness statewide. Fifteen states and the District of Columbia require diagnostic or development testing of prekindergartners. At the federal level, new performance measures are being used to evaluate Head Start programs, including their impact on children's math and literacy skills.

Efforts also are under way to rethink how states pay for early care and education. Many states, for instance, are seeking new sources of money to support their efforts, such as beer and cigarette taxes or state lottery proceeds.

Despite the economic downturn, many believe that the continued push for better academic performance in the elementary years could well compel states to pay more attention to early learning for years to come.

Index

Index

Test Your Knowledge Form

We encourage you to photocopy and use this page as a tool to assess how the articles in *Annual Editions* expand on the information in your textbook. By reflecting on the articles you will gain enhanced text information. You can also access this useful form on a product's book support Web site at *http://www.dushkin.com/online/*.

NAME: _____   DATE: _____

TITLE AND NUMBER OF ARTICLE: _____

BRIEFLY STATE THE MAIN IDEA OF THIS ARTICLE: _____

_____

LIST THREE IMPORTANT FACTS THAT THE AUTHOR USES TO SUPPORT THE MAIN IDEA:

_____

_____

WHAT INFORMATION OR IDEAS DISCUSSED IN THIS ARTICLE ARE ALSO DISCUSSED IN YOUR TEXTBOOK OR OTHER READINGS THAT YOU HAVE DONE? LIST THE TEXTBOOK CHAPTERS AND PAGE NUMBERS:

_____

_____

LIST ANY EXAMPLES OF BIAS OR FAULTY REASONING THAT YOU FOUND IN THE ARTICLE:

_____

_____

LIST ANY NEW TERMS/CONCEPTS THAT WERE DISCUSSED IN THE ARTICLE, AND WRITE A SHORT DEFINITION:

We Want Your Advice

ANNUAL EDITIONS revisions depend on two major opinion sources: one is our Advisory Board, listed in the front of this volume, which works with us in scanning the thousands of articles published in the public press each year; the other is you—the person actually using the book. Please help us and the users of the next edition by completing the prepaid article rating form on this page and returning it to us. Thank you for your help!

ANNUAL EDITIONS: Early Childhood Education 03/04

ARTICLE RATING FORM

Here is an opportunity for you to have direct input into the next revision of this volume.
We would like you to rate each of the articles listed below, using the following scale:

1. **Excellent: should definitely be retained**
2. **Above average: should probably be retained**
3. **Below average: should probably be deleted**
4. **Poor: should definitely be deleted**

Your ratings will play a vital part In the next revision.
Please mail this prepaid form to us as soon as possible.
Thanks for your help!

RATING	ARTICLE	RATING	ARTICLE
	1. Overview of Existing Policies and Programs for Young Children		27. Guidance & Discipline Strategies for Young Children: Time Out Is Out
	2. Does Universal Preschool Pay?		28. Reinforcement in Developmentally Appropriate Early Childhood Classrooms
	3. Eager to Learn—Educating Our Preschoolers: Executive Summary		29. Bullying Among Children
	4. How Do Education and Experience Affect Teachers of Young Children?		30. Use the Environment to Prevent Discipline Problems and Support Learning
	5. Concern Turns to Preschool Facilities		31. Helping Children Cope With Stress in the Classroom Setting
	6. Skills for School Readiness—and Life		32. Children and Grief: The Role of the Early Childhood Educator
	7. Look Who's Listening		
	8. What's the Difference Between Right and Wrong: Understanding How Children Think		33. Learning Centers: Why and How
	9. Gender Expectations of Young Children and Their Behavior		34. Blocks as a Tool for Learning: Historical and Contemporary Perspectives
	10. Encouraging Fathers to Participate in the School Experiences of Young Children: The Teacher's Role		35. Improving Public Health Through Early Childhood Movement Programs
	11. Developing High-Quality Family Involvement Programs in Early Childhood Settings		36. Using Documentation Panels to Communicate With Families
	12. No Time for Fun		37. The Right Way to Read
	13. Talking to Kids About Race		38. Fostering Language and Literacy in Classrooms and Homes
	14. Cartoon Violence: Is It as Detrimental to Preschoolers as We Think?		39. Helping Preschool Children Become Readers: Tips for Parents
	15. Who's Watching the Kids?		40. Children Are Born Mathematicians: Promoting the Construction of Early Mathematical Concepts in Children Under Five
	16. Creating Home-School Partnerships		
	17. For America's Infants and Toddlers, Are Important Values Threatened by Our Zeal to "Teach"?		41. Salting the Oats: Using Inquiry-Based Science to Engage Learners at Risk
	18. All They Do Is Play? Play in Preschool		42. Young Children & Technology
	19. 10 Signs of a Great Preschool		43. The "Failure" of Head Start
	20. Study: Full-Day Kindergarten Boosts Academic Performance		44. Accountability Shovedown: Resisting the Standards Movement in Early Childhood Education
	21. The Child-Centered Kindergarten: A Position Paper		45. Class-Size Reduction in California
	22. Measuring Results		46. Putting Money Where It Matters
	23. Different Approaches to Teaching: Comparing Three Preschool Program Mo		47. 'All Children Can Learn': Facts and Fallacies
	24. Examining the Reggio Emilia Approach to Early Childhood Education		48. In Early-Childhood Education and Care: Quality Counts
	25. The Silencing of Recess Bells		
	26. Guidance Techniques That Work		

(Continued on next page)

BUSINESS REPLY MAIL
FIRST-CLASS MAIL PERMIT NO. 84 GUILFORD CT

POSTAGE WILL BE PAID BY ADDRESSEE

McGraw-Hill/Dushkin
530 Old Whitfield Street
Guilford, Ct 06437-9989

NO POSTAGE
NECESSARY
IF MAILED
IN THE
UNITED STATES

ABOUT YOU

Name

Date

Are you a teacher? ☐ A student? ☐
Your school's name

Department

Address

City

State

Zip

School telephone #

YOUR COMMENTS ARE IMPORTANT TO US!

Please fill in the following information:
For which course did you use this book?

Did you use a text with this ANNUAL EDITION? ☐ yes ☐ no
What was the title of the text?

What are your general reactions to the *Annual Editions* concept?

Have you read any pertinent articles recently that you think should be included in the next edition? Explain.

Are there any articles that you feel should be replaced in the next edition? Why?

Are there any World Wide Web sites that you feel should be included in the next edition? Please annotate.

May we contact you for editorial input? ☐ yes ☐ no
May we quote your comments? ☐ yes ☐ no